*The Gorehound's Guide to
Splatter Films of the 1960s and 1970s*

The Gorehound's Guide to Splatter Films of the 1960s and 1970s

by SCOTT AARON STINE

McFarland & Company, Inc., Publishers
Jefferson, North Carolina, and London

Frontispiece: *The Monster of Piedras Blancas.*

Library of Congress Cataloguing-in-Publication Data

Stine, Scott Aaron, 1968–
    The gorehound's guide to splatter films of the 1960s and 1970s / by Scott Aaron Stine.
       p.   cm.
    Includes index.
    ISBN 0-7864-0924-X (softcover : 50# alkaline paper) ∞
    1. Horror films — History and criticism. 2. Horror films — Catalogs. I. Title.
PN1995.9.H6S76   2001
791.43'6164 — dc21   00-66454

British Library cataloguing data are available

©2001 Scott Aaron Stine. All rights reserved

Front cover design by Scott Aaron Stine

No part of this book may be reproduced or transmitted in any form or by any means, electronic or mechanical, including photocopying or recording, or by any information storage and retrieval system, without permission in writing from the publisher.

Manufactured in the United States of America

McFarland & Company, Inc., Publishers
  Box 611, Jefferson, North Carolina 28640
    America.www.mcfarlandpub.com

Acknowledgments

The following sources were consulted while I was writing this book:

The Amazing Herschell Gordon Lewis, Asian Trash Cinema, Asian Cult Cinema, Bizarre Sinema!, Brutarian, Carnage, Castle of Frankenstein, Cinefantastique, Cinema: A Critical Dictionary, Cult Movies, Deep Reed, The Deep Red Horror Handbook, Delirium, Demonique, Dracula—The Vampire Legend on Film, Draculina, Ecco, L'Ecran Fantastique, The Encyclopedia of Science Fiction Movies, European Trash Cinema, Eyeball, Famous Monsters of Filmland, Fangoria, Fantastic Cinema Subject Guide, Fatal Visions, Fear, Film Directors: A Complete Guide, Film Threat, Film Threat Video Guide, The Film Yearbook, Filmfax, Flesh & Blood, For One Week Only, Foreign Affairs, G.A.S.P., GICK!, Giallo Pages, Gore Creatures, The Gore Gazette, The Gore Score, Gorezone, Grindhouse, Headpress Magazine, Highball, Horror Fan, Horror Holocaust, House of Horror, Imagi-Movies, Immoral Tales, Is It... Uncut?, Killing for Culture, Knights of Terror, Little Shoppe of Horrors, Magick Theatre, Midnight Marquee, Midnight Movies, Monster International, Movie Fantastic, Naked! Screaming! Terror!, Necronomicon, Obsession, The Official Splatter Movie Guide, Oriental Cinema, Outré, The Overlook Film Encyclopedia of Horror, Painful Excursions, Photon, Psychotronic, The Psychotronic Encyclopedia of Film, Reflections of a Teenage Gorehound, Samhain, Scarlet Street, Scary Monsters, Schlock-O-Rama—The Films of Al Adamson, Scream Queens Illustrated, The Seal of Dracula, Sex-Murder-Art, The Shape of Rage, Shivers, Shock Value, Shock X-Press, Sickoid, Slaughter House, The Sleaze Merchants, Sleazoid Express, Spahetti Splatter Holocaust!, Splatter Movies, The Splatter Times, Starburst, Terror on Tape, Toxic Horror, Trash Compactor, Trashola, Trauma, The Underground Film Bulletin, Uncut, Ungawa, Variety Movie Guide, Video Junkie Magazine, Video Movie Guide, Video Watchdog, Videooze, Videosonic Arts, and *World of Fandom.*

Special thanks go to Lorren

Acknowledgments

Bell, Devon Bertsch, Charles Dawson, Laurie Dawson, Duane Eilf, Robin Harris, Ben Radford, Gerald Stine, Judy Stine, Tim Towns, Michael von Sacher-Masoch, and T. Andrew Wahl for their invaluable assistance and contributions.

Additional thanks go to Jim Becker, Gary Hill, Hugh Newton, Peter Gilmore and Larry Schemel.

Any suggestions for additions or revisions will be greatly appreciated. These and any questions or comments can be sent to the author in care of the publisher.

Contents

Acknowledgments
v

Preface
1

A Brief History of the Splatter Film
11

The Splatter Films
37

Appendix 1. Snuff: The Making of an Urban Legend
249

Appendix 2. Video Sources
259

Index
263

Preface

Welcome, fellow splatterpunks and trash film aficionados, to *The Gorehound's Guide to Splatter Films of the 1960s and 1970s*. This handy reference book should make it a little less of a chore for completists and genre enthusiasts to track down information pertaining to their favorite films and most beloved filmmakers' output.

Being one of the aforementioned film geeks, I know what it is like to be at a loss as to just who "A. Frank Drew White" actually is, or to wonder what the original Spanish title for *Don't Open the Window* is, or if *Il Tuo Vizio é una Stanza Chiusa a Solo Lo Ne Ho la Chiave* actually means something in Italian. Of at least equal importance are: is this film available on video, what label released it, and what are the running times of the available prints?

Of course, this information is geared more towards the lost souls who, like myself, live and breathe this dreck; for those who are simply curious about a particular film (and are—for some odd reason—hung up on finding out if the film in question is actually *good* before they spend their hard earned bucks on what could be a turkey), I also took the time to review each and every one of these cinematic killing sprees. (Considering some of the crap I've had to wade through, you should be extremely thankful that I've actually taken the time to, you know, actually watch—or fast forward through—each and every film just so I can warn you about which ones to steer clear of.)

So whether you're a dedicated enthusiast praying for an invaluable tool in sorting through the bloody mess that comprises the splatter genre, or you're a burgeoning fan browsing for a primer into the world of celluloid carnage, this book should have what you're looking for. (By the way, if you answered Jesús Franco Manera, *No Profanar el Sueño de los Muertos*, and "Your Vice Is a Closed Room and Only I Have the Key" to the above three queries, you're obviously one of the former. God help you.)

Originally, this compendium was to be a complete overview of

Preface

splatter films as a genre from 1963 to the end of the century. When problems of sheer scale arose, I was forced to make several revisions, not the least of which was breaking it up into three separate volumes. The first of these volumes you now hold, and encompasses those films made from 1963 through 1979. (The second planned volume will span 1980 through 1989, and the third—I'm sure you can see it coming—1990 through 1999.)

Now, on to the essentials.

To avoid any confusion as to exactly what constitutes a splatter film, I will now attempt to define it as clearly and succinctly as humanly possible (a not easy task, I assure you):

> **Splatter Film** *n.* **1.** Any motion picture which contains scenes of extreme violence in graphic and grisly detail, especially those films which also fall into the broader categories of the horror film and, specifically, the slasher film.
> **2.** Those films produced since 1963 that focus on blood-drenched special effects, often at the expense of minor technicalities like, well, everything else.

Admittedly, this definition is still vague—especially to those individuals unfamiliar with the genre—but most film buffs tend to accept this as the criterion "splatter" films must meet. Since my standards might vary slightly in certain areas (especially concerning "fringe" productions), I will attempt to clarify why certain films which otherwise might qualify under the above definition didn't make it into my guide, or why others seemingly not up to snuff did.

The biggest stipulation I would like to add to the above definition is that "blood alone doth not a splatter film make." Unless the red stuff is in copious amounts, it is the open wound itself that usually garners a film the "splatter" labeling. Before I start getting too clinical, I would like to add that, yes, I might on occasion stray from the rules I myself have set, but only if I feel that the film in question is otherwise important contribution to the genre.

One distantly related genre that I took great pains to avoid, though, was the *mondo* film. The term "mondo" is casually applied to those documentaries which employ a wide range of shock tactics, and is derived from the infamous *Mondo Cane* [*A Dog's World*] (1962), a film which is directly responsible for such unpleasantries as the *Faces of Death* series and its inbred kin. Although many of these films fall within the definition of the splatter film, for the most part they employ real-life footage of death, dismemberment, and mutilation (usually newsreel footage or staged animal butchery), unlike the special effects upon which splatter films are so reliant.

(If I were to include every film that simply depicts the real thing, I would have to make room for traffic safety films, war atrocity propaganda, PBS wildlife documentaries, and the like. And—contrary to what would appear to be a widely held view—

most splatterpunks have little or no use for scenes of real-life bloodshed.)

Our interests lie with filmmakers, special effects, and—in most cases—the catharsis that *staged* bloodshed offers.

As one can probably foresee, it was not always easy to decide which films are in and which are out. Since it is difficult to measure the blood quart for quart and the wounds inch by inch, much of the decision making process was subjective. I will be the first to admit that some of the films really don't qualify under the given criteria, but how could I *not* include such films as *The Texas Chain Saw Massacre* (1974) and *Halloween* (1978). These films are not all that gory (except maybe to those who haven't actually *seen* them), but they have undoubtedly influenced more splatter films than the entirety of Herschell Gordon Lewis' groundbreaking oeuvre.

The Texas Chain Saw Massacre made everyone realize that cannibalism was hot, whereas *Halloween* jump-started the ailing psycho killer subgenre, giving it a new lease on life as the slasher flick. Other films that have managed to weasel their way into this book may not have the same clout as these three, but—for whatever reason—I still felt inclined to include them.

Be warned: If you rent or buy a video because you found it listed herein, and it's *not* the gore-ridden wonder you expected, stop to think before sending me any nasty letters. A large number of these films have been released on domestic video trimmed, cut, or completely hacked by American distributors in an effort to conform to the MPAA's puritan standards. (This is usually the case with the more extreme foreign productions, at least those which are somehow lucky enough to make it through Customs. I think it's safe to assume that films are among the most difficult of contraband to smuggle through our ports.)

Although my tastes continue to "mature" with age and the scope of my interests broaden, I have been a devout splatterpunk for half of my life now (and undoubtedly will be until the end). Since an early age, my greatest obsession was horror, in particular the monster movies shown on television after hours or on weekend afternoons.

Ironically, it is because of these films I am literate. My mother—tired of having to read me the listings in the *TV Guide*—told me that if I learned to read it myself I could watch anything that made its way to the tube. Not only did I learn to read long before I ever set a foot in school, I also picked up an idiosyncratic habit from this. Since the most opportune time to watch monster movies was on Friday nights, thanks to *Nightmare Theater* and its vampiric, Barnabas Collins–wannabe host, I would read the *TV Guide* backwards from end to beginning. I do so to this day.

Unfortunately, the monster movies I passionately sought to ingest became progressively campier as I got older. And—like most television and film addicts—I continued to search for something new: Films that went further into the uncharted territory that the others only hinted at.

By my early teens, things weren't looking too good. Television continued to show the same old tired prints of movies I had seen religiously a few times too many. Along the way, I had become quite familiar with the adult-oriented horror magazines put out by Warren Publishing (*Eerie*, *Creepy*, *Vampirella*), Skywald Enterprises (*Psycho*, *Nightmare*, and *Scream*), and—of course—Eerie Publications, whose sleazy knock-offs (*Terror Tales*, *Weird*, *Tales from the Tomb*, etc.) are surprisingly difficult to find considering the innumerable titles and availability of them. What I wanted to know was if they made *films* that were similarly intense; productions which dared to show the aftermath that was only implied or alluded to in the films with which I was intimately familiar. Or—better yet—the carnage in progress.

On occasion, *Famous Monsters of Filmland* would mention a film or—if you were lucky enough—print a still from a production that let younger readers know that, yes, there was life after Boris Karloff and Bela Lugosi. Almost overnight I noticed that television began running ad spots for a lower caliber of film than it had previously, piquing my interest even more.

One of the earliest trailers to expose me to more hardcore horrors was *Squirm* (1976), and shortly thereafter I came across a copy of *Starlog* magazine that showed stills from *The Incredible Melting Man* (1977). ("Incredible" in that the special effects here were well beyond the toilet paper and oatmeal-derived prosthetics I had learned from the many how-to books I collected fervently.) This stuff made even Hammer's grisly fare (by far the most visceral films I'd seen up until then) pale in comparison.

(I also vividly remember—now bear with me—being handed a dog-eared copy of *Fangoria* #3—in church, of all places—and finding myself dumbfounded by the blood-drenched photos of *The Brood*, and—more specifically—the shots of Samantha Eggar licking the amniotic gore off of her newborn kid. Ahhh... the memories of youth.)

Although the gears were already in motion, it was a significant event in 1979 that was responsible for sealing my pact with the devil and devoting my life to trash. My father—in a moment of profound wisdom (or temporary insanity, take your pick)—invested in the family's first VCR. (Long before the craze had hit the country, I might add. This was back in the old days when top-loading Betas—cheap at fifteen hundred bucks—were considered top of the line, and to rent a film we had to drive thirty miles to the nearest video rental outlet and lay down a hundred dollar deposit for each and every video we took home. Needless to say, this monthly excursion was a religious, although often disappointing, experience as this store probably had fewer horror titles than most 7-Elevens have nowadays.)

Pretty soon I had convinced my parents that these films weren't really as bad as the gruesome video box art made them out to be, and within the year I had seen a film that diverted my cinematic interests away from the monster flicks from yesteryear, namely John Carpenter's *Halloween* (1978). Although the bloodshed was sparse (okay... damn near nonexistent), it was such a high-tension, brutal film that I was forever sold on this new celluloid high. By the time I had waded through enough low-rent slasher fare for it to be considered cruel and unusual punishment, I came across a film that is still considered the pinnacle of the genre by most fans.

Then came *Dawn of the Dead* (1979), which showed everything. *Everything.* Every piece of excavated viscera was held out lovingly for all to see. Aghast, I found myself witness to an epic crash course in death and dismemberment, and was unable to look away for fear of missing something that would contribute to the nightmares I cherished in my sleeping hours.

(Okay, okay... the first time out, I spent much of the film watching my parents out of the corner of my eye. The looks on their faces during the really nasty moments were worth the price of admission alone. Why they never hit the eject button, I'll never know, although the threat seemed prevalent at the time. Maybe in the backs of their minds they only realized that *that* would have made things *worse*.)

But — as most loyal fans would be happy to exclaim — the violence was just the icing on a very bloody cake. Once one had gotten over the hard-hitting realism of most of the effects work (still fairly convincing by today's standards), one realized that this messy little film was *good*. Even my mother — appalled by the violence — found the rest of the film engaging. (Or at least she *feigned* interest.) Despite a modest budget, director George Romero succeeded in creating what was undoubtedly the most enjoyable vision of apocalypse ever brought to the screen. Characterization, drama, an unpredictable script, satire, an examination of socio-political themes, and some serious taboo-bashing were all combined to make one of the most intense and visceral horror films ever made.

(Personally, I feel that 1985's *Day of the Dead* succeeds on numerous other levels as well — and is in my mind the superior film — but I have yet to find anyone who wholeheartedly agrees with me. Chalk it up to a chronic case of nostalgia on their parts, I suppose.)

Although I quickly discovered — much to my dismay — that films of this caliber were quite uncommon, I sallied forth, and was able to dig up enough winners to nurture my enthusiasm. It wasn't long before I also gained an appreciation (purely out of necessity?) for truly *bad* films, particularly the no-budget, drive-in, exploitation fare of the 60s and 70s. I could safely say that my introduction to films of the "so-bad-they're-great" variety was

H.G. Lewis' *The Wizard of Gore* (1970). (Up until a few years ago, I could recite a great deal of its dialogue verbatim, in particular Ray Sager's droning monologues, i.e. "Torture and terror have always fascinated mankind, perhaps..." yadda yadda yadda.) Within a few years, I became just as excited over finding a new Dario Argento or David Cronenberg film as I was about unearthing another *Corpse Grinders* or *Blood Freak*. Hook, line, and sinker.

Having currently tired of mainstream dreck (such Hollywood franchises as *Friday the 13th*, *A Nightmare on Elm Street*, and *Child's Play* come immediately to mind), I now spend my time musing about the horrors of Blood Island, or futilely trying to sort out the chronology of El Hombre Lobo's or Ilsa's respective histories, or biding the time until Amando de Ossorio Rodríguez gets off his tired butt and films the fifth *Blind Dead* film. Obviously, the nostalgic yearnings for a repressed childhood plays a large part in my current interests.

How to Use This Book

This main section is, essentially, an attempt to compile a complete list of works which fall within the definition of a splatter film. They are arranged alphabetically and are accompanied by information that the film student or casual reader might find important, or information they may simply find insightful or interesting:

Original title of film (year of production)

Production company [country of origin]

DIR: Director/s
PRO: Producer/s
SCR: Screenwriter/s
     [Availability of source material and or movie novelization and author]
DOP: Director/s of Photography
EXP: Executive Producer/s
SFX: Special Effects
MFX: Makeup Effects
VFX: Visual Effects
MUS: Music Composer/s
STR: Cast (All are alphabetized by last name. Single names—usually dogs or strippers—are alphabetized thus.)
AKA: Alternate titles
     Note: In case of alternate versions where additional footage is added and the film is rereleased under a new title, original years of production are given as well.
     Approximate running time; B&W or Color [3-D, if applicable]
NOV: Availability of film novelization and author [publisher]
SND: Availability of soundtrack [record label]
VID: Availability on video (Video label [format of tape if not standard NTSC]; stated running time of print; language of print and subtitles, if not in English;

widescreen letterboxing [LBX], if available; and—if applicable—any double- or triple-bill features the video may contain)
Note: When the running time of a particular videocassette is erroneously stated on the box or label, the actual running time is noted in parentheses immediately following the stated time; I have also done the same with "compressed" running times of non–NTSC formats. As a rule, I tend to round the running time to the nearest minute. Also, RTU means running time unknown.

ADL: A selected adline used to promote the film for either its theatrical or video release.

Of utmost importance are the highly biased, often unrelenting reviews of the film which immediately follow the more technical information. I have done my best to point out any redeeming qualities of each and every film (not an easy chore, I assure you).

Just for fun, I will occasionally include a synopsis of the film culled from the back of the video box, *especially* if they are completely erroneous and misleading. (If they *are* way off the mark, I'll take the time to vent my frustrations at having been deceived and set the record straight.) Sometimes, though, these breakdowns just happen to capture the essence of the film succinctly and with much more grace than yours truly can muster. Whatever the case, a synopsis will directly precede my review, and be set off by quotation marks.

For the politically correct gorehound, I have also included a warning if a particular film contains scenes of animal cruelty or slaughterhouse footage. (I use these two terms to differentiate, loosely, whether the scenes are before or after-the-fact.) This information is geared specifically towards those individuals who wish to avoid or simply be prepared for such footage, and is not meant to blacklist such films. If you don't care, ignore it. (I hold a number of these films in high regards despite these scenes... but that won't stop me from bitching about it incessantly.)

On a similar note, I've included a warning if the film contains actual surgery footage. (Although I'm not morally offended by these particular scenes, I do find them unnerving and I do like *some* forewarning as to what to expect... even though my finger never strays far from the fast-forward button.)

I have given a "hardgore" rating to those films which, in reference to sheer quantity of bloodshed, go way beyond the required excesses of an already frowned upon genre. All of the films I chose to receive this honor contain—in lingering detail—the most graphic dismemberments and eviscerations ever depicted onscreen. These are the heavyweights, or—to put it more poetically—the "dogs that like to revel in their own stink." Those films that fall into this category are marked with a ☠☠☠ (a bastardization of the triple-X rating) immediately following my review. This delineation is aimed towards those unrepentant gorehounds who have no use for any substance in their entertainment outside that of simple evisceration, and indiscriminately search out the nastiest fare they can find.

Although I have not bothered to list the original MPAA ratings for the films (it's safe to assume that most are R, whatever the case), I have marked those films which contain hardcore sex footage with the classic **XXX** rating. (Of course, this rating doesn't actually exist and is not recognized by the MPAA. For those who don't know, this was originally a ploy by adult filmmakers to convince their audience that *their* films were "harder" than the usual adult fare, thus deserving three Xs as opposed to one.) This is simply to warn people who do not wish to see penetration shots outside of the violent, metaphorical variety that can be found in most slasher pics.

I have also issued several "warnings" as to whether a film contains scenes of animal cruelty and or slaughterhouse footage 🐾🐾🐾, and autopsy footage and or actual surgery footage 🩸🩸🩸.

Non–English-language titles make up almost a fifth of the films included in the filmography, certain classifications may be helpful in avoiding any confusions that might arise as a result of language barriers.

First, (non–English titles are arranged alphabetically by the first word other than articles (i.e., as in English one ignores "a", "an" or "the"). Lest you feel you need to drag out your trusty old foreign dictionaries, here is a list of common articles for French, German, Italian, Portuguese, and Spanish below:

A	Der	El	Il	Le	O	Une
As	Die	Gli	L'	Les	Un	Uno
Das	Ein	I	La	Lo	Una	

Second, standard transliterations of non–Romanized (i.e., Asian) titles are listed when a Romanized version of the title is not available. (It would be very difficult for me to reproduce these titles using the actual Asian ideograms. And how I would go about alphabetizing them is beyond me.) Romanized (transliterated) Asian titles are listed alphabetically, and are followed by translations whenever available.

The Appendices

"Appendix 1. *Snuff*: The Making of an Urban Legend" is an exposé detailing the sordid history of America's, nay, the *world's* most infamous splatter film to date. Despite what one may think of the film itself, **Snuff**'s importance in exploitation cinema is indisputable, and it remains one of the most interesting cases of mass hysteria and sensationalism.

Included herein are known pseudonyms of major players in the genre, with the pseudonyms referring back to the individual's given name (whether they like it or not). Pseudonyms may include Americanized pseudonyms for Asian and European players, and even commonly documented misspellings for some individuals. For pseudonyms used to blanket co-directors, an entry is included for both names.

"Appendix 2. Video Sources" is for you hardcore videohounds out there. I have included a listing of video companies, distributors, and those who sell "from one collector to another" to aid you in tracking down those titles not carried by video store.

Helpful Sources

Some books and articles that were of considerable aid come in compiling this work are listed here.

Brunvand, Jan Harold. *Curses! Broiled Again!* New York: W.W. Norton, 1990.

Kerekes, David, and David Slater. *Killing for Culture*. Creation Books, 1995.

Lynch, Jay. "The Facts About the Snuff-Film Rumors." *Oui* 7 (1976): 69-70, 86, 117-118.

McCarty, John. *Splatter Movies*. New York: St. Martin's Press, 1984.

Meyers, Richard. *For One Week Only*. New Jersey: New Century Publishers, 1983.

Palmerini, Luca M., and Gaetano Mistretta. *Spaghetti Nightmares*. Florida: Fantasma Books, 1996.

Sanders, Ed. *The Family—The Story of Charles Manson's Dune Buggy Attack Battalion*. London: Panther Books, 1976.

Smith, Jack. "Snuff Myth—The Bloody Truth About On-Screen Sex Slayings." *Escapade* 8 (1982): 22-25, 92-94.

Vale, V., and Andrea Juno. *Re/Search #10—Incredibly Strange Films*. San Francisco: Re/Search Publications, 1986.

Weisser, Thomas, and Yuko Mihara Weisser. *Japanese Cinema Encyclopedia*. Florida: Vital Books, 1997.

A Brief History of the Splatter Film

Since the advent of film, filmmakers have employed grisly and horrific images to depict the darker side of man. Although most of the early pioneers who experimented with what was perceived as more questionable methods of expression chose (or were forced by producers) to do so within the more acceptable restraints of the horror film, there were always the ostracized few who chose (usually for more artistic reasons) to ignore the moral standards of the day. (Tod Browning's 1932 film **Freaks** being an excellent example of subversive filmmaking during this time period.) With these filmmakers, the visceral quality of a film was just as important as the psychological since the two were intricately bound by catharsis, as it relates to the viewer and the artist alike.

One of the earliest and best examples—both reviled and applauded by critics of its time—is a film far removed from the type of cinema this book focuses on, both in time and artistic intent. Still, this movie exploits the same macabre fascination with the flesh as does each and every film casually labeled "splatter." Luis Buñuel's **Un Chien Andalou** [*An Andalousian Dog*] (1929) is a visual assault of seemingly unrelated nightmarish images that would still garner a reaction from modern filmgoers, despite the fact that its intents to shock the viewer does not adhere to simple geek philosophy. Some of the more extreme scenes include a dismembered hand being consumed by hungry ants, and an unsettling close-up of a straight razor slicing open a woman's eye as she sits complacently. These images—products of co-scenarist Salvador Dalí's fevered genius—are violent, but artistically viable attacks on the establishment of his time. It can be argued, though, that these statements still remain valid. Although it was wholly intended as political and social commentary by disgruntled surrealists, the film was—unfortunately—recognized more for its graphic, unrelenting nature, and was disregarded by many as a serious piece of work worthy of attention.

For decades thereafter, the hands of cinema and its progenitors were kept bound by conservatism's apron-strings; if unspoken taboos were breached, and a stern scolding failed to do the trick, a backhand usually sufficed in silencing them. Sex and violence in its purest forms weren't even conceivable; filmmakers were too busy making sure married couples kept to themselves in separate beds, and mobsters riddled with bullets spilled nary a single drop of blood on the sterile setpieces. It was a world of fantasy... but the need to represent the results of man's basest nature would eventually become a pressing issue, and the world of fantasy would become a very unpleasant place indeed. Theatergoers would tire of seeing this unreal, stale representation of a world that ended just off screen, and would demand to be shown something more without sacrificing the escapist elements which are the cornerstones of modern film. As could be expected, this chancre finally burst, initiating an entire genre whose sole purpose was to actually show the aforementioned taboos kept under lock and key for all those years. The year was 1963, but first, more on the years leading up to it.

The signs of socio-political repression figured prominently in the previous decade. The 1950s were a time of McCarthyism, the looming threat of nuclear catastrophe, and—last but not least—the growing menace of juvenile delinquency. The rise in underage crime was not attributed as a predictable surge in rebellion, but was instead blamed on the slight loosening of censorship's belt, especially in respect to film and literature. (Particularly comic books, it would seem. Dr. Frederic Wertham and his puritan attacks on EC Comics were some of the most publicized attempts to reinstall the quickly failing control system the conservatives used to dictate "art," the reverberations of which could still be felt twenty years later with the label "Approved by the Comics Code Authority." Film, though, was allowed to reach something akin to maturity—a stunted growth at best—decades before comics were able to shed some of its stigma.) By the end of the 1950's, the gears were already in motion.

Hammer Studios, a UK production company whose previous output consisted primarily of dramas and murder mysteries, jumped feet first into the horror genre. Even though their initial genre efforts were essentially remakes of the old, by now familiar Universal classics (**Curse of Frankenstein** and **Horror of Dracula**, 1957 and 1958 respectively), they were able to draw on an entirely new audience by injecting sex and violence into the stale proceedings. Although the bloodletting is still fairly tame by today's standards (television still insists on airing cut prints, more than likely for reasons of availability), these films helped open the floodgates. Other companies quickly followed suit and began breaking the unwritten laws that held jurisdiction over the depiction of film violence by producing similarly strong fare. At first it was a slow, gradual process, but within a decade's passing Hammer found themselves having difficulty in keeping up with the trend they themselves helped to initiate.

Films like **The Brain That Wouldn't Die** (1959), **The Monster of Piedras Blancas** (1959), **Les Yeux sans Visage** [*The Eyes Without a Face*] (1959), and **The Flesh Eaters** (1963) were intent on showing groundbreaking scenes of gore-laden effects to spice up their typical monster-on-the-loose and science-gone-awry formulas. Dismemberments—key shocks in the former two films—were shown on screen, as it happened, the black and white film stock unable to soften the blow as blood was spilled in the name of entertainment. The third—considered by some a stylish classic of the genre—depicted unnerving scenes of skin graft experiments. The fourth film on the list took the idea of mutilation even further, giving the viewer a taste of what it would be like to be eaten alive by what were essentially microscopic piranha.

Unlike the above films, Nobuo Nakagawa took advantage of the trend—for more artistic reasons—and gave us **Jigoku** [*Hell*] (1960), a compelling film whose intent was more like **Un Chien Andalou** in its attempts to make the viewer confront their darker side as opposed to reveling in it. With few restraints, Nakagawa wholly succeeded in depicting Hell as a bloodied tapestry of death and mutilation rivaled only by Dante's troubled visions. Even today, viewers aren't likely to forget the messages **Jigoku** proffers, thanks in no small part to its use of confrontational imagery.

But it was the aforementioned year of 1963 when it all came to a head. Herschell Gordon Lewis and David F. Friedman (the selfsame men who pioneered the "nudie" films that became the foundation of today's adult film industry) introduced a film so repulsive and unbelievably abhorrent that it has been officially cited as the first true splatter film by historians... and deservedly so. **Blood Feast** was released on an unsuspecting public who were wholly unprepared for such a bloodied spectacle despite the growing acceptance of violence in the cinema. Nobody knew what to make of this poorly made, artistically and—in most people's minds—socially irredeemable little film that illustrated in unprecedented grisly acts of dismemberment and evisceration conceivable. And—to the chagrin of critics and concerned parents alike—this monstrosity was apparently conceived in the name of *entertainment*.

And before anyone had a chance to catch their breath, the same team followed up their infamous epic with two more exercises in bad taste, namely **Two-Thousand Maniacs** (1964) and **Color Me Blood Red** (1965). Although both of these films boasted better production values than their predecessor, and despite the fact they toned down the gore—if only slightly—they were still mutually reviled...

but not so much that they weren't viable box-office draws.

Only in the last few years has it been brought to the attention of genre enthusiasts that another lesser-known filmmaker (a Brazilian who is known more popularly under the slightly erroneous moniker of Coffin Joe) was producing work in his own country that—although not nearly as over the top as Lewis' fieldwork—clearly secures him a similar title as a pioneer in the field of genre filmmaking. Also to this man's credit is his unyielding career; it is of little surprise that he continues to produce films to this very day, and has yet to shy away from the narcissistic furor that has dominated his work from early on. (Although having been at it longer than Spanish director Jesús Franco Manera, he has yet to equal the sheer quantity of work Franco has produced in an equally impressive career.) In 1942, José Mojica Marins started off his career as a filmmaker, and although he toyed with graphic violence in many of his early shorts and feature length productions, he didn't make his first "legit" splatter film—**À Meia-Noite Levarei Sua Alma** [*At Midnight I'll Take Your Soul Away*]—until 1963. (Ironically, it was also one of the first Brazilian horror films, a tradition which didn't take root until many years later.) Marins continued to explore the then-uncharted territories of the gore film for a decade before it became commonplace to show such violent excursions. Even when splatter films lost their initial shock value, "Coffin Joe" continued to revel in its excesses, sometimes to startling effect. Most fans familiar with Marins' work would be hard pressed to argue that the man's love of film might even exceed that of the prolific Franco, if only because of the hardships he was forced to endure in order to get his films seen.

Exploitation films of this variety were becoming more and more popular, although few other filmmakers dared to go to the lengths Lewis' films did. Numerous other sexploitation directors decided to test the waters as well, and some jumped in altogether, leaving their T&A-stained past behind them. (By this time, the innocuous nudie films were a dime a dozen, and to survive they would eventually incorporate the sadistic elements more common to the splatter film. These "roughies" would in turn be abandoned for the hardcore sex films that would come into marketable prominence in the late 1960s and early 1970s.) Of notice is the late Andy Milligan, a Staten Island resident whose bargain-basement productions made Lewis' aforementioned classics look good in comparison. His career as a genre filmmaker spanned three decades, from **The Ghastly Ones** (1968) (which he remade in 1978 as **Legacy of Blood**) to **The Weirdo** (1988). His persistence alone is enough to garner him recognition as a pioneer in the field.

Other sex-cum-splatter filmmakers include Jack Curtis and the previously mentioned **The Flesh Eaters**; Harold Hoffman, whose only recently rediscovered **The**

Black Cat (1966) was a lost but not forgotten gore classic for the many years it was out of circulation; Ted V. Mikels, who gave us **Astro-Zombies** (1968) and **The Corpse Grinders** (1971); and Michael and Roberta Findlay, the duo ultimately responsible for **Slaughter** (1971), a film that was repackaged as the now-infamous **Snuff** four years after the fact. (Roberta, who went on to direct a string of acclaimed hardcore films after her husband's death in 1975, returned to horror/splatter films with a slough of straight-to-video releases in the 1980s.) Even Russ Meyer would eventually add heavy doses of violence into his already rough sex epics.

Exploitation filmmakers weren't the only ones taking advantage of this breech of peace; the underground art community that was established by disenfranchised art students took it as a calling as well. Such cinematic anarchists as John Waters, whose films traipsed a fine line between satire and camp, sought to garner some of the same reactions from audience members as his idol H.G. Lewis did. Even Andy Warhol and his troupe would go to bloody extremes to further their somnambulistic statements on pop culture. Halfway across the world, critically acclaimed director Pier Paolo Passolini took the same liberties (which culminated with the swan song **Salo, o le 120 Giornate di Sodoma** [*Salo, or the 120 Days of Sodom*] (1975), a film released shortly before his murder), as did Alejandro Jodorowsky, an artist whose work strikes a similar chord as that of early surrealists like Buñuel and Dalí. Jodorowsky's dark masterpiece **El Topo** [*The Mole*] (1970) and its "sequel" **La Montana Sagrada** [*The Holy Mountain*] (1973) quickly garnered a cult following rivaling that of David Lynch and his similarly discordant **Eraserhead** (1978), another splatter-cum-art exercise that packed them in at midnight showings.

Even with the sudden surge of screen violence, it wasn't until a few years later that some critics began taking the genre a little more seriously. In 1968, George Romero and a small Pittsburgh-based film crew who specialized in commercials and industrial films scraped together their pennies and embarked on what would be their feature-length screen debut. Despite a few scenes of graphic cannibalism (among other still heretofore taboos), **Night of the Living Dead** actually received some praise from its contemporaries. Considering its shoestring budget, the film was fairly well made (especially so when compared to other genre outings made up until then), and it managed to strike a chord with its audience. (Part of this is because—some claim—it alluded to a number of issues plaguing America at the time: Our involvement in the Vietnam war, the disintegration of the nuclear family, etc.) And despite its use of what could be considered geekshow gore, it relied more on psychological horror to raise the hackles on one's neck (unlike most of the films that preceded it, and many of those which immediately in its wake as well).

Night of the Living Dead became the film to kickstart an entirely new subgenre: the zombie flick. (Unrelated, of course, to earlier zombie films where the walking dead never even thought about chewing on one's intestines.) It was also indirectly responsible for the Italian-produced cannibal films that took the subject of anthropophagia to then-unrealized extremes... but more on that shortly.

By the 1970s, zombie flicks had taken up where Lewis' films left off. Benjamin Clarke (of **Porky's** fame) gave us the black comedy **Children Shouldn't Play with Dead Things** (1972), a twisted little romp that culminates with a bleak, nihilistic ending that would be lifted by a number of other zombie gorefests soon thereafter. Spain's Jorgé Grau Sola made his mark with **Non Si Deve Profanare il Sonno dei Morte** [*Do Not Disturb the Sleep of the Dead*] (1974), a film more widely recognized as **Don't Open the Window** and **Breakfast at Manchester Morgue**. This film—as could be seen in retrospect—gave a better indication of the genre's direction than its predecessors.

The gore quotient wouldn't be topped until Romero himself followed up his trend setting film with the instant cult classic **Dawn of the Dead** (1979), a sequel that took everything to the extreme. On a $1.5 million budget, Romero had produced the pinnacle of the splatter genre: an unrepentant gorefest that successfully combined drama, horror, and black humor in a way that no one else had succeeded in doing before. With a strong cast, an intelligent script, and manipulative pacing, horror fans were given a film which reached heights that other genre efforts couldn't even hope of achieving.

Released in Europe as **Zombie** (in an alternate version overseen by Italian splatter maestro Dario Argento), **Dawn of the Dead** added fuel to an already growing fire. Director Lucio Fulci (known more for his *giallo* thrillers up to that point, described later) decided to try to outdo said film. The result was the unrelated **Zombi 2** (1980), released here in the States as—ironically enough—**Zombie**. This low-budget schlockfest didn't come close to equaling **Dawn of the Dead** in any way save one, and that was its propensity to upset, shock and or gross out the viewer. Hailed by fans as Fulci's *pièce de résistance*, this nasty excursion into brutality offers the required gallon drum of pig gut strewn about the setpieces, but it lacks the humor usually present to blunt the horrific nature of the crimes; this, it could be argued, is also its greatest strength. Here, the kick-in-the-teeth ending (which owes everything to the aforementioned **Children Shouldn't Play with Dead Things**) is truly chilling. This was an example of the zombie film at its most visceral, as repellent as it was and still remains.

To this day, Italy can be held responsible for the bulk of the **Dawn of the Dead**–inspired zombie flicks. Of notice are Andrea Bianchi's **Le**

Notte del Terrore [*The Night of Terror*] (1979), released here on video as **Burial Ground**; Umberto Lenzi's **Incubu sulla Cittá Contaminata** [*Nightmare in the Contaminated City*] (1980), released here as **City of the Walking Dead**; Bruno Mattei's **Inferno dei Morti-Viventi** [*Inferno of the Living Dead*] (1981), released here as **Night of the Zombies**, and as **Zombie Creeping Flesh** in other parts of Europe; and finally Lucio Fulci's more refined gross-outs **Paura nella Cittá dei Morti Viventi** [*Fear in the City of the Living Dead*] (1982) — more commonly known as **The Gates of Hell** — and its exemplary sequel **L'Aldilá** [*The Beyond*] (1983), released here as **The Seven Doors of Death**. (Even Fulci's **Quella Villa Accanto al Cimitero** [*The House by the Cemetery*] [1981] could — with little stretch of the imagination — be included in this popular subgenre.)

The only post–**Dawn of the Dead** zombie film that deserves to be mentioned alongside **Dawn** with equal reverence, though, is Romero's own **Day of the Dead** (1985) which — despite last minute budget restrictions and script rewrites — is felt by some to even surpass **Dawn**. Having honed his already adept direction to a razor's edge, the original innovator of this subgenre not only created a film that exhibited all the polish of a Hollywood film, but did so *without* sacrificing the bite of his own skewed vision. Tom Savini, the mastermind effects wizard behind **Dawn**, returned with a vengeance, creating a barrage of illusions that would have made a remarkable swan song to his career had he passed on soon after. To accommodate Romero's gritty scenario, Savini contributed what could arguably be the most disturbing and high-tech gore effects ever seen in a zombie flick. Unfortunately, many of **Dawn**'s diehard fans were disappointed in the darker tone of the film and the resulting lack of humor, and were thus compelled to label it inferior to its predecessor. (Humor does punctuate numerous scenes, but Romero spent more time on the characterization, a facet which he considered more important to this installment, and this writer tends to agree with his decision to avoid what would have been superfluous slapstick.)

Although Romero has reported that he wished to make a fourth and final film (utilizing concepts which had been trimmed from **Day**'s original script due to last minute budgetary constraints) tentatively titled **Twilight of the Dead,** no plans have been announced in the ten-plus years since **Day**'s release. Until then, fans will have to settle with the inferior straight-to-video fare that is continually being churned out by impatient fans.

As mentioned earlier, **Night of the Living Dead** was at least indirectly responsible for one of the more reviled subgenres, one that barely spanned two decades: namely, the "cannibal epic." Instead of following another country's lead, Italy was this time the prime mover and — with the exception of a few Spanish imports — completely dominated the market on said films.

The aforementioned Umberto Lenzi introduced the world to **Il Paese del Sesso Selvaggio** [*A Nation of Sex Savages*] (1972), released here and abroad as **Deep River Savages** and **The Man from Deep River**. This film was a bastard crossbreed between the zombie film (replacing the hungry dead with very much alive cannibals) and the *mondo* shockumentaries that had become popular with more jaded filmgoers. The usual doses of high-voltage gore (for which **Il Paese del Sesso Selvaggio** seemed tame when compared to the other films which followed in its wake) were now accompanied by very real scenes of animal butchery and mutilation, usually performed by the perfunctory natives. No matter what the intentions of the filmmakers, it was geek show gore that appealed only to the viewers' basest nature.

Although these films were reasonably few and far between, people turned out in mobs to catch them at their local drive-ins, wondering how the producers would outdo the previous additions to the genre. Most notable were Ruggero Deodato's **Ultimo Mondo Cannibale** [*The Last Cannibal World*] (1976) and his exemplary **Holocausto Canibal** [*Cannibal Holocaust*] (1979); Aristide Massaccesi's **Emanuelle e gli Ultima Cannibali** [*Emanuelle and the Last Cannibals*] (1976), known hereabouts as **Trap Them and Kill Them**; Sergio Martino's **Il Montagna del Dio Cannibale** [*The Mountain of the Cannibal God*] (1977), released here as **Slave of the Cannibal God**; Umberto Lenzi's **Mangiati Vivi** [*Eaten Alive*] (1980), released here as **The Emerald Jungle**, and—last but not least—**Cannibal Ferox** [*Ferocious Cannibals*] (1981), known worldwide as **Make Them Die Slowly**.

Animal rights activists everywhere will be happy to know that stricter laws dealing with animal cruelty have put a damper on the production of these types of films. Still, most are available on videocassette and continue to do very well in both sales and rentals.

By the end of the sixties, there was a surge in splatter productivity, again thanks to the success of **Night of the Living Dead**. On the home front, H.G. Lewis continued to churn out (at a slower, more sporadic pace) the type of films that had made him famous, while other filmmakers and less talented opportunists continued to fill the growing demand for splashier fare. Before long, even the general horror output from independent studios began exploiting the need for more explicit violence, a necessity born out of a highly competitive market. Films like **The Undertaker and His Pals** (1967), **Scream, Baby, Scream** (1969), and **Flesh Feast** (1970) haunted drive-ins across country, coyly daring the more adventurous moviegoers to sit through them in their entirety. Although the sixties were coming to an end, the reign of cinematic taboo-bashing wasn't even close to peaking.

Conditions were similar everywhere. As mentioned earlier, filmmakers abroad had just started taking advantage of these newfound freedoms. In England, Hammer Studios found themselves being pushed aside by fare that avoided the old clichés altogether. By 1970, they were injecting as much gore and sex into their tiring productions as international laws would allow, but it was too little, too late. The only English director (working exclusively outside of Hammer and its rivals at Amicus) with enough credits to garner a following was Peter Walker, a talented independent filmmaker who began his career—like many others—making adults only films. Starting with **Die Screaming, Marianne** (1970) (a borderline genre effort, at best) he made a handful of films which—although dismissed by most critics at the time as inept schlock—are actually well written, adeptly directed. At their best, they are quite thought provoking; at their worst, they are entertaining.

Italy and Spain, on the other hand, were responsible for the majority of splatter films being made at the time. (On average, over half the genre films released in the United States in the early to mid-1970s were imports, although most bore pseudonymous credits to mask the fact they weren't homegrown.)

In the 1960s, Italy was becoming known for its cultivated output of *giallo* thrillers. ("Giallo" translates as "yellow," and refers to the color of book covers that were common to a brand of pulp-writing popular in that country, the genre being referred to under the same name.) Essentially, these were grittier variations on the ever-popular murder mystery, the story usually hinging on an unseen, gloved killer whose motives were more psychological than that of their predecessors. (Although most of them are the counterparts of today's serial killers, revenge, the procedural elimination of eyewitnesses, and other classical modus operandi usually played a part as well.)

Giallo as it applied to cinema was first brought to light by master filmmaker Mario Bava with his stunning **Sei Donne per l'Assassino** [*Six Women for a Murderer*] (1964), released here as **Blood and Black Lace**. (Unfortunately, he would only try his hand at the genre occasionally through his exemplary career. These include the disappointing **Cinque Bambole per la Luna d'Agosto** [*Five Dolls for an August Moon*] [1969] and the highly influential **Antefatto** [*Before the Fact*] [1972], a film which secured the link between *giallo* and the phenomenon which would come to be known as the slasher film by the end of that decade.)

The second wave of *giallo*'s long-standing popularity—which had only begin to wane in the last decade—was kickstarted by the film **L'Uccello dalle Piume di Cristallo** [*The Bird with the Crystal Plumage*] (1969), the premiere film from auteur Dario Argento. Even though it was decidedly more brutal than most giallo fare, it wasn't until his fourth genre excursion—**Profundo Rosso**

[*Deep Red*] (1975)—that gorehounds began to take real notice of his penchant for graphic violence. With inimitable camerawork, ear-bursting scores, and dizzying choreography, Argento brought an unnatural beauty to the brutality that punctuated his films. His already recognizable style was taken to greater extremes with **Suspiria** (1977). Despite a threadbare storyline, this surreal excursion into the supernatural remains his most popular work to date, and is still as unrelenting as it was two decades ago. (A feat in itself considering how poorly many horror films stand the test of time.)

Argento now spends much of his time producing others' works (in particular, his protégé Michele Soavi—who made a name for himself with **Dellamorte, Dellamore** [*Of Love, of Death*] [1993]) aka **Cemetery Man**—and Lamberto Bava, son of the famed Mario and director of the 1985 cult favorite **Demoni** [*Demons*]), but he hasn't abandoned his place behind the camera. New generations of splatterpunks everywhere continue to discover and be amazed by his impressive catalogue of films, even though his work since the under-appreciated **Opera** (1988) has been less than satisfactory. Like his contemporaries (Romero, Hooper, Craven, etc.) Argento has joined the solemn ranks of filmmakers who have—somewhere along the way—lost the spark that once made them visionaries to be reckoned with.

In the 1970s when filmmakers working within the genre found the limits to which they could push, taking advantage of censorship's inevitable decline. (Part of this could be attributed to the adult film industry and its sudden jump from mail-order only stag films to theatrically released productions whose budgets swamped that of many independent features. With all eyes on the rise of porn, few were paying much attention to the parallel rise of screen violence.) In 1972, H.G. Lewis had made his last and most excessive gore film to date, namely the ruthlessly twisted **The Gore-Gore Girls** (1972). Despite the desperate decision to include as much T&A as he could into his now formulaic butchery, the whole bloody mess barely raised an eyelid. Although he managed to excel beyond what constituted "bad taste," similar productions weren't far behind in their ability to shock and offend. Because of this saturation, the audience was quickly becoming jaded to Lewis' charming abattoirs.

Viscera was being thrown at indiscriminate theater patrons by the bucket load, which they continued to consume in the flurry of newfound freedoms, or so it seems. (It also needs to be taken into account that most of these productions never made it past the drive-ins whose attendees weren't always there for the show; whether it was fertilizer or filet mignon they were being served, they often times didn't care.) For once though, the claims these films were making about their grisly contents weren't all hype. Of course, one would more than likely be wading through abysmal production values and poorly dubbed soundtracks, but at least you knew you would probably get your money's worth. (And this was before the special effects in a film were given any real importance... before being a special makeup artist was a respectable position, taking precedence over gaffer and best boy.)

The roughies had, by this time, been all but absorbed into these new genre pics, since graphic nudity and even softcore sex had made its way into more mainstream films. Sex and violence would never again be so uncomfortably close; it was the year of the body count, and the victims—for the most part—had forgotten where they had left their clothes.

Unfortunately, this convenient coupling of exploitation's greatest weapons in the war of the buck gave a stronger foothold to aspects which have always plagued their respective parents. Sexism had been rampant in exploitation films, even the most innocuous outings. Now, blatant misogyny was given reign in the proceedings. The fairer sex was not only there to titillate male viewers while she was alive, but to be a readily disposable unit when it was time for the blood to start flowing. Women were being considered "slabs of meat" in more ways than one.

One film in particular came out during this time that was guilty of the above crime, but—it could be argued—for most of the right reasons. Although everything about it reeked of exploitation, it forced the viewer into a position where they had to think twice about the degradation of the characters (whose places were usually reserved for the obligatory "pieces of meat") which would only be titillating to the true sadist. It was a disturbing piece of celluloid that somehow transcended the same genre that gave birth to it.

Last House on the Left (1973) truly left its mark on the drive-in crowd, quickly securing its place in horror film history (as well as garnering a cult following for first-time director Wes Craven who went on to develop **A Nightmare on Elm Street**'s franchise). Although its rape/revenge formula became a popular (and overused) theme in the 1970s (having itself borrowed the basic premise from Ingmar Bergman's **The Virgin Spring** (1959), a film particularly disturbing for its time), none of these knock-offs managed to be anything more than cheap exploitation. The only other notable film of this much-maligned subgenre would be the exceptionally powerful **Day of the Woman** (1977), which would eventually make film history as **I Spit on Your Grave**. Thanks to Roger Ebert and his perpetulant lambasting of said film on his syndicated TV show **Sneak Previews** (which he and cohort Gene Siskel left for **At the Movies** some years later), this film garnered a great deal of notoriety and received a cult status for all of the wrong reasons.

As a side note, this theory (that bad press was infinitely better than no press at all) was taken to an unprecedented extreme by the film

Snuff (1976), a 1971 film (released unsuccessfully as **Slaughter**) that was repackaged by producers who—after adding some unconvincing gore footage—coyly tried to convince the public that, yes indeedy, it was the real thing. They even went so far as to hire actors to pose as FBI agents and question patrons as they entered the theaters as to the possible whereabouts of the filmmakers. They also made an effort to alert special interest groups to the groups claims, who immediately went and began picketing the theaters who had the nerve to "profit from the murder of innocent people." By the time most of the public figured out it was all a put-on (many naïve individuals *still* believe it's the real McCoy), it had already raked in a tidy sum at the box-office. (For more information, check out the Appendix for an in-depth look at the roots of the snuff film phenomenon.)

It could also be argued that 1973 was the year splatter infiltrated the mainstream. All it took was one big-budgeted Hollywood production to prove that gore was no longer an independent commodity. (Although not explicitly gory, the violent bodily eruptions and supernaturally-driven self-mutilation that punctuates this film elicit the same kind of response out-and-out gore would have, and proved that even more conservative moviegoers were in the wont for something more intense.) William Peter Blatty's novel of demonic possession was brought to the silver screen by director William Friedkin in an attempt to give the public the likes of which they had never seen, but neither creator had any clue as to the impact (and the resulting furor) their somewhat unpleasant film would cause. **The Exorcist** employed the same sort of shocking effects that drew the disenfranchised youth to the drive-ins and midnight marquees, but backed up its excesses with Oscar-level performances, a literate script, and some of the most high-tech effects ever employed in a film (courtesy of Dick Smith). Many were appalled by what the film depicted; reports of people throwing up or passing out were not uncommon (although they were undoubtedly exaggerated by the press on many occasions). Its success could be easily gauged by the slough of copycats that flooded the drive-ins for years soon after. Films like Ovidio Assonitis' **Chi Sei?** [*Who Is It?*] aka **Beyond the Door**, Alberto de Martino's **L'Antichristo** [*The Antichrist*] aka **The Tempter**, and **La Endemoniada** [*The Possessed*] aka **Demon Witch Child** (all 1974) were churned out as quickly as possible in an effort to take advantage of the phenomenon.

The splatter film—for all intents and purposes—was now legit.

Over the previous ten years, Hollywood had been gradually allowing filmmakers more leeway when it came to things previously considered taboo. But, with a few exceptions (like Sam Peckinpah's unbelievably violent westerns), there were still unspoken rules you didn't break and unstated lines it was best not to cross. By the early 1970s, though, the trickle had eroded enough of these walls away to allow access for more visceral material. **The Exorcist** wasn't the first, but it is undeniably one of the largest stepping stones in the acceptance of gore-laden effects in American films.

The next film that helped further the genre was not a Hollywood production, but a small independent feature that seems to have garnered a bad reputation, despite the fact it's not nearly as graphic as even its name implied. Still, **The Texas Chain Saw Massacre** (1974) was a grueling, unprecedented foray into cannibalism and serial murder. It was harangued by critics for what proved to be its greatest strength; instead of the glitz and/or artsy pretensions most films strove for, it approached its subject with a documentary-style sensibility. An onscreen claim of historical authenticity ("The film which you are about to see is an account of the tragedy which befell a group of five youths...") is hogwash, but it added to the disturbing tension despite its fallaciousness. (The crimes committed by the fictitious cannibals herein were obviously inspired by the morbid activities of the infamous Illinois resident Ed Gein, but in no way is it anything other than a work of fiction. All too often, though, I run into someone who claims they had a friend or relative in Texas who "lived just down the road from where it happened.")

Very few films have managed to evoke the same of sense of intensity as Tobe Hooper's unequaled classic (although **Henry—Portrait of a Serial Killer** [1986] is a very close contender indeed, being the only film ever to be rejected by the MPAA on the grounds of its "tone"). Even Hooper's own **The Texas Chainsaw Massacre II** (1986)—a nauseating but fun little ditty in its own right—made no effort to try to recapture its predecessor's magic, falling back on black humor for its overall approach. (I'll conveniently overlook **Leatherface—The Texas Chainsaw Massacre III** [1989] and the upcoming "remake" that is currently in the works as they are not worth mentioning.)

Even with the rise of splatter-oriented productions in the United States, the majority of genre films (as mentioned earlier) were imported from Europe. Repackaged with new, often misleading titles, and the names of cast and crew "Americanized" for finicky consumers, these outings tended to be nastier than their homegrown counterparts. Unfortunately, U.S. ratings board did not approve of Europe's liberal standards; a great deal of these films were immediately shorn of their more excessive moments. (It's hard to imagine considering that countries like Great Britain and Germany now vehemently censor anything that does not follow their strict moral agendas.)

Hands down, Italy led the pack, producing enough blood-stained *giallo* fare and gothic-inspired sleaze (let alone the occasional cannibal epic) to quell the average fan's needs. Spain followed closely behind, exposing confused Americans to their own peculiar brand of horror. Along with the type of fare that could be expected from their Roman neighbors, Spanish filmmakers combined splatter with what could be described as the traditional monster movie. This awkward (but very popular) subgenre aided the career of one of Europe's biggest B-film stars (outside of the UK), a man who was almost singularly responsible for kickstarting the selfsame trend in Spain. Although he preferred to take screenwriting credit under most—if not all—of his given name Jacinto Molina Alvarez, it was under the Americanized stage name of Paul Naschy that he gained most of his attention.

An ex-wrestler, Paul Naschy began his film career with **La Marca del Hombre Lobo** [*The Mark of the Wolfman*] (1967), a well-received exploitation flick that would kick off one of the longest running genre-oriented series to date. (**Friday the 13th**, with nine installments under its belt, is the only other one even in the running.)

Combining explicit violence, abundant nudity, and recycled storylines, Naschy starred in (as well as occasionally scripting and directing) ten films as Waldemar "El Hombre Lobo" Daninski, a sympathetic lycanthrope who—when not seducing the local maidens—was often pitted against other stock monsters. (i.e. **Dr. Jekyll y el Hombre Lobo** [*Dr. Jekyll and the Wolfman*] (1971), **La Maldición de la Bestia** [*The Curse of the Beast*] (1975) aka **The Werewolf and the Yeti**, etc.) In **Los Monstruos de la Noche** [*The Monster of the Night*] (1969), his third outing as Daninski, the filmmakers went for broke and utilized aliens, the Frankenstein monster, the mummy, and Dracula, thus creating what could only be described as a sexy, gory updating of **House of Frankenstein** or **House of Dracula** (both 1945). Apart from the "El Hombre Lobo" series, Naschy also took out time to portray the mummy in 1973 (**La Venganza de la Momia** [*The Vengeance of the Mummy*]), Dracula in 1972 (**El Gran Amor del Conde Dracula** [*The Great Love of Count Dracula*]), the devil himself (**La Rebellión de las Muertas** [*The Rebellion of the Dead Women*], also 1972), and a host of other horror film standbys.

Oddly enough, Naschy (despite his extensive filmography) never worked with Spain's most prolific director (genre or otherwise). Jesús Franco Manera (aka Jesse Franco) has spent a career spanning five decades producing low-budget, patchwork films which range from children's fare to sadistic hardcore pornography—some within the same year! Still, horror seems to be the one genre from which he never strays far.

Beginning with his first feature **Tenemos 18 Años** [*We Are 18 Years Old*] (1959), Franco can lay claim to a long list of often poorly made (abysmal, to be blunt) but usually interesting, narcissistic productions that are as much exploitation as they are personal visions. Since his first horror outing (**Gritos en la Noche** [*Screams in the Night*] (1961), a classic by most horror aficionados), his films have been marked by violently fetishistic imagery and engaging symbolism. (This is particularly evident in such odd early-70s films as **Vampyros Lesbos—Die Erbin des Dracula** [*Vampire Lesbians—The Heiresses of Dracula*] [1970], **La Comtesse aux Seins Nus** [*The Bare-Breasted Countess*] [1973], and the like.) Obviously, sex and violence are an integral part of his inconsistent and eclectic oeuvre.

Except for a few one-offs, France had little to offer in the way of genre films (let alone filmmakers), the one major exception being the inimitable Jean Rollin. Although he treads similar territory as Franco (particularly in respect to the films mentioned above), Rollin's early films were singularly distinct in their vision. Their approach was more art school–oriented (surreal imagery and scant dialogue forms the crux of these efforts), with a heaping helping of comic book eroticism thrown in for good measure. As he matured, so did his work, without losing the flavor of his initial attempts.

With the bulk of his output reserved for vampiristic themes, Rollin produced a series of unrelated films that built upon the last in the explicitness of sex and violence on display. (**Requiem pour un Vampire** [*Requiem for a Vampire*] [1971] is — to this writer's knowledge — the only one of his horror films to be released to a general public in America. As could be expected, it was heavily edited and released under such ridiculous titles as **Caged Virgins, Crazed Vampire**, and **The Virgins and the Vampires**.) Also to his credit are several zombie flicks and even a few slice'n'dicers, but it is due to his trademarked vampire films that he has secured himself a place in film history. Sadly, he eventually turned to hardcore porn like so many others in an effort to keep making films. (Franco and Aristide Massaccesi also followed this path at some point in their long careers; for Massaccesi, it seems he has focused all of his current energies on direct-to-video hardcore.) Luckily — after a long hiatus — Rollin has been given the opportunity to return to his old stomping grounds. Although unreleased in the states at the time of this writing, **Les Deux Orphelines Vampires** [*The Two Vampire Orphans*] (1995) has been received with much fanfare, and shows that he has yet to lose his spark for filmmaking.

Crossing the border back to Spain, another European filmmaker from this period that made himself a name is Amando de Ossorio Rodríguez (more widely recognized without the final surname), a western director turned horror film maestro who is recognized almost solely for his "Blind Dead" films. Starting with **La Noche de las Muerte Ciego** [*The Night of the Blind Dead*] (1971) and culminating with **La Noche de las Gaviotas** [*The Night of the Seagulls*] (1975) — a film which does extremely well considering its sequel status — this entrancing quartet of undead flicks succeeded (technically and financially) despite their low budgets. Even Romero's zombies couldn't hold a finger against the decayed and ominous grandeur of the eyeless Templars that highlighted de Ossorio's nihilistic outings. (Only the second has anything even remotely resembling a Hollywood-style happy ending, and even this is dubious.)

Other Spanish directors, lacking the notoriety but no less influential, include Javier Aguirre, Carlos Aured Alonso, León Klimovsky (all having worked with Naschy at some point, on some of the films mentioned earlier), and the aforementioned Jorgé Grau Sola. As could be expected, most of their collective output at the time was gore-drenched period pieces and—on occasion—*giallo*-related thrillers.

Also popular at the time (which conveniently fell in step with Spain and Italy's predilection for period pieces at the time) were the inquisition/witchhunter films, which were then incorporated in with the post-**Exorcist** possession films once it had lost some steam. These sordid, but rarely historically accurate storylines gave—to the viewer's delight—the filmmakers ample opportunity to depict gratuitous sex and violence, all the while claiming to "make a statement" about morality and the dangers of religious extremism. More often than not, though, it was simply an excuse to show unclad women being tortured in the name of God. Of these, Naschy's own **Inquisición** [*Inquisition*] (1976) is still one of the best—or worst—of the lot, depending on one's point of view.

Although Italy and Spain were responsible for the majority of these persecution-minded productions, England actually kickstarted it years earlier with Michael Reeves' **The Witchfinder General** (1968) aka **The Conqueror Worm**, and the minor Vincent Price vehicle **Cry of the Banshee** (1970), but it was the German co-production **Brenn, Hexe, Brenn** [*Burn, Witch, Burn*] (1970) which really turned heads. Well, maybe not under this title, but as **Mark of the Devil** it gained enough notoriety to become a cult classic, thanks almost entirely to its relentless promotion. (Not only did it claim to have been banned in 21 countries, theatergoers were also given, upon admission, a barf bag with the film's ad art printed on its face.) Although **Mark of the Devil** wasn't nearly as graphic as promoters—and censors, for that matter—would have led one to believe, the successful ad campaign sparked a flood of imitators that usually outdid said film when it came to the gore.

Other sado-oriented fare grew in popularity around the same time, the most noticeable of which being the Nazi concentration camp films. (I prefer to refer to them as "atrocity" films since this is actually what they exploit—the fact that most of them are pretty atrocious notwithstanding.) Instead of confessions, the tormentors are only interested in forced sexual services and or extracting "vital" medical knowledge from their human guinea pigs, again most of whom are young *frauens*. Judaism—instead of witchcraft—seem to be their most unexonerable crime. Although originating during the flood of late 1960's roughies (the 1968 shocker **Love Camp 7** being one of the more noteworthy—if not first—of such efforts), the first formidable entry in the subgenre was the U.S. production **Ilsa, She-Wolf of the SS** (1974), a nasty little film (inspired by the "Olga" series of the 1960's) whose popularity guaranteed its star, buxom Dyanne Thorn, a place in exploitation's hall of fame. Despite a self-imposed X-rating, **Ilsa** was no more graphic than most R-rated fare at the time. This (arguably the best of the atrocity films) spawned two official sequels, namely **Ilsa, Harem Keeper of the Oil Sheiks** (1976) and **Ilsa, Tigress of Siberia** (1977). An unofficial sequel followed in their wake as well, Jesse Franco's **Greta, Haus Ohne Männer** [*Greta, House Without Men*] (1977), a women's prison film in which Ms. Thorn reprised her role, but here as a sadistic wardeness without the infamous given name. (Distributors saw the connection and re-released it as **Ilsa, the Wicked Warden** to cash in on the notorious series.) Although this last film isn't nearly as gory as it predecessors, Franco made up for it by injecting as much sadism as he could into its typical women-behind-bars formula.

Somehow, this stagnant subgenre persisted into the late 1980s, yet it never regained the momentum it had in the 1970s. (The producers of the **Ilsa** films recognized the self-imposed restrictions of the subgenre and opted to change the locales of each sequel—as well as their time frames, making "Ilsa" a symbol of evil incarnate instead of a specific character whose exploits carry over from film to film. This probably could have been carried further had the general audience member recognized this; instead, many individuals were getting a little irate that Ilsa would show up in each new film, unscathed, with no explanation as to how she escaped her previous film's fate... and why she hadn't aged more than a couple of years when twenty- or-more had passed. Such is the stuff—and logic—of drive-in films.)

By the mid–1970s, most horror fare (especially independent features) in the U.S. had embraced the use of graphic violence to accentuate the horrifying elements on which they were dependent. Not only had standard scare tactics lost most of their effectiveness with the public, most independent filmmakers found it was easier to employ pure shock effects than spend the allotted time building up suspense. Viewers desensitized by the horrors of Vietnam and Kent State had to look further for thrills that would effectively shake them up, and filmmakers everywhere were again more than happy to give in to these demands.

Some directors refused to follow either camp, successfully employing both devices in their product. (It isn't a surprise that quite a few of these individuals eventually wound up in Hollywood when producers saw the importance and or marketability of their work.) Having already mentioned the likes of

Romero, Craven and Hooper, independent filmmakers such as David Cronenberg (**The Brood** [1979] and **Scanners** [1981] etc.) Larry Cohen (**It's Alive!** [1974] and **Q—The Winged Serpent** [1982], etc.) Brian de Palma (**Sisters** [1973], **Carrie** [1976], etc.), and other less talented (but no less viable) directors like Benjamin Clark and William Girdler (both mentioned earlier) are excellent examples.

Another aspiring filmmaker, John Carpenter, followed quickly in their footsteps, and with his third try at directing created one of the most influential horror films of all time. **Halloween** (1978) breathed new life into the "psycho" genre, redefining it for a new generation of filmgoers. Thus was born the modern day slasher flick—a subgenre that has become essentially synonymous with the splatter film (*and* its inherent downfalls as an art form). (Ironically, **Halloween**'s gore quotient was quite mild when compared to the slough of mindless slaughterfests that followed in its wake.) No longer was the killer simply a pathetic, mentally deranged mama's boy that begged for the viewer's sympathy; now, he (or she) was an unstoppable killing machine that asked for nothing more than the bloody retribution of its peers.

The first generation of post-**Halloween** slice'n'dicers was catapulted further by the much more violent **Friday the 13th** (1980), which—thanks to the work of Tom Savini—boasted some of the most realistic gore effects featured in such a film. Unfortunately, it lacked the *frissons* that Carpenter's film evoked, and it did its best to blind the viewer to the fact by spraying as much stage blood in their faces as the producers and distributors would allow.

The trend continued, undaunted. For years it was difficult to scan the entertainment section of the newspaper without being accosted by the ad art for yet another incompetent slasher flick that was invariably revolved around a holiday or other annual event (e.g. **New Year's Evil** [1980], **My Bloody Valentine** [1981] **April Fool's Day** [1986], **Mother's Day** [1980], **Prom Night** [1980], **Graduation Day** [1981], **Silent Night, Deadly Night** [1984], etc.). Although most of these seem pretty abysmal at the time, it is fairly safe to say that—in retrospect—many of them aren't nearly as slipshod when compared to the recycled backwash which continued to flourish far into the 1980s.

Of course, there were exceptions (as few as they were) which actually *did* something with the genre. Case in point is the much-maligned **Maniac** (1980), which took the nastiness to an extreme with its grimy, documentary-like approach (not that far removed from **The Texas Chainsaw Massacre** in that aspect), or the socially conscious **Mother's Day**, mentioned earlier but lost amidst the glut all the same. Unfortunately, though (retrospect notwithstanding), most of it can be dismissed as uninspired pabulum for the most undiscriminating gorehounds.

Spanning two decades and with eight sequels under its frayed belt, **Friday the 13th** has essentially outlived its peers (with the exception of **Halloween**, a franchise that—despite the fact it preceded the former—has fewer outings to its credit), a remarkable feat considering the progressive lack of originality and self-sustaining acts of auto-cannibalism to which it has been inevitably driven. Each subsequent film promises to be the last, but ticket-buyers are slowly becoming savvy to the fact that, if they continue to see them, the studios will continue to churn them out.

Also during the late 1970s, another substantial (but less prolific) subgenre was spawned—but not by low-budget profiteers. Like **The Exorcist**, **Alien** (1979) was payrolled by a big studio, and probably wouldn't have succeeded had this not been the case. A larger budget was required to bring to life (in what was essentially an updated version of the 1958 film **It! The Terror from Beyond Space**) the realistic setpieces and groundbreaking effects work that the project demanded. The technical superiority it held over most science fiction fare was only the means to an end, though, setting the stage for a superbly crafted, well-written suspense film that stands the test of time. *And* it offered a few of the grisliest, most disturbing gore scenes ever contrived.

These shocking scenes, which shamelessly played on the viewer's xenophobia, have since been copied endlessly in other "aliens-on-the-loose" offerings. Since most filmmakers attempting to cash in on **Alien**'s popularity lacked the backing for an interplanetary setting, they invariably moved the trappings to Earth. **Alien Contamination** (1980), **The Return of the Aliens: The Deadly Spawn** (1981), **Alien Predator** (1985), and the like all proffered exploitive, downbeat alternatives to the more optimistic **Close Encounters of the Third Kind** (1977) and **E.T. The Extra-Terrestrial** (1982). With little subtlety, these films explored how the always-hungry intruders would fare on our turf... but with an unlimited number of "hosts" at their disposable in which to impregnate, infect, and or devour in the most unorthodox of ways. Not since the 1950's had humankind been on the threshold of such alien-assisted Armageddon. (At least during the days of McCarthy they only wanted to *conquer* us... not *rape* and *eat* us.)

Even today these unpleasant, unexpected guests are popular in film. They've evolved beyond the mindless balls of teeth and protoplasm, and are usually more intelligent than man himself. (*And* more bloodthirsty. Imagine *that*.) **Predator** (1987) and its sequel made a valiant attempt at redefining the subgenre, but they ultimately proved to be little more than extremely gory Hollywood fare contrived as vehicles for wisecracking heroes.

The onset of the 1980s also saw the rise of a lesser known genre of film that—although it quite often employed the use of extreme violence and other shocking imagery—was not a subgenre unto itself but an entirely new school of filmmaking. "Transgression Cinema" as it has come to be known (a term apparently coined by one of its founding fathers, Nick Zedd) was a punk rock interpretation of art school filmmaking, taking its cues from 1960s filmmakers like Kenneth Anger, Andy Warhol, Jack Smith, John Waters, et al.

Rarely making the running time of full-length features, these shorts ran the gamut from documentary-style expositions to hallucinatory vignettes to what could easily be classified as music videos for underground and experimental rock bands. Most were technically inept, reflecting the DIY (do it yourself) ethics that still underlie the punk rock culture. And—since most were reflective of their environment—graphic violence was immediately accepted as a staple in these productions. (It is not uncommon, however, for the violence depicted therein to be *real*; like the mondo films, you are just as likely to see a senseless act of self-mutilation as you are to see a staged effects sequence.)

Although a little has been written about Transgressive Cinema in above-ground press, the films themselves are rarely accessible, so few of the filmmakers have succeeded in reaching a general audience. Besides Zedd, fellow New Yorker Richard Kern is one of the few filmmakers to receive any kind of widespread distribution for his works. (I purposefully avoid calling them simply "directors" as they more often than not handle almost *all* of the chores, from filming, producing, writing and editing, to even starring in their own works.) Even artists like Kern wouldn't be known outside of his own city had it not been for video companies like Film Threat Video, an independent packager and distributor that specializes in underground and independent works that are not given their dues elsewhere. Not surprisingly, they are also the ones who gave America an opportunity to see the films of a young German filmmaker whose works preceded him, previously available only as grainy third-generation bootlegs.

Jörg Buttgereit may not be a common household name, but anyone who knows anything about underground filmmaking are familiar—at least by reputation—with his work, primarily the infamous **Nekromantik** (1987). Having started a career in film that closely followed the tilt of the trangressionists, Buttgereit eventually moved into the world of feature films, choosing necrophilia as the subject of his full-length debut. Since it is—in most people's eyes—an extremely unpleasant subject indeed, he decided to approach it thus, and turned out one of the most unsettling films of all time. Ultra-graphic gore, and fairly convincing post-mortem love play were enough to get the film banned in several European countries... including his own. Even though all of his subsequent productions are more adeptly made, they are similarly downbeat (embracing taboos that even genre filmmakers tend to avoid), and all are undeniably artistic and far from the purely exploitational excesses censors lead the public to believe. As could be expected, authorities continue to do their best to hinder not only their distribution, but their production as well. Despite all this, Buttgereit continues to bring his unrelenting visions to light.

With the rise and immediate popularity of slasher films in the late 1970s and early 1980s, there was a significant portion of films being made which fell into other subgenres that help to collectively make up the splatter film. Surprisingly, mainstream efforts like **Jaws** (1975), **Raiders of the Lost Ark** (1981), and **Poltergeist** (1982) continued to inject high-tech gore into their otherwise accessible offerings. Even the independently produced **A Nightmare on Elm Street** (1984) was a far cry (technically) from Craven's earlier efforts. (Since **Last House on the Left**, he had kept his feet firmly planted in the horror business, directing such films as **Deadly Blessing** (1981) and—what is arguably his best film ever—**The Hills Have Eyes** (1977). To this day he plies the same trade, but with much less vigor than what he once did.)

Next to **Friday the 13th**'s Jason Vorhees, **Nightmare**'s villain Freddy Krueger is easily the most widely recognized horror icon of what has been referred to as the MTV generation. (I find it rather ironic that a supernaturally-animated child molester/serial killer is so popular among children, so much that he has spawned a franchise that includes everything from action figures to trading cards to "Underoos." Strange world, indeed, but not at all surprising from a psychological point of view. Every generation needs their bogeyman, and as times get more "intense," so do the darker manifestations of our own troubled psyches.)

Another Hollywood-level film from the early 1980s that marked a major stride for special effects (and gore films in general) was John Landis' **An American Werewolf in London** (1981). Featuring never-before-seen effects wizardry and a hefty helping of strewn viscera, this mainstream hit helped further splatter's legitimization. *And* it helped give a much-needed updating to the tired-and-true werewolf myth. Unfortunately, it managed to eclipse its just-as-eventful peer, **The Howling** (made and released the same year). Ironically, **The Howling**'s effects artistry was provided by Rob Bottin, a student of Rick Baker, the man responsible for **An American Werewolf**'s spectacular effects. (**The Howling**'s only crime is that—unlike Landis' film—it gave birth to insofar five sequels, all stillborn and unworthy of their progenitor's namesake.)

In the mid-1980s, while most exploitation filmmakers were busy churning out slice'n'dicers in an effort to make a quick, guaranteed buck, more inspired or innovative fare had a better chance of being noticed. One such film, **The Re-Animator** (1985), was based on a serialized pulp story (originally appearing in the long-running magazine **Weird Tales** in the 1930s) by the cult horror writer Howard Phillips Lovecraft. Although a loose adaptation at best, director Stuart Gordon and producer Brian Yuzna gained genre acclaim for this highly visceral dark comedy. Although both went on to do more competent work, neither has been able to reclaim the cult success that this film brought them.

Another influential film—the debut of Sam Raimi—was the homegrown cult hit **The Evil Dead** (1982). Made on a budget that was eclipsed by what H.G. Lewis was forced to contend with in the 1960s, this no-holds-barred splatter flick somehow managed to attract a following which eventually secured Raimi a comfortable career as a Hollywood filmmaker. (Despite my respect for Raimi, I still have difficulty seeing how anyone could have spotted his talent in this meager gore offering. A few flashes of talent do occur, but there is much to belie the brilliance that is more evident in some of his later work.) Disguised as a sequel, **Evil Dead 2—Dead by Dawn** (1987) followed several years later; all of this was capped off by the disappointing **Army of Darkness** (1991), which did little to add to the tenuously-cited "trilogy."

The biggest name in horror films during the 1980s (and into the 1990s) is not a filmmaker (although he does have one film to his directorial credit), but a universally known writer by the name of Stephen King. Countless work has been written about the man, so I will keep this obligatory mention succinct.

Having started in the 1970s writing short stories for such men's magazines as **Cavalier** and **Gent**, a number of his early gore-drenched novels were adapted to the screen by such luminaries as De Palma (with the aforementioned **Carrie**), Stanley Kubrick (**The Shining**, in 1980), and David Cronenberg (**The Dead Zone**, in 1983). Literally dozens of films later, his name—which usually precedes the title of the productions themselves—continues to draw in substantial box-office receipts. Even though (currently, anyway) I find him overrated at best, his films are undeniably popular and his influence on the horror/splatter genre—despite the medium—hard to overlook. (At one point—fed up with filmmakers not doing his books justice—King decided to try his own hand at it. Suffice it to say, **Maximum Overdrive** (1986) was no better than the sludge that took advantage of having his name tagged onto them. Go figure.)

Another writer by trade has broken into the film industry and—although he isn't nearly as universally recognized as Stephen King—has produced an intense body of work. With his directorial debut in 1987 with **Hellraiser**, Clive Barker proved to the world that he could certainly do more than just write elegant and visceral horror stories, and that his vision transcended the borders between literature and film. (The first two films based on

Barker's work failed miserably, spurning him into the director's chair, and was a comfortable position considering he had made several "student" films in the 1970s, and had worked extensively with play productions before he tried his hand at writing exclusively.)

With two more films under his belt (**Nightbreed** and **Lord of Illusions**, 1989 and 1994 respectively), and a number of authorizations (franchises on **Hellraiser** and **Candyman**), Barker continues to offer filmgoers unique horror films which refuse to insult the viewers' intelligence, and offer the gorehound an imaginative alternative to the usual Hollywood body-counters which have squelched the life from the genre.

Taking a momentary reprieve from the films and the filmmakers themselves, the difference between 1970s gore and the slough of splatter fare in the 1980s couldn't have been much greater. Whereas most of the earlier decade's films were—by today's standards—nastier (and less politically correct), 80s fare tended to break fewer rules. They compensated by offering the viewer better technical values and effects work, showing that which their predecessors could not show successfully because of limited budgets and still-maturing effects technology. The extra gloss could be attributed to Hollywood's rising interest in what was primarily an independent dominated genre.

By the turn of the decade, being a make-up effects artist had become a respectable—and much sought after—position. Names like Tom Savini, Rob Bottin, Rick Baker, and the like (all having given their propers to Dick Smith, a pioneer in the field) were now drawing in fans who would see a film solely on the merits of the effects artist.

Scenes of violence could now overstep the usual throat slashing, decapitations, dismemberments, and occasional eviscerations. Prosthetics, sometimes mechanically-controlled, added a never-before-imagined dimension to the old parlor tricks used to suspend the viewer's disbelief. Suddenly, lopped off hands needn't be concealed under an elongated stump; the severed limb could be controlled with a remote so as to depict it twitching even as it was removed from the body. Upgraded bladders would further convince the audience that the setpieces were truly being showered by actual blood, brain matter, what have you. In short, the open wound had just gotten deeper, and easier to poke around in.

Unfortunately, most genre producers and filmmakers didn't take advantage of these tools to advance the films themselves. Instead, they began to depend solely on the effects as a selling point, while the movies became sorry reiterations of proven sellers. (Although a broad generalization, this observation becomes more apparent with the more films watched from this two-decade stretch. I've realized that even the films I *like* from the latter decade are usually strained variants of earlier fare—a fact not wholly sanctioned to the genre to be sure, but prevalent nonetheless.)

Because of the more graphic displays in horror films, they were quickly becoming fair game to zealous religious activists. (No one seemed to notice the moral underpinnings of said films, or aware that the films were—thanks to Hollywood's growing involvement—less racist and sexist [or even blatantly misogynist] than their 1970s counterparts. Maybe the bible-thumpers were unconsciously pining over the old days, basing their decisions on fare made ten years previous; regardless, the cathartic depiction of violence offended them more than the numerable "isms" mentioned earlier.) With a horde of "concerned parents" at their side, the moral majority began blaming society's century-old woes on a genre that had barely reached adulthood. Unbeknownst to them, the constant attacks only bolstered interest amongst rebellious and disenfranchised teens, helping turn what was once relegated to Saturday-night entertainment into a cult-like phenomenon. (Much in the same way punk rock secured its roots in the fabric of our society. What doesn't hurt us only makes us that much stronger.)

A war had begun that is still being fought even to this day.

Censorship became an issue that is now as synonymous with films—particularly horror—as it was with music. In America, a large number of productions are forced to remove excessive violence or suffer the debilitating wrath of an NC-17 rating, a boon to almost any genre, let alone horror. "Art" films usually aren't shown in multiplexes, where all of the earnings for theatrical releases are made nowadays (may drive-ins rest in peace), and—most importantly—they don't depend on the patronage of teenagers, the natural audience of horror films.

And this—the morally right knows—is how they can do the most damage: by making the films inaccessible to its target audience. It's not so much a matter of "are teenagers mature enough to watch and properly digest violent films"; anyone with even the most basic grasp of psychology knows that teenagers are no more impressionable than adults, and that if they are somehow "influenced" by the films they watch, it is a much deeper problem than "monkey see, monkey do." In situations as these, any type of stimuli might trigger the individual into performing sociopathic acts. It has even been shown that such films can and do act as a catharsis, giving such troubled individuals a more socially acceptable way in which to vent—not fuel—their sociopathic desires. (Much in the same way that most forms of "pornography"—in a controlled and legalized environment—actually help to alleviate sex crimes. [The liberal climate in many European countries—and the resulting decline in sex crimes since such laws were initiated—attest to this.] This is not to say that violent films will eliminate violent crimes, but in a large number of individuals it can act as a safety valve—a necessity in a society plagued by the adverse effects of overpopulation.)

With most studio fare under stricter ratings standards, it has been up to the fans to keep the tradition going on a more grass roots level. Unfortunately, the cost of professional film equipment—and especially the rising cost of film stock itself—is so expensive that these fans are forced to utilize more accessible means of getting their films made... namely, video. To the dismay of film purists everywhere, videocassette not only makes whatever films lensed with it look like cheap home movies or—at best—low budget teleplays, it has also given the means to make films to those who lack any credentials or experience whatsoever. Now, any one can rent a camera for a weekend, and bribe a bunch of friends with a six-pack in contributing to his no-budget rehash of his/her favorite horror flick.

To give credit where credit's due, there are a few talented individuals working within this field who deserve the backing to do more professionally-oriented work... but only a few. The amount of jack being made and distributed by most videocam guerrillas is overwhelming, and it is no surprise that the only ones who really take this dreck seriously are the filmmakers themselves.

With shot-on-video being the primary source of product for today's splatterpunks, it would seem to be a sad eulogy—not far from what has befallen the adult film industry. (Video has become the standard in the industry, with *filmed* productions a rarity.) It seems that in both markets, originality or intelligent storylines are swept aside in favor of the tried-and-true devices that quickly introduce the obligatory hardcore sex or gore-laden effects. For the most part, newer technology such as "film-look" is a desperate attempt to cover up the stink with cheap perfume... yet some of us—myself included—find it better than nothing.

I want to apologize if at times I sound hypocritical or narrowminded. My love for the genre remains despite the fact that I have waded through enough shit to disillusion even the more ardent fans. And it is because of my adoration for this sick, malformed child that I can't help but to point out its shortcomings. Admittedly, I'll criticize it for its sad state and lament over the salad days, then turn around and comment on how it has come further in twenty, thirty years than mainstream film itself has. This is because the subject—splatter films—is an enigma ripe with contradictions, and any critic who has decided to dedicate his/her life to this unwanted beast must conform to the rules in order to understand, and accept it before doing so.

And whether or not I am worthy to be a spokesperson is irrelevant; I'm going to continue to watch and review this dreck—for better or for worse—until there's nothing left to watch. And in the process I'm going to do what I can to remind people that—even with splatter films—there's sometimes more to it than what meets the eye. Even if it is one of Lucio Fulci's very ominous splinters of glass.

The Splatter Films

À Meia-Noite Levarei Sua Alma [At Midnight I'll Take Your Soul Away] (1961)

Indústria Cinematográfica Apolo [Brazil]; Approximately 81m; B&W
DIR: José Mojica Marins; PRO: Arildo Iruam, Geraldo Martins Simões, and Ilídio Martin Simões; SCR: José Mojica Marins; DOP: Giorgio Attili; VFX: Produções Cinemattográfica Indrikis Kruskops
STR: Robinson Aielo, Almir Barbosa, Suzy Barros, Cardoso, Genê Carvalho, Claudiane, Nivaldo de Arildo Iruam, Mário Lima, Luana, Raul Malentaquii, Antônio Marins, Carmen Marins, José Mojica Marins, Magda Mei, Renato Melo, Avelino Morais, Cicero Paulino, Vânia Rangel, Tomás Sebastião, Euripidesda Silva, Ilídio Martins Simões, Valéria Vasquez, Landro Vieira, and José Vilar
VID: **At Midnight I'll Take Your Soul Away** [Something Weird Video; 81m; In Portuguese w/English subs]

Zé do Caixão is a vigilant and sadistic atheist terrorizing the inhabitants of a small town. Apparently, he's a little ticked off that his wife cannot conceive a child—continuing his bloodline seems to be an obsession with him—and takes out his frustrations on the townsfolk who he believes are beneath him. Eventually, he sets his sights on his friend's fiancée, Terezinha, and so decides that wifey has got to go (as well as anyone else who gets in the way). Needless to say, being a horror film, the dead have a hell of a time staying dead, and decide to exact revenge on their murderer.

In this, the first screen appearance of Marins' malevolent alter ego Zé do Caixão (better known by the mistranslated moniker of "Coffin Joe"), the director gets ample opportunity to chew the scenery—so much that he inevitably spent most of post-production picking the splinters out of his gums. (Or wads of cardboard, if one takes the production values into consideration.)

Occasionally quoted by modern historians as being denied the official "first gore film" status by the later **Blood Feast** (1963), it's safe to say that H.G. Lewis won't be losing any sleep over this claim. Although **À Meia-Noite Levarei Sua Alma** does proffer some scenes undeniably gruesome for its time (some finger-cutting and eye-gouging being the most notable), the bloodshed is sparse and not as integral to the production as the over-the-top gore was for Lewis' groundbreaking effort.

The film itself is fairly interesting and not entirely without historical merit. Paving the way for his future, often blood-soaked offerings, Marins created a film that not only gave him a direction in his prolific career, but single-handedly introduced the horror film (as well as the splatter film) to his home country of Brazil. Today's generation of filmgoers, though, will more than likely find his work both pretentious and juvenile, and will be put off by the dimestore visual effects that punctuate Marin's films. (Not to mention that his later efforts are painfully meandering as well, thanks to their patchwork editing.)

For Coffin Joe fans and hardcore film aficionados only.

Un Accetta per la Luna di Miele
  see **Il Rosso Segno della Follia**

Alarido *see* **Suspiria**

Alice, Sweet Alice (1977)

Allied Artists [USA]; Approximately 112m; Color

DIR: Alfred Sole; PRO: Richard K. Rosenberg; SCR: Rosemary Ritvo and Alfred Sole [Based on the novel **Communion** by Frank Lauria]; DOP: John Friberg and Chuck Hall; SFX: Illusions, Inc.; MUS: Stephen Lawrence

STR: Gary Allen, Dick Boccelli, Peter Bosche, Mary Boylan, Beth Carlton, Mildred Clinton, Alphonso de Noble, Leslie Feigen, Libby Fennelly, Sally Anne Golden, Patrick Gorman, Marco Guazzo, Lucy Hale, Michael Hardstark, Louise Horton, Jane Lowry, Niles McMaster, Linda Miller, Kathy Rich, Antonino Rocca, Drew Roman, Joseph Rossi, Lillian Roth, Paula E. Sheppard, Brooke Shields, Tom Signorelli, Ted Tinling, Michael Weil, Ronald Willoughby, Rudolph Willrich, and Maurice Yonowsky

AKA: **Communion; Holy Terror**
NOV: **Communion** by Frank Lauria [Bantam Books]
VID: **Alice, Sweet Alice** [Anchor Bay Entertainment; 112m]; **Alice, Sweet Alice** [Congress Video; 108m]; **Alice, Sweet Alice** [Goodtimes Video; 112m]; **Alice, Sweet Alice** [Program Hunters, Inc.; 108m]; **Communion** [VCL (PAL); 102m]; **Holy Terror** [Marquis Video; 96m]

Karen's first communion doesn't go so well as the whiny brat is strangled and set aflame only minutes before her turn arrives. Of course, pretty much everyone suspects her

older, highly neurotic and obviously vindictive sister Alice. We—the viewer—know better, even when others are viciously attacked by a masked assailant wearing her very raincoat and galoshes.

Despite the fact this is Ms. Shield's screen debut, she is quickly dispatched in the first ten-or-so minutes (to no one's chagrin, I'm sure). But—surprisingly—there are a number of *other* reasons to take time out to watch this late 70s mystery that undoubtedly owes more to the Italian *giallos* of the previous fifteen years than the whole of American whodunits.

Compelling, and not entirely predictable, Sole's first (and only truly worthwhile) effort is driven by strong anti-Catholic messages (*à la* Peter Walker) and—even more pertinent—littered with unflinchingly disturbing scenes of violence that are reminiscent of Argento's earlier handling of brutality. (Mr. Alfonso, an overweight and effeminate landlord who eventually gets knifed, also harks back to the eccentric supporting players of Dario's earlier thrillers.) Despite all the similarities to the aforementioned *giallos* and—in particular—Mr. Argento's inimitable work, **Alice, Sweet Alice** is far from derivative, showing how a talented director can be inspired by his peers without simply emulating what has already been brought to the screen.

The violence isn't overtly gory, but is nonetheless quite unnerving. A well-used butcher knife—the killer's weapon of choice—is usually aimed at a person's more sensitive areas, not to mention a particularly grueling scene involving a man's teeth getting smashed in with the heel of the killer's shoe.

The only bone I have to pick with the film is a scene involving cat handling that looks particularly inhumane. (Let's just hope it's an extremely effective edit and nothing more.) Until I know for sure, I'll hold off on my "cruelty to animals" warning.

As I alluded to earlier, director Sole helmed a couple of lame follow-ups, namely the well-meaning but absent-minded **Tanya's Island** (1981) and the inexcusably unfunny comedy **Pandemonium** (1982).

Alien (1979)

Brandywine Productions [UK]; Approximately 124m; Color
DIR: Ridley Scott; PRO: Gordon Carroll, David Giler, and Walter Hill; SCR: Dan O'Bannon; DOP: Derek Vanlint and Denys Ayling; EXP: Ronald

Alien

Shusett; MFX: Carlo Rambaldi; MUS: Jerry Goldsmith [Soundtrack available]
STR: Bolaji Badejo, Veronica Cartwright, Ian Holm, Helen Horton, John Hurt, Yaphet Kotto, Tom Skerritt, Harry Dean Stanton, and Sigourney Weaver
AKA: **Le 8ème Passager** [The Eighth Passenger]
NOV: **Alien** by Alan Dean Foster [Warner Books]
VID: **Alien** [CBS/Fox Video; 116m]
ADL: *In space, no one can here you scream...*

This effective, gothic-cum-splatter film disguised as a modern bent on 50s B science fiction is *still* the last word in the entire aliens-on-the-loose subgenre it helped to redefine. (If all of the copycats were even *half* as scary as they were visceral, those like myself wouldn't be so apt to pass them by in the local video stores.) Despite its similarities to one film in particular—**It! The Terror from Beyond Space** (1958)—**Alien** still manages to come across as groundbreaking, defying the categorical restraints that commonly plague exploitation or genre-related productions. (It also steals one of the more effective scenes from Mario Bava's **Terrore nello Spazio** [1965] aka **Planet of the Vampires**, but we'll overlook this if only because they do such a damn good job of pilfering it.)

The relentless pacing exploits the claustrophobic setpieces for all they're worth, instilling in the viewer the nightmare's mandate of "you can run, but you can't hide." With an average cast and crew, this would add up to little more than cheap shocks; with an impeccable group of actors and filmmakers, it becomes the pinnacle of the horror film. **Alien** is about as frightening as a fantasy film can get, surpassing the low expectations that are unfortunately inherent to the genre.

Also contributing to the film's success—almost as important but more often cited than the above reasons—are the alien designs, contributed by Swiss painter H.R. Giger. Internationally acclaimed for his nightmarish brand of surrealism that incorporates occult oriented symbolism and "bio-mechanical" imagery, Giger helped the film succeed where others inevitably failed by creating an adversary that is truly "alien" despite its humanoid stature. (Those who are interested in the paintings which inspired the alien's countenance are urged to check out Giger's **Necronomicon** from Big O Publishing, as well as any other books collecting his work.)

Recommended viewing.

The Alien Dead (1979)

Firebird Pictures Inc. [USA]; Approximately 87m; Color

DIR: Fred Olen Ray; PRO: Fred Olen Ray and Chuck Sumner; SCR: Martin Alan Nicholas and Fred Olen Ray; DOP: Fred Olen Ray; EXP: Henry Kaplan; MFX: Allen Duckworth; MUS: Franklyn Sledge and Chuck Sumner

STR: Mike Bonavia, Ellena Contello, Buster Crabbe, Nancy Karnz, George Kelsey, John Leirier, Linda Lewis, Martin Alan Nicholas, Norman Riggins, Roy Roberts, Edi Stroup, Dennis Underwood, and Rich Vogan

AKA: **It Fell from the Sky; Swamp of the Blood Leeches**

VID: **The Alien Dead** [Academy Home Entertainment; 87m]; **The Alien Dead** [Genesis Home Video; 87m]

This is one of those not-so-rare homemade films which prompts even the most simple-minded couch potato to exclaim "Hey... I can do better than that!" **The Alien Dead** is bottom-of-the-barrel zombie sludge that—despite liberal doses of gore—has nothing to offer outside of the whir of the camera's motor every time the microphone gets too close to the cameraman. Even taking into account the cut-rate production values, one is surprised by how bad the cast is; you would have to take great pains to assemble a troupe of actors as inept as those involved with this backyard effort. (Except, of course, for Buster Crabbe, star of the original **Flash Gordon** and **Buck Rogers** serials. Not surprisingly, this was his last film. Apparently, he couldn't live with the humiliation of having been in this sorry flick, and kicked the metaphorical bucket less than four years later.)

Better left untouched.

L'Alliance Invisible *see* **Tutti i Colori del Buio**

Altar of Blood *see* **Ivanna**

Alucarda *see* **Alucarda—La Hija de las Tinieblas**

Alucarda—La Hija de las Tinieblas [Alucarda—The Daughters of Darkness] (1975)

Films 75 [Mexico] and Yuma Films [Mexico]; Approximately 94m; Color

DIR: Juan López Moctezuma; PRO: Max Gueffen and Eduardo Moreno; SCR: Alexis T. Arroyo, Juan López Moctezuma, and Yolanda L. Moctezuma; DOP: Xavier Cruz; SFX: Abel Contreras; STR: Claudio Brook, Betty Catania, Lily Garza, Susana Kamini, Martin Lasalle, Adriana Roel, Tina Romero, and David Silva

AKA: **Alucarda; Innocents from Hell; Mark of the Devil 3; Sisters of Satan**

VID: **Innocents from Hell** [Neon Video; 94m]; **Sisters of Satan** [Academy Home Entertainment; 94(76)m]

ADL: *They gave their souls to Hell... but the devil wanted MORE!*

Life just doesn't get any better than this.

Although it adheres to the nun exploitation film formula, **Alucarda** sets itself apart from its peers by dwelling more on the gore than the inherent taboo-pitched sexual shenanigans that are usually prevalent in such outings. (Recovering Catholics shouldn't fret, though, as there is still ample footage of unclothed nuns gallivanting about and feeling up each other. I almost wished I had been brought up in a

this actually intensifies the violence and makes it that much more effective.)

Not for the timid, or the easily offended. (Did I mention the nekkid nuns?) ☠☠☠

American Cannibale *see* **Snuff**

Amok *see* **Schizo**

L'Amour Parmi les Monstres *see* **El Espanto Surge de la Tumba**

Andy Warhol's Bad (1977)

New World Pictures [USA]; Approximately 107m; Color

DIR: Jed Johnson; PRO: Jeff Tornberg; SCR: George Abagnalo and Pat Hackett; DOP: Alan Metzger; EXP: Fred Hughes; MUS: Mike Bloomfield

STR: Barbara Allen, Matthew Anton, Carroll Baker, Susan Blond, Mary Boylan, Kitty Bruce, Stefania Casini, Richard Cummings, John Dunn, Michael Forella, Jane Forth, Cyrinda Foxe, Tito Goya, Robert Hodges, Tamara Horrocks, Barbara Hunt, Ruth Jaroslow, Perry King, Joe Lambie, Susan Landau, Charles McGregor, Gordon Oas-Heim, Renee Paris, Brigid Polk, Tom Quinn, Matthew Reich, Jerry Rosenberg, Cathy Roskam, Geraldine Smith, Maria Smith, John Starke, Michael Sullivan, Tere Tereba, Lawrence Tierney, Susan Tyrrell, Vasco Valladares, Pat Way, and Charles Welch

VID: **Andy Warhol's Bad** [Embassy Home Entertainment; 107m]

ADL: *A picture with something to offend absolutely everybody.*

more religiously strict environment just so I could appreciate the taboo elements on a more, uhm, *profound* level.) Throw in one of the more convincingly staged Black Masses put to celluloid and you have a film that is guaranteed *not* to be approved by the Pope.

Despite its over-the-border origins, **Alucarda** was filmed in English. (Not that I really miss the awful dubbing we would've most certainly been subjected to had it been recorded in Spanish; it's just nice to see the dialogue match the actors' lips for a change.) The average production values are boosted by some intense imagery (almost all crucifixion-oriented), and some industrial strength bloodshed. (Unfortunately, most of the gore and geysers of blood are relegated to the last third of the film, but it can also be argued that

Since director Jed Johnson died just a few years back in a plane crash, I thought I'd take the time to honor him by reviewing his swan song, and what is undoubtedly his finest accomplishment. (Okay... so I have no

Andy Warhol's Bad

clue if he actually directed anything else, but with such a fine film to his credit, who cares, right?)

Andy Warhol's Bad is an utterly tasteless black comedy that brings to mind what John Waters might have done if he decided to cut the camp and play it straight around the time of **Desperate Living**. Don't believe me? Carroll Baker runs an electrolysis business that is actually a front for a group of female "hitmen" who will do just about anything if the money's right. One is hired to kill a lady's unwanted baby, but the desperate mother decides—at the very last minute—to save herself some money and do the job herself by throwing the tike out of a five-story window. Another customer wants revenge against her neighbor (Lawrence Tierney) who had made rude comments about her flabby thighs, so she hires a white trash take on the Doublemint twins to waste the ex-cop's beloved dog. Things go from manageable to out of control, though, when Perry King (a Dallesandro-type stud) takes up a room in Baker's establishment and accepts the job of killing a rich couple's autistic son to cover his rent. Also on hand for the fun is Susan Tyrrell (in one of the most unexpected roles of her career) and Stefania Casini (from Argento's **Suspiria**). Without a single, sympathetic character in the bunch, most people probably won't get a whole lot of enjoyment out of watching this film. (If you're anything like *me*, though...)

Gore? Yeah, there's some, although probably not quite enough to justify it being in this book. Besides the baby-toss mentioned earlier, there's also a pretty disturbing scene involving a lift in an auto repair shop and an unfortunate mechanic's vulnerable legs. Even without the over-the-top mayhem of Andy Warhol's **Dracula Vuole Vivere—Cerca Sangue di Vergina!** and **Il Mostro è in Tavola... Barone Frankenstein** (both 1973), splatterpunks will get a kick out of the overall nastiness Warhol's troupe offers the unwary viewer. (If you're anything like me, that is.)

Andy Warhol's Dracula *see* **Dracula Vuole Vivere—Cerca Sangue di Vergina!**

Andy Warhol's Frankenstein *see* **Mostro è in Tavola... Il Barone Frankenstein**

L'Antéchrist *see* L'Antichristo

Antefatto [Before the Fact] (1971)

Nuova Linea Cinematografica [Italy]; Approximately 81m; Color
DIR: Mario Bava; PRO: Giuseppe Zaccariello; SCR: Mario Bava, Sergio Canevari, Filippo Ottoni, Francesco Vanorio, and Giuseppe Zaccariello; DOP: Mario Bava and Antonio Rinaldi; SFX: Carlo Rambaldi; MUS: Stelvio Cipriani
STR: Claudine Auger, Chris Avram, Laura Betti, Guido Boccaccini, Roberto Bonnanni, Nicoletta Elmi, Ilker Inanoglu, Isa Miranda, Giovanni Nuvoletti, Luigi Pistilli, Anna Maria Rosati, Paola Rubens, Brigitte Skay, Leopoldo Trieste, and Claudio Volonté
AKA: **Bahia de Sangre** [Bay of Blood]; **La Baie Sanglante** [The Bloody Bay]; **Blood Bath**; **Carnage**; **L' Ecologia del Delitto**, [Ecology of a Crime]; **Last House on the Left II**; **Reazione a Catena** [Chain Reaction]; **Twitch of the Death Nerve**
VID: **Bay of Blood** [MPI Video; 85(81)m]; **L'Ecologia del Delitto** [Redemption Video (PAL); 80m; LBX]

Why this film is slighted by most Bava fans (some of whom tout it as an "unambitious" effort) I can't say for certain, but I would have to assume that—being fans of more traditional horror—they cannot look past what would be in a lesser director's hands gratuitous violence. Oh, well. Bava's expertise is still more than apparent this far into his career, proving that splatter films can attain to be something more than dime-store *guignol*.

The overused inheritance-driven plot-device is given a new reign on life with this film's *giallo* approach (a genre that Bava helped to create with his groundbreaking **Sei Donne per l'Assassino** [1964] aka **Blood and Black Lace**) and over-the-top excesses inherent to the gore film. Bava also—in a rare breech of tradition—utilizes black humor in what I assume is an attempt to dampen the wave of self-destruction that **Antefatto** initiates within the first few frames. The redemption played out before the camera's unblinking eye is just short of textbook nihilism, and is saved only by a perversely ironic ending.

As a murder mystery, **Antefatto** barely makes the grades. The goings on are

just a little too complex to make sense of in one sitting. (A scorecard similar to that used in the board game **Clue** should have been handed out at screenings. Viewers are advised to make their own.) If you were one of the few individuals able to grasp Dario Argento's **Tenebre** (1982) in its entirety during the initial viewing (which would make you one up on me), be advised that you may need to rely on that same ability here.

It will also interest splatterpunks that many of the situations and means of death were pilfered several years later by the makers of **Friday the 13th**, so any feelings of déjà vu you may have aren't at all unwarranted.

Definitely worth your effort.

L'Antichristo [The Antichrist] (1974)

Capitolina Produzioni Cinematografiche [Italy]; Approximately 112m; Color

DIR: Alberto de Martino; PRO: Edmondo Amati; SCR: Gianfranco Clerici, Alberto de Martino, and Vincenzo Mannino; DOP: Aristide Massaccesi; SFX: Biamonte Cinegroup; MUS: Ennio Morricone and Bruno Nicolai

STR: Ernesto Colli, George Colouris, Mel Ferrer, Remo Girone, Carla Gravina, Arthur Kennedy, Umberto Orsini, Mario Scaccia, Anita Strindberg, and Alida Valli

AKA: L'Antéchrist [*The Antichrist*]; **The Tempter**

VID: **The Tempter** [Embassy Home Entertainment; 96m]

This is one of the sorriest **Exorcist** rip-offs I've been forced to endure, and yours truly has been unlucky enough to have suffered through pretty much the lot of them. **L'Antichristo** *does* boast a particularly distasteful scene involving a newly converted witch performing analingus on an indifferent goat during her first Black Mass—severely edited in the U.S. print—but this and other exploitable taboos (sacrilege, incest, etc.) aren't nearly enough to make it a film worth seeing, even for its precarious geek value.

L'Antichristo is boring exploitation fodder whose questionable highlights include poor optical effects, excremental performances, and tired shocks. (Have you figured it out yet that I really didn't enjoy this one? Sorry if I'm getting bitchy, but *you* sit through this film and try to take it in stride.)

Only for diehard fans looking for tasteless obscurities, no matter how ineffectual they may be. (Include me in this category if you must, but I fell asleep to this sucker twice. And believe you me, it didn't make for a very pleasant nightcap.)

Apartment on the 13th Floor *see* **La Semana del Asesino**

Asesino *see* **Scream Bloody Murder**

Assignment Terror *see* **Los Monstruos de la Noche**

Asylum Erotica *see* **La Bestia Uccide a Sangue Freddo**

Asylum of the Insane (1973)

Heritage Ltd. [UK]; Approximately 97m; Color

Asylum of the Insane

DIR: Peter Walker; PRO: Peter Walker; SCR: Alfred Shaughnessy; DOP: Peter Jessop; MUS: Cyril Ornadel STR: Carol Allen, Robin Askwith, Kent Baker, Patrick Barr, Stuart Bevan, Elizabeth Bradley, Ray Brooks, Jane Cardew, Jess Conrad, Alan Curtis, Rodney Diak, Candace Glendinning, Jenny Hanley, David Howey, Michael Knowles, Sally Lahee, Judy Matheson, Tom Mennard, Penny Meredith, Luan Peters, Tristan Rogers, Brian Tully, Peter Walker, Raymond Young, and John Yule

AKA: **The Flesh and Blood Show**; VID: **The Flesh and Blood Show** [Monterey Home Video; 97m]; **The Flesh and Blood Show** [Wizard Video; 97m]

ADL: *An Appalling Amalgam of Carnage and Carnality...*

A group of young, mostly hard on their luck actors get offered parts in a stage production called "The Flesh and Blood Show." (The theater is located on a pier, ominously isolated from most of civilization. Imagine that.) They spend most of their time either jumping each other's bones or playing dead; as for the latter, they get more than enough opportunities to do it for real once an unknown killer begins stalking the lot of them, covering his/her tracks with mind games and the like.

Asylum of the Insane is another charming Walker production, although more primitive than his later horror-oriented offerings. (The lighting seems unusually bad, although this might be due to the shoddy prints obtained by American video companies. Whatever the reason, it's a real shame as the old waterfront theater makes a wonderful backdrop, its nuances responsible for most of the atmosphere, hence much of the suspense the film generates.) The acting is above par, and the script keeps the viewer on their toes. An engaging murder mystery, **Asylum of the Insane** bears more than a passing resemblance to the *giallo* thriller **Deliria** [*Delirium*] (1987), and not just because of the shared setting. (That film was also released here under a more descriptive title, **Stage Fright**.)

At this point in time, Walker was still in the process of shifting his focus from sexploitation pics to horror flicks, and it shows. Despite its more common (and more apt) moniker of **The Flesh and Blood Show**, **Asylum of the Insane** boasts more flesh than blood; there is an abundance of T&A, but the gore is spread relatively thin. Regardless, it's another effective film from a much-underrated English director.

At Midnight I'll Take Your Soul
see **À Meia-Noite Levarei Sua Alma**

El Ataque de los Muertos sin Ojos [The Attack of the Blind Dead] (1973)

Ancla Century Films [Spain] and Belen Films [Spain]; Approximately 91m; Color

DIR: Amando de Ossorio Rodríguez; PRO: Ramón Plana; SCR: Amando de Ossorio Rodríguez; DOP: Miguel F. Milá; SFX: Amando de Ossorio Rodríguez; MFX: José Luis Campos; MUS: Anton Garcia Abril

STR: Luis Barboo, Franco Braña, José Canalejas, Ramon Cantenero, Juan Cazalilla, Lone Fleming, Ramon Lillo, Esther Ray, Maria Nuria Rodriguez, Esperanza Roy, Betsabe Ruiz, Fernando Sancho, Francisco Sanz, Paco Sanz, Luciano Stella, José Telman, and Loretta Tovar

AKA: **La Cavalcata dei Morti Senza Occhi** [*The Calvary of the Blind Dead*]; **El Retorno del Terror Ciego** [*The Return of the Blind Terror*]; **El Retour des Morts-Vivants** [*The Return of the Living Dead*]; **Return of the Blind Dead; Return of the Evil Dead; Die Rückkehr der Reitenden Leichen** [*The Return of the Riding Dead*]; **De Terugkeer der Gemaskerde Lijken** [*The Terror of the Blind Dead*]

VID: **Return of the Evil Dead** [Bingo Video Inc.; 91m]; **Return of the Evil Dead** [JTC; 87m]; **Return of the Evil Dead** [Precision Video (PAL); RTU]; **Return of the Evil Dead** [Redemption Video (PAL); RTU]

For the most part, de Ossorio's follow-up to **La Noche de las Muerte Ciego** (1971) doesn't offer anything new (except for maybe a higher body count), but if you like the Blind Dead films even half as much as I do, this won't mean squat. Even the most tiring entry of the series (a choice I'll leave for the fans to make) is a trashy little gem like no other. Just the sight of the Blind Dead's hairy little chinbones is enough to make us gape like an eight-year-old horror fan; they're just too damn cool for words.

Unlike its predecessor and—especially—*Ataque*'s sequel **El Buque Maldito** (1974), this entry cuts to the quick, letting our favorite resuscitated corpses make lunch meat out of an entire town who are—speak of the devil—celebrating the one-hundred-year anniversary of the knights' mass execution. (Historically speaking, the Templars had long since disbanded or been wiped out by the 1800s, but we'll forgive the scriptwriters for this little *faux pas*.) The last two-thirds of the film is the expected **Night of the Living Dead**-style goings-on as a small group of survivors hole up in a church and do their damnedest to

fend off the vengeful horde until help arrives. Production values are overall a step up from its predecessor, and—the kind folks that the filmmakers are—they upped the ante on the gore as well.

For the uninitiated, this is pretty spooky stuff that falls somewhere between George Romero's aforementioned zombie classic and John Carpenter's **The Fog** (1980). Just turn out the lights, think back to what it was like being eight years old, do your best to ignore the horrendous dubbing, and you shant be disappointed.

Austria 1700 *see* **Brenn, Hexe, Brenn**

Autopsy *see* **Macchie Solari**

Axe *see* **The Axe**

The Axe (1977)

Childs Associates Films Ltd. [USA] and Frederick Productions [USA]; Approximately 66m; Color
DIR: Frederick R. Friedel; PRO: J.G. Patterson, Jr.; SCR: Frederick R. Friedel; DOP: Austin McKinney; EXP: Irwin Friedlander; MUS: George Newman Shaw and John Willhelm
STR: Suzy Bertoni, Lynne Bradley, Jack Canon, Don Cummins, Frederick R. Friedel, Ray Green, David Hayman, Frank Jones, Graddie Lane, Leslie Lee, Jeff MacKay, Carol Miller, Douglas Powers, Jacqueline Pyle, George Newman Shaw, Hart Smith, Beverly Watterson, and Ronald Watterson
AKA: **Axe**; **The Axe Murders**; **California Axe Massacre**; **California Axe Murders**; **Lisa**; **Lisa, Lisa**
VID: **Axe** [Best Film & Video;

66m; Double-bill w/**A Scream in the Streets**]; **The Axe** [Continental Video; 66m]; **The Axe** [SW Video; 66m]; **California Axe Massacre** [Malibu Video; 75(66)m]; **California Axe Massacre** [Wizard Video; 66m]
ADL: *Total terror—you'll be scared to breathe..!*

"Three killers lurk in a secluded home waiting for their victims to return. After torturing the couple and killing the young husband, they flee to an isolated old house. Their nightmare begins when the hysterical wife follows them to their hideout and begins to slowly get her revenge... with a well-sharpened axe!"

Once again, the publicity department for the video company (Best Film & Video, in this case) didn't even bother to *watch* the film before writing a synopsis for the back of the box. First and foremost, the "couple" is comprised of two gay men, and the one they don't kill throws *himself* to his death immediately thereafter. The "isolated" farmhouse is owned by a girl and her wheelchair-bound father, *she* being the one to exact revenge after the killers torment and abuse the two for several days, not the nonexistent wife.

The Axe (Articles can make a world of difference, you know?) is typically brutal 70s trash that boasts just enough character development and inspired directorial touches to keep things interesting. Director Friedel made a similar (but much more obscure) effort, **Date with a Kidnapper** (1978), which—despite the lack of gore—will still be found endearing to fans of this effort. (What's most puzzling, though, is how hard this film is to find, considering the fact it has been released on video no less than five times in the US alone. **Date with a Kidnapper** suffers the same odd fate.) The gore herein is nothing too terribly substantial either, but the film itself should be of interest to splatterpunks who like reveling in 70s filth.

And, yes, it *was* produced by the director of **The Body Shop** (1974) (aka **Dr. Gore** and **Dr. Gore's Body Shop**), also the same man responsible for the wonderfully high-tech makeup effects which graced many an H.G. Lewis film.

The Axe Murders *see* **The Axe**

Back to the Killer *see* **La Vergine di Norimberga**

Bad Girls *see* **Penetration**

Bahia de Sangre *see* **Antefatto**

Bay of Blood *see* **Antefatto**

Bay of Blood, Part Two *see* **Il Rosso Segno della Follias**

Beast *see* **Beast of the Yellow Night**

Beast of Blood (1970)

Hemisphere Pictures Inc. [Philippines/USA]

DIR: Eddie Romero; PRO: Eddie Romero; SCR: Eddie Romero; DOP: Justo Paulino; EXP: Kane W. Lynn; SFX: Teofilo Hilario; MUS: Tito Arévalo

STR: John Ashley, Liza Belmonte, Angel Buenaventura, Alfonso Carvajal, Eddie Garcia, Johnny Long, Beverly Miller, Bruno Punzalan, and Celeste Yarnall

AKA: **Bestia de Sangre** [Beast of Blood]; **Beast of the Dead; Blood Devils; Horrors of Blood Island; Return to the Horrors of Blood Island**

Approximately 90m; Color

ADL: *Stunning, squirming, SHOCKING terror as a human head transplant creates a new horror creature more fantastic than science—more frightening than fantasy!*

In this sequel to **The Mad Doctor of Blood Island** (1968), Bill Foster (John Ashley) returns to the infamous island and finds things have not settled down much since the supposed disposal of the dreaded Dr. Lorca. The natives have become restless following a series of mysterious abductions by "the evil one." It seems that not only has the mad doctor survived—albeit horribly disfigured—he has managed to keep alive not only the body of the "blood

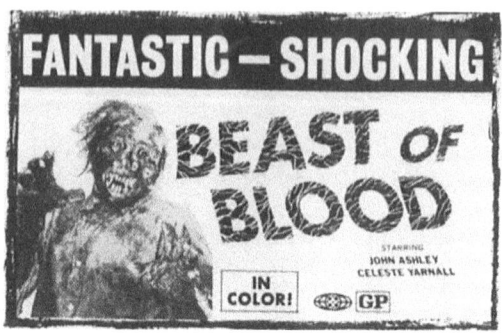

monster" responsible for his unsightly appearance, but its decapitated head as well. So, it's up to 60s cut-rate teen heartthrob Ashley to clean up the mess and save the poor ignorant natives from being used as human pigs. (Guess he got tired of lounging around with Annette Funicello and Frankie Avalon, those wussies.)

For those who love low-rent splatter from the Philippines, this is the third in a trilogy of "Blood Island" films. (The second I've already mentioned; the first was the similarly titled **Brides of Blood** [1966], which also featured John Ashley as the hero and Eddie Romero calling the shots. Hey, one shouldn't fix what's not broken, right?) Production values are still about ten, maybe twenty years behind the time, the script is still fettered with a politically incorrect charm, and the gore is still cheap and nasty. Unfortunately, the filmmakers called it quits with this particular franchise after **Beast of Blood**, and went on to do a couple of other somewhat inferior, but still loads of fun trash horror flicks. (Okay, so **The Twilight People** [1972] might as well have been an entry in the Blood Island series, even though it was painfully bereft of gore.)

So now that I got me a **Mark of the Devil** barf bag, where can I snag one of those fake ten dollar bills with the **Beast of Blood** ad art printed on the backside?

Beast of the Yellow Night (1970)

Four Associates Ltd. [Philippines/USA]

DIR: Eddie Romero; PRO: John Ashley and Eddie Romero; SCR: Eddie Romero; DOP: Justo Paulino; EXP: David J. Cohen and Beverly Miller; SFX: Teofilo Hilario; MUS: Nestor Robles

STR: John Ashley, Carpi Asturias, Andrés Centenera, Crisalda, Vic Diaz, Joonee Gabboa, Eddie Garcia, José García, Ruben Gastia, Don Liaman, Johnny Long, Peter Magurean, Ken Metcalfe, Nora Nunez, Jose Roy, Jr., Leopoldo Salcedo, James Spencer, and Mary Wilcox

AKA: **Beast; La Bestia de la Noche Amarilla** [*The Beast of the Yellow Night*]

Approximately 87m; Color

VID: **Beast** [Delta Video (PAL); 90(87)m]; **Beast of the Yellow Night** [Cult Video; 80m]; **Beast of the Yellow Night** [Edde Entertainment; 87m]; **Beast of the Yellow Night** [United Home Video; 87m]

A criminal's life is spared by the devil himself, in exchange for—what else?—his soul. Part of the package, though, is a curious side effect whereupon our anti-hero turns into a crusty-faced monster and feeds upon some of the other islanders.

Sound like a sure bet for a trashy horror film? You bet.

Despite some mild racism and horrendously bad makeup (both of which are pretty typical of a Filipino horror film), this is a fairly ambitious effort considering those involved. (Being another John Ashley vehicle helmed by the not-so-illustrious Eddie Romero, you would assume it to be a *lot* worse than it really is.)

Not only are the production values a cut or two above the usual, **Beast of the Yellow Night** boasts a reasonably original and thought-provoking screenplay. (Of course, the script often falters into low-rent melodrama; when asked a simple "Who are you?" Ashley replies "As far as you're concerned, I am, and can only be, whoever or whatever you think I am." Whatever you say, John.) Ashley, a Naschy-inspired anti-hero, gets to overstep what is usually required of him in Romero's films, namely seducing young native girls and destroying whatever cut-rate monster is on the rampage. (If only because he *is* the cut-rate monster on the rampage.) Like Naschy's "El Hombre Lobo," the angst is laid on pretty thick; unfortunately, though, he doesn't quite have the chops to back it up. Still, he's just so damn *cool*... it's almost stifling.

The gore is fairly extreme, and not bad considering the usual level of competence in Romero's flicks. Still, **Beast of the Yellow Night** will probably only appeal to those viewers who have already been stricken by the Philippines' native charms.

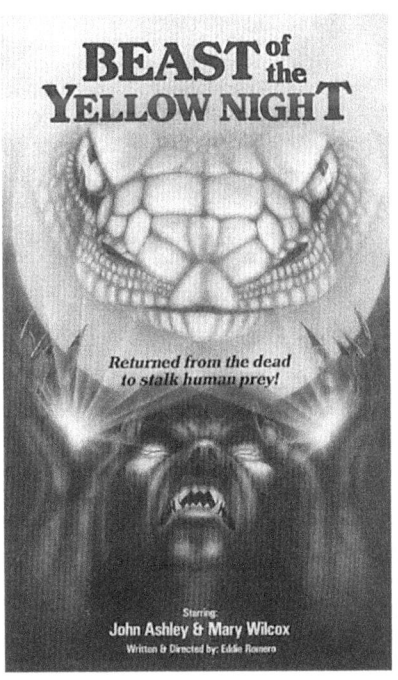

Bebere Tu Sangre *see* **I Drink Your Blood**

Bebo Tu Sangre *see* **I Drink Your Blood**

Die Bestia aus dem Totenreich *see* **La Orgia de los Muertos**

La Bestia Uccide a Sangue Freddo [The Beast Kills in Cold Blood] (1971)

Cineproduzione Daunia 70 [Italy] DIR: Fernando di Leo; PRO: Tiziano Longo and Armando Novelli; SCR: Fernando di Leo and Nino Latino; DOP: Franco Villa; MUS: Silvano Spadaccino

STR: Giulio Baraghini, Ettore Ceri, Fernando Cerulli, Gidia Desideri, John Eley, Jane Garret, John Karlsen, Klaus Kinski, Margaret Lee, Rosalba Neri, Antonio Radaelli, Sandro Rossi, and Monica Strebel

La Bestia Uccide a Sangue... 52

AKA: **Asylum Erotica; La Cliniques des Horreurs** [*The Hospital of Horrors*]; **La Cliniques des Ténèbres** [*The Hospital of Darkness*]; **The Cold-Blooded Beast; Hotel Erotica; Les Insatisfaites Poupées Érotiques du Dr. Hichcock** [*The Insatiable Sex Dolls of Dr. Hichcock*]; **Les Poupées du Professeur Hichcok** [*The Dolls of Professor Hichcock*]; **Les Poupées Sanglantes du Docteur X** [*The Bloody Dolls of Doctor X*]; **Das Schloß der Blauen Vögel** [*The Castle of the Blue Bird*]; **Slaughter Hotel; Der Triebmörder** [*The Sex Killer*]

Approximately 89m; Color

VID: **Asylum Erotica** [Meteor Video; 72m]; **La Bestia Uccide a Sangue Freddo** [Video Clak (PAL); 89m; In Italian]; **Les Poupées du Professeur Hichcok** [Farah Film Production (PAL); 85(89)m; In French]; **Slaughter Hotel** [MPI Home Video; 100(89)m]

ADL: *Carved out of today's headlines! See the slashing of 8 innocent nurses! Slaughter Hotel...*
A place where nothing is forbidden!

La Bestia Uccide a Sangue Freddo is ultra-sleazy Eurotrash which boasts Kinski as a not-too-convincing psychiatrist at a clinic for women and who may or may not be a killer slaughtering the patients while they lounge around in various stages of undress. The sloppy handheld camerawork (one almost wonders if the cinematographer had imbibed a few too many spirits) is enough to make viewers with even iron constitutions reach for the Dramamine. There is a hell of a lot of early 70s gore and nudity (a failed attempt to pad out what is a pretty slipshod murder-mystery), but even the most hardcore exploitation junkies will find it an effort to wade through the proceedings.

As you may have noticed, the original ad campaign (as well as the film's finale) was devised to mirror and cash in on the still-lingering notoriety of the massacre of eight student nurses by sicko Richard Speck. The promoters of this film, it seems, aren't much better. And—just in case this bag ain't sleazy enough for you—there is rumored to be a version containing hardcore footage making the rounds, but this has yet to be substantiated.

Beyond the Darkness *see* Buio Omega

Beyond the Fog *see* Tower of Evil

Beyond the Living *see* Nurse Sherri

Beyond the Living Dead *see* La Orgia de los Muertos

Big Snuff *see* Snuff

The Black Frankenstein see Blackenstein

Black Magic III *see* Ratu Ilmu Hitam

Black Magic Queen *see* Ratu Ilmu Hitam

Black Magic Rites—Reincarnation *see* Riti, Magie Nere e Segreto Orge nel Trecento...

Black Magic Terror *see* Ratu Ilmu Hitam

Blackenstein (1972)

FRSCO Productions Limited [USA]
DIR: William A. Levey; PRO: Frank R. Saletri; SCR: Frank R. Saletri; DOP: Robert Caramico; EXP: Ted Tetrick; SFX: Ken Strickfadden; MFX: Gordon Freed; MUS: Cardella de Milo and Lou Frohman

STR: Dale E. Bach, Nick Bolin, Don Brodie, Bob Brophy, Andy C, James Cousar, Cardella de Milo, Joe de Sue, Marva Farmer, Daniel Fauré, Beverly Hagerty, John Hart, Robert L. Hurd, Roosevelt Jackson, Andrea King, Karin Lind, Liz Renay, Yvonne Robinson, Jerry Soucie, and Ivory Stone

AKA: **The Black Frankenstein; Return of Blackenstein**

Approximately 92m; Color

VID: **Blackenstein** [Media Home Entertainment; 87(86)m]

This one's a doozy of a rotten film, but it's also a bit too slow to make the ranks of the "So Bad It's Great" hall of fame. That shouldn't stop trash fiends from enjoying this blaxploitation flick that dishes up low-rent actors delivering precariously stilted dialogue that would make Ed Wood proud, with production values

Blood and Lace

More Bizarre Than The Original
BLACKENSTEIN
Starring JOHN HART, IVORY STONE, LIZ RENAY

equally dismal. (For a scene involving a quadriplegic—who is eventually fashioned into the resident patchwork monster—the effects department decided to save time and money by throwing a sheet over the supposedly limbless man. C'mon, they could have at least spent the time to cut holes in the mattress in an attempt to conceal the amputated limbs, for cryin' out loud, but I for one am almost glad they didn't.) Best of all, though, is **Blackenstein**'s monster himself, who belies his dated fashion sense by sporting a flattop afro.

The film barely lives up to a PG rating (let alone the issued R) for the first two-thirds of the film; it looks as if the filmmakers suddenly realized (none too soon) the possibility of ticket buyers demanding their money back and decided to go for broke by laying on the sex and violence in the last reel. The gore—mostly dismemberments and disembowelings—is really primitive, and is usually preceded by our monster ripping off his victims' blouses. (Any attempts at making a grand sociopolitical statement are—thankfully—buried beneath the sleazy excesses heaped onto this shoddy production.)

Blackenstein is ludicrous and hackneyed blaxploitation fare that is only recommended to bad film aficianados.

Blade of the Ripper (1970) see Lo Strano Vizio della Signora Wardh

Blade of the Ripper (1976) see Schizo

Blind Dead, The *see* La Noche del Terror Ciego

Bloedige Heksenjacht *see* Brenn, Hexe, Brenn

Bloedlink *see* Profondo Rosso

Blood and Lace (1970)

Carlin Company Productions [USA] and Contemporary Film-Makers [USA]

DIR: Philip Gilbert; PRO: Ed Carlin and Gil Lasky; SCR: Gil Lasky; DOP: Paul Hipp; ART: Lee Fischer; EFX: Dennis Marsh [Makeup]; MUS: John Rons

STR: Peter Armstrong, Ben Besser, Dennis Christopher, Maggie

Corey, Joe Durkin, Gloria Grahame, Terri Messina, Melody Patterson, Milton Selzer, Louise Sherrill, Ronald Taft, and Vic Tayback

Approximately 86m; Color
VID: **Blood and Lace** [HBO Video; 87(86)m]
ADL: *SHOCK! After SHOCK! as desire drives a bargain with DEATH!*

A sleeping hooker and her john are attacked by an unseen assailant with a claw hammer. The woman is killed (not only does she wail like she's in the throes of an orgasm, her lover isn't even roused out of his stupor by the commotion), and both are set on fire. While a police detective is looking into the case, the prostitute's surviving teenage daughter is put in the care of the Deere Youth Home, an orphanage with rather strict rules: Anyone attempting to run away is brutally dispatched with a meat cleaver. (Sounds fair to me.) Those who stay suffer at the hands of an abusive matron and her sleazy, opportunistic henchman. And, to keep the fun moving along, everyone is doing their best to hide their closeted skeletons from the other players while avoiding the various sharp instruments.

Blood and Lace boasts more R-rated fun than any other PG-rated film I've ever seen: bloody clawhammer killings, sleazy old men referring to underage girls as "good breeding stock," a hand lopped off by a well-aimed meat cleaver (and another lodged in someone's spine), freezerburnt teens, implied incest, and—best of all—not one likable or sympathetic character in the bunch. (Where's the guy in the purple robe and sunglasses wielding the aforementioned clawhammer that graces the movie poster and ad art? Instead, we have to settle with what looks like a chunky Freddy Krueger.) Oh, and did I mention the clawhammer cam? (Don't make me explain, all right?)

Not real heavy in the gore department, but the seedy atmosphere more than makes up for it (as does the multiple twist endings that cap off this sleazy offering).

Blood Castle *see* **Ceremonia Sangrienta**

Blood Ceremony *see* **Ceremonia Sangrienta**

Blood Devils *see* **Beast of Blood**

Blood Feast (1963)

Box Office Spectaculars [USA]
DIR: Herschell Gordon Lewis; PRO: David F. Friedman, Stanford S.

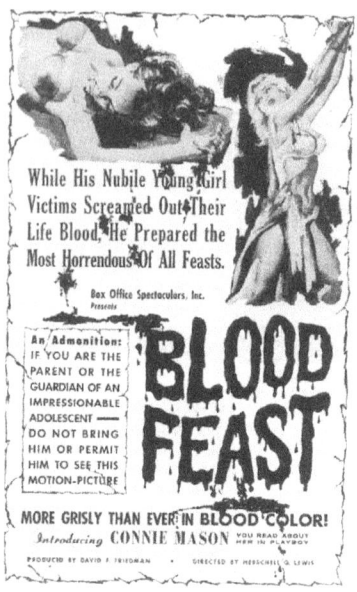

Kohlberg, and Herschell Gordon Lewis; SCR: Allison Louise Downe; DOP: Herschell Gordon Lewis; SFX: Herschell Gordon Lewis; MUS: Herschell Gordon Lewis

STR: Mal Arnold, Lyn Bolton, Toni Calvert, Gene Courtier, Jerome Eden, David F. Friedman, Al Golden, Scott H. Hall, Louise Kamp, William Kerwin, Ashlyn Martin, Connie Mason, Craig Maudslay, Jr., Astrid Olson, Hal Rich, Sandra Sinclair

Approximately 75m; Color

NOV: **Blood Feast** by Herschell Gordon Lewis [Novel Books]; **Blood Feast** by Herschell Gordon Lewis [Fantaco Enterprises]

SND: **Blood Feast** [Rhino Records; Split LP w/**Two-Thousand Maniacs**]

VID: **Blood Feast** [Comet Video; 75m]; **Blood Feast** [Cult Video; 75m]; **Blood Feast** [Rhino Video; 75m]

ADL: *Nothing so appalling in the annals of horror!*

This is it... the film that kick-started a trend and made gore films a legitimate genre separate from its cinematic progenitor, the horror film. Virtually made by a mild-mannered, one man killing machine (albeit bankrolled and promoted by David F. Friedman, grandfather of the adult film industry), Herschell Gordon Lewis gained instant cult status by crossing every cinematic taboo related to the theme of violence. Not only was stage blood spilled to an unprecedented extent, he dug a little deeper, showing us the

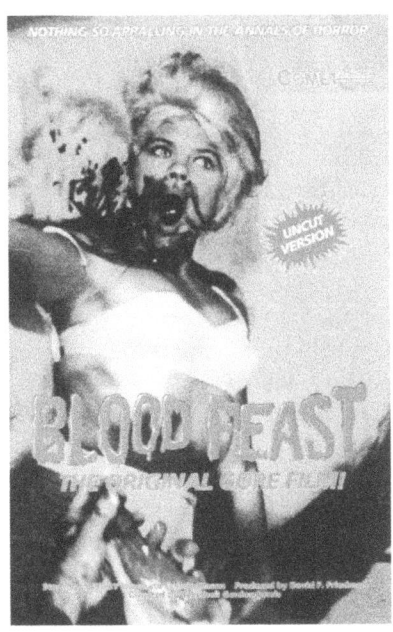

things second-year medical students become quite familiar with. The story was only a device to get from one gruesome killing to the next (a contrivance which would haunt the genre to the present day, being used by opponents to prove its lack of artistic merit and social relevance). Many would try to outdo said film (even Lewis himself spent the next ten years trying to live up to his own standards), but few would even touch the same nerve (or gag reflex, take yer pick) that **Blood Feast** did in 1963.

For those unfamiliar with the film, **Blood Feast** chronicles the killing spree of Fuad Ramses, an Egyptian caterer who offers blood sacrifices to the goddess Ishtar. (Represented here by a mannequin wrapped in tin foil and gauze.) That's about it, folks. To make things worse (or better, depending on your tolerance for trash filmmaking), all of the production values are substandard, even as far as horror and exploitation films went at the time. Thirty-some-odd years later, it seems even more miserable, but—despite the abundance of splatter films and the advances in special effects—one can still appreciate the spark generated by this single production. It might not be a *good* film, but it is easily the most *influential* film of all time. (Having seen more films—directly or indirectly—inspired by said film than even *I* can recall, I can say this with the utmost conviction.)

Required viewing, if only for its historical merit. ☠☠☠

Blood for Dracula *see* **Dracula Cerce Sangue di Vergine... Mori di Sete**

Blood Freak (1971)

Production company unknown [USA]

DIR: Brad F. Grinter and Steve Hawkes; PRO: Brad F. Grinter and Steve Hawkes; DOP: Ron Sill; MUS: Gil Ward

STR: Tera Anderson, Dana Cullivan, Bob Currier, Dolores Currier, Randy Grinter, Jr., Dominik Grutta, Steve Hawkes, Heather Hughes, Sandy Kneelen, Lee Morris, Linda Past, Linda Preuwet, Anne Shearin, Francis Sipek, Debbie Smith, Sam Taker, Jane Tarber, Steve Vaughan, and Larry Wright

AKA: **Blood Freaks**

Approximately 86m; Color

VID: **Blood Freak** [New Horizons Home Video; 86m]; **Blood Freak** [Regal Video; 86m]

ADL: *A Dracula On Drugs!*

Blood Freak

This is one of those notoriously awful trash wonders that you stumble across only if Lady Luck is truly with you. Here's the scoop: a drifter (a Vietnam vet with nasty burns, an addiction to morphine, and an unpredictable accent, played by co-director Hawkes) is picked up and taken home by a Bible-thumping cutie, only to fall for her hippie sister. With her airhead charms and rabid Kewpie-doll voice, she seduces him (with the aid of an unspecified, highly addictive drug). Somewhere along the line, he gets a job working at a turkey farm where they just so happen to be testing out some experimental drugs. He passes out after they decide he would make a dandy guinea pig, and is left by the farmhands in a field where he spends the remainder of the day, unconscious and suffering from some very severe seizures. He eventually recovers, but—to his dismay—he's not quite the man he once was. He now boasts a large (obviously papier-mâché) turkey head, and an insatiable predilection for the blood of junkies. And, well... it gets worse. (Gods be praised.)

Onscreen narration (gratiously supplied by co-director Grinter) about God and the downfalls of drug abuse, an unbelievably bad script recited by inept actors who seem a little too distracted by the cue cards on which they sorely depend, an overused set of post-synched looped screams, and a *lot* of spurting blood being lapped up by our deformed anti-hero gobbling like a turkey round out the proceedings. (An ensuing sex scene between the "Blood Freak" and his true love, cut short during the onscreen foreplay, is sure to wake up even the most jaded filmgoer. Truly, truly touching, that.)

No holds barred, **Blood Freak** is probably the worst, most audacious film I've ever seen. Ain't life grand? 🐱🐱🐱

Blood Freaks *see* **Blood Freak**

Blood Hunger *see* **Vampyres**

Blood Moon *see* **La Noche de Walpurgis**

Blood of Frankenstein *see* **Dracula vs. Frankenstein** (1971)

Blood of the Undead *see* **Schizo**

Blood Orgy *see* **The Gore-Gore Girls**

Blood Rites *see* The Ghastly Ones

The Blood Seekers *see* Dracula vs. Frankenstein (1971)

Blood Stalkers *see* Bloodstalkers

Blood Sucking Freaks *see* The Incredible Torture Show

Blood Tide (1977)

Athon Productions [Greece] and Conaught International [UK]
DIR: Richard Jeffries; PRO: Donald Langdon and Nico Mastorakis; SCR: Richard Jeffries and Nico Mastorakis; DOP: Ari Stavrou; EXP: John D. Schofield; SFX: Yannis Samiotis; MFX: Vince Jeffords; MUS: Jerry Moseley
STR: Lydia Cornell, José Ferrer, James Earl Jones, Lila Kedrova, Martin Kove, Spyros Papafrantziz, Rania Photiou, Annabel Schofield, Sofia Seirli, Deborah Shelton, Despina Tomazina, Irini Tripkou, and Mary Louise Weller
AKA: The Red Tide
Approximately 82m; Color
VID: **Blood Tide** [Continental Video; 82m]
ADL: *It feeds on human flesh!*

A young man follows his missing sister to a secretive Greek isle, and finds not only his loopy sibling, but a Shakespeare-spouting, machete-wielding "archaeologist" who inadvertently unleashes a primeval critter from its watery imprisonment. Unfortunate for everyone involved, the already paranoid natives are forced to revive certain traditions which involve virgins and blood sacrifices. (Can't have one without the other, now can we?)
This small scale monster flick is exceptional for a number of reasons, not the least of which is the presence of James Earl Jones, a powerful actor who brings a certain amount of depth to even the most tawdry productions he appears in. (Not to imply **Blood Tide** is cheap genre fodder; low-rent, maybe, but exceptional considering the budget.) Also of note is the film's unrelenting atmosphere; despite the formula, the filmmakers keep the proceedings tense, instilling an essential sense of dread that is sorely missing from most horror films in this day and age. (Remember when monster flicks used to be scary?)
Although the gore is not gratuitous, the few scenes that punctuate this film are far from tame. The only real letdown—in reference to special effects or otherwise—is the monster itself; fortunately, we are spared the sight of its rubbery hide for all but a few frames.
Since the title on the U.S. print of **Blood Tide** was videoburned, I think it is safe to assume that it was originally released under another title, but I have yet to find reference to the elusive moniker anywhere.
If monster flicks are your thing, check it out.

Bloodlust *see* Mosquito der Schander

Bloodstalkers (1975)

Bloodstalkers Ltd. [USA]
DIR: Robert W. Morgan; PRO: Robert W. Morgan; SCR: Robert W. Morgan; DOP: Irv Rudley; EXP: Ben Morse; SFX: Doug Hobart; MUS: Stan Webb

Bloodthirsty Butchers

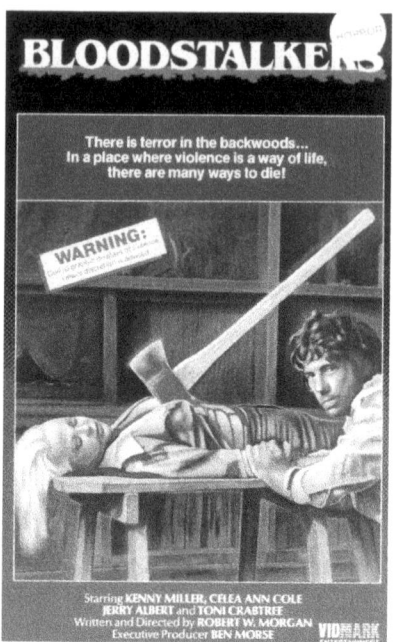

STR: Jerry Albert, Nina Baeza, Lane Chiles, Celea-Ann Cole, Toni Crabtree, Ted Ernst, Herb Goldstein, Joe Hilton, John R. Meyer, Kenny Miller, Robert W. Morgan, David Paris, Michael Polesnek, Joanne Rettew, Irv Rudley, Kristina von Mueller, Jerry Watson, Stan Webb, Karen Williams, and Chuck Yates
AKA: **Blood Stalkers**
Approximately 91m; Color
VID: **Bloodstalkers** [Vidmark Entertainment; 91m]
ADL: *In a place where violence is a way of life, there are many ways to die!*

Despite warnings from a small town's inbred populace (they prefer the label of "cranky old swamp rats," thank you very much), two couples vacationing in the Florida Everglades refuse to steer clear of an isolated cabin owned by one of the men. Before they've even had the opportunity to sweep out the cobwebs, the four saps find themselves being stalked by a dime-store bog beastie who has a penchant for farming implements. (Remember **The Prey**'s wonderful adline which boasts "It's not human... and it's got an axe?" Apparently, our resident bloodstalker isn't so limited with what he uses to dispatch people.)

If you *have not* read the blow-by-blow synopsis on the back of the video jacket, you will probably find **Bloodstalkers** an unpredictable, albeit melodramatic obscurity that ranks in there as one of the better no-budget swamp monster flicks. Unfortunately, the screenwriters decided to relegate all of the gore to the last ten-or-so minutes; this, of course, was not the smartest of moves as—being an exploitation film—the screenplay isn't always enough to hold the viewer's interest for the first hour-plus. (Ya' gotta spread it around a little, guys, or else we're going to be reaching for the fast-forward button on our remotes. Of course, this was made shortly before home video became an accessible medium, but still...)

Quite charming, as far as dross is concerned. (If this floats yer boat, check out the Findlay's similarly-orchestrated **Shriek of the Mutilated** [1974] for more of the same.)

Bloodsucking Freaks *see* **The Incredible Torture Show**

Bloodthirsty Butchers (1970)

Constitution Films, Inc. [UK/USA]
DIR: Andy Milligan; PRO:

Bloodthirsty Butchers

William Mishkin; SCR: John Borske and Andy Milligan; DOP: Andy Milligan; EFX: Marcia Neilson

STR: Ann Arrow, Shirley Ashdown, Dickson Bain, William Barrel, George Barry, Susan Cassidy, Michael Cox, Linda Driver, Frank Echols, Jane Hilary, Jonathan Holt, Berwick Kaler, John Miranda, David Pike, and Annabella Wood

Approximately 78m; Color

VID: **Bloodthirsty Butchers** [Midnight Video; 80(78)m]

ADL: *Their prime cuts were curiously erotic... but thoroughly brutal!*

For some reason, this is the film that has become synonymous with the creator, Andy Milligan. Although it is representative of Milligan and his no-rent exercises in gratuity and clotheshorse melodrama, it is by no means his best film. Still, this gory adaptation of Sweeney Todd—a *grand guignol* favorite—is truly worthy of mention, and a must-see for those who appreciate Milligan's stunted charms. (Sure, the severed-breast-in-a-meat-pie scene is quite silly, but it's the thought that counts.)

For those unaware of the pitfalls of a Milligan feature, be prepared for a truly inept exercise. Editing is harried and slipshod, the photography (in respect to any scenes involving action) invariably culminates with the camera spinning wildly out of control, select stock music is used liberally (with several incongruous pieces overlapped at one point), and the acting on par with most high school play productions, at best. But, oh, the sideburns... the sideburns make it all seem worthwhile.

Debatably, it's a notch above **The Ghastly Ones**. (And even ends on a similar note with an airborne meat cleaver planting itself in the villain's noggin. How's that for convenience?)

Yes, it really is bad, and suggested only for truly desensitized trash fiends like myself.

Bloody Countess *see* **Ceremonia Sangrienta**

The Bloody Exorcism of Coffin Joe *see* **Exorcismo Negro**

Das Blutegerecht der Reitenden Leichen *see* **La Noche de las Gaviotas**

Blutmesse der Zombies *see* **El Espanto Surge de la Tumba**

Blutmesse für den Teufel *see* **El Espanto Surge de la Tumba**

The Body Shop (1974)

Metrolina Motion Picture Corporation [USA]
DIR: J.G. Patterson, Jr.; PRO: J.G. Patterson, Jr.; SCR: J.G. Patterson, Jr.; DOP: Harry M. Joyner; EXP: Robert M. McClure; SFX: J.G. Patterson, Jr.; MFX: J.G. Patterson, Jr.; MUS: William B. Girdler and Bill Hicks
STR: Jeannine Aber, Chris Allen, Reggie Belk, Jan Benfield, Don Brandon, Judy Calloway, Vince Carmen, Mike de Skram, Jenny Driggers, Bill Ennis, Linda Failo, Candy Furr, Dave Graig, Jack Hamell, Bill Hicks, Kerry Joyner, Jerry Kearns, Joe B. Lamb, Linda Lindsey, Roy Mehaffey, Vickie O'Neal, Nita Patterson, Bill Simpson, Ken Simpson, and Howard Stewart
AKA: **Doctor Gore; Doctor Gore's Body Shop**
Approximately 83m; Color
VID: **Body Shop** [Paragon Video Productions; 75m]; **Doctor Gore** [United Home Video; 90(83)m]

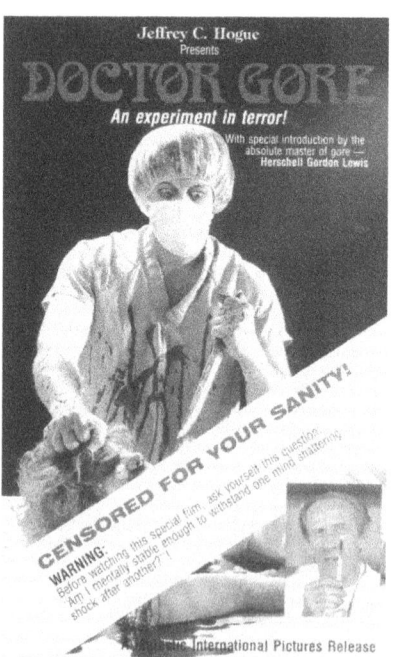

A doctor, obsessed with reviving his dead wife, goes to gore-drenched extremes to resuscitate his one true love. Say, now *there's* an original idea for a horror film. (Yawn.)

This is little more than an H.G. Lewis–style production sans the self-deprecating humor that pervades his films and makes them such an unmitigated joy to watch. (I guess it should come as no surprise then that Patterson worked on several of Lewis' films, primarily as an effects artist. Of course, the term "artist" is used in the loosest sense.) There are a few scenes that are worthy of a chuckle, but even these are a little forced. (A dead girl wrapped in tin foil and accidentally baked by our resident mad scientists is responsible for one of the better attempts at humor.) Otherwise, it's your typical love-shorn mad scientist fare. (Which, of course, wouldn't be complete without the obligatory hunchbacked assistant. Can't forget him, now can we?)

Although the lead is played by one Don Brandon (billed as "America's No. 1 Magician" in the opening credits), I have a sneaking suspicion that this is none other than J.G. Patterson hiding behind a pseudonym. (Don't ask ... call it a hunch.) I would also swear Ray Sager (of **The Wizard of Gore** "fame") makes an appearance as a prison guard. (In this case, I'm probably mistaken as I don't see any reason for *him* to use an alias.)

Be warned: You may have to view this film with the sound off.

The entire soundtrack consists of Patterson—oops—Brandon himself singing (ad infinitum) a verse from a "bowdlerized" children's song which claims "Sugar and spice, and everything nice. That's what little girls are made of. But as they get bigger, they take on a figure, and some are much nicer than others." Trust me… you'll be screaming for earplugs before the film hits the second reel.

Rumor has it that Patterson died shortly after the completion of this film, and that the only existing print was dug out of his garage almost ten years later. Quite possible, but it's sad to think that **The Body Shop** would be his swan song. ☠☠☠

The Bogeyman and the French Murders see **La Casa d'Appuntamento**

The Boogeyman (1977)

Interbest American Enterprises [USA]
DIR: Ulli Lommel; PRO: Ulli Lommel; SCR: David Herschel, Ulli Lommel, and Suzanna Love; DOP: Jochen Breitenstein and David Sperling; EXP: Wolf Schmidt; SFX: Craig Harris; MUS: Tim Krog
STR: Raymond Boyden, John Carradine, Katie Casey, Gilian Gordon, Howard Grant, Ron James, Nicholas Love, Suzanna Love, Ernest Meier, Felicite Morgan, Claudia Porcelli, Jane Pratt, Bill Rayburn, Stony Richards, Natasha Schiano, David Swim, Catherine Tambini, Llewelyn Thomas, Jay Wright, and Lucinda Zeising
Approximately 82m; Color
VID: **The Boogeyman** [Magnum Entertainment; 81(82)m]; **The Boogeyman** [Wizard Video; 86(82)m]
ADL: *The most terrifying nightmare of childhood is about to return!*

Since the video box synopsis tells you everything you ever wanted to know about the goings-on, I'll get to the point. (Talk about Cliff Notes. Sheesh.) Although adequate, **The Boogeyman** is little more than a supernaturally-driven rip-off of **Halloween** (1978). Save for the plot (and even this is quite derivative), everything seems to have been lifted from Carpenter's preeminent slasher film: music, staging, et al. Despite its stalk'n'slash leanings, the script focuses on the supernatural aspects (even though the poltergeist's origin is similar to Michael Myer's indoctrination into psychodom).

Lommel (and the respective crew members) should be given some credit in maintaining a particularly spooky and somber atmosphere throughout (again, with tricks obviously borrowed from Mr. Carpenter, but who's keeping track). If only they could have pulled it off again for the unbelievably inept sequel.

Overrated, but not utterly without merit. (Of course, any dues should probably be given to John Carpenter, but...)

Le Bossu de la Morgue see **El Jorobado de la Morgue**

Breakfast at Manchester Morgue see **Non Si Deve Profanare il Sonno dei Morto**

Brenn, Hexe, Brenn [Burn, Witch, Burn] (1970)

Hi-Fi Stereo 70-KG [West Germany]

DIR: Michael Armstrong and Adrian Hoven; PRO: Adrian Hoven;

SCR: Michael Armstrong and Adrian Hoven; DOP: Ernst W. Kalinke; MFX: Günther Kulier and Alena Heidankova; MUS: Michael Holm

STR: Johannes Buzalski, Dorothea Carrera, Günter Clemens, Gaby Fuchs, Herbert Fuchs, Bob Gerry, Adrian Hoven, Curd Jürgens, Udo Kier, Herbert Lom, Michael Maien, Reggie Nalder, Marlies Petersen, Ingeborg Schoener, Doris von Danwitz, and Olivera Vuco

AKA: **Austria 1700; Bloedige Heksenjacht** [*Bloody Witchhunt*]; **Hexen Bis Aufs Blut Gequält** [*Witches Tortured Until the Blood Flows*]; **Mark of the Devil; Satan; Les Sorcières Sanglantes** [*The Bloody Sorcerers*]

Approximately 97m; Color

VID: **Mark of the Devil** [Anchor Bay Entertainment; 90(97)m; LBX]; **Mark of the Devil** [Lightning Video; RTU]; **Mark of the Devil** [Redemption Video (PAL); RTU]; **Mark of the Devil** [T-Z Video; 97(96)m]

ADL: *Positively the most horrifying film ever made! Likely to upset your stomach!*

Udo (**Andy Warhol's Frankenstein** and **Dracula**) Kier stars as an assistant witchfinder general who comes to learn that some of his elders have a tendency to abuse their positions of office for their own twisted ends. (Doesn't take much suspension of disbelief here, now

does it?) Herbert Lom and Reggie (**Salem's Lot** and **The Dead Don't Die**) Nalder are the aforementioned witch hunters who want to ensure that Kier doesn't overstep his bounds and ruin it for them. The film's culmination—surprising even by today's standards—will surely leave a sour taste in the mouths of even the more callused gorehounds. (Still unreleased is a version which boasts a different finale altogether; this alternate ending ditches the more nihilistic cap for one where the victims of the witchfinder general rise from the grave to exact retribution. Needless to say, this poorly calculated stab of poetic justice would have quashed the film's serious tone.)

Forget all of the hoopla surrounding this infamous witchburning flick and enjoy it for what it is. Despite all of the lambasting by critics over the years, **Brenn, Hexe, Brenn** is easily one of the best films of this once-popular subgenre. Although not "vomit-inducing" like the film's American promoters claimed (theater goers were given free barf bags with the film's ad art printed on its face), it is actually quite disturbing, for all the right reasons. (Furthermore, it's actually quite *moving* in parts, God forbid.)

Speaking of "moving," does anyone out there have an extra **Mark of the Devil** barf bag they want to part with?

Brides of Blood (1966)

Hemisphere Pictures, Inc. [Philippines/USA]

DIR: Gerardo de Leon and Eddie Romero; PRO: Eddie Romero; EXP: Kane W. Lynn

STR: Angelita Alba, John Ashley, Andres Centenera, Eva Darren, Carmelita Estrella, Beverly Hills, Oscar Keesee, Quiel Mendoza, Mario Montenegro, Pedro Navarro, Bruno Punzalan, Ely Ramos, Jr., Ben Sanchez, Kent Taylor, and Willie Tomada

AKA: **Brides of Blood Island; Brides of Death; Brides of the Beast; Grave Desires; The Island of Living Horror; Orgy of Blood; Terror on Blood Island**

Approximately 92m; Color

VID: **Brides of the Beast** [New Horisons Home Video; 85(90)m]; **Brides of the Beast** [Regal Video; 85(90)m]

ADL: *A marriage made in hell!*

This low-rent creature flick—the first in a series of "Blood Island" films that include **The Mad Doctor of Blood Island** (1968) and **Beast of Blood** (1970)—stars the ever-suave,

ever-chivalrous John Ashley. This first time out, the villain is a scientist who, after being exposed to radiation from nearby atomic bomb tests (Bikini Atoll. Natch.), becomes a hulking dime-store beastie who—like all good Filipino monsters—likes to rape and kill young native girls. Lucky for him, the superstitious populace are more than happy to sacrifice their virgin daughters to keep his bloody appetite sated. (And if to make everyone's plight more unbearable, the island on which the mad doctor conducts his experiments is plagued by flesh-eating banana trees with a hankering for the natives. Oh, and there's a shape-changing killer moth. Also, did I mention the dwarf servants? I *think* that's everything now...)

Although not nearly as racist as many of these films tend to be, the undercurrent of sexism is particularly heavy in this one. Of course, being a disposable horror flick, one is inclined to take the proceedings with a grain of salt. (Granted, the metaphorical grain of salt is in high demand when it comes to early sleaze horror, but that shouldn't keep one from enjoying the film on a purely superficial level. Aesthetics aside, of course.) There is some liberal bloodshed, although the filmmakers upped the gore quotient considerably for the next entry in this apparently popular series.

Of little interest to those besides fans of Filipino horror and John Ashley.

Brides of Blood Island *see* **Brides of Blood**

Brides of Death *see* **Brides of Blood**

Brides of the Beast *see* **Brides of Blood**

The Brood (1979)
New World Pictures [Canada]
DIR: David Cronenberg; PRO: Claude Heroux; SCR: David Cronenberg; DOP: Mark Irwin; EXP: Pierre David and Victor Solnicki; SFX: Allan Kotter; MFX: Dennis Pike and Jack Young; MUS: Howard Shore

STR: Henry Beckman, Christopher Britton, Nicholas Campbell, Samantha Eggar, John Ferguson, Nuala Fitzgerald, Art Hindle, Cindy Hinds, Susan Hogan, Jerry Kostur, Michael Magee, Oliver Reed, Rainer Schwarz, Joseph Shaw, Feliz Silla, Robert Silverman, Larry Solway, and Mary Swinton

AKA: **La Clinique de la Terreur**
Approximately 93m; Color

The Brood

VID: **The Brood** [Embassy Home Entertainment; 92m]
ADL: *If they get their hands on you you're better off... dead!*

Quoted as being Cronenberg's askew interpretation of **Kramer vs. Kramer**, this low-key horror film remains one of the director's most personal, thus most effective efforts. A troubled marriage results in the mother being institutionalized for severe personality disorders, leaving the father to care for his young daughter. When the girl comes back from visiting her mother covered with bites and bruises, the concerned parent tries to forbid her visiting rights. Her doctor insists that this is not in everyone's best interest, and if to make his point, friends and relatives of the broken family begin falling like flies, murdered by seemingly inhuman assailants.

Oliver Reed puts in one of his best genre performances as the institute director, the person responsible for unleashing the brood, transubstantiations of the mother's troubled id through his patented and controversial "Psychoplasmics" therapy. Even Cronenberg's darker films contain enough humor to keep them from becoming too oppressive; **The Brood**, however, avoids this defense mechanism, leaving nothing to soften the blows. The analogies are quite clear: Child abuse is a vicious circle, with the abused inevitably spawning potential abusers.

Outside of more recent offerings, Cronenberg has never been particularly conservative when it comes to bloodletting. Although not over-the-top as some filmmakers, he's never shied away from the depiction of graphic violence, using it sparingly and more effectively when compared to most splatter filmmakers. The "birthing" scene that punctuates **The Brood** is one of the most unsettling scenes ever to grace the silver screen; despite the fact that so many others have imitated and tried to outdo this *coup de grace* since its conception, this scene remains as powerful as it was twenty years ago.

Really nightmarish stuff. Highly recommended.

Brutal Nights *see* **Emanuelle in America**

Buio Omega [Dark Holocaust] (1979)

D.R. per le Communicazioni di Massa [Italy]
DIR: Aristide Massaccesi; PRO: Marco Rossetti; SCR: Ottavio Fabbri; DOP: Aristide Massaccesi; MUS: Goblin
STR: Simonetta Allodi, Kieran Canter, Anna Cardini, Luccia d'Elia, Sam Modesto, Cinzia Monreale, Mario Pezzin, Klaus Rainer, Franca Stoppi, Walter Tribus, and Edmondo Vallini
AKA: **Beyond the Darkness; Buried Alive; Demonoia** [*Demon*]; **Folie Sanglante** [*Bloody Madness*]; **In Quella Casa Buio Omega** [*In the House of the Blue Holocaust*]
Approximately 91m; Color
VID: **Buried Alive** [Thriller Video; 85(91)m]

If you're in the mood for a nasty necrophile flick and Buttgereit's **Nekromantik** isn't handy, try this sick little number (which predates Jörg's celluloid atrocities by a decade). **Buio Omega** is a sordid mess to be sure: Blackmail, implied incest, cannibalism, and—last but not least—necrophilia are all thrown together in a tasteless melange that is sure to please the palate of hardcore splatterpunks everywhere. The man responsible for this is also the lost soul who brought us **Emanuelle e gli Ultima Cannibali** (1976) aka **Trap Them and Kill Them**, and **Anthropophagous** (1981), aka **The Grim Reaper**; with a track record like this, how could we be disappointed?

By far, this is one of Massaccesi's strongest contributions to the genre. (It still smells like cheap Italian trash, to be sure, but it approaches the subject with a certain amount of flair not found in similar productions.) To up the ante is a soundtrack by Italian progressive rock group Goblin that is sure to please their fans. (Some sources claim that the soundtrack was actually performed by I Libra, a group formed by ex–Goblin member Walter Martino shortly after he left the band in the mid–70s, but the print states otherwise.)

Splatterpunks and Eurotrash aficionados should agree that **Buio Omega** is a must-see, whether the rumors concerning the alleged special effects are true or not. (Rumors had it that a real corpse was used for the film in an effort to add to the realism; everyone involved denied these allegations, of course. Some of the gore *is* particularly convincing, though, so one can only wonder.) You know the score. ☠☠☠

El Buque Maldito [The Cursed Ship] (1974)

Ancla Century Films [Spain] and Belen Film [Spain]
DIR: Amando de Ossorio Rodríguez; PRO: J.L. Bermudez de Castro; SCR: Amando de Ossorio Rodríguez; DOP: Raul Artigot; SFX: Pablo Perez; MFX: Carlos Paradela; MUS: Anton Garcia Abril
STR: Manuel de Blas, Blanca Estrada, Carlos Lemos, Margarita Merino, María Perschy, Barbara Rey, and Jack Taylor
AKA: **Das Geisterschiff der Schwimmenden Leichen** [*The Ghostship of the Swimming Dead*]; **The Ghost Galleon; Horror of the Zombies; Le Monde des Morts-Vivants** [*The World of the Living Dead*]; **La Noche del Buque Maldito** [*The Night of the Cursed Ship*]; **Ship of Zombies**

El Buque Maldito

Approximately 106m; Color
VID: **Horror of the Zombies** [Super Video; 90(89)m]; **Horror of the Zombies** [VidAmerica; 90(89)m]
ADL: *They exist on the flesh of beautiful young women.*

The plot is thin (a small group of people find themselves lost at sea on a ghost ship), so I'll just skip to the heart of the matter. The script offers a nice departure from the stomping grounds which usually accommodates the bloody proceedings, replacing the Spanish countryside with a rotting galleon. Although easily the weakest entry in de Ossorio's infamous Blind Dead series, this third outing for the Knights Templar is still heavy on the selfsame atmosphere and suspense that makes the other entries so popular.

Although **El Buque Maldito** does improve with repeated viewings, it still suffers considerably from the lack of screen time given to the undead knights. Not only is it nearly an hour into the film before the Templars decide to show their crusty hides, they are barely onscreen for a total of eight minutes before the end credits roll. Unfortunately, their screen time is cut even shorter with domestic prints which are shorn of the gore (not that there is a lot of this to begin with, thanks to a lack of human fodder). As disappointing as all of this is, though, it seems a small price to pay in order to see everyone's favorite zombies in action again. (Well, they're *my* favorite zombies, anyway.)

The film's only real sore point is the miniature boat used for the finale, set aflame and conveniently filmed in someone's bathtub. (De Ossorio's last film, **Serpiente de Mar** [1985]—released pseudonymously, no surprise there—suffers from similarly atrocious effects work. Surprisingly, though, that one wasn't released from VidAmerica's World's Worst Video line, as sorry effects are the *least* of its crimes.)

This one's for Blind Deadheads only. Those who have not been introduced to the Templars' charms should check out the earlier outings prior to viewing **El Buque Maldito**, otherwise they might not be able to see what all the fuss is about.

Burial Ground *see* **La Notte del Terrore**

Buried Alive *see* Buio Omega

California Axe Massacre *see* The Axe

California Axe Murders *see* The Axe

Le Camp des Filles Perdues *see* SS Campo Extermination

Canibales *see* Cannibal Girls

Cannibal *see* Ultimo Mondo Canibale

Cannibal Girls (1973)

Scary Pictures Productions [Canada]
DIR: Ivan Reitman; PRO: Daniel Goldberg; SCR: Robert Sandler; DOP: Robert Saad; EXP: Ivan Reitman; SFX: Michael Lotosky and Richard White; MUS: Doug Riley
STR: Randall Carpenter, David Clement, Joan Fox, Doug Ganton, Alan Gordon, May Jarvis, Bunker Kingfish, Eugene Levy, Ray Lawlor, Lyn Logan, Nell Lundy, Rick Maguire, Gino Marrocco, Andrea Martin, Bob McHeady, Bonnie Neilson, Mira Pawluk, Earl Pomerantz, Allan Price, Marion Swadron, Julie Thilpot, and Ronald Ulrich
AKA: **Canibales** [Cannibals]
Approximately 84m; Color
VID: Cannibal Girls [CIC; 84m]

After their car breaks down in a remote town, two young hippies check into an inn that was rumored to be the site of a cannibalistic massacre years before. Before long, the couple get the feeling that no one in town wants them to leave. Turns out, not only is the folk story true, but that its culinary influence has spread beyond that of the title trio.

Some people say that everyone's got at least one skeleton in their closet, but I think that this—if anything—proves that every filmmaker's got at least one good film under their belt. (Reitman also had the decency to produce some of David Cronenberg's earlier films before going on to do big-budget crap like **Ghostbusters** and **Twins**.) Although there are some gory highlights (the audience is warned of the impending carnage by a bell), the film is unavoidably comic, thanks to the presence of SCTV members Levy and Martin, both of whom have gone on to take supporting roles in innumerable Hollywood films, as well as a TV series.

Cannibal Girls is a charming obscurity that has yet to get a decent video release in this country.

Cannibal Holocaust *see* Holocausto Canibal

The Cannibal Man *see* La Semana del Asesino

Cannibal Massaker *see* Holocausto Canibal

Cannibal Terror *see* Terror Caníbal

Cannibals *see* **Ultimo Mondo Canniballe**

The Captive Female *see* **Scream Bloody Murder**

Carnage (1972) *see* **Antefatto**

Carne per Frankenstein *see* **Mostro è in Tavola... Il Barone Frankenstein**

Carnival of Blood (1970)

Kirt Films International [USA]
DIR: Leonard Kirtman; PRO: Leonard Kirtman; SCR: Leonard Kirtman; DOP: David Howe; MUS: The Brooks Group and Heskel Brisman
STR: Martin Barolsky, Earle Edgerton, William Grinell, John Harris, Glen Kimberley, Linda Kurtz, Kaly Mills, Eve Packer, Judith Resnick, Gloria Spivak, and Burt Young
AKA: **Death Rides a Carousel**
Approximately 89m; Color
VID: **Carnival of Blood** [Spectrum Video; 80(89)m]; **Carnival of Blood** [United American Video; 80(89)m]
ADL: *A Flashing Midway of Murder and Mystery.*

Inexplicably, patrons of a midway carnival begin losing their heads—and other vital organs—during spats with their better halves. Who is responsible? Is it Tom, the effeminate matchmaker with a thing for teddy bears? What about Gimpy, the scarred half-wit whose precarious temper with unruly patrons precedes him? Maybe it's the old gypsy fortune teller who foresees the victims deaths in her cards? Who cares? The tepid mystery is the *last* thing trash fiends will be paying attention to when viewing this bargain-basement splatfest.

The production values are, for the most part, inept. Actors can barely remember their lines, the cinematographer can barely remember how to run the camera, and the director can barely remember what he's getting paid to do. At least a third of the film's running time is—surprise!—carnival footage. (Did I hear someone say "filler?") Outside of the tiring midway shots, **Carnival of Blood** has much of the "so bad it's good" charm that trashoholics thrive on. And the sometimes extreme gore is a bennie; those who like the pre-prosthetics effects work (pig offal doused in red paint) shant be disappointed by the carnage herein. Throw in a weirded out electronic score, and the most obnoxious, unconvincing drunk this side of Lucille Ball, and we have a winnah!

Fans of H.G. Lewis are sure to appreciate this no-budget atrocity. (Did I mention the teddy bear stuffed with human entrails?)

Carnivorous *see* **Ultimo Mondo Cannibale**

Carole *see* **Una Lucertola con la Pelle di Donna**

Carrie (1976)

Red Bank Films [USA]
DIR: Brian De Palma; PRO: Paul Monash; SCR: Lawrence T. Gordon; [Based on the novel **Carrie** by Stephen King]; DOP: Mario Tosi; SFX: Gregory M. Auer; MUS: Pino Donaggio
STR: Nancy Allen, Betty Buckley, Doug Cox, Cindy Daly, Cameron de

Palma, Anson Downes, Stefan Gierisch, Harry Gold, Amy Irving, William Katt, Sydney Lassick, Piper Laurie, Edie McClurg, Noelle North, Priscilla Pointer, P.J. Soles, Sissy Spacek, Rory Stevens, Michael Talbott, and John Travolta
Approximately 98m; Color
SND: **Carrie** [Rykodisc]
VID: **Carrie** [CBS/Fox Video; 98m]
Carrie [MGM/UA Home Video; 97(98)m]

Do you remember when King actually wrote some palatable horror novels? Can you even recall that some of these better books were successfully translated to film by talented directors? Can you remember when John Travolta was a household name for all the wrong reasons? Well, here's a little reminder in case you've forgotten "the good old days."

Taking it's cue from Juan Buñuel's **Au Rendez Vous de la Mort Joyeuse** [*To the Appointment of the Joyful Dead*] (1972), aka **Expulsion of the Devil**, an awkward young girl's burgeoning womanhood begins to manifest itself in ways not commonly associated with puberty. Her Bible-thumping mother only aggravates her vengeance-driven psychokinesis, which reaches its bloody crescendo on the night of the prom.

Carrie exploits the rarely forgotten anxiety of puberty, using these valid fears to ground the film's supernatural leanings. De Palma deftly avoids the traps which have befallen every single film in **Carrie**'s wake; those films rarely rise above the level of tired hokum, whereas **Carrie** remains compelling and unnerving twenty years later. (Those who had difficulty fitting in at school will be particularly empathetic towards the film's tortured protagonist, but will find themselves no less disturbed by the series of events which befall her peers.)

De Palma's knack for high-tension editing and violent imagery is complimented by a top-notch cast; although never surpassing her performance herein, Spacek established a career which resulted in favorable reviews for such films as **Coal Miner's Daughter** and **The Raggedy Man**.

Recommending viewing for both horror fans and more "discriminate" filmgoers.

La Casa d'Appuntamento [The Appointment House] (1972)

Production company unknown [Italy]
DIR: Ferdinando Merighi; PRO: Marius Mattei and Dick Randall; SCR: Marius Mattei, Ferdinando Merighi, and Ramiro Oliveros; DOP: Mario Mancini and Gunter Otto; MFX: Carlo Rambaldi; MUS: Bruno Nicolai

STR: William Alexander, Eva Astor, Barbara Gutcher, Rolf Eden, Anita Ekberg, Evelyn Kraft, Pietro Martellanza, Rosalba Neri, Alessandro Perrella, Ada Pometti, Renato Romano, Robert Sacchi, Mario Lippert, and Piera Viotti

AKA: **The Bogeyman and the French Murders; Murder in Paris; Paris Sex Murders**
Approximately 83m; Color

A psychopathic thief is smitten by the charms of a four-bit prostitute, and when she gets knocked off, all fingers point at him. A Bogie impersonator is put on the case and promptly tracks down their only suspect. The thief is sentenced to death, denying his guilt and threatening to come back from the grave to exact revenge on those who falsely accused him. He escapes from prison, but ends up getting in a fatal motorcycle accident while the authorities are in pursuit. A doctor (Franco fixture Howard Vernon) somehow receives custody of the poor man's head, but before anyone can close the case, the killings continue. (Natch.)

Who is the real killer? Why does he insist on caving in people's faces with lamps, of all things? What is Vernon doing with the hoodlum's head? What possessed the producers to hire a Bogie impersonator to play the lead? Before all is said and done, only one of these questions will be answered, and done so in a most unconvincing manner, even as far as most *giallos* go.

This slightly bent *giallo* thriller seems driven to give Eurotrash a bad name. **La Casa d'Appuntamento**'s only real point of interest is the gore; although mostly offscreen to begin with, the brutal acts of violence become progressively bloodier until it has reached a level of gratuity rarely found in others from the time. (Just to up the ante, some surgery footage is tossed in, that of some poor soul's eye being split open with a scalpel—quite forcefully and with little grace.)

Unfortunately, the remainder of the film doesn't attempt the same level of realism they reach with the special effects. The script is poorly contrived, the actors' performances lack credibility as well; the action sequences are staged with such ineptitude as to almost garner laughs from the viewer. (The killer's demise is particularly amusing, and will not convince even the most braindead viewer.)

Not bad enough to be good, and not good enough to be considered competent. 🎥🎥🎥

Castle of Terror *see* **La Vergine di Norimberga**

Cat's Victims, The *see* **Il Gatto dagli Occhi di Giada**

Cavalcatta dei Morti senza Occhi, La *see* **El Ataque de los Muertos sin Ojos**

Cemetery Girls *see* **El Gran Amor del Conde Dracula**

Cemetery Tramps *see* **El Gran Amor del Conde Dracula**

Ceremonia Sangrienta [Blood Ceremony] (1972)

X Film [Italy] and Luis Films [Spain]

DIR: Jorgé Grau Sola; PRO: José María Gonzalez Sinde; SCR: Sandro Continenza, Jorgé Grau Sola, and Juan Tebar; DOP: Fernando Arribas; EXP: José María Gonzalez Sinde; SFX: Basilio Cortijo; MUS: Carlo Savina

STR: Francisco Agudin, Sergio Alberti, Ewa Aulin, Me Paz Ballesteros, Lucía Bosè, Miguel Buñuel, Fabian Conde, Roberto Daniel, Fernando de Bran, Antonio de Mossul, Anna Farra, Rafael Frias, Lola Gaos, Ghika, Estanis Gonzalez, Franca Gray, Angel Menéndez, Sofia Nogueras, Racquel Ortuño, Juan José Otegui, Antonio Puca, Joaquín

Pueyo, Puca, Angel Rodal, Ismael Garcia Romeu, Espartaco Santoni, Adolfo Thous, Dolores Tovar, Silvano Tranquili, Rafael Vakero, Maria Vigo, and Enrique Vivó
 AKA: Blood Castle; The Bloody Countess; Countess Dracula; The Female Butcher; Lady Dracula; The Legend of Blood Castle; Le Vergini Cavalcano la Morte [*The Virgins Ride the Dead*]
 Approximately 87m; Color
 VID: **The Legend of Blood Castle** [Consolidated Video; 84m]
 ADL: *A horror chamber of blood and gore, depraved, documented in the pages of the Guinness Book of World Records!*

This is one of the better horror films derived from the infamous crimes of Elisabeth de Báthory, a Hungarian countess from the early seventeenth century who may well have murdered over six-hundred young women, bathing in *and or* drinking their blood in the hopes of resuscitating her fading youth. (The only other film which remains superior is Hammer Studios' **Countess Dracula** [1970], despite that film's penchant for supernatural tomfoolery.) Having yet to reach his peak, director Jorgé Grau Sola (who later brought us **Pena de Muerte** [*Death Penalty*] and **Non Si Deve Profanare il Sonno dei Morti** [*Do Not Disturb the Sleep of the Dead*], 1973 and 1974, respectively) offers a fairly realistic dramatization of the events leading up to the Countess' incarceration, yet doesn't hesitate to exploit the more sordid facets of the case. (This was the 70s, after all.)

The gore—at least in U.S. prints—is pretty minimal, but fairly gratuitous considering the PG rating the MPAA slapped on it for its U.S. release. (Unfortunately, still intact were the scenes of live doves being drained of their blood and being brutally torn apart by trained hawks. As much as I love the 70s, there are some things about that decade's cinematic transgressions that I don't miss, flagrant scenes of animal cruelty being the most paramount.)

Now if only someone would do a similar treatment for Vlad Tepes...

Chair pour Frankenstein
see Monstro è in Tavola... Il Barone Frankenstein

The Child (1977)

Panorama Films [USA]
 DIR: Robert Voskanian; PRO: Robert Dadashian; SCR: Ralph Lucas; DOP: Mori Alavi; EXP: Harry H. Novak; MFX: Jay Owens; MUS: Robert Wallace
 STR: Anoosh Avan, Ruth Ballen, Laurel Barnett,

Children Shouldn't Play...

Chick Cavanaugh, Rosalie Cole, Jim Dickson, Richard Hanners, Wendell Hudiberg, Frank Janson, Slosson Bing Jong, Ralph Lucas, Rod Medigovich, and Chris Tieken

AKA: **Kill and Go Hide!**; **Zombie Child**
Approximately 95m; Color
VID: **The Child** [Best Film & Video; 82m; Double-bill w/**Dungeon of Terror**]; **The Child** [Magnum Entertainment; 83m]; **Zombie Child** [CIC Video; 90m]

A governess has the unfortunate luck of being hired to watch over a strange little girl who has the curious ability to resuscitate the dead. To no one's surprise, they're a bit grumpy, and are more than eager to take out their dissatisfaction on the young girl's enemies (of which there are plenty). To the governess' chagrin, she gets on the girl's bad side, and the expected mayhem ensues.

Despite a grating score and some really poor post-synch dubbing, this is a fairly taut and well made little low-budget zombie flick. Most of the gory mayhem is relegated to the last third of the film, but the remainder of this low-key film is (surprisingly) engaging. To its credit, the hokum (in this case, the young girl's paranormal abilities) are kept grounded reasonably well, avoiding the flashy visual effects which usually accompany such fare. The makeup effects on the girl's crusty playmates are a bit primitive by today's standards, but this adds to the film's diseased charm without being too terribly distracting. (And for some inexplicable reason, this particular breed of the living dead prefers to rip the faces off of their victims as opposed to actually eating them. Inexplicable, that is, until we realize that the producers wanted to get their money's worth from a one-size-fits-all latex "ripped face" prosthetic after running out of funds for pig offal. At least they had the smarts to film each killing from a different angle.)

A charming obscurity that deserves a look-see.

Children Shouldn't Play with Dead Things (1972)

Brandywine [USA] and Motionarts [USA]
DIR: Benjamin Clark; PRO: Ben-

jamin Clark and Gary Goch; SCR: Benjamin Clark and Alan Ormsby; DOP: Jack McGowan; MFX: Alan Ormsby; MUS: Carl Zittrer
STR: Alecs Baird, Harry Boehme, Curtis Bryant, Peter Burke, Jean Cark, Paul Cronin, Debbie Cummins, Jane Daly, Roy Engleman, Gordon Gilbert, Jeffrey Gillen, Andy Herbst, Jerry Hoffer, Paula Hoffer, Brendan Kenny, Sandra Laurie, Camille MacDonald, Valerie Mamches, Al McAdams, Jane McAdams, Stuart Mitchell, Lee O'-Donnell, Alan Ormsby, Anya Ormsby, Chester Phebus, Robert Philip, Carl Richardson, Robert Sherman, Seth Sklarey, Robert Smedley, Jack Sohmer, Bruce Solomon, Stephanie Solomon, and Trey Ward
AKA: **Revenge of the Living Dead**
Approximately 86m; Color
VID: **Children Shouldn't Play with Dead Things** [VidAmerica, Inc.; 86m]; **Children Shouldn't Play with Dead Things** [Video Communications, Inc.; 85(86)m]; **Revenge of the Living Dead** [True World Video; 85m]
ADL: *YOU'RE INVITED TO ORVILLE'S "COMING OUT" PARTY... It'll Be A Scream... YOURS!!*

A theater troupe decides to hammer out their new production in an isolated graveyard (home to mostly murderers and rapists) off the coast of New York. To add a touch of realism to their rehearsal, they enlist the aid of a reasonably fresh cadaver they christen "Orville." After some premeditated hijinks on the part of the director, they take the disinterred remains of their new friend to a small house nearby for an impromptu party, unaware that they have upset some of the other residents as well.

This post–**Night of the Living Dead** gut-muncher remains a decent low-budget shocker, built around one of the most memorable exploitation film titles of all time. (The moniker may not be as recognizable or witty as **I Dismember Mama**, but at least this film has other things going for it.) Mostly awful makeup is compensated for by underexposed photography; unfortunately, they couldn't do the same for the lame jokes with the wonderfully noisy soundtrack. (Ads hyped this as a comedy, debatable as that may be.)

The film's charm lies in its fannish, DIY approach, much like that of **The Demon Lover** (1976). Instead of naming characters after comic book personalities, though, **Children Shouldn't Play with Dead Things** has its players named after the actors themselves, making one wonder if they are *playing* themselves as well. (Alan Ormsby—hamming it up as the tyrannical leader with a macabre sense of humor—

may not be on the mark, but with everyone else it seems a distinct possibility.) The film's final note also gives it some weight; Lucio Fulci must have found it particularly effective as well, for he copied it in his own **Zombi 2** eight years later.

After directing a couple of other notable low-budget horror films (**Night Walk** and **Black Christmas**, 1972 and 1974, respectively), filmmaker Clark finally hit the big time with outings like **Porky's**. I guess his muse got fed up with him. (Screenwriter/star Ormsby co-directed the wonderful **Deranged** [1974] before finding what he thought to be his calling as a makeup effects artist. To each their own.)

Claw of Terror *see* Scream Bloody Murder

La Clinique de la Terreur *see* The Brood

La Cliniques des Horreurs *see* La Bestia Uccide a Sangue Freddo

La Cliniques des Ténèbres *see* La Bestia Uccide a Sangue Freddo

Code Name Trixie *see* The Crazies

The Cold-Blooded Beast *see* La Bestia Uccide a Sangue Freddo

La Colina del Terror *see* The Hills Have Eyes

La Colline a des Yeux *see* The Hills Have Eyes

Color Me Blood Red (1965)

Box Office Spectaculars [USA]
DIR: Herschell Gordon Lewis; PRO: David F. Friedman; SCR: Herschell Gordon Lewis; DOP: Herschell Gordon Lewis
STR: Cathy Collins, Candi Conder, Jerome Eden, Scott H. Hall, William Harris, Jim Jackel, Don Joseph, Patricia Lee, Iris Marshall, and Elyn Warner
AKA: **Model Massacre**
Approximately 70m; Color
NOV: **Color Me Blood Red** by Herschell Gordon Lewis [Novel Books]; **Color Me Blood Red** by Herschell Gordon Lewis [Fantaco Enterprises]
VID: **Color Me Blood Red** [Continental Video; 70m]; **Color Me Blood Red** [Rhino Video; 70m]; **Model Massacre** [BFPI; 70m]
ADL: *The Color of Terror... Is Red*

A pretentious, beatnik-ish painter is pushed over the deep end having been snubbed by the art community for quite some time. After his girlfriend accidentally cuts herself in his studio, he discovers that—lo and behold!—blood offers the very same pigment he'd been searching for all this time! It doesn't take him long to realize, though, that he can only give so much of his own before he's of little use to anybody, so he's off, looking for victims with which to supply him with an endless supply of "paint." (Forget the fact that blood darkens considerably as it dries, even turning black if laid on thick enough.)

Cited as the third in Lewis' infamous "gore trilogy," and the last collaboration between him and producer Friedman, this splatter-oriented take on Corman's **A Bucket of Blood** (1959) improves on the production values of his previous two entries, erstwhile toning down the gratuity of the gut-stained proceedings. (Gore is plentiful, to be sure, but the viewer is allowed to take some extended breathers between the scenes of obligatory carnage.)

Don Joseph makes an admirable psychopath, and the paintings used in the film (and ruthlessly burned at film's end) would be the cherished possessions of any cult-film aficionado. The film boasts other trashy charms as well, but—despite all of these—**Color Me Blood Red** is often considered inferior to its predecessors by Lewis' fans. (Me? I have a soft spot in my heart for this one. Don't ask, but I will say it has something to do with the subject matter. Now where did my brushes go..?)

The Comeback (1977)

Heritage Ltd. [UK]
DIR: Peter Walker; PRO: Peter Walker; SCR: Murray Smith; DOP: Peter Jessop; MUS: Stanley Myers
STR: Patrick Brock, June Chadwick, David Doyle, Penny Irving, Richard Johnson, Jack Jones, Sheila Keith, Bill Owen, Holly Palance, Jeff Silk, Pamela Stephenson, and Peter Turner
AKA: **The Day the Screaming Stopped; Encore; Hallucinations; I Wake Up Screaming; The Sixth Gate of Hell**
Approximately 100m; Color
VID: **The Comeback** [Karl-Lorimar Home Video; 100m]; **Encore** [Saturn Productions, Inc.; 100m]
ADL: *The Nightmare Continues...*

An American pop singer (Jack Jones. Yes, *the* Jack Jones) and his acquaintances are being stalked and picked off while he's in London

recording a new album. Suspicions are thrown back and forth, and the killers are revealed only after everyone but them and Jones are left standing.

Although easily one of Walker's slicker efforts, it is far from his best, lacking the dark edge that gave his earlier films their "oomph." There's no lack of juicy gore or effective shocks, but that is all. (To aggravate the viewer even further—at least those expecting Walker's penchant carnage—there is a lag of an hour between the first and second death.) Worse, there are too many poorly orchestrated red herrings, and a rather unsatisfactory ending that hampers it from being a truly successful thriller. (Oh, and let's not forget Jones' perfunctory crooning. That I could have done without.)

On the up side, we have "Bosley" from TV's **Charlie's Angels** as a sleazy, cross-dressing music executive (obviously one of the aforementioned red herrings). Okay, so maybe that doesn't qualify as a bonus, but it sure didn't hurt matters any.

Recommended for Peter Walker fans only.

Communion *see* **Alice, Sweet Alice**

Computer Killers *see* **Horror Hospital**

I Corpi Presentato Tracce di Violenza Carnale [The Bodies Exhibit Signs of Sexual Violence] (1973)
Compagnia Cinematografica Champion S.P.A. [Italy]
DIR: Sergio Martino; PRO: Carlo Ponti; SCR: Ernesto Gastaldi and Sergio Martino; DOP: Giancarlo Ferrando; EXP: Antonio Cervi; MUS: Guido de Angelis and Maurizio de Angelis
STR: Patrizia Adiutori, Cristina Airoldi, Tina Aumont, Luciano Bartoli, Roberto Bisacco, Carla Brait, Ernesto Colli, Angela Covello, Suzy Kendall, Luc Merenda, and John Richardson
AKA: **Torso**
Approximately 89m; Color
VID: **Torso** [Prism Entertainment; 91(89)m]

Like so many other *giallo*-cum-slasher flicks, a masked killer is making short work of young women enrolled in a school for fine arts. (Occasionally, he pokes out their eyes and cuts down the unwieldy remains with a hacksaw, nice guy that he is.) A scarf is found tied around one of the corpse's necks, and is identical to one worn by a rather obsessive student. Four friends retreat to a hillside villa to get away from the escalating carnage, only to find out that the killer has followed them.

Before the beginning credits even start rolling, one will recognize **I Corpi Presentato Tracce di Violenza Carnale** as being the kind of sleazefest those wacky Italians are so gosh darn good at, especially in the permissive seventies. Gratuity is the key word here, as this enjoyably distasteful thriller swaps suspense for shocks, piling on the brutality in order to distract the viewer from all else. (Of course, the liberal nudity and softcore sex is used in much the same manner.)

For those who don't mind taking a shower after watching a film. A *hot* one, that is.

The Corpse Grinders (1971)

Geneni Film Distribution [USA]
DIR: Ted V. Mikels; PRO: Ted V. Mikels; SCR: Joseph L. Cranston and Arch Hall, Jr.; DOP: Bill Anneman; SFX: Gary R. Heacock; MUS: Music Industries
STR: Warren Ball, Vince Barbi, George Bowden, Mary Ellen Burke, Carl Burman, Andy Collings, Ray Dennis, Don Ellis, J. Byron Foster, Charles Fox, Zena Foster, Ellis Garrison, Drucilla Hoy, Monika Kelly, Sean Kenney, William Kirschner, Stephen Lester, Harry Lovejoy, Curtis Matson, Sanford Mitchell, and Ann Noble
Approximately 75m; Color
VID: **The Corpse Grinders** [Wal-

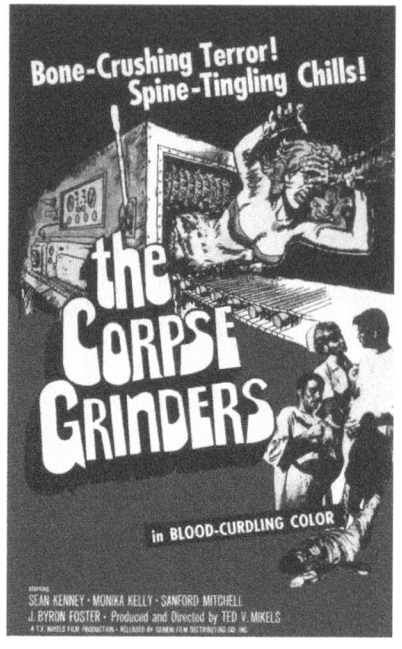

terscheid Productions, Inc.; 75m]; **The Corpse Grinders** [World Video; 73m]

ADL: *Bone-Crushing Terror! Spine-Tingling Chills! The Corpse Grinders turn bones and flesh into screaming, savage bloody death!*

"Sudden, inexplicable attacks, by cats on their human owners, paralyze a metropolis! It's soon learned that an exotic cat food turns these gentle pets into ravenous man-eaters! Apparently, some diabolically disreputable types, operating a cat food factory, have run shy of raw material. They soon overcome that obstacle by finding a new source—*fresh cadavers!*"

Well, that's the film in a nutshell. **The Corpse Grinders** is wonderfully cheap, drive-in quickie that has it all: bottom-of-the-barrel special effects, actors who are probably still working day jobs, an outrageous storyline that could only have been swiped from **The Weekly World News**, and one of the greatest, oft-quoted monikers of all time. (Would've made a great double-bill with **Shriek of the Mutilated**, don't you think? How about **Three on a Meathook**?) Reminiscent of Lewis' later efforts, minus much of the gore and with actors who actually took a moment to study their lines before stepping before the camera, **The Corpse Grinders** will quickly endear itself with fans of 60s and 70s trash horror. (Director Mikels was also responsible for such "classics" as **Astro-Zombies** and **Blood Orgy of the She-Devils**, 1968 and 1973, respectively. Unfortunately, the latter of those two inept horror flicks doesn't live up to the promise of his earlier efforts.)

Cat lovers should take heed, though, for they'll either be unnerved by the starving felines who have acquired a taste for human flesh, *and or* appalled by their manhandling by stagehands as they're thrown at their intended victims. (One seriously wonders how many of the resulting cat scratches are real or not.)

It makes my top twenty "so-bad-it's-good" list; with a recommendation like that, how can you go right?

Cosa Avete Fatto a Solange? *[What Have They Done to Solange?] (1972)*

Italian International Film [Italy] and Rialto Film [West Germany]

DIR: Massimo Dallamano; PRO: Fulvio Lucisano and Leonardo Pescarolo; SCR: Bruno di Geronimo and Massimo Dallamano (Based on a novel by Edgar Wallace); DOP: Aristide Massaccesi; EXP: Horst Wendlandt; MUS: Ennio Morricone

STR: Karin Baal, Carlo Badessi, Claudia Botenuth, Pilar Castel, Giovanna di Bernardo, Joachim Fuchsberger, Cristina Galbo, Camille Keaton, Maria Monti, Rainer Penkert, Günther W. Stoll, Fabio Testi, and Emilia Wolkowicz

AKA: **Das Geheimnis der Grunen Stecknadel** [*The Secret of the Green Pin*]; **The School That Couldn't Scream**; **What Have You Done to Solange?**; **Who's Next?**

Approximately 102m; Color

VID: **What Have You Done to Solange?** [Redemption Video (PAL); 100m]

While making out with her gym teacher on a paddleboat, a young woman witnesses a murder. The victim turns out to be a schoolmate, and—in one of the more disturbing scenes—an X-ray of the dead girl's pelvic region is shown the parents, which proudly displays a rather large knife inserted into her privates. The teacher becomes a prime suspect, but is unwilling to come clean about his involvement because it could cost him his job and his marriage.

This is an interesting *giallo*-style whodunit filled with unexpected twists, and is guaranteed to keep even the more avid mystery fans on their toes. Technically, it is competent, boasting some inspired edits and above-average performances. There are some particularly bloody deaths, equal in number to

the numerous shower scenes. (What do you expect when the victims are all schoolgirls?)
One of the better films of its type, and similar to the also exemplary (but undoubtedly sleazier) Enigma Rosso (1978).

Count Dracula's Great Love *see* **El Gran Amor del Conde Dracula**

Countess Dracula (1972) *see* **Ceremonia Sangrienta**

The Craving *see* **El Retorno del Hombre Lobo**

The Crazies (1973)
Cambist Films [USA]
DIR: George A. Romero; PRO: Alvin C. Croft; SCR: George A. Romero; DOP: S. William Hinzman; SFX: Tony Pantanello and Regis J. Survinski; MUS: Bruce Roberts
STR: Edith Bell, Roger Brown, Lane Carroll, Norman Chase, Roy Cheverie, Walton Cook, Will Disney, Richard France, Ross Harris, S. William Hinzman, Lloyd Hollar, Harold Wayne Jones, Robert Karlowsky, William C. Kennedy, Richard Lewicki, Stephen Liska, Lynn Lowry, A.C. MacDonald, Robert J. McCully, W.G. McMillan, David Meek, MaLynda Parker, Ned Schmidtke, Tony Scott, Kim Smith, Harry Spillman, Leland Starnes, Vincent D. Survinski, W.L. Thunhurst, Jr., Peg Tilbrook, and Jack Zaharia
AKA: **Code Name Trixie**; **The Mad People**
Approximately 103m; Color
VID: **The Crazies** [Anchor Bay Entertainment; 103m]; **The Crazies** [Redemption Video (PAL); 103m]; **The Crazies** [Vista Home Video; 103m]
ADL: *ALL HELL BREAKS LOOSE! ...MAN BECOMES AN ENDANGERED SPECIES!*

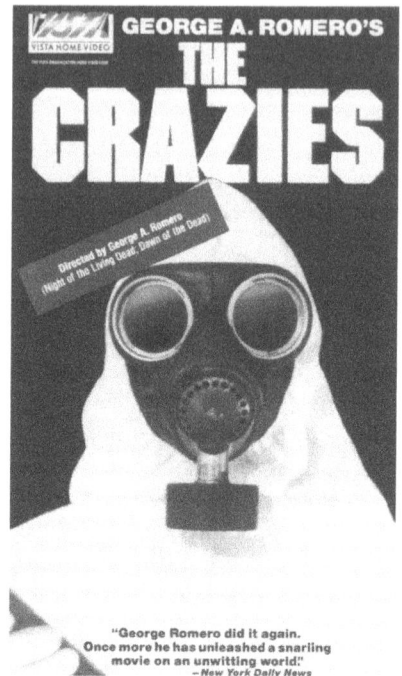

A small town is besieged by a genetically-engineered virus that turns anyone exposed into raving, usually homicidal maniacs. The government steps in to clean up their little mess, ready for the worst. An ex-Green Beret, his pregnant girlfriend, and some cohorts take foot, trying to break the perimeters of the quarantined town. Although he appears to be naturally immune to the mutant flu, his friends aren't so lucky.
Treading dangerously similar ground as that of his debut **Night of the Living Dead** (1968), Romero begins to show the inimitable style that flourishes in **Martin** (1977) and **Dawn of the Dead** (1978). (It can also be seen, in retrospect, that Romero reused much of this film's formula in the latter groundbreaking

splatter epic. Entire scenes have been copped—albeit improved upon—for the latter effort.)

Although a film of obvious merit, **The Crazies** suffers from the usual primitivisms, but is only truly hindered by some atrocious editing, both in the case of film and sound. The gore is not extreme, but there is more than enough bloodshed to sate the thirsts of most gorehounds. Its most outstanding feature, though, is its nihilism; **The Crazies** is exceptionally downbeat, made that much more effective by decent characterizations and its socio-political subtexts.

Some of the faces you might find familiar are Lynn Lowry, who has inadvertently become synonymous with killer disease flicks (**The Parasite Murders**, **I Drink Your Blood**, etc.), Bill Hinzman (the lead zombie from **Night of the Living Dead**), Richard Liberty (Dr. Logan from **Day of the Dead**), and even that TV guy with the eyepatch from **Dawn of the Dead**. (I don't recall his name, but damn if he ain't a great over-actor.)

Crimen Sin Huella see **Giallo a Venezia**

Criminally Insane (1973)

IRMI Films [USA]
DIR: Steve Millard; PRO: Frances Millard; SCR: Steve Millard; DOP: Karil Ostman
STR: Priscilla Alden, Robert Copple, Charles Egan, Lisa Farros, Michael Flood, Jane Lambert, Sonny Larocca, C.L. Lefleur, Cliff McDonald, Gina Martine, and Sandra Shotwell

Approximately 61m; Color
VID: **Criminally Insane** [World Video; 61m]
ADL: *250 POUNDS OF MANIACAL FURY!*

"A 250 lb. female psychopath is prematurely released from an asylum for the criminally insane. What little is left of her mind soon gives way, as her gluttonous appetite for food is shockingly equaled by her appetite for blood!"

There isn't much I can add to the succinct video box synopsis without being redundant; if this piques your interest, you'll probably get a kick out of this no-budget wonder. If not, don't bother, as its charm depends solely on its geek value. (For some of us, geek value is more than sufficient.) Filmed on what I suspect is Super 8, **Criminally**

Insane boasts the wonderfully droll Priscilla Alden as Ethel, who is responsible for what has to be some of the most inept murders ever committed to celluloid. (They must've had a hell of a time scraping that red paint off of the lens, I tell you.) Herky jerky editing, flagrant mannequin abuse, and intended humor *that works* are all crammed into its conservative hour running time. (Okay, so maybe they could've taken a little more off the top. Just a little, though.)

Millard directed the similarly atrocious **Satan's Black Wedding** (1974), as well as a write-off sequel to **Criminally Insane**, the patchwork tosser **Crazy Fat Ethel II** (1987).

Crypt of the Blind Dead *see* **La Noche del Terror Ciego**

Curse of the Cannibal Confederates *see* **The Curse of the Screaming Dead**

Curse of the Confederate Cannibals *see* **The Curse of the Screaming Dead**

Curse of the Devil (1972) *see* **Hexen Geschändet und zu Tode Gequält**

Curse of the Devil (1973) *see* **El Retorno de Walpurgis**

The Curse of the Screaming Dead (1976)
Little Warsaw Productions [USA]
DIR: Tony Malanowski; PRO: Tony Malanowski; SCR: Lon Huber; MFX: Bart Mixon; MUS: Charlie Barnett
STR: Rebecca Bach, Jim Ball, Judy Dixon, Christopher Gummer, Mimi Ishikawa, Mark Redfield, Bump Roberts, Richard Ruxton, and Steve Sandkuhler
AKA: Curse of the Cannibal Confederates; Curse of the Confederate Cannibals
Approximately 88m; Color
VID: The Curse of the Screaming Dead [Mogul Communications; 90(88)m]

Three hippie couples on a hunting trip stumble across a graveyard which dates back to the time of the Civil War. Unfortunate for them, the stumbling scriptwriter decided to cut their little nature hike short by resurrecting the members of a platoon buried therein, and giving them voracious appetites to boot. (Not soon enough, I'm inclined to point out. The viewer must sit through well over an hour's worth of them bickering amongst themselves before the bloodthirsty regiment has a chance to administer the propers.) And, you see, it's all over a stupid flag. (The socio-political allusions are just so *profound*... donchya' think?)

Being a 70s zombie flick, **The Curse of the Screaming Dead** dutifully goes through the motions, with scads of unwitting extras gnawing on pig gut and latex. (The scenes of cannibalism are actually quite funny, although I don't think guffaws are quite what the filmmakers were expecting. Still, you can't help but laugh at scenes of old men in smeared greasepaint slurping up a storm, chewing on viscera draped over unscathed bellies. It would probably be even funnier if these scenes didn't go on, and on, and on, and on, and...) Not only are the zombies unconvincing, but when it's time for them to be dispatched, their noggins are replaced by exploding papier-mâché heads, with stock fireworks footage superimposed over the lame action. Now *that's* what I call top notch optical effects. (It would make the late Al Adamson proud, I assure you.)

As could be expected, the crappy production values are topped off by an equally dungy script; my guess is that it was probably prepared for a short film, and not a full-length feature. (Lucky, lucky us they decided to go for broke.)

Although the credits insist that this mess was cooked up in 1982, it's obvious from the unwashed hippie stink that this sucker probably came to fruition sometime in the mid-70s.

Da Dove Vieni? *see* **Non Si Deve Profanare il Sonno dei Morti**

Dans les Griffes du Loup Garou *see* **La Maldicion de la Bestia**

Dawn of the Dead (1978)
Laurel Group [USA]
DIR: George A. Romero; PRO: Dario Argento and Richard P. Rubenstein; SCR: George A. Romero; DOP: Michael Gornick; MFX: Tom Savini; MUS: Dario Argento and Goblin
STR: John Amplas, Jim Baffico, Fred Baker, Pasquale Buba, Butchie, Sharon Caccatti, Pam Chatfield, David Crawford, Jese del Gre, Daniel Dietrich,

David Early, David Emge, Ken Foree, Christine Forrest, Richard France, John Harrison, Dave Hawkins, Clayton Hill, Jeannie Jefferies, Tom Kapusta, Jim Krut, Lenny Lies, Patrick McCloskey, Clayton McKinnon, Joe Plato, Scott H. Reiniger, Rudy Ricci, George A. Romero, Gaylen Ross, Tom Savini, Marty Schiff, Joe Shelby, Howard Smith, Taso N. Stavrakos, Rod Stouffer, Jay Stover, Nick Tallo, and Larry Vaira

AKA: **In de Greep van de Zombies** [In the Grip of the Zombies]; **Zombi—El Regresso de los Muertos Vivientes** [Zombie—The Return of the Living Dead]; **Zombie**; **Zombies—Dawn of the Dead**

Approximately 144m; Color

NOV: **Dawn of the Dead** by George A. Romero and Susanna Sparrow [St. Martin's Press]

SND: **Dawn of the Dead** [Varèse Sarabande]

VID: **Dawn of the Dead** [Anchor Bay Entertainment; 139m; Director's Cut; LBX]; **Dawn of the Dead** [HBO/Cannon Home Video; 126m]; **Dawn of the Dead** [Thorn EMI Video; 126m]; **In de Greep van de Zombies** [Movies Select Video (PAL); RTU]; **Zombi—El Regresso de los Muertos Vivientes** [Izaro Films (PAL); RTU]; **Zombie** [ADB Video; 125m; In English w/Spanish subs]

ADL: *When there's no more room in Hell, the dead will walk the earth!*

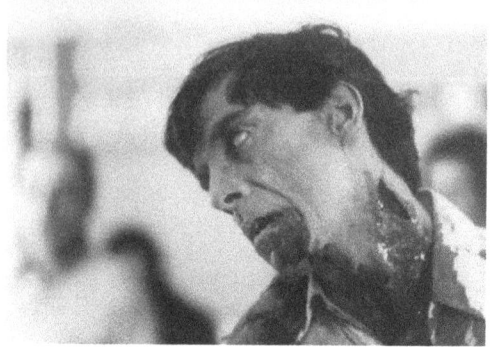

Picking up where **Night of the Living Dead** (1968) left off, the world is in the process of being overrun by the walking corpses whose sole ambition is to eat their living kith and kin. Four individuals—a newscaster, her boyfriend, and two SWAT team members—hightail it out of the big city, eventually making a place for themselves in a deserted mall... deserted, save for the hungry dead that are drawn to the suburban haven like flies to a dead hog. Not only do they have zombies to contend with, but survivalists and—worst of all—themselves as well.

This is it... what most splatterpunks consider the pinnacle of the genre, both in quality of the film and quantity of the grue. The gore is over-the-top and—although a little primitive by today's standards—still fairly shocking. Unlike similar fare, though, **Dawn of the Dead** spends as much time depicting taboo-bashing scenes of violence as it does examining the lives of four individuals who are separated from the standards of a normal life, and are forced to reconsider the politics of "The American Dream." Romero not only offers subtle sociopolitical subtexts within the context of the film, but confronts the viewer with the myths of consumerism. But don't worry about grabbing a bottle of Tylenol before settling in to watch **Dawn**; the viewer never has to wait long before someone is eviscerated, alleviating any headaches one might get while trying to dissect the finer points of the film. There's also enough tongue-in-cheek humor that keeps the film from getting too serious for its own good. (Wisely, Romero decided to save the darker approach for **Day of the Dead**, the third and insofar final entry in the series.)

The cast is superb; even when their performances are awkward, they manage to create very sympathetic, very real characters. In this way, **Dawn of the Dead** manages to stand out from most films, regardless of the genre. The scaled down versions of the film originally offered during theatrical runs do suffer from rather awkward edits, some of which create continuity problems and other anomalies.

Fans of Romero's other films will probably notice that the formula used here is nearly identical to that used in his earlier effort **The Crazies** (1972), although here it is used to greater effect, and on a much grander scale.

As for varying running times, **Dawn of the Dead** was originally filmed as a 144m film. From this, director Romero culled his own 126m edit for the American market (under the title of **Dawn of the Dead**) and Argento did the same for Europe with a completely different 125m version (released abroad as **Zombie**). In 1996, Anchor Bay Entertainment released a remastered Director's Cut that runs 139m, insofar the most complete cut to have an official release, although a bootleg of the 144m version is still in circulation.

Recommended viewing... although anyone reading this book will probably have already seen it. Many, many times. ☠☠☠

Day of the Maniac *see* **Tutti I Colori del Buio**

Day of the Woman (1977)

Cinemagic Pictures [USA]
DIR: Meir Zarchi; PRO: Meir Zarchi and Joseph Zbeda; SCR: Meir Zarchi; DOP: Yuri Haviv; SFX: Berlau Picaro and Bill Tasgal
STR: Isac Agami, Traci Ferrante, Ronit Haviv, Camille Keaton, Gunter Kleemann, Alexis Magnotti, Anthony Nichols, Richard Pace, Eron Tabor, Bill Tasgal, Tammy Zarchi, and Terry Zarchi
AKA: **I Hate Your Guts; I Spit on Your Grave; Mulher Violada** [*Violated Woman*]
Approximately 102m; Color
VID: **I Spit on Your Grave** [Wizard Video; 102m]; **Mulher Violada** [Top Video; RTU; In Portuguese]
ADL: *This woman has just cut, chopped, broken, and burned five men beyond recognition... but no jury in America would ever convict her!*

This is the film even I avoided for so many years because of all the negative hype surrounding it, most of which can be traced back or accredited to Roger Ebert during his **Sneak Previews** days. Now, I'll be spending the rest of my life trying to live down the ignorance and conformist passivity shown on my part.

Without a doubt, **Day of the Woman** is one of the most effective cinematic diatribes against misogyny and rape. Far from being entertaining (except maybe to the select few sadists of the kind this film depicts), **Day of the Woman** goes head on against the popularly depicted view of rape as glamorized in the films of the 70s (particularly in the exploitation market). Even as a male of the species, one will find it a harrowing experience, making it at least partly successful in its attempts to convey the seriousness of such reprehensible acts. Unfortunately, once this rape/revenge film begins to capitalize on the latter half of this popular formula, some of the previous images become trivialized, exposing it as nothing more than a well-meaning exploitation film. But even as it makes its descent into splatter territory, one can still taste the blood it had drawn in its first half.

Technically, Zarchi apparently decided (with good reason) that a more succinct, documentary-style approach would be more effective. Even the lack of a soundtrack helps to close the gap between the work and its audience. As previously mentioned, there is gore to be found amidst the deaths of the rapists; it is not as appealing as it is trite, and seems unnecessary, except as a possible warning or to show the severity of such crimes. If it turns out there is a case for life imitating art, let's just hope **Day of the Woman** manages to put a damper on the burgeoning rape fantasies of those who may actually act upon them.

Required viewing, if one can stomach it.

The Day the Screaming Stopped see **The Comeback**

Death at the Villa see **Delirio Caldo**

Death Carries a Cane see **Passi di Danza Su una Lama di Rasoio**

Death Line (1972)

K-L Productions [UK]
DIR: Gary A. Sherman; PRO: Paul Maslansky; SCR: Ceri Jones; DOP: Alex Thomson; SFX: John Horton; MFX: Harry Frampton; MUS: Will Mallone and Jeremy Rose
STR: Hugh Armstrong, James Cossins, Gerry Crampton, James Culliford, Hugh Dickson, Sharon Gurney, David Ladd, Christopher Lee, Colin McCormack, Ron Pember, Gordon Petrie, Donald Pleasence, Terence Plummer, Norman Rossington, Heather Stoney, Clive Swift, June Turner, Gary Winkler, Suzanne Winkler, and Jack Woolgar
AKA: **Raw Meat**
Approximately 88m; Color
VID: **Raw Meat** [Carlton Video (PAL); 83m]
ADL: *The most terrifying journey you will ever make... to the land of the hungry dead!*

An American economics student and his Brit girlfriend come across a man—apparently unconscious—in the subway. Unbeknownst to them, he's with the Ministry, so

the authorities are more than a little interested when they tell the police their story. Suspicions fall on the couple, though, when the authorities arrive on the scene and find the body missing... yet another addition to a long string of odd disappearances. As it turns out, the culprits are the descendants of workers trapped in a cave-in circa 1892, who, out of necessity, acquired a taste for—c'mon, you already knew it before I got this far—*human flesh*. (Is it just me, or shouldn't the 70s be remembered as the decade of the cannibal?)

Although all of the ads obliterate any of the surprises this film may have once held for the viewer, this virtually lost film is a great 70s shocker that is deserving of a decent stateside release. (Bootlegs from a now out-of-print UK tape are—as far as I know—the only copies in circulation as of this writing.) But despite its wonderfully exploitive demeanor, this is actually one of the more, how should I put this, *poignant* cannibal flicks to cross my path. (Call me a bleeding heart, but I really felt sorry for these pathetic wretches; Christ, all they need is a little love. And support. And a lifetime membership to Anthropophagus Anonymous.) Despite its sometimes dated charm, **Death Line** still manages to be quite effective. Part of the film's success lies in its intentionally slow pacing, and its use of silence to compliment the sparse score, both tools used to heighten the tension. Unfortunately, today's generation—dependent on non-stop action to keep their limited attention spans—will not be able to fully appreciate such a film.

And, yes, there is some gruesome after-the-fact gore, but it—like the music—is used conservatively to great effect. (The only scene which would constitute over-the-top is our first view of the cannibals' lair-cum-abattoir, a set strewn with corpses which—although underexposed—is just as unnerving as it is truly repugnant. Even *without* the realistic corpses, it is a scene which would likely evoke shivers.)

If that isn't enough for you, remember that Christopher Lee—albeit in a small part—and Donald Pleasence (as a fairly chipper but abrasive police detective) are on hand to spice things up.

Hey, Anchor Bay Entertainment is looking for other titles to release in their definitive versions; I suggest anyone with a few minutes of spare time go and drop them a line about this flick. It's worth a shot.

Death Rides a Carousel *see* **Carnival of Blood**

Death Trap *see* **Eaten Alive**

Deep Red *see* **Profondo Rosso**

Deep Red Hatchet Murders *see* **Profondo Rosso**

Delirio Caldo [Hot Delirium] (1972)
G.R.P. Cinematografica [Italy]
DIR: Renato Polselli; SCR: Renato Polselli; DOP: Ugo Brunelli; MUS: Gianfranco Reverberi

STR: Krista Barrymore, Rita Calderoni, Katia Cardinali, Tano Cimarosa, William Darni, Mickey Hargitay, Stefano Oppedisano, Raoul, Steffy Stefen, and Carmen Young
AKA: **Au-Delà du Désir** [*Beyond Desire*]; Death at the Villa; **Delirium**
Approximately 92m; Color
VID: **Delirium** [Empire Video (PAL); 90(92)m; In English w/Dutch subtitles]

A Vietnam vet is killing off young women; after being questioned by police, he not only gets off but—being a criminal psychologist by trade—is offered the chance to help crack the case by authorities. His wife knows something is up, but doesn't seem too perturbed by her hubby's extra-curricular activities. (If anything, she gets worked up by his violent advances, and even goes so far as to provoke him into them.)

This gory thriller is almost in a class by itself; but then again, what do you expect from the man who brought us **Riti, Magie Nere e Segrete Orge nel Trecento**... the same year? (**Delirio Caldo** even cannibalizes footage from this other Polselli film, shown here as funky, sleaze-ridden dream sequences.) Granted, this film is a less chaotic effort, and can actually lay claim to having a coherent storyline, but it still has much of the same "charm."

Aside from the stock Vietnam war footage, the innumerable nude women in chains, and some interesting plot twists, we also are graced by the presence of Mickey Hargitay (who also starred in that other Polselli flick) and a wonderfully overbearing soundtrack. (Fuzzed-out guitars, jazzy drums, and even an occasional, abused Moog synthesizer comprise most of the score.)

Not a good film, but a hell of a lot more engaging than many of its peers.

Deliríos de um Anormal [Deliriums of the Abnormal] (1977)

Ribalta Filmes [Brazil]
DIR: José Mojica Marins; PRO: José Mojica Marins; SCR: Rubens Francisco Lucchetti and José Mojica Marins; DOP: Giorgio Attili; MFX: Nilcemar Leyart; MUS: Clayber de Souza and Beto Strada
STR: Neiva Aparecida, José Barbosa, Natalina Barbosa, Lírio Bertelli, Alex Brandwira, Jayme Cortez, Shirley da Conceição, João da Cruz, Sandoval Félix, Elza Ferreira, Lenira Galdino, Anadir Gói, Orival Gonçalves, José Mojica Marins, Magna Miller, José Nivaldo, Jorge Peres, Vítor Perrici, Lourenço B. Rocha, Walter Setembro, Luzia Zaracausca, and Maria Helena Zeferino
AKA: **Hallucinations of a Deranged Mind**
Approximately 86m; B&W and Color
VID: **Hallucinations of a Deranged Mind** [Something Weird Video; 86m; In Portuguese w/English subs]

First and foremost, this patchwork atrocity contains footage from several of Marins' earlier efforts, namely **Esta Noite Encarnarei No Teu Cadaver** (1966), **O Estranho Mundo de Zé do Caixão** (1966), **Ritual dos Sádicos** (1969), and **Exorcisma Negro** (1974). For those who haven't seen any of these no-budget wonders, **Deliríos de um Anormal** will make a good primer for those unfamiliar with the man's work; for those who have, and still wish to see more of his oeuvre, then nothing I say will deter you from watching this one as well. There is some new footage, but this is just a talky attempt to tie all of the unrelated sequences together. (Much like Al Adamson, Marins seems obsessed with reusing footage indefinitely if he can find a way to do so.)

The wraparound sequence stars the director (natch) in a dual role, portraying himself and his antithetical creation "Coffin Joe" (or, if you prefer the proper name, Zé do Caixão). Marins attempts to add some depth to the proceedings by either spewing unconvincing, pseudo-philosophical psychobabble, or—if Coffin Joe has the floor—ranting and raving and generally chewing the scenery as dime-store nightmares assault the viewer. (A few are pretty intense—the addition of real piercings and other mondo-style footage gives the fake blood a much-needed touch of realism—but other scenes are simply quite silly. A mob of bare asses painted up to resemble Coffin Joe's countenance is not nearly as frightening as the filmmaker probably intended.)

To make the viewing experience unusually painful is the downright sloppy editing and migraine-inducing sound production; the fact that the source footage is culled from both color and black & white sources can also be quite jarring. As for the quality of the recycled footage, well, let's just say that it's difficult to distinguish the old from the new.

For Coffin Joe fans only.

Delirium (1972) *see* Delirio Caldo

Delirium (1977)

Worldwide and Odyssey [USA]
DIR: Peter Maris; PRO: Peter Maris and Sunny Vest; SCR: Richard Yalem; DOP: John Huston and Bill Mensch; EXP: Mark Cusumano; SFX: Bob Shelly; MUS: David Williams

STR: Decatur Agnew, David Basch, Garrett Bergfeld, Terry Ten Broek, Eugene Camp, George Cantner, Jr., Turk Cekovsky, Debi Chaney, Chris Chronopolis, Carol Emory, Jon Frankel, Letty Garris, Jack Garvey, Glen Gelber, Harry Gorsuch, Melissa Higgins, Richard Jones, Mike Kalist, Pat Knapko, Myron Kozman, Charlotte Littrell, Gary Mandrell, Allen Maris, Stephanie Maris, Rick Miller, Nick Panouzis, Joe Pollack, Lloyd Schattyn, Randy Shulman, James Barry Simmerman, Dana Smith, Sherri Stevens, Bill Thomas, Mike Tierney, Julie Hauck Vest, Todd Vest, Jennifer C. Voges, Police Officer Walleman, Barron Winchester, Bob Winters, and Richard Yalem

AKA: **Psycho Puppet**
Approximately 85m; Color
VID: **Delirium** [Academy Home Entertainment; 86(85)m]
ADL: *He's waiting to kill you... Poor Charlie—you'll die when you meet him.*

Not to be confused with Renato Polselli's **Deliria Caldo** (released as **Delirium** as well), this flick *also* features a crazed Vietnam vet stalking and killing young women. This effort, though, avoids the traditional formula entirely, as the killer whose exploits the film focuses on is himself killed not an hour into the movie, whereupon **Delirium** veers off into conspiracy thriller territory.

There is some nasty gore, but—despite the off-kilter plot

Deranged

construction—**Delirium** is wholly unengaging. (Unless, of course, one likes low-rent, low-key 70s crime fare; but even then, one would be hard-pressed to consider this anything exemplary.)

By the way, I'm guessing that the Vietnam war footage is not authentic, nor is it filmed on location. I think it's all the powerlines that end up in the shots that make me think otherwise.

Demonoia see **Buio Omega**

Demons of the Dead see **Tutti I Colori del Buio**

Deranged (1974)

Karr International Pictures [USA]
DIR: Jeffrey Gillen and Alan Ormsby; PRO: Tom Karr; SCR: Alan Ormsby; DOP: Jack McGowan; EXP: Benjamin Clark; MFX: Jerome Bergson, Alan Ormsby, and Tom Savini; MUS: Carl Zittrer
STR: Roberts Blossom, Leslie Carlson, Marcia Diamond, Arlene Gillen, Cosette Lee, Jack Mather, Robert McHeady, Micki Moore, Alan Ormsby, Patt Orr, Brian Smeagle, Marion Waldman, and Robert Warner
Approximately 82m; Color
VID: Deranged [Moore Video; 82m]
ADL: *Pretty Sally Mae died a very unnatural death! ...but the worst hasn't happened to her yet!*

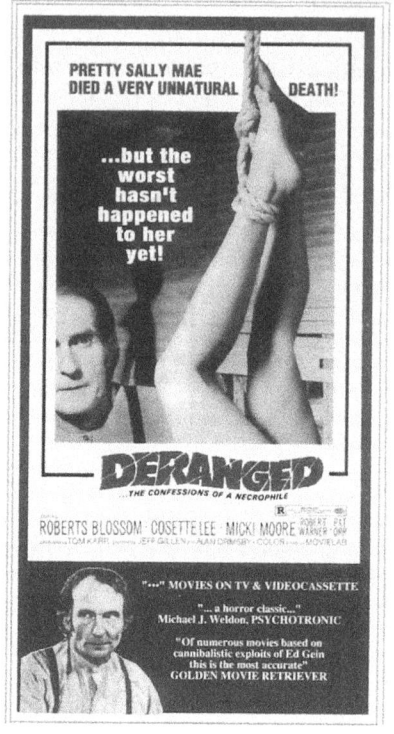

Deranged opens with the claim "The motion picture you are about to see is absolutely *true*. Only the names and locations have been changed." Although it is obviously based on the exploits of famed necrophile-cum-cannibal Ed Gein, the screenwriters didn't hesitate to take some artistic license with the facts. (Several other films have been influenced by the case—**Psycho**, **The Texas Chain Saw Massacre**, and **Three on a Meathook** come immediately to mind—**Deranged** is by the far the most accurate of the lot.) Despite any liberties taken, **Deranged** deserves (at least in part) the recent claims of being a rediscovered cult classic.

Roberts Blossom (the old man in Carpenter's **Christine** [1983] who shows up just long enough to sell the accursed car of the same name) makes his film debut in **Deranged** as the charmingly loony Ezra Cobb, a repressed mama's boy with some macabre inclinations. After the death of his domineering mother, Ezra decides to take up a career in grave robbing and—when the graves start to run dry—murder. His rather esoteric hobbies tend to get in the way of him acquiring anything even remotely resembling a social life. But that's okay, 'cause he'll always have mama to turn to for company.

This is one of those films that benefits greatly from the low budget; the intensity of the subject matter would have been lost had it the luster of higher productions. The budget restrictions also force the filmmakers to rely more on innovation and a documentary-like approach, much like the aforementioned **The Texas Chain Saw Massacre**, made the previous year. There are a few distracting chuckles (supplied by scriptwriter Alan Ormsby, who also had a hand in **Children Shouldn't Play with Dead Things**), but—thankfully—these are few and far between.

This charming sickie received an official video release only a few years back. (For almost twenty years, desperate collectors were forced to rely on grainy fourth generation bootlegs from questionable sources just to see it.) To commemorate the occasion, the producers included previously unseen (and quite nasty) gore footage that was trimmed prior to its initial theatrical release. (Not to mention a bonus documentary on the Gein case, filmed in the early 80s shortly before Gein himself passed away while incarcerated.) Rumors have it that the director is planning a remake.

La Dernier Maison sur la Gauche *see* **The Last House on the Left**

Le Dernier Monde Cannibale *see* **Ultimo Mondo Cannibale**

El Descuartizador de Binbrook *see* **Necrophagus**

O Despertar da Besta *see* **Ritual dos Sádicos**

The Devil and Dr. Frankenstein *see* **Il Mostro è in Tavola... Barone Frankenstein**

The Devil's Eye *see* **Gatti Rosso in un Labirinto do Vetro**

I Diabolici Amori di Nosferatu *see* **El Gran Amor del Conde Dracula**

Disciple of Death (1972)
Chromage Productions Ltd. [UK]
DIR: Tom Parkinson; PRO: Churton Fairman and Tom Parkinson; SCR: Churton Fairman and Tom Parkinson; DOP: William Brayne; MUS: Johanne Sebastian Bach
STR: Betty Alberge, Nicholas Amer, George Belbin, Stephen Bradley, Daisika, Joe Dunlop, Rusty Goffe, Marguerite Hardiman, Louise Jameson, Ronald Lacey, Mike Raven, and Virginia Wetherell
Approximately 82m; Color
VID: **Disciple of Death** [Unicorn Video; 90(82)m]

Two young lovers accidentally revive a devil worshipper dead for fifty years. With his sights set on the girl,

Doctor Death

Starring: Mike Raven, Ronnie Lacey and Stephen Bradley

he spends his off hours sacrificing and zombifying the village maidens. An overzealous parson and the girl's desperate boyfriend enlist the aid of an absent-minded Jewish alchemist to defeat the bloodthirsty count. ("This is none of your Christian shmutas... this is your kosher Yiddisha magic!" he exclaims at one point.)

Not only is this a fairly clumsy attempt to repeat the success of Hammer's period offerings, it's a clumsy attempt at a horror film altogether. (The lackluster production values somehow make it look more like U.S. trash than the British fare it tries to emulate.) **Disciple of Death** is ultimately worse than what one is initially lead to believe, as the filmmakers had difficulty covering up their ineptitude as the film progressed. (This may be what lead to the decision to begin hamming it up halfway through, as the aforementioned Yiddish sorcerer will clearly attest.) Distracting close-ups, stilted dialogue, tacky stop-motion photography, an anticlimactic finale, and a conjured devil (a dwarf sans makeup save for a pair of cheap plastic fangs) all help to contribute to this abysmal shocker. There is some gore, but this is mostly relegated to some *guignol*-inspired scenes of hearts being removed from the sacrificial virgins.

The film's single high point is Mike Raven (a poor man's Christopher Lee who starred in Hammer's **Lust for a Vampire** two years earlier). Although not a great actor by any means, what charisma the man boasts is hopelessly lost amidst the hackneyed scriptwriting. If he had been thinking about a career, **Disciple of Death** probably put a kibosh on any chance he had of establishing one.

After an hour and a half of this, I was beginning to look like one of Raven's pasty faced ghouls as well, so approach at your own risk.

Doctor Bloodbath *see* **Horror Hospital**

Doctor Death—Seeker of Souls (1972)

Freedom Arts Picture Corporation [USA]

DIR: Eddie Saeta; PRO: Eddie Saeta; SCR: Sal Ponti; DOP: Emil Oster and Kent Wakeford; VFX: Van der Veer Photo; MUS: Richard la Salle

STR: Sivi Aberg, Leon Askin, Robert Ball, Anna Bernard, Barbara Boles, Eric Boles, Jim Boles, Barry Coe,

John Consadine, Denise Denise, Patrick Dennis-Leigh, Pierre Gonneau, Lin Henson, Jeffrey Herman, Moe Howard, Athena Lorde, Florence Marly, Cheryl Miller, Joe Morrow, Stewart Moss, Larry Rogers, Larry Vincent, and Leon Williams

    AKA: **Dr. Death**
    Approximately 89m; Color
    VID: **Doctor Death** [Prism Entertainment; 90(89)m]
    ADL: *To Make Them Whole, He Needs Your Soul!*

Obsessed with bringing his dead wife back to life, a desperate man employs the dubious talents of a doctor who claims he can do just that. Despite some rather tasteless stage theatrics, our title conjurer turns out to be the real McCoy... but even he has his limits. When the good doctor finds himself unable to come through for the bereaved husband, the man decides to call it quits. But not the persistant doctor; he's determined to hold up his end of the bargain, even if it means killing every woman in the city in order to make it so.

After a slow start, **Doctor Death—Seeker of Souls** actually manages to prove itself rather enjoyable once the hokum kicks in. Despite a low budget, the production values are quite passable. (comparable to what could be found in made-for-TV films from the same time), and the script offers some commendable tongue-in-cheek humor. (the better jokes are actually stabs at horror films, which—although effective—makes one wonder where the filmmakers' loyalties lie.) Gore is sparse, but the splatter effects are quite gruesome when it does rear its ugly face. (And some ugly faces they are, with a nasty decap, and a time-lapse meltdown, the latter of which could have done without the super-imposed flames.)

Look for Moe Howard (of Three Stooges fame) as a participating audience member.

Would make a good double-bill with **Love Me Deadly** (1972). Oh, the sideburns...

Doctor Gore *see* **The Body Shop**

Don't Go in the House (1979)
    Turbine Films Inc. [USA]
    DIR: Joseph Ellison; PRO: Ellen Hammill; SCR: Joseph Ellison, Ellen Hammill, and Joseph R. Masefield; DOP: Oliver Wood; SFX: Matt Vogel; MFX: Tom Brumberger; MUS: Richard Einhorn

    STR: Charlie Bonet, Ralph D. Bowman, David Brody, Tom Brumberger, Johanna Brushay, Mary Ann Chin, Ruth Dardick, Jim Donnegan, Eileen Dunn, Charlie Foits, Johnny G., Dan Grimaldi, John Hedburg, Dennis M. Hunter, Christine Isadore, Ken Ketsch, Nikki Kollins, D'Mara Leary, Sean Manning, David McComb, Colin Moinnes, Connie Oaks, Robert Osth, Rosy Peschi, Bill Ricci, Kim Roberts, Darcy Shean, Susan Smith, Maria Srymkovicz, Gail Turner, Lois Verkruspe, Pat Williams, and Denise Woods

    Approximately 83m; Color
    VID: **Don't Go in the House** [Arcade Video (PAL); 83m]; **Don't Go in the House** [Medie Home Entertainment; 90(83)m]; **Don't Go in the House** [Video Treasures; 90(83)m]
    ADL: *You have been warned.*

A young boy is ritually abused by his mother (she has a particular penchant for holding his hand over an open fire), and grows up to be a serial killer who has equipped his house with specially insulated rooms where he can incinerate his victims to his heart's content. And that, folks, is about all she wrote.

Although it strikes similar chords as William Lustig's **Maniac** (made the following year), **Don't Go in the House** isn't nearly as effective. Production values are subpar, the lead psychopath is far from convincing, and the storyline too threadbare to carry the weight of the film. (Let's just say it's a particularly *long* hour and a half.) To its credit, the scenes of young women being burned alive are quite unnerving, but this does little to justify what is, ultimately, highly exploitive and sadistic fare.

At least Joe Spinell was scary.

Don't Look in the Basement (1973)

Camera 2 Productions [USA] Century Studios [USA]
DIR: S.F. Brownrigg; PRO: S.F. Brownrigg; SCR: Tim Pope; DOP: Robert Alcott; EXP: Walter L. Krusz; SFX: Jack Bennett; MUS: Robert Farrar
STR: Camilla Carr, Betty Chandler, Robert Dracup, Hugh Feagin, Jessie Lee Fulton, Michael Harvey, Rosie Holotik, Jessie Kirby, Rhea MacAdams, Ann McAdams, William McGhee, Gene Ross, Harryette Warren, and Annabelle Weenick
AKA: **The Forgotten**
Approximately 95m; Color
VID: **Don't Look in the Basement** [MPI Home Video; 95m]; **Don't Look in the Basement** [VCI Home Video; 95(89)m]; **Don't Look in the Basement** [VidAmerica; 82m]

ADL: *Take a look at what happens when the insane take over the asylum.*

A new nurse arrives at Stephens Sanitarium the selfsame day the director and head nurse are murdered by the patients. She introduces herself to one venerable resident who recites the poem "Up the airy mountain, down the rushing glen, you never can go hunting for fear of little men." (She is apparently fond of this as it seems to be the old woman's catchall response to any question thrown her way; guess she watched **Willy Wonka and the Chocolate Factory** one too many times.) The interesting characters don't end there: There's Sam, a lollipop sucking lobotomy who just wants to play with his toy boat; Danny, a hyena-like loony tune who bears a passing resemblance to another Danny (that Bonaduce kid from **The Partridge Family**); Liz, a psychotically obsessive nymphomaniac; and the appropriately named Sarge (a shell shocked Nam vet) and Judge (who has apparently seen **Pena de Muerte** one too many times). Before long, the nurse (and anyone else who perchances upon the place) find themselves imperiled by the touch-and-go inmates.

Considered a minor cult classic by fans of 70s trash horror, this charming gem was enough to garner director Brownrigg something of a fan following (even though none of his other films—all exemplary shockers in their own right—made much of an impact). Brownrigg's penchant for palpable characterization and tongue-in-cheek humor push **Don't Look in the Basement** above the level of most low-budget shock horror exercises. (The downbeat ending is immediately followed with cast credits, names accompanied by shots of the actor drenched in the blood and gore of the preceding carnage, a little reminder from the director that it's all entertainment.) There is some decent 70s splatter, but it's not the "real gorefest" that the video boxes claim. (What's ironic is that these selfsame prints are shorn of the gorier moments, even though the end credit stills showing what was cut are left intact.)

If you've seen **Alone in the Dark** (1982), you might find yourself overcome by a sense of *déjà vu*;

conscious or not, it appears that much of that film was derived from Brownrigg's cruder, albeit more effective shocker.

Don't Open the Window *see* **Non Si Deve Profanare il Sonno dei Morti**

Dr. Gore's Body Shop *see* **The Body Shop**

Dr. Jekyll and Mr. Blood (1972)

Constitution Films Inc. [UK]
DIR: Andy Milligan; PRO: William Mishkin; SCR: Andy Milligan; [Based on the novel *The Strange Case of Dr. Jekyll and Mr. Hyde* by Robert Louis Stevenson]; DOP: Andy Milligan; MUS: David Tike

STR: Guido Adorni, William Barrell, Jeremy Brooks, Simon Coady, April Conners, Raymond Cross, Doreen Davies, Dennis de Marne, Frank

Dougherty, Gay Feld, Angela Hill, Berwick Kaler, Jacqueline Lawrence, Katherine Maitland, Craig Malcomson, Tony Parkin, Louis Raynes, Janis Servals, Bryan Southcombe, Grahame Steane, Jennifer Summerfield, Karina Tamahine, Patricia Thorn, Mary Ann Turner, and Jim Wilson
AKA: **The Man with Two Faces; The Man with Two Heads**
Approximately 80m; Color
VID: **The Man with Two Heads** [Midnight Video; 80m]
ADL: *FLESH CURDLING EXPERIMENTS! SADISTIC SUFFERING!*

More wonderfully inept trash from Statton Island's premiere filmmaker. (Admittedly, though, the work of the late Andy Milligan is an acquired taste.) Of his earlier splatter-oriented efforts, this is one of the best looking and best scripted; even the actors seem to be on the ball for a change. (I'm starting to feel guilty for calling it "inept trash" but, oh, well... life goes on.)

As to be expected, there is a fair amount of grade-Z gore (he's still the only filmmaker who insists on using modeling clay as a substitute for flesh), but this—sadly— looks good in comparison to the slapdash stage makeup the poor lead had to endure. To Milligan's credit (an ex-dressmaker by trade), there is some convincing period costuming; this helps to distract the viewer from the innumerable anachronisms that constantly plague his period pieces.

All in all, it's fairly endurable, and might even make a good introduction to those unfamiliar with Milligan's charming oeuvre. Hey, I sat through at least a dozen of his films before I could truly appreciate the man and his work. Now *that's* the definition of dedication.

Dr. Jekyll and the Wolfman see **Dr. Jekyll y el Hombre Lobo**

Dr. Jekyll et le Loup Garou see **Dr. Jekyll y el Hombre Lobo**

Dr. Jekyll vs. the Werewolf see **Dr. Jekyll y el Hombre Lobo**

Dr. Jekyll vs. the Wolfman see **Dr. Jekyll y el Hombre Lobo**

Dr. Jekyll y el Hombre Lobo [Dr. Jekyll and the Wolfman] (1971)

Arturo González P.C. [Spain]
DIR: León Klimovsky; PRO: Arturo González; SCR: Jacinto Molina Alvarez; DOP: Francisco Fraile; EXP: Alfredo Fraile; SFX: Antonio Vidal Molina; MUS: Antón García Abril
STR: Jacinto Molina Alvarez, Barta Barri, Shirley Corrigan, Luis Gaspar, Luis Induñi, Montserrat Julio, José Marco, Mirtha Miller, Jack Taylor, Lucy Tiller, Adolfo Tohus, Jorge Vico, and Elsa Zabala
AKA: **Dr. Jekyll et le Loup Garou; Dr. Jekyll vs. the Werewolf; Dr. Jekyll vs. the Wolfman; Die Nacht der Blutigen Wolfe** [*The Night of the Bloody Wolf*]
Approximately 96m
VID: **Dr. Jekyll and the Wolfman** [Sinister Cinema; 88m]

A man returns to his home town of Baliavasta in the Carpathian mountains. (It turns out his parents had been hacked to death with an axe, a macabre account that has absolutely nothing to do with the rest of the film. Go figure.) An innkeeper warns him and his wife to stay away from Castle Inri, but before he has a chance to take him up on his dare, he is killed by some villagers who also take it upon themselves to rape his wife, Justine. Before you can say "knight in shaggy armor," good old Waldemar Daninsky shows up to save the day. Although spooked at first, she eventually succumbs to his somber, wooden charms. (Our brooding hero is also aided by a scaly-faced leper; guess they were all out of hunchbacks this time around.) The surviving villagers decide to raid the castle and kill Waldemar, but their plans are quashed by everyone's favorite Polish lycanthrope.

With his newfound love, Daninsky flies to London and is put in the care of Dr. Henry Jekyll (Eurotrash fave Jack Taylor looking mighty suave in his sideburns and goatee) who is not only the head of a "Biological Research Clinic," but the great grandson of... c'mon, one guess. *Anyway*, Jekyll gets the keen idea to inject Waldemar with the infamous Hyde formula just prior to his inevitable transformation. But, hey, the fun's just beginning...

By far the silliest entry in the "el Hombre Lobo" series, **Dr. Jekyll y el Hombre Lobo** still packs in more sleazy Spanish fun in an hour and a half than most. Sure, Paul Naschy (*né* Jacinto Molina Alvarez) looks pretty foolish walking around modern day London in a prototypical Hyde getup. And, sure, he spends the other half of the film drooling profusely. (Oh, wait, he slobbers a lot as Hyde too, so make that two-thirds of the film.) But it's a Paul Naschy film, so just shut up and enjoy. (At least they didn't rewrite his origin for this one; trying to keep track of those gives me a migraine.)

Gore is everything that could be expected: Innumerable throats are torn out, while Naschy in his fuzzy jumpsuit poses for the camera with hunks of raw meat hanging out of his mouth. **Dr. Jekyll y el Hombre Lobo** also boasts some groovy optical effects, a tacky transformation sequence set in a crowded elevator, and some chilly location shooting. (Daninsky must've forgotten to pay his electric bill as you can see everyone's breath in his castle domain.)

So when's he going to be pitted against Jack the Ripper? How about a swamp creature?

Dracula Cerca Sangue di Vergine e... Morì di Sete!!! *see* **Dracula Vuole Vivere—Cerca Sangue di Vergina!**

Dracula—The Bloodline Continues *see* **La Saga de los Draculas**

Dracula—The Terror of the Living Dead *see* **La Orgia de los Muertos**

Dracula Jagt Frankenstein *see* **Los Monstruos de la Noche**

Dracula vs. Frankenstein (1969) *see* **Los Monstruos de la Noche**

Dracula vs. Frankenstein (1971)
Independent-International Pictures [USA]

Dracula vs. Frankenstein

DIR: Al Adamson; PRO: Al Adamson and John van Horn; SCR: William Pugsley and Samuel M. Sherman; DOP: Paul Glickman and Gary M. Graver; EXP: Mardi Rustam; MFX: Tony Tierney; VFX: Bob le Bar; MUS: William Lava

STR: Forrest J Ackerman, John Bloom, William Bonner, John Cardos, Lon Chaney, Jr., Greydon Clark, Albert Cole, Jim Davis, Lu Dorn, Anthony Eisly, Roger Engel, Barney Gelfan, Regina Gelfin, Sean Graver, Gary Kent, Bruce Kimball, Maria Lease, Anne Morrell, J. Carrol Naish, Connie Nelson, Angelo Rossitto, Ervin Saunders, Russ Tamblyn, and Shelly Weiss

AKA: **Blood of Frankenstein; The Blood Seekers; Revenge of Dracula; Satan's Bloody Freaks; Teenage Dracula**

Approximately 90m; Color
VID: **Dracula vs. Frankenstein** [Entertainment Programs International; 90m]; **Dracula vs. Frankenstein** [Vid-America; 90m]; **Revenge of Dracula** [Dura Vision Inc.; 85(86)m]

Dracula (Zandor Vorkov né Roger Engel sporting cheap plastic fangs, pancake makeup and a white man's afro, and equipped with a ring that shoots lightning bolts) digs up the remains of the Frankenstein monster (buried in a California cemetery.) who has come to resemble a burnt marshmallow in combat boots. Meanwhile, someone is decapitating young women with an axe underneath peers in Venice (the center for drug pushing and white slavery activity, one cop insists) and stealing the corpses. One of the unfortunate girls is the sister of grade-Z starlet Regina Carrol, who decides to conduct her own investigation into the disappearance of her sibling, schmoozing with hippies and worse. Nearby is a carnival spookshow, a front for the work of Dr. Duree, the last descendant in the infamous Frankenstein lineage. He is aided by a dwarf (Rossitto) who displays "amazing" feats of legerdemain, and Grotin (Chaney, shortly before his death and looking it), a half-wit servant sent out to collect bodies for the doctor after being injected with a drug that turns him into a drooling madman. (What the obviously illegal substance is, they refuse to specify; as contrived as everything is, they should've just said it was Mr. Hyde's infamous elixir mixed with LSD.) Duree is approached by Dracula, who wants him to revive the monster so as to aid him in his plan for world domination. And this, my dear readers, is only the first twenty minutes of this brain-damaged classic. (I wasn't the first to apply this term to **Dracula vs. Frankenstein**—this credit goes out to Duane Eilf—but it is so fitting that I couldn't resist plagiarizing it.)

This one's so bad it has to be seen to be believed. Forrest J (No Period) Ackerman of **Famous Monsters of Filmland** fame shows up just long enough to get manhandled by Frankenstein's creation, and also functions as the film's "technical advisor." Russ Tamblyn (Dr. Jacobi of TV's **Twin Peaks**) plays Rico, again typecast as a sleazy druggie/biker/punk, the only role he was ever offered in the 60s and early 70s. And—the most horrifying of all—Regina Carrol (née Gelfin) headlining a musical number!

But wait, there's more! One cop spends his screen time talking about man's subconscious and the meaning of life; his half-baked observations are a real hoot, and much more interesting than Naish's somnambulistic monologues that repeatedly encroach on the film's precious running time. **Dracula vs. Frankenstein** also boasts the *worst* acid trip ever committed to celluloid. Not to mention the wonderfully garish credits sequence; you'll know if it's your bag before they even finish rolling. "What are we protesting tonight?" a hippie asks her boyfriend at one point. "I don't know, but I bet it's fun." (I assumed they were referring to adept filmmaking, in which case this film qualifies as a true rebel. And it is fun.)

Brief nudity, gore, an attempted gang rape, drug abuse ... all of the things you would expect from a film rated GP. (That's "General Public" to baby boomers too young to remember the old ratings board. Boy, those were the days.)

Just to prove that there is life after **Plan Nine from Outer Space**.

Dracula Vuole Vivere—Cerca Sangue di Vergina! (1973)

Compagnia Cinematografica Champion S.P.A. [France/Italy]
DIR: Antonio Margheriti and Paul Morrissey; PRO: Andrew Braunsberg; SCR: Antonio Margheriti and Paul Morrissey; DOP: Luigi Kuveiller; EXP: Carlo Ponti, Jean Pierre Rassam, and Jean Yanne; SFX: Carlo Rambaldi; MUS: Claudio Gizzi
STR: Inna Alexeievna, Gil Cagne, Emi Califri, Stefania Casini, Joe Dallesandro, Dominique Darel, Vittorio de Sica, Silvia Dionisio, Arno Juerging, Udo Kier, Maxime McKendry, Roman Polansky, Milena Vukotic, and Eleonori Zani
Approximately 106m; Color
AKA: **Andy Warhol's Dracula**; **Dracula Cerca Sangue di Vergine e... Morì di Sete!!!**; **Du Sang pour Dracula** [*The Blood for Dracula*]; **Young Dracula**

VID: **Andy Warhol's Dracula** [Air Video; 106m]; **Andy Warhol's Dracula** [Triboro Entertainment; 91m; R-Rated Version]; **Andy Warhol's Dracula** [Triboro Entertainment; 106m; Unrated Edition]; **Andy Warhol's Dracula** [Video Gems; 106m]

As with **Il Mostro è in Tavola... Barone Frankenstein**, Udo Kier takes centerstage, this time as an emaciated and feeble Dracula. (A far cry from the unyielding, virile creature as the Count is usually portrayed.) Slowly dying from lack of nourishment, he moves away from his homeland in search of "wergin" blood. (Apparently, virgin blood is the only sustenance he can keep down; quite literally. One of the more unpleasant sights the film offers is Dracula heaving up his guts after making the dreadful mistake of presuming his victim to be chaste.) When he does perchance upon a young girl (the youngest daughter of a well-to-do household) who fits his strict dietary requirements, a race ensues between him and a young handyman (Joe Dallesandro, still sporting a Brooklyn accent) who is determined to beat the vampire to the punch. So to speak.

Made back to back with **Il Mostro è in Tavola... Barone Frankenstein**, this garish updating of Bram Stoker's classic places its emphasis on sex and violence, although here the sexual aspects get a lot more attention than they did in the same team's updating of the Frankenstein legend. This film is similarly garish, and has its tongue firmly planted in its cheek as well. It is also just as politically incorrect, its tone summed up by the scene where not only the hero rapes the only virgin so as to save her from Dracula's clutches, but with the desperate vampire then lapping off the floor the blood from her torn hymen.

Production values bear all the markings of the previous film, although the cinematography doesn't suffer from having things thrust into the camera; unlike **Il Mostro è in Tavola...** this production wasn't filmed in 3-D. Gore is sparse, and most of that is relegated to the finale where our pathetic bloodsucker is dismembered by the underdog hero and his well-sharpened axe. But, if you like to watch incestuous vampire lesbians in period costuming doing their thing, you'll find more than enough here of interest.

Although Morrisey receives sole directorial and screenwriting credit on most film prints, it has been cited by Margheriti himself in several interviews that he co-scripted and directed much of the film. Morrisey denies such claims, so it hasn't been fully substantiated. Regardless, he has been given co-credit for both.

If you haven't, check out the aforementioned **Il Mostro è in Tavola... Barone Frankenstein**, as it's just as bad if not *more* so.

Dracula's Blood *see* **El Gran Amor del Conde Dracula**

Dracula's Great Love *see* **El Gran Amor del Conde Dracula**

Dracula's Virgin Lovers *see* **El Gran Amor del Conde Dracula**

The Driller Killer (1979)

Navaron Films [USA] and Rochelle Films [USA]
DIR: Abel Ferrara; PRO: Rochelle Gail Weisberg; SCR: Nicholas St. John; DOP: Ken Kelsch; MUS: Joseph Delia and the Roosters
STR: Chris Amato, Thomas Baeza, Dicky Bittner, Rich Bokun, Steve Brown, Michael Canosa, Andrea Childs, Gary Cohen, Hallie Coletta, Tom Constantine, John Coulakis, Steve Cox, Janet Dailey, Baybi Day, Bob de Frank, Abel Ferrara, Joyce Finney, John Fitze, Paul Fitze, Rita Gooding, Frank Hazrd, Maria Helhoski, Richard Howorth, Victoria Keiler, Jack MacIntyre, Claire Mailer, Carolyn Marz, Louis Mascolo, Karl Metner, Rhodney Montreal, Butch Morris, Paula Nichols, James O'Hara, Anthony Picciano, Chuck Saaf, Tommy Santora, Greg Schirrira, Harry Schultz, Stephen Singer, Trixie Sly, Lanny Taylor, Laurie S. Taylor, Alan Wynroth, and Peter Yellen
AKA: **Driller Killer**
Approximately 94m; Color
VID: **Driller Killer** [Magnum Entertainment; 88(94)m]; **Driller Killer** [Wizard Video; 84(94)m]
ADL: *As the drill finds its victim... the blood runs in rivers... and the drill keeps tearing through flesh and bone*

Although this seedy little flick has reached a cult status to where it has become overrated, **The Driller Killer** is an ambitious no-budget effort that successfully captures the grime of the Lower East End. There is some innovative use of editing, complemented by occasionally striking imagery, but little else.

Unfortunately, not much work is put into personal motivations; the "reasons" are clear, but the characters are little more than unsympathetic, two-dimensional lowlifes that blend in with the woodwork. (Of course, this may be the filmmakers' intentions, depicting the players as desensitized automatons, but it doesn't make for very engaging cinema. At times, you get the feeling you're watching nothing more than a home movie perpetrated by a bunch of downtrodden, yet uninteresting twenty-somethings.)

The film would have been improved considerably, though, had less time been spent on the Roosters, a really awful 70s punk band who—for reasons unknown—get more screen time than the title anti-hero. (They may have helped finance the project, but I find that hard to believe, if only because I don't see them earning a penny from their "musical" endeavor.)

The violence is staged very matter-of-factly, and it is all the more disturbing because of it. (Pretty grisly stuff, I assure you.) The vague ending is sure to disappoint most viewers, although a traditional approach wouldn't have set well with those who can appreciate the movie for what it is: a stark portrayal of one man's desperate attempt to keep his identity in a cold and uncaring city. Although the film's pretensions keep it from being a solid film, they are also what help separate this from the many sordid mass murderer exploitationers common to dead end drive-ins in the 70s.

Ferrara covered similar ground in 1992 with **The Bad Lieutenant**, replacing an artist struggling with his own sanity with a cop corrupted by the power of his position.

Drive-In Massacre (1976)

S.A.M. Productions, Inc. [USA]
DIR: Stuart Segall; PRO: Stuart Segall; SCR: George Flower and John F. Goff; DOP: Kenneth Lloyd Gibb; EXP: Rochelle Gail Weisberg; MUS: Lon John Productions
    STR: Michael Alden, Catherine Barkley, Jake Barnes, George Flower, Verkina Flower, Marty Gatsby, Myron Griffith, Douglas Gudbye, Frank Hollowell, Patricia James, Tiffany Jones, Adam Lawrence, Newton Naushaus, Norman Sherlock, and Valdesta
    Approximately 74m; Color
    VID: **Drive-In Massacre** [Magnum Entertainment; 78(74)m]; **Drive-In Massacre** [Cult Video; 78(74)m]

A typical teen-ridden drive-in theater becomes the site of a series of grisly and brutal murders. (There is no apparent motivation save for thinning the zit-laden herd, so cops are understandably stumped.) The owner—who used to run a carnival fifteen years previous on the selfsame piece of land—is somewhere on vacation, leaving his old carny friends in charge, all of whom are suspects. Is it van Heusen, the unaccounted-for owner? How about Mr. Johnson, the abrasive manager who still harbors jealousy for van Heusen? What about Germy, the geek-cum-janitor who has traded in chickens for a broom? Could it be Mr. Engleston, a peeping prevo into back-seat bumping who frequents the theater? Does it matter? No, because the killer is never identified, the case left unresolved to accommodate the following gimmick. Just as the last suspect is dispatched by the faceless psychopath, the film grinds to a halt, and is followed by the announcement "Ladies and gentlemen, this is the manager. Do not panic. There is a murderer loose in the theater. I repeat... do not panic. The police are on the way." I doubt anyone bought this clever promotional tactic upon its theatrical release, but it's a hell of a lot more memorable than had they taken the more traditional route.

    Needless to say, I have a soft spot for this hunk of 70s trash. Opening with a really messy decap (which is worth checking out frame by frame), this film continues to pile on the grue, the bloody proceedings accompanied by a weird electronic score, numerous red herrings, and interesting characterization. **Drive-In Massacre** was co-written by everyone's favorite B-movie stand-in George "Buck" Flower (who also contributes an uncredited performance as a mental case—one of the aforementioned red herrings—and the father of a girl who is his real life daughter, Verkina).

    Now if only someone would devise a gimmick like this that would be effective for video consumers...

Dungeon of Death *see* **Torture Dungeon**

Eaten Alive (1977)

Mars Production Corporation [USA]
DIR: Tobe Hooper; PRO: Mardi Rustam; SCR: Kim Henkel; DOP: Robert Caramico; EXP: Mohammed Rustam; SFX: A&A Special Effects; MUS: Wayne Bell and Tobe Hooper
    SCR: Janus Blythe, Neville Brand, Marilyn Burns, David Carson, Betty Cole, Roberta Collins, Ronald W. Davis,

Eaten Alive

Robert Englund, Mel Ferrer, William Finley, James Galanis, Tarja Leena Halinen, David Haward, Carolyn Jones, Lincoln Kibbee, Valerie Lukeart, Jeanne Reichert, Kyle Richards, Sig Sakowicz, Christine Schneider, Scuffy, Crystin Sinclaire, Caren White and Stuart Whitman

AKA: **Death Trap; Horror Hotel Massacre; Legend of the Bayou; Murder on the Bayou; Starlight Slaughter**
Approximately 88m; Color
VID: **Eaten Alive** [Ace Video; 96(88)m]; **Eaten Alive** [Prism Entertainment; 96(88)m]

A reluctant prostitute stumbles across the Starlight Hotel, a seedy dive situated, apparently, in the middle of the bayou. (Surprisingly, she's not the only one who decides to take refuge in this pay-as-you-leave septic tank.) The place is owned and run by Neville Brand (to call him "nutters" would be an understatement) and his pet croc. By the time she realizes the predicament she's gotten herself into, it's too late, so it's up to Daddy and sis to find out just what happened to her.

Although **Eaten Alive** is not nearly the film **The Texas Chain Saw Massacre** was, it is a sorely underrated, nearly forgotten entry in the annals of 70s shock horror. Much of the claustrophobic atmosphere has been carried over—quite successfully—from **Chain Saw**, thanks at least in part to Bell and Hooper's unnerving ambient score. Although he's no replacement for the entire Sawyer family, Neville Brand does an admiral job filling in their flea-bitten shoes, offering the best Cajun psycho ever to make it to the silver screen.

Aware that they probably couldn't recreate the pure intensity of **Chain Saw**, the filmmakers tried to make up for this by upping the sex and violence; not only is there scads of gratuitous T&A, the gore is much heavier. (There are no chainsaws, but Brand seems to make do with a scythe and—of course—his saurian sidekick Scuffy.)

Marilyn Burns (proving she hadn't lost her scream appeal since **Chain Saw**) has a small part, as does Robert (Freddy Krueger) Englund as troublemaker Buck (whose name, he likes to point out, conveniently rhymes with "fuck").

All in all, a tense shocker worthy of recognition. (Hey, Hooper hasn't made anything this good in the twenty years since, although Texas Chain Saw Massacre II is worth a mention.)

Ecologio del Delitto see Antefatto

Le 8ème Passager see Alien

Emanuelle and the Last Cannibals see Emanuelle e gli Ultima Cannibali

Emanuelle e gli Ultima Cannibali [Emanuelle and the Last Cannibals] (1976)

Flora Film [Italy] Fulvia Cinematografica [Italy] and GICO Cinematografica [Italy]
DIR: Aristide Massaccesi; PRO: Aristide Massaccesi; SCR: Aristide Massaccesi and Romano Scandariato; DOP: Aristide Massaccesi; MFX: Fabrizio de Angelis; MUS: Nico Fidenco
STR: Giuseppe Auci, Bona Bono, Massimo Cipriari, Anne Marie Clementi, Geoffrey Coplestone, Dirce Funari, Laura Gemser, Percy Hogan, Maria Gabriella Mezzetti, Nieves Navarro, Donald O'Brian, Gabriele Tinti, Pierluigi Cervetti Valle, Al Yamanouchi, and Monica Zanchi
AKA: **Emanuelle's Amazon Adventure; Trap Them and Kill Them**
Approximately 93m; Color
VID: **Emanuelle and the Last Cannibals** [Twisted Dreams Home Video; 93m]; **Trap Them and Kill Them** [Twilight Video; 93m]

This film claims to be the true story of a journalist (Gemser) who gets involved with a case of cannibalism in New York; a tattoo on the perpetrator leads them to an isolated tribe in South America that still practices the unpleasant custom of eating their fellow man. (Usually raw, I might add.) Sound familiar? The selfsame premise found its way into Marino Girolami's **La Regina dei Cannibali** (1980), re-edited and released here as **Dr. Butcher, M.D.**; to further the comparison, that film's antagonist was played by Donald O'Brian, who is on hand here as an equally sleazy—but not nearly as crazed—individual.

This installment in Europe's ever-popular Emanuelle series (not to be confused with the Emmanuelle films initiated by Sylvia Kristel) is little more than the type of cannibal fare we've come to expect from Italy. Although Laura Gemser's ambitious journalist is a key figure in the film, the generic archetype has been recycled and remolded to fit the needs of every cannibal epic made since. Granted, sex is quite often more predominate than the gore (being an Emanuelle film and all), but the brutal violence is still overwhelming (something else which these vehicles for Gemser never shy away from). Surprisingly, the animal cruelty which became a staple for such films in the subgenre is at a minimum, so people who avoid such films because of the geek show gore will find little to be distressed over herein.

Production values are average at best (poor dubbing, and an annoying disco soundtrack tend to make it seem worse than it actually is), but—as mentioned earlier—the film gets bogged down with the perfunctory softcore sex. (Having never been a Laura Gemser fan, her innumerable romps in the sack come across as little more than tired filler, thus keeping the film from gaining any momentum.) Xenophobia is also high, the inherent racism in these films never so painfully obvious; the voice-over for the native chief is so badly marked that one can't help but laugh. Still, I don't think he felt nearly as humiliated in retrospect as Gemser must have been while giving her closing speech.)

Hey, what did you expect? It's a Joe d'Amato film, after all. 🐱🐱🐱
🐱🐱🐱

Emanuelle en America *see* **Emanuelle in America**

Emanuelle in America (1976)

New Film Production [Italy]
DIR: Aristide Massaccesi; SCR: Maria Pia Fusco; DOP: Aristide Massaccesi; MFX: Maurizio Trani; MUS: Nico Fidenco

STR: Efrem Appel, Salvatore Baccaro, Giulio Bianchi, Lars Bloch, Roger Browne, Matilde dall'Aglio, Lorraine de Salle, Carlo Foschi, Maria Renata Franco, Laura Gemser, Marina Hedman, Giulio Massimini, Stefania Nocilli, Maria Piera Regoli, Riccardo Salvino, Paola Senatore, and Gabriele Tinti

AKA: **Brutal Nights; Emanuelle en America** [Emanuelle in America]; **Emanuelle Negra en America** [Black Emmanuelle in America]

Approximately 99m; Color

VID: **Emanuelle Negra en America** [Grabaciones Selecvision Home Video; 95(99)m; In English w/Spanish subs]; **Emanuelle in America** [Vid-America; 95(93)m]; **Emanuelle in America** [Video for Pleasure (PAL); 93m; In English w/Dutch subs]

ADL: *She does it all for Old Glory!*

Emanuelle in America

Yet another entry in the infamous "Black Emanuelle" series showcasing Gemser's talents (whatever they may be). As per usual, the inquisitive reporter wanders from one misadventure to another, crossing as many borders (literally and metaphorically) as she can over the course of ninety-plus minutes. From nude photography to white slavery, gun-running, to aristocratic debauchery to, well, snuff films, this film tries to cover all the bases. (The latter is the only reason the film made it into this guide, but more on that shortly.)

Sex and skin is in abundance, with enough crotch shots to make Jesse Franco blush. Gemser's cure for everything is sex, and she doesn't hesitate to get herself out of a tight squeeze by using her body. (Sex is power, to be sure, but in these films the credo is quite insincere, as the scriptwriter tries desperately to obscure the film's exploitive nature with feeble-minded rhetoric.)

The final vignette in this aimless film has Emanuelle stumbling across a snuff film. She tracks it down to its source, and—although drugged—gets to witness the making of one first hand. By far, this is the most effective, most disturbing, most downright nauseating mock-snuff footage ever made. The footage is grainy, silent, and its hand held photography hurried. It takes place in what appears to be a South American prison, where a handful of women are being viciously beaten and sexually assaulted by sleazy guards. The violence escalates until they are tortured and finally killed in a fashion more unsettling than anything ever captured in a horror film. It would be easy to see how this could be mistaken for the real thing if ever it was taken out of context. Even knowing the proceedings are faked, it is unsettling; even moreso in that it is the finale in a hardcore sex film. (Of course, most accessible prints are truncated R versions that retain only the nudity and softer sex scenes, and are similarly missing much of the snuff footage, but the association is perturbing nonetheless.)

Highly recommended to those interested in the urban legend known as the snuff film; everyone else, though, should use extreme caution. XXX

Emmanuelle Negra en America
see **Emanuelle in America**

Emanuelle's Amazon Adventure
see **Emanuelle e gli Ultima Cannibali**

The Emerald Jungle *see* **Mangiati Vivi**

Encore *see* **The Comeback**

L'Enfer des Zombies *see* **Zombi 2**

Erotic Blue *see* **Perche Quelle Strane Gocce di Sangue sul Corpo di Jennifer?**

Erotic Nights of the Living Dead
see **Le Notti Erotiche de Morti Vivent**

Erotico Profondo *see* **Jack the Ripper—Der Dirnenmorder von Lodon**

El Espanto Surge de la Tumba [Horror Rises from the Tomb] (1972)

Profilmes S.A. [Spain]
DIR: Carlos Aured Alonso; SCR: Jacinto Molina Alvarez; DOP: Manuel Merino; EXP: José Antonio Pérez Giner and Ricardo Muñez Suay; SFX: Antonio Vidal Molina; MUS: Carmelo A. Bernaola
STR: Victor Alcazar, Jacinto Molina Alvarez, María José Cantudo, Juan Cazalilla, Ramón Centenero, Luis Ciges, Montserrat Julio, Francisco Llinas, Francisco Nieto, Julio Peña, Emmanuela Beltrán Rabola, Betsabé Ruiz, Helga Lina Stern, Cristina Suriana, and Elsa Zabala
AKA: **L'Amour Parmi les Monstres** [*Love Among the Monsters*]; **Blutmesse der Zombies** [*Blood Mass of the Zombies*]; **Blutmesse für den Teufel** [*Blood Mass for the Devil*]
Approximately 88m; Color
VID: **Horror Rises from the Tomb** [Alpha Video; 90(80)m]; **Horror Rises from the Tomb** [Charter Video; 90(88)m]
ADL: *The cursed come back to haunt you...*

France, 1454. A knight (Alvarez *aka* Paul Naschy) is beheaded for some petty crimes, namely "drinking human blood and eating the flesh of both the living and the dead, celebrating Black Mass with the bloody sacrifices of the newborn and young girls," and in general "adoring Satan." He curses everyone involved with his sentence, including his disfigured brother. Five-hundred-plus years later, his descendant makes the mistake of having a medium help locate his infamed ancestor's head, which has been conveniently preserved in a chest and buried near his ancestral home. In no time the head of the family has most of the cast under his control. With a little help, he's soon back on his feet again, and just when you think you're watching a rehash of a Hammer Dracula film (sans exsanguination), the film throws the viewer some unexpected punches.

Naschy is at it again, playing his bad old sulking self. (Except, of course, when he's playing the role of the dead knight, head shoved up through a hole in the table looking all wild eyed.) As per 70s Spanish horror fare, sex and violence is served up in liberal quantities (cut from most American prints), and the proceedings are decidedly downbeat. Also, production values are as good (or bad) as could be expected from a Euro-film of this caliber.

Another no-budget classic from the Golden Age of sleazy horrors. (It ain't an "El Hombre Lobo" pic, but it'll do in a pinch.)

Esta Noite Encarnarei No Teu Cadáver [Tonight I'll Incarnate Your Corpse] (1966)
Ibéria Filmes [Brazil]
DIR: José Mojica Marins; PRO: Augusto Pereira; SCR: José Mojica Marins; DOP: Giorgio Attili
STR: Salvador Amaral, Renato Azevedo, Arlete Lobo Brazolin, Marina Brito, José Carvalho, Dina Cristina, Sebastiana Dantas, Wilson Gomes de Araújo, Nivaldo de Lima, Terezinha de Oliveira, Osvaldo de Souza, Maria del Carmen, Antônio Fracari, Nádia Freitas, Paulo Gaeta, Ivair Gomes, Sebastião Grandim, Lya Laguette, Mário Lima, Enio Lôbo, Denise Maria, Antônio Marins, Cármen Marins, José Mojica Marins, Elidio Martins, Tânia Mendonça, Mina Monte, William Morgan, Palito, Paula Ramos, Vânia Rangel, Roque Rodrigues, Roque Romeu, Esmeralda Ruchel, Dario Santos, Ilídio Martins Simões, Nélson Stasionis, and Tina Wohlers
Approximately 107m; Black & White and Color
AKA: **This Night I Will Possess Your Corpse**
VID: **This Night I Will Possess Your Corpse** [Something Weird Video; 107m]

Zé do Caixão is back in this direct sequel to **A Meia Noite Levare Tua Alma**, still obsessed with spawning in order to perpetuate his bloodline and create "the perfect man" that will spell the future of mankind. After recovering from wounds received in the finale of the first film, "Coffin Joe" makes his way to a small town where he "appropriates" the town's young women with a little help from his hunchbacked assistant. He puts his newfound harem through several tests in order to weed out those unworthy of his seed, but it is met with little success. Eventually, he discovers a "superior" woman who approaches him, much to the chagrin of her brother.

Unlike his later patchwork creations, this is one of Marins' most consistent and accessible productions, and is sure to please those fans who can only handle so much of his more meandering and auto-cannibalistic fare. **Esta Noite Encarnarei No Teu Cadáver** culminates, though, in the type of dime-store Dante's **Inferno**-style shenanigans with which his name would become synonymous. (Gripped by delirium, the lead character finds himself in a hell of his own making, the film switching from grainy black and white to a spectrum of garish colors. Here, the usual display of Coffin Joe atrocities are put on exhibit, although it is much tamer than what would inevitably make it into later productions.) The gore is never more explicit than what is was in the previous installment, and is still quite primitive in execution. The focus, as could be expected, is on Marins, chewing the scenery, ranting about life, death, and "the perfect man."

One of the more solid films in José Mojica Marins' oeuvre.

Estranho Mundo de Zé do Caixão [The Strange World of Zé do Caixão] (1968)

Ibéria Filmes [Brazil]
DIR: José Mojica Marins; PRO: José Mojica Marins and Jorge Michel Serkeis; SCR: Rubens Francisco Lucchetti; DOP: Girgio Attili; MUS: Édson Lopes & Titulares do Ritmo
STR: Anselmo Alves, Marlene Alves, Salvador Amaral, Édson Antunes, Nelita Aparecida, Arnaldo Brasil, Iris Bruzzi, Rosalvo Caçador, Aparecida Calixto, Carlos Campos, Toni Cardi, Jayme Cortez, Abigail de Barros, Nivaldo de Lima, Messias de Melo, Leila de Oliveira, Terezinha de Oliveira, Osvaldo de Souza, Bettyr Dorifer, Wilson dos Santos, Kátia Dumont, Carlos Farah, Geni Franci, Sebastião Grandim, João José, Verônica Krimann, Cristiane Lemei, Mário Lima, France Lore, Ana Maria, José Mojica Marins, Guilhermina Martins, Vany Miller, Palito, Luís Sérgio Person, Paula Ramos, Antônio F. Ravagnoli, Nidi Reis, Jeff Ribeiro, Romeu Rocha, Esmeralda Ruschel, Tabajara Sales, Dario Santos, Ponti Santos, Jorge Michel Serkeis, Ademir Silva, Jean Silva, Antonia Siqueira, Carla Sotis, and Luiz Carlos Viana
AKA: **The Strange World of Coffin Joe**
Approximately 81m; B&W
VID: **The Strange World of Coffin Joe** [Something Weird Video; 81m; In Portuguese w/English subs]

More madness from Brazil's most enduring filmmaker, José Mojica Marins (known stateside as "Coffin Joe"), this anthology consists of three EC-style shorts stamped with his indelible style.

The first, "O Fabricante de Bonecas" ["The Maker of Dolls"], tells the story of an old dollmaker's revenge on five men who had beat him and raped his five daughters. The comic book approach makes the ensuing rape fantasies quite deplorable, with the results of the dollmaker's vengeance unable to make up for this breach of etiquette. The second segment, "Tara" ["Obsession"], is a simple, almost surreal ode to necrophilia, and is as heartwarming as Marins' work ever gets. There is no gore to speak of, but this is more than made up for in "Ideologia" ["Ideology"], the third segment. Here, Marins cuts loose, brandishing the full-tilt boogie approach that has garnered him a reputation. Obviously a vehicle for the director and his insidious alter ego Zé do Caixão, the storyline is, shall we say, threadbare. Every minute of the segment's running time is spent depicting a mélange of horrors, from the staged (loving close-ups of H.G. Lewis-style mutilation, with one neck wound being an assault to even hardcore splatterpunks) to the real (body piercings, and the usual menagerie of creepy crawlers: snakes, toads, spiders, etc.).

There is little or no dialogue throughout (although Marins does take the opportunity to chew the scenery a bit in "Ideologia"), and as if to justify the nasty proceedings, Coffin Joe's palace of perversions is destroyed by (what I assume to be, anyway) God. (It may even be a simple nuclear warhead, I'm still not sure.) A biblical verse appears onscreen immediately thereafter.

If you were ever interested in checking out Marins' work, this would make for a good introduction as it covers his range as a filmmaker, both good and bad.

Evil Force see **Hollywood Meat Cleaver Massacre**

Excite Me see **Il Tuo Vizio e una Stanza Chiusa è Solo Lo ne Ho la Chiave**

Exorcismo Negro [Black Exorcism] (1974)

Cinedistri [Brazil]
DIR: José Mojica Marins; PRO: Aníbal Massaíni Neto; SCR: José Mojica Marins and Adriano Stuart; DOP: Antônio Meliande
STR: Ariane Arantes, Geórgia Gomide, Wanda Kosmo, José Mojica Marins, Merisol Marins, Alcione Mazzeo, Marcelo Picchi, Jofre Soares, Adriano Stuart, and Walter Stuart
AKA: The Bloody Exorcism of Coffin Joe
Approximately 94m; Color
VID: The Bloody Exorcism of Coffin Joe [Something Weird Video; 76m]

Although made to cash in on the worldwide success of **The Exorcist**, this—one of Marins' more professionally made productions—bears only a peripheral resemblance to Friedkin's film. As in **Delirios de um Anormal** [*Deliriums of the Abnormal*] (1977), Marins plays both the parts of director José Mojica Marins (who else?) and his diabolical creation come to life Zé do Caixão (*aka* Coffin Joe). After denying the existence of his malevolent alter ego at a press conference, Marins decides to spend some time at a friend's country house, and finds that he was a little hasty in his claims. Supernatural occurrences plague the director and his friends, the work of Coffin Joe, who is pissed off that his creator has repudiated him. Not content with shuffling furniture about, he begins possessing anyone within spitting distance of poor Marins.

Although more structurally sound than his earlier splatter-oriented offerings, it is initially quite restrained, saving his trademarked Z-grade shock-surrealism for the last ten-or-so minutes. The Z-grade trick photography, cheap Halloween-ish props, abundant nudity, and H.G. Lewis-style gore which has become synonymous with his work is a long time coming, and will surely disappoint fans who look forward to the cheap thrills which has become expected of him. (Although hardly worth the wait, the gore is above par for Marins; a tongue is ripped out, an ear cut off and eaten, people dismembered... all very convincingly, I might add.) Since most of the footage later turned up in the aforementioned **Delirios de um Anormal**, it might be worth your while just to check that one out instead.

For Coffin Joe completists only.
🐱 🐱 🐱

L'Exorcists N.2' see **Un Urlo dalle Tenebre**

Eye of the Black Cat see **Il Tuo Vizio è una Stanza Chiusa a Solo Lo ne Ho la Chiave**

Eye of the Evil Dead see **L'Occhio del Male**

Eyeball *see* Gatti Rosso in un Labirinto do Vetro

Eyes *see* Mansion of the Doomed

Eyes of Dr. Chaney *see* Mansion of the Doomed

Les Fantômes de Dracula *see* La Marca del Hombre Lobo

Fascination (1979)
Les Films ABC [France] and Comex Productions [France]
DIR: Jean Rollin; PRO: Joe de Lara; SCR: Jean Rollin; DOP: Jean-Claude Couty; MUS: Philippe d'Aram
STR: Agnes Bert, Joe de Lara, Vincent Gardair, Dominique Journet, Jean-Marie Lemaire, Fanny Magier, Franka Mai, Jacques Marboeuf, Muriel Montossé, Sophie Noel, Bernard Papineau, Alain Plumey, Jacques Sansoul, Cathy Stewart, Evelyne Thomas, Brigitte van Meerhaegue, and Myriam Watteau
AKA: **Filles Traquees** [*Hunted Girls*]; **Night of the Cruel Sacrifice**
Approximately 80m; Color
VID: **Fascination** [Redemption Video (PAL); 78m; In French w/English subs; LBX]; **Fascination** [Video Search of Miami; 76m; In French w/English subs; LBX]

A thief holes up in a desolate chateau, hiding from his jilted cohorts in crime. There he comes across two women who are waiting for the owners to arrive, and who waste no time in initiating a series of mind games. Once their hosts arrive, the robber and his cronies find out—much to their chagrin—that these people have some rather odd tastes.

Although another "vampire" film from a director who just can't seem to get enough of them, **Fascination** itself is inspired not by European folklore, but by factual cases concerning blood fetishism. (Specifically, the historical evidence of aristocratic cults whose impetus is the drinking of fresh blood, preferably human. The socio-political subtext is unmistakable, taking this film into territories where Rollin's earlier efforts rarely tread.) The lack of a fantastical basis also helps to ground the film, making it that much more visceral than his earlier work.

Not as lyrically haunting as **La Morte Vivante** [*The Living Dead Girl*] (1982), this films is no less memorable, walking the selfsame fine line between art and exploitation. Unlike the later film, the gore is more restrained, as well as more successful in its execution. (Neither Rollin films or French cinema in general is known for their groundbreaking effects work; with his more splatter-oriented productions, the effects are usually the most lacking as far as production values go, imminently hindering them from reaching their potential as truly good films.) Sex is, as with the violence, a crucial part of the proceedings. and—like in many of his films—indivisible. (Rape seems to be a common theme, and would seem to be a euphemism if it wasn't handled no differently than sleazy titillation. This seems odd in that the strongest, and—at the very least—the most sympathetic characters in all of his films are of the female persuasion.)

To quote one of the film's characters "People like us are called sick... degenerates. But it's not fair... no, we are just different." One can't help but wonder if Rollin was speaking of himself and his fans.

Highly recommended.

The Female Butcher *see* Ceremonia Sangrienta

La Figlia di Frankenstein *[The Daughter of Frankenstein] (1971)*

Condor International Pictures [Italy]
DIR: Ernst R. von Theumer; PRO: Ernst R. von Theumer; SCR: Umberto Borsato, Egidio Gelso, and Aureliano Luppi; DOP: Riccardo Pallotini; EXP: Humbert Case, Harry C. Cushing, and Jules Kenton; SFX: CIPA; MUS: Alessandro Alessandroni

STR: Richard Beardley, Joseph Cotten, Herbert Fuchs, Mickey Hargitay, Johnny Joffrey, Renate Kasché, Peter Martinov, Paul Müller, Rosalba Neri, Ada Pometti, Andrew Ray, Lorenzo Terzon, Adam Welles, and Peter Whiteman

AKA: **La Fille de Frankenstein** [*The Daughter of Frankenstein*]; **Lady Frankenstein**; **Lady Frankenstein, Cette Obsedée Sexuelle** [*Lady Frankenstein, Her Sexual Obsession*]; **Madame Frankenstein**

Approximately 99m; Color

VID: **Lady Frankenstein** [Embassy Home Entertainment; 84m]; **Lady Frankenstein** [United American Video Corporation; 84m]

"The silent evil that haunts Transylvania emerges again in Lady Frankenstein, daughter of the late and eminent Doctor Frankenstein. Obsessed with the desire to create her perfect man she sets out to piece together her lover from dismembered qualified candidates. Murder and mayhem abound as this amorous mad scientist produces not only her lover but a horrific and terrifying love story."

Unfortunately, **La Figlia di Frankenstein** is not nearly as insipid as the video box makes it out to be; had it been worse, it may at least have been amusing. As it stands, the film is a forgettable shocker that sticks to the formula established forty years previous. (Of course, being the 70s, **La Figlia di Frankenstein** does not shy away from that decade's excesses. Sex and violence is gratuitous, although most of this is missing from American prints, making it that much more difficult to sit through prints of the stateside release.)

The Fog (1979)

Similar to **Andy Warhol's Frankenstein**, except that this film is bereft of everything but the most exploitive elements and lacks a talented cast and crew to make it work.

La Fille de Frankenstein *see* **La Figlia di Frankenstein**

Fin de Semana Para los Muertos *see* **Non Si Deve Profanare il Sonno dei Morti**

Flesh and Blood Show, The *see* **Asylum of the Insane**

Flesh for Frankenstein *see* **Mostro è in Tavola ... Il Barone Frankenstein**

Avco-Embassy Pictures Corp. [USA]
DIR: John Carpenter; PRO: Debra Hill; SCR: John Carpenter and Debra Hill; DOP: Dean Cundey; EXP: Charles B. Bloch; SFX: Richard Albain, Jr., and A&A Special Effects; MFX: Rob Bottin and Dean Cundey; VFX: James F. Liles; MUS: John Carpenter and Dan Wyman

STR: Laurie Arent, Lindsey Arent, Tom Atkins, Adrienne Barbeau, Rob Bottin, James Canning, John Carpenter, Christopher Cundey, Jamie Lee Curtis, Charles Cyphers, George Flower, Fred Franklyn, John F. Goff, Jim Haynie, Hal Holbrook, John Houseman, Darrow Igus, Jay Jacobs, Shari Jacoby, Darwin Joston, Janet Leigh, Nancy Loomis, Ty Mitchell, Ric Moreno, Charles Nicklin, Lee Sacks, John Strobel, Bill Taylor, John Vic, Regina Waldon, and Tommy Lee Wallace

Approximately 89m; Color
VID: **The Fog** [Embassy Home Entertainment; 94(89)m]; **The Fog** [Magnetic Video Corporation; 94(89)m]
ADL: *What you can't see won't hurt you... it'll kill you!*

A charter ship transporting a leper colony is led to its doom by the founding fathers of Antonio Bay. On the hundred year anniversary of the "accident," strange things begin happening in the otherwise quiet little fishing town, not the least of which being a glowing fog inhabited by some very pissed off ghosts who use it as cover.

The Fog is underrated spookshow fare that seems to owe much to Amando de Ossorio Rodríguez' **El Ataque de los Muertos sin Ojos** (1973), but successfully captures the once patented style and chills of

John Capenter's early output. Although it displays a remarkable sense of storytelling, the focus is on atmosphere (which doesn't let up for a second, I might add); even the hokum is remarkably effective. Outside of direction, much of the film's success can be attributed to Cundey's mood-drenched cinematography and Carpenter's evocative score. Although there are a few gory murders, perpetrated by the worm-infested, waterlogged ghouls conveniently armed with gaff hooks, swords, and sickles, most of the violence is offscreen, accompanied by very grisly sound effects. (The scene involving two very vulnerable eyes should be played loud for best effect. It sounds like it hurt, anyway.)

The cast is mutually comprised of Carpenter regulars and old pros. Of the former are Jamie Lee Curtis, Tom Atkins and Nancy Loomis, among others; the latter include John Houseman, Hal Holbrook, and Adrienne Barbeau (Carpenter's real-life wife). Even Carpenter makes a rare cameo, showing why he took up filmmaking and not acting as a career. Sorry, John. (Oh, and let's not forget George Flower with his great gravel-coated deliverance of "There's no fog bank out there." You gotta' love this guy.)

Guaranteed to raise some goosebumps.

Folie Sanglante *see* **Buio Omega**

Foltermühle der Gefangenen Frauen *see* **Les Raisin de la Mort**

The Forbidden (1978)

Production company unknown [UK]

DIR: Clive Barker; SCR: Clive Barker
STR: Peter Atkins, Clive Barker, and Doug Bradley
Approximately 36m; B&W
VID: **The Forbidden** [Redemption Video USA; 36m; Double-bill w/*Salome*]

In case you weren't aware of it, Clive Barker directed several underground films years before he became a best-selling author. (He also directed, produced, and starred in a number of plays, most of which have been well documented in several books on this multi-talented individual.) Of the handful of these films, **The Forbidden** will hold the most interest for splatterpunks as it is an obvious precursor to **Hellraiser** (1987), his first professional film; although started in 1975, this short wasn't finished until three years later.

Short on story but a wealth of imagery (as are many student "art" films), **The Forbidden** is loosely adapted from the timeless Faust legend; what remains, though, are only the most basic concepts, and are used to accommodate Barker's more fervent imagination and esoteric visions. As in **Hellraiser**, there is a predominate puzzle motif, and a grueling scene of a man being skinned alive by "angels" (which could easily be interpreted as his trademarked Cenobites). As intense as the film is, it may prove to be a bit tiring for those people accustomed to more conventional cinema.

And, yes, there is a particularly distracting scene (which takes up way to much screen time) of Barker himself spinning around frenetically, nude and with a rather prominent erection. (Not only did he authorize this video release, he also re-edited the unfinished footage that comprises **The Forbidden**.)

It's probably safe to say that **The Forbidden** is for Barker completists only.

The Forgotten *see* **Don't Look in the Basement**

Frankenstein (1973) *see* **Mostro è in Tavola... Il Barone Frankenstein**

Frankenstein (1973) *see* **Mosaico**

Frankenstein '80 *see* **Mosaico**

Frankenstein 1980 *see* **Mosaico**

Frankenstein and the Monster from Hell (1973)
Hammer Film Productions Limited [UK]
DIR: Terence Fisher; PRO: Roy Skeggs; SCR: Anthony Hinds; DOP: Brian Probyn; SFX: Les Bowie; MUS: James Bernard
STR: Norman Atkyns, Shane Briant, Sydney Bronley, Christopher Cunningham, Peter Cushing, Sheila d'Union, Mischa de la Motte, Lucy Griffiths, Janet Hargreaves, Tony Harris, Andrea Lawrence, Bernard Lee, Charles Lloyd-Pack, Peter Madden, Norman Mitchell, Clifford Mollison, David Prowse, Winifred Sabine, Madeline Smith, John Stratton, Patrick Troughton, Philip Voss, Elsie Wagstaff, Michael Ward, Jerold Wells, and Victor Woolf
AKA: **Frankenstein en het Monster van de Hel** [*Frankenstein and the Monster from Hell*]; **Frankenstein et le**

Frankenstein and the Monster   118

Monstre de l'Enfer [*Frankenstein and the Monster from Hell*]
Approximately 99m; Color
VID: **Frankenstein and the Monster from Hell** [Paramount Home Video; 93(83)m]

In this, the last entry in Hammer Studios' long-running Frankenstein franchise, Peter Cushing (as gaunt as ever) plays Dr. Frankenstein for the sixth and final time. Being the series' swan song, the filmmakers decided to go out with a splat, upping the gore quotient far beyond Hammer's already liberal gratuity.

This time around, an aspiring medical student following in the good doctor's footsteps is charged with sorcery and sentenced to five years in a sanitarium. Much to his surprise and delight, Dr. Frankenstein—under the not-so-clever pseudonym of Dr. Karl Victor—is the resident doctor on the premises.

Once he has proven his worth, the young man is brought on as his mentor's assistant, and the two are up to their old tricks again. Having proved "unsuccessful" with reanimating corpses, though, the two seem happy enough with performing simple brain transplants, the result being what is probably the most ape-like interpretation of the monster to date. (The lumbering creature is played by Prowse, the man who donned Darth Vader's cape four years later in **Star Wars**.)

Although pretty typical of Hammer's output, **Frankenstein and the Monster from Hell** should appeal not only to fans of the UK's preeminent studio, but those who like 70s sleazy period pieces as well. Once forerunners in violent genre films, Hammer found themselves lagging behind by the early 70s, unable to inject enough sex and violence for a more "discriminating" market. **Frankenstein and the Monster from Hell** may not have much in the way of flesh (as Hammer's last few Dracula films displayed), but it is gory enough to be included herein (unlike the others in this series). Unfortunately for U.S. fans, all domestic prints are bereft of the gore, making for a completely awkward and almost unenjoyable experience.

The film was left open-ended to accommodate further sequels; sadly, the opportunity and or demand never arose.

Frankenstein en het Monster van de Hel *see* **Frankenstein and the Monster from Hell**

Frankenstein et le Monstre de l'Enfer *see* Frankenstein and the Monster from Hell

The Frankenstein Experiment *see* Il Mostro è in Tavola... Barone Frankenstein

Frankenstein's Bloody Terror *see* La Marca del Hombre Lobo

Frightmare (1974)

Heritage Ltd. [UK]
DIR: Peter Walker; PRO: Peter Walker; SCR: David McGillivray; DOP: Peter Jessop; EXP: Tony Tenser; MUS: Stanley Myers
STR: Kim Butcher, Fiona Curzon, Jack Dagmar, Rupert Davies, Deborah Fairfax, Pamela Farbrother, Gerald Flood, Leo Genn, Paul Greenwood, Anthony Hennessey, Nicholas John, Noel Johnson, Edward Kalinski, Sheila Keith, David McGillivray, Tricia Mortimer, Andrew Sachs, Sue Shaper, Michael Sharvell-Martin, Victor Winding, Tommy Wright, and Jon Yule
AKA: Frightmare II; Once Upon a Frightmare; Schizophrenic Murder; Terror sin Habla [*Terror Without Words*]
Approximately 85m; B&W and Color
VID: Frightmare II [Prism Entertainment; 86(85)m]
ADL: *Two Generations of Evil Haunted by a Deadly Past.*

London, 1957. A man in need of help calls on an old friend, and is brutally murdered for his troubles. A married couple is found guilty of the crime but—due to extenuating circumstances—are institutionalized until they are deemed rehabilitated seventeen years later. About this time, their eldest daughter becomes worried by her sister's erratic behavior and rebellious attitude. When not dealing with her delinquent sibling, she is sneaking out of the house, delivering mysterious parcels to her clearly unbalanced mother in order to keep the old woman content.

Despite a rather conservative stance towards rehabilitation and the death penalty, Peter Walker—England's premiere splatterpunk—dishes up another well-executed shocker. Production values are a bit gritty, although competent; as could be expected, though, Walker makes up for any shortcomings with the selfsame ingenuity that has graced his films for most of his career. As per usual, there are some truly disturbing moments, and numerous surprises in store for the viewer as well, even though much of the revelations are telegraphed far in advance. The exemplary performances only strengthen the material that much more.

Although the gore may be too sparse for most splatterpunks, the then-taboo subject matter and overall bleak tone of the film should more than please them, as well as fans of low-budget 70s horror.

Frightmare II *see* **Frightmare**

Frissons *see* **The Parasite Murders**

Les Frissons de l'Angoisse *see* **Profondo Rosso**

The Funhouse (1977)

Today Productions, Inc. [USA]
DIR: Roger Watkins; PRO: Norman F. Kaiser; SCR: Brian Laurence; DOP: Alexander Tarsk; SFX: Kevin Heatley; MFX: Kevin Heatley; MUS: Claude Armand
  STR: Barbara Amunsen, Lawrence Bornman, Alan Cooper, Ronald Cooper, Dennis Crawford, Doreen Ellis, Alex Kregar, Steven Morrison, Howard Neilsen, Elaine Norcross, Paul Phillips, Helene Roberts, Geraldine Saunders, Janet Sorley, Franklin Statz, and Nora Tucker
  AKA: **Last House on Dead End Street**
  Approximately 76m; Color
  ADL: *It's back! The evil that had you screaming... IT'S ONLY A MOVIE!*

"Nobody's interested in sex anymore... they're lookin' for something else."
A loser is drawn towards making snuff films as a way to lash out at society. (Seems he has difficulty blaming himself for getting put away for a year after a big drug bust.) As it turns out, though, he seems to be doing society a favor by eliminating seedy underworld filmmakers and their ilk with his new pastime-slash-business venture.

As could be expected, having been released while **Snuff** was still fresh in everyone's minds, **The Funhouse** not only tries to cash in on that film's infamy, but even goes so far as to reiterate the now classic ending of said film almost verbatim. (Except that the victim here is particularly tenacious, putting up a fight even after she's been eviscerated and had both her legs sawn off.)

The Funhouse could have been an effective film (as bleak as it is) had it not been so shoddy a production. (True, its inherent graininess—as well as the cast and crew's stalwart ineptitude—would seem to lend itself well to the subject matter, but it's ultimately self-defeating as it makes the film simply unwatchable.) And, worst of all, it's direly tedious and dull. By the time the keynote events take place, the viewer is cold to the proceedings. (Had that been intended, it would have made an interesting statement by the filmmakers about our jaded culture, but alas...) Even on a purely exploitive level, the film is difficult to appreciate; I would never have thought that scenes involving a half-nude woman in blackface being whipped by partygoers, or a man forced to deep throat a deer's hoof could be boring. In poor taste, maybe, but not boring.

Despite the expected low-rent gore, **The Funhouse** boils down to little more than ninety minutes of "insightful" narration being supplied by filthy people who smoke too much. (I'm not surprised that this film is as rare as it is.) 🐱🐱🐱

Fureur Muertriere *see* **Non Si Sevizia un Paperino**

changed in order to accommodate the proceedings. (It's interesting that someone who was entombed until 1967 would end up teaching at a medical university only four years later. You'd think it would be tough studying for a medical degree when you spend so much time howling at the moon, fighting monsters, and getting killed once a year.) In this one, Waldemar Daninsky is a doctor who has discovered his wife to be unfaithful; his wife and her lover sabotage his car. The resulting accident brings him closer to a woman who claims to have discovered a cure for his malady... but first he has business to attend to. Sporting fur and fangs, he returns to his adulterous wife and begins the divorce proceedings in a rather bloody fashion.

La Furia del Hombre Lobo
[The Fury of the Wolfman]
(1971)
Plata Films S.A. [Spain]
DIR: Enrique López Eguiluz and José Mariá Zabalza; PRO: Maximiliano Perez Plores; SCR: Jacinto Molina Alvarez; DOP: Leopoldo Villaseñor; EXP: Cesar Gallego; MUS: Angel Arteaga and Anna Satrova
STR: Jacinto Molina Alvarez, Francisco Amorós, Fabián Conde, Perla Cristal, Ramón Lillo, Verónica Luján, José Marco, Diana Montes, Javier Rivera, and Pilar Zorrilla
Approximately 85m; Color
VID: **The Fury of the Wolfman** [Unicorn Video; 85m]

Obviously, you can't keep a good werewolf down, as this entry in the string of "El Hombre Lobo" attests. Again, though, his origin is

Paul Naschy (*née* Alvarez) puts in another angst-ridden performance as everyone's favorite barrel-chested, mohair-faced lycanthrope. Here, his adversaries are a jilted ex-lover-cum-mad doctor, her henchman who thinks he's the Phantom of the Opera, and his infected ex-wife. Although not the most contrived film in the series, it is probably the worst, albeit no less enjoyable an entry. Production values are awkward, due in part to the change of hands midway through. Still, **La Furia del Hombre Lobo** is pretty typical of the series, with an ever-increasing quota of sex and violence to spice up the low-rent horrors.

On an interesting note, the opening scenes of **La Furia del Hombre Lobo** were directed by Enrique López Eguiluz, who was replaced by producers shortly after filming began. This film also uses excerpts from **La Marca del Hombre Lobo** (1967) which were helmed by Eguiluz as well.

The Fury of the Wolfman *see* **La Furia del Hombre Lobo**

Las Garras de Loreli [The Lorelei's Grasp] (1972)

Compagnia Cinematografica Astro [Spain] and Profilmes S.A. [Spain]
DIR: Amando de Ossorio Rodríguez; PRO: Ricardo Sanz and Ricardo Muñoz Suay; SCR: Amando de Ossorio Rodríguez; DOP: Miguel F. Milá; EXP: Ricardo Sanz and Ricardo Muñoz Suay; SFX: Abobaq and Alfredo Segoviano; MUS: Antón García Abril
STR: Cristino Almodovar, Luis Barboo, Javier de Rivera, Mary Sol Delgado, Vicky Hernandez, Luis Induñi, Josefina Jartin, Sergio Mendizabal, Angel Menéndez, Francisco Nieto, Antonio Orengo, Betsabé Ruiz, Luciano Stella, Helga Lina Stern, José Telman, Sylvia Tortosa, Loretta Tovar, and María Vidal
AKA: **When the Screaming Stops**
Approximately 102m; Color
VID: **When the Screaming Stops** [Lightning Video; 86(85)m]
ADL: *You'll never sleep alone again!*

A scaly, reptilian critter in a robe is terrorizing a small coastal community, ripping out the hearts of young women who aren't aware that leaving one's window open at night in a horror film is a no-no. The town's blind man claims it is the fabled *Lorelei*, who needs to devour

Gatti Rossi in un Labirinto...

human hearts every so often to keep her human countenance. Justifiably worried, the director of an all girls' school hires a big game hunter to track down the beastie responsible.

Borrowing fantasy elements from the Nibelungen myth, de Ossorio tries almost vainly to break away from the standard horror formula for which he was quickly becoming known for at the time. Although not nearly as accomplished as the films in his Blind Dead series, **Las Garras de Loreli** is by far one of the director's better films. (Sure, it's not the Templars, and sure, the critter here looks like the "phony" fish-monster from **They Bite**, but it's much better than de Ossorio's **La Endemoniada** or **Serpiente de Mar**.) The effects are passable for the budget, and the damage inflicted by the Lorelei's dark side is pretty extreme. (Part of the film's publicity campaign had the screen flash red just prior to any scenes of carnage so as to warn the more faint-hearted viewers of the bloodshed to come.)

Fans of the Blind Dead will surely recognize and appreciate de Ossorio's trademarked flare; anyone else will probably wonder what all the fuss is about.

Gatti Rossi in un Labirinto di Vetro [Red Cats in a Maze of Glass] (1974)

Pioneer [Italy] and Estela Films S.A. [Spain]
DIR: Umberto Lenzi; PRO: José Maria Cunilles; SCR: Umberto Lenzi and Antonio Troisio; DOP: Antonio

Millan; EXP: Joseph Brenner; MUS: Bruno Nicolai
STR: Martine Brochard, Martha May, Mirtha Miller, Ines Pellegrini, John Richardson, George Rigaud, and Silvia Solar
AKA: **The Devil's Eye; Eyeball; The Secret Killer; Wide-Eyed in the Dark**
Approximately 87m; Color
VID: Eyeball [Prism Entertainment; 87m]
ADL: *A Tale of Blinding Horror!*

A bus full of tourists hopping the Spanish countryside becomes the focus of a deranged killer with a penchant for cutting out the victim's left eye. (There's no gaping eye sockets here though, folks; a very noticeable red eyepatch is circulated among the victims by a very cheap effects department.) Obviously, one of the passengers is responsible, so it's up to viewers and targets alike to try and figure out this convoluted whodunit, which can only be done by throwing all logic to the wind.

A fairly inept, but almost enjoyable *giallo* thriller from hackmeister Lenzi. (If you've seen **Incubo sulla Città Contaminata** aka **City of the Walking Dead**—by far the worst zombie flick to ever come out of the Big Boot—you already have a pretty good idea of the dreck this man can churn out.) Production values are bottom-of-the-barrel, but are made to seem even more gauche by the horrendous English dubbing and the aforementioned special effects. (You'd think, being the primary focus of the film, the filmmakers would've put *some* effort into the gore and not settle with cheap Halloween theatrics.)

If you've been eyeing the garish box art, you just might want to leave it at that.

Il Gatto dagli Occhi di Giada
[The Cat with the Eyes of Jade] (1975)

Elis Cinematografica [Italy]
DIR: Antonio Bido; PRO: Gabriella Nardi; SCR: Antonio Bido, Roberto Natale, Vittorio Schiraldi, and Aldo Serio; DOP: Mario Vulpiani; MUS: Trans Europa Express
STR: Giuseppe Addobbati, Inna Alexeievna, Roberto Antonelli, Gianfranco Bullo, Fernando Cerulli, Franco Citti, Paolo Malco, Corrado Pani, Giuseppe Pennese, Cristina Piras, Jill Pratt, Gaetano Rampin, Paola Tedesco, Bianca Toccafondi, and Giovanni Vannini
AKA: **The Cat's Victim; Watch Me When I Kill**

Approximately 95m; Color
VID: **The Cat's Victim** [Redemption Video (PAL); 91(95)m; LBX];
Watch Me When I Kill [Thorn EMI Video; 95(94)m]
ADL: *When I go berserk ... you're better off dead!*

A pharmacist is killed while the store is closed, and after a girl comes to the door and hears his voice as he tries to shoo her away, he decides it's better to be safe than sorry. After he fails the first attempt on her life, she moves in with her on-again, off-again boyfriend. Interestingly enough, *his* neighbor has been getting weird phone calls, a pre-recorded cacophony of overdubbed noises. He starts an investigation of his own, and finds out that those killed—as well as his harassed neighbor—all shared jury duty on a murder case, and that the accused broke out of prison only months before the murders erupted. Although not released here until six years after the fact in 1981 by schlockmeister Herman Cohen, this *giallo* thriller is a bit more interesting than most. Not to say that it is exemplary in any way; not even. The film's sole charm stems from its insistent knack for emulating the far superior thriller **Profondo Rosso** [*Deep Red*] (1975), right down to the punchy staging and overwhelming prog-rock score. (The latter mimics Goblin's classic soundtrack almost to the point where it could be considered flagrant copyright infringement.) It also wallows in its own complexities, but whereas Argento's pinnacle of the genre overcame its convoluted nature through sheer force of style, **Il Gatto dagli Occhi di Giada** becomes simply confusing. Additionally, the script is so weighted down with conveniences and coincidences that one's suspension of disbelief is equally beleaguered.

The violence, albeit brutal, is fairly unimpressive, with the best scenes copied from its inspiration as well. The biggest point of departure for this film from its obvious influence is its penchant for sloppy hand-held camerawork. Argento's cinematography is often cited as balletic in its grace. In comparison, the photography here is not unlike a half-blind wino stumbling around in the dark.

Despite the harsh commentary (remember: This film obviously decided not to be judged on its *own* merits) **Il Gatto dagli Occhi di Giada** should appeal to fans of Italian *giallo* fare.

Geheimnis der Grunen Stecknadel *see* **Cosa Avete Fatto a Solange?**

Das Geheimnis des Gelben Grabes *see* **L'Etrusco Uccide Ancora**

Das Geisterschiff der Schwimmenden Leichen *see* **El Buque Maldito**

Gently Before She Dies *see* **Il Tuo Vizio e una Stanza Chiusa e Solo Ne Ho la Chiave**

The Ghastly Ones (1969)

J.E.R. Pictures Inc. [USA]
DIR: Andy Milligan; PRO: Jerome-Fredric; SCR: Andy Milligan and Hal Sherwood; DOP: Andy Milligan; MFX: Jerry Rowe
STR: Robert Adsit, Hal Borske, Niel Flanagan, Eileen Haves, Fib la Blaque, Anne Linden, Ada McAllister, Veronica Radburn, Maggie Rogers, Richard Romanos, Hal Sherwood, Carol Vogel, and Don Williams
AKA: **Blood Rites**
Approximately 81m; Color
VID: **Blood Rites** [Scorpio Video (PAL); 81m]; **The Ghastly Ones** [Video Home Library; 81m]
ADL: *Mad creatures of the night existing only for sensual sadistic moments of HUMAN SLAUGHTER!*

Having filled the marriage requirements of their father's will, three sisters and their hubbies are then requested to stay for three days in their family home ("in sexual harmony") before the estate of their

The Ghastly Ones

dead father can be dispensed between his surviving family members. (The island property has been kept up and looked after by three servants: two spinsters, and a bucktoothed moron whose talents never rise very far above capturing small animals and eating them raw.) Despite a warning to give up their claims (a half eaten rabbit with the accompanying note "Blessed are the meek, for they shall inherit"), the greedy guests are undeterred. Within days of their visit (and, boy, will it seem like days to the viewer), the three couples find themselves victim of a rather ghoulish assassin.

This was Milligan's first foray into horror (having previously relegated his "talents" to seedy grindhouse fare); apparently, he found this to be his calling as—save for a few exceptions—he continued to produce genre films until his dying day twenty years later. What convinced him this was his niche, though, is difficult for anyone but him to see. **The Ghastly Ones** is, in almost every way, completely incompetent. Direction, cinematography, editing, acting, special effects, you name it—all bad. (What's most surprising is that a film of this caliber—no better

than an elaborate home movie, really—actually received some sort of theatrical distribution.) Regardless, this film, like every other film in Milligan's oeuvre, is imbued with a certain amount of naive charm. Although much of this lies with their ineptitude, it is also due to the man's perseverance, learning the craft while he did the one thing which he enjoyed: making movies. (And, being one of Milligan's beloved period pieces, one has to keep from being distracted by the myriad anachronisms inherent to his productions.)

Outside of H.G. Lewis' gory groundbreakers, this one of the earliest films to wallow in gratuitous bloodshed. Limbs are hacked off right and left, people are eviscerated in loving detail, pitchforks rammed through their more vulnerable parts... all for the viewer's benefit. Of course, the effects are so clumsily conceived that even those theater goers convinced by **Snuff**'s authenticity would laugh them off as being bad. (Not only is the smell of rubber almost stifling, the distinct earthiness of modeling clay isn't far behind.)

Truly, truly awful. (At least he thought the material showed promise, for he remade it in 1978 as **Legacy of Horror**... without—it seems—the prequisite sex and gore. So what else is left? Don't ask...)

The Ghastly Orgies of Count

Dracula *see* **Riti, Magie Nere e Segrete Orge nel Trecento...**

The Ghost Galleon *see* **El Buque Maldito**

Giallo a Venezia [Giallo in Venice] (1979)

Elea Cinematografica [Italy
DIR: Mario Landi; PRO: Gabriele Crisanti; SCR: Aldo Serio; DOP: Franco Villa; EXP: Marcello Spingi; MFX: Mauro Gavazzi; MUS: Berto Pisano
STR: Jeff Blynn, Eolo Capritti, Eleonora Crisofani, Gianni Dei, Giancarlo del Duca, Maria Angela Giordano, Vassili Karamesinis, Mario Mancini, and Michele Renzullo
AKA: **Crimen sin Huella** [Crime Without Footsteps]; **Gore in Venice**
Approximately 91m; Color

A police investigator who only eats hardboiled eggs is heading a case involving a sadistic killer who likes "sticking it to" women of questionable moral ethics. In the meantime, a couple is facing a bit of a hurdle when the guy can only get aroused while whipping his girlfriend or looking at antique erotica. Eventually, he forces her into a threesome, and finally into more dangerous realms of sex play, much to her chagrin.

The very first frame of the film depicts a brutal stabbing, but **Giallo a Venezia** soon wanders into a different territory, wallowing in unrestrained sleaze until the second murder occurs almost forty minutes into the film. The gore is sparse, but the few scenes the film boasts have gained it a reputation as a video nasty, a title it justly deserves. Not only is the violence brutal and graphic, it is also unnervingly sexual, making much of it difficult to watch by anyone with any compunctions. (Director Landi also brought us the equally tasteless **Patrick Vive Ancora** the following year.)

Outside of the unsettling violence-towards-women bent, **Giallo a Venezia** is pretty standard, low-rent Eurotrash that will appeal to anyone with a hankering for politically incorrect mysteries.

Il Giustizere Sfida la Polizia *see* **Una Libelula para Cada Muerto**

God's Bloody Acre (1975)

Production company unknown [USA]
DIR: Harry E. Kerwin; PRO: Wayne Crawford and Andrew Lane; SCR: Wayne Crawford and Harry E. Kerwin; DOP: William J. Walsh; MUS: Michael Shaw
STR: Claudette Bawmgardner, Lane Chiles, Wayne Crawford, Freddie Dawson, Raymond Diaz, Richmond Farren, Thomas Ferguson, Fredrick Fryer, Gary Glover, Paul Goeld, Jennifer Gregory, Charles Hines, April Hirsch, Pat Hopwood, Robert Hudson, Jerry James, Lynn Kava, William Kerwin, Bruce Kronenberg, Anthony Lane, Gwenn Lane, Lori Lane, Nancy Larson, David Lipsick, Kaye Lynn, Sam Moree, Jack Nuber, Luis Ramos, Sheila Riley, Robert Rosano, Carlos Sanchez, Daniel Schweitzer, Michael Shaw, Adrian Sherman, Gerald Shulman, Berry Sweeting, Rob Torokvei, B.M. Troop, Michael Waldfogel, Judy Weinstein
Approximately 86m; Color
VID: **God's Bloody Acre** [TransWorld Entertainment; 85(86)m]

ADL: *The vacation getaway that everyone's trying to get away from...*

This low-rent shocker centers around three pseudo-hillbillies trying to fudge up the attempts of the government to covert the land they're squatting on into a camping ground. After cutting one poor worker in half with his own Caterpillar, they realize there's no turning back and begin going after not only them but some premature campers hanging out nearby.

God's Bloody Acres offers nothing more than the scads of other backwoods horror flicks that were geared towards drive-in theater goers in the mid-70s. There is a fair amount of sex and violence, but the latter is usually quite misogynistic, with a brutal gang rape by the sleazy rednecks being particularly repellent. (What's particularly unnerving is to hear some of the same stock music used in **Dawn of the Dead** accompanying that scene.) Even the downbeat ending does little to distinguish it from similarly inclined fare. (Give me **The Hills Have Eyes** any day, thank you very much.)

If you're in the mood for some mudraking, be my guest.

Gomar—The Human Gorilla *see* La Horriplante Bestia Humana

The Gore Gore Girls (1972)
Lewis Motion Picture Enterprises [USA]
DIR: Herchell Gordon Lewis; PRO: Herchell Gordon Lewis; SCR: Alan J. Dachman; DOP: Eskandar Ameripoor; MFX: Robert Lewis, Herschell Gordon Lewis, and Allison Louise Downe; MUS: Herschell Gordon Lewis
STR: Nora Alexis, Eskandar Ameripoor, Russ Badger, Marlene Berger, Corlee Bew, Lena Bousman, Vicki Carr, Luba Cherewchenko, Alan J. Dachman, Harry Dachman, Norman Dachman, Amy Farrell, Frank Kawsh, Jim Killen, Frank Kress, Jackie Kroeger, Phil Laurensen, Hedda Lubin, Menda MacPhail, Emily Mason, Jeanne Mocen, Lauren Obeda, Alex Petrovic, Frank Rice, Ray Sager, Marina Salli, Peter Sande, John Sezonov, and Henny Youngman
AKA: **Blood Orgy**
Approximately 84m; Color
VID: **The Gore Gore Girls** [Midnight Video; 84m]; **The Gore Gore Girls** [Something Weird Video; 84m]
ADL: *Notice: Persons with heart conditions prohibited from entering this theater.*

Someone is murdering local strippers, mutilating their features beyond recognition. A pompous and belligerent investigator with an extraordinary track record is hired by a tabloid newspaper to crack the case, on the condition that they retain all story rights. Aided by a young female reporter, he begins scouring the local dives, and finds himself with more suspects than he bargained for. (Despite having done as many splatter flicks in ten years, this is Lewis' first film where the killer's identity is a secret, and remains so until the finale.)

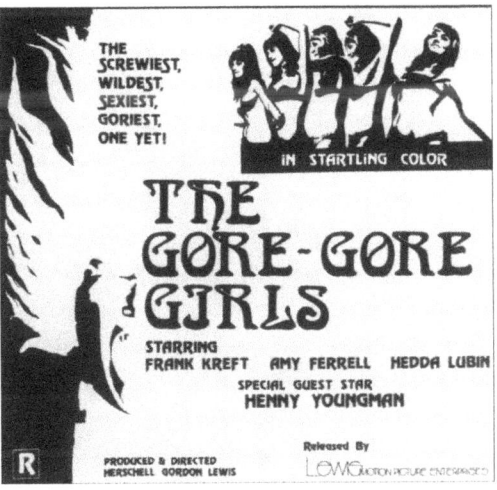

All of his H.G. Lewis' trademarks are here: stilted dialogue, awkward performances, cut-rate production values, and—of course—loads of shoddy gore effects. Little, it seems, had changed since the days of **Blood Feast** (1963) except that **The Gore Gore Girls** is Lewis' first film to combine carnage with sexploitation. (Lewis actually broke into the business in the late 50s doing nudie flicks with adult film veteran David Friedman, so it's actually quite surprising that he didn't do this sooner; it's even more ironic he waited until his last film to combine his favored genres.) It also needs to be said that the gore is probably the most extreme, the most brutal to appear in a Lewis production; because of the conscious effort to integrate the sex and violence, **The Gore Gore Girls** is also fairly misogynistic, with women being killed whenever they show even the slightest hint of sexuality. The only strong female character is an ineffectual journalist whose single contribution to cracking the case comes when she gets drunk and flaunts her wares, luring the killer out so our machoistic investigator can wrap things up.

Even more discomforting, **The Gore Gore Girls** is presented as a comedy, of sorts. Not only does stalwart comedian Henny Youngman appear as a strip joint owner, but in-jokes are even inserted into some of the bloody deaths. (The most notorious involves a young woman getting her nipples cut off. The killer collects the milk from each snipped breast in a glass; although one is predictably white, the other spews chocolate milk.) Even more so than any other Lewis film, the crew is comprised of innumerable eccentrics. (Ray Sager, immortalized as Montag the Magician in **The**

Wizard of Gore, plays a bartender, and is probably one of the most innocuous actors of the lot. Scary.) Thanks in part to its relentless gratuity, **The Gore Gore Girls** is one of Lewis' more interesting films; unfortunately, it also has a tendency to leave the selfsame bad taste in one's mouth as, say, **The Incredible Torture Show** (1976). ☠☠☠

El Gran Amor del Conde Dracula [The Great Loves of Count Dracula] (1972)
Janus Films, S.L. [Spain]
DIR: Javier Aguirre; PRO: Francisco Lara Polop; SCR: Javier Aguirre, Jacinto Molina Alvarez, and Alberto S. Insua; DOP: Raúl Pérez Cubero; SFX: Pablo Perez; MUS: Carmelo A. Bernaola
STR: Victor Alcazar, Jacinto Molina Alvarez, Alvara de Luna, Ingrid Garbo, Susana Latour, José Manuel Martín, Mirtha Miller, Benito Pavon, Julio Peña, Haydée Politoff, Leandro San José, Charo Sorlano, Rossana Yanni
AKA: **Cemetery Girls; Cemetery Tramps; Count Dracula's Great Loves; I Diabolici Amori di Nosferatu** [*The Diabolic Loves of the Vampire*]; **Dracula's Blood; Dracula's Virgin Lovers; Le Grand Amour du Comte Dracula** [*The Grand Loves of Count Dracula*]; **Vampire Playgirls**
Approximately 95m; Color
VID: **Count Dracula's Great Loves** [MPI Home Video; 95m]

A box is delivered to the clinic of Dr. Kargos; the delivery men are dispatched for their troubles (one quite brutally with an axe). A coachman is then "accidentally" kicked to death by his horse, and his four female passengers are then forced to take refuge in the aforementioned sanitarium. Despite all of the foreshadowing given the viewer, the young women are unaware that their host is none other than Dracula himself having taking the doctor's name. With all of this "new blood" walking the halls, the old Count has difficulty keeping his teeth to himself.

Although **El Gran Amor del Conde Dracula** doesn't stray far from standard vampire fare, it was probably the goriest film of its type up until this point in time. (The screenwriters do throw in a few surprises; people you expect to be the heroes are bitten almost right off the bat, and spend the rest of the film generally making nuisances of themselves.) It's also noticeable for the presence of Paul Naschy (*né* Jacinto Molina Alvarez), who made a name as everyone's favorite lycanthrope in the "El Hombre Lobo" series during the 70s. Granted, it's not much of a stretch from the Waldemar Daninski character he made famous; his angst-ridden performances make him well suited for the roles of sympathetic monsters. Unfortunately, it's a downhill slide once he puts on the obligatory cape and fangs. (The abysmal narration-style overdubs that accompanies the revelation that he is the infamous bloodsucker of legend don't go over very well either.)

The film's greatest success is with the production values. **El Gran Amor del Conde Dracula** is, by far, one of Nashy's best looking outings; the sets are elegant, the photography lush. The gothic atmosphere is exemplary as far as similar Spanish outings are concerned as well. Unfortunately, this is all that is left in the only available print in the U.S., as MPI's print is a sterile TV print that has been shorn of all sex and violence. (Save for the initial axe murder, which is also shown five times during the opening credits sequence, each time progressively slower than the last.)

Recommended to Spanish horror enthusiasts.

Le Grand Amour du Comte Dracula see **El Gran Amor del Conde Dracula**

Grand Guignol Cannibale see **Holocausto Canibal**

Grave Desires see **Brides of Blood**

Graveyard of Horror see **Necrophagus**

Grim Company see **Last House on the Left**

The Gruesome Twosome (1967)
Mayflower Pictures, Inc. [USA]
DIR: Herschell Gordon Lewis; PRO: Herschell Gordon Lewis; SCR: Allison Louise Downe; EXP: Fred M. Sandy; MUS: Larry Wellington
STR: Andrea Barr, Rodney Bedell, Marcelle Bichette, Yom Brent, Elizabeth Davis, Joseph Delino, C.A. Dukes, Ronnie Gass, Barbara Kerwin, Sherri Lane, Michael Lewis, Robert Lewis, Chris Martel, Donna Merrill, Dianne Raymond, Sherry Robinson, Ray Sager, Frank Slander, Irene Speel, Irene Stoeber, Karl Stoeber, Mike Todd, Barrie Walton, Kay Warden, Gretchen Welles, and Dianne Wilhite

Approximately 72m; Color
VID: The Gruesome Twosome [Midnight Video; 72m]
ADL: *A hairy story about a little old lady and her wigged-out son!*

A buggy old woman and her halfwit son make ends meet by running a wig shop (specializing in 100 percent human hair) and renting out rooms in their house to college girls. Unbeknownst to those looking to rent a room, this is only a scam with which to lure unsuspecting women into their home, women who unwittingly supply the "gruesome twosome" with the resources to produce more wigs. Oh, and let's not forget their stuffed bobcat, Napoleon, with whom the batty old woman converses and supplies fresh liver on Tuesdays.

Lewis' first film to combine intentional comic relief with the obligatory butchery, **The Gruesome Twosome** falls short of his other films, if only because it really isn't all that funny. (He should've stuck to playing it straight as *that's* where the real laughs begin.) The gore is typical Lewis, although it is a little scarce when compared to his other gore epics. **The Gruesome Twosome** is further belabored by

padding; the film came up short of the prerequisite running time, so additional footage was shot and tacked on, the worst being a pre-credits sequence that focuses on a very unfunny conversation between two styrofoam heads. Still, the film displays a certain amount of naïve charm that could have only been born of the sick sick sixties, and it will remain a footnote in the history books for as long as splatter films are given their due. For H.G. Lewis fans only.

Die Gruft der Lebenden Leichen see **La Vergine di Norimberga**

Una Hacha para la Luna de Miel see **Il Rosso Segno della Follia**

Hall of the Mountain King see **La Maldicion de la Bestia**

Halloween (1978)
    Falcon International Productions [USA]
    DIR: John Carpenter; PRO: Debra Hill; SCR: John Carpenter and Debra Hill; DOP: Dean Cundey; EXP: Irwin Yablans; MUS: John Carpenter
    STR: Brian Andrews, Nick Castle, Jamie Lee Curtis, Charles Cyphers, John Michael Graham, Peter Griffith, Adam Hollander, Sandy Johnson, David Kyle, Brent la Page, Nancy Loomis, Arthur Malet, Tony Moran, George O'Hanlon, Robert Phalen, Donald Pleasence, Kyle Richards, Will Sandin, P.J. Soles, Nancy Stephens, and Mickey Yablans
    AKA: **La Nuit des Masques** [*The Night of Masks*]
    Approximately 91m; Color
    NOV: **Halloween** by Curtis Richards [Bantam Books]

VID: **Halloween** [Anchor Bay Entertainment; 93(91)m; LBX]; **Halloween** [Media Home Entertainment; 90(91)m]; **Halloween** [M.I.A. (PAL); 87m]
    ADL: *The night HE came home!*

Okay, so there's hardly any gore in it, but I *had* to include it, if only for posterity. Despite the lack of bloodshed, **Halloween** is the father of the modern day slasher film. (Okay, so **Psycho** is the granddaddy, and you want to know why I didn't include *that* film, huh? Well, uhm...)
    You probably already know the story, and if you don't, all you really need to know is that **Halloween** is the film that every other stalk'n'slash quickie made since uses as a blueprint. (Except, of course, the obligatory shower scene, which was swiped from that other film I did fail to include.) Even the films which try to cash in on the long-running success of **Friday the 13th** owes their livelihood to John Carpenter's inimitable suspense flick.
    Required viewing, even if it is a little dated by now (thanks to all of the dreck that followed in its wake).

Hallucinations see **The Comeback**

Hallucinations of a Deranged Mind see **Delirios de um Anormal**

The Hanging Woman see **La Orgia de los Muertos**

Hardgore (1972)
    Production company unkown [USA]

STR: David Brook, Joan Devlin, Justina Lynn, Tony Scott, and John Seeman
Approximately 64m; Color
VID: **Hardgore** [Alpha Blue Archives; 63m]

Insofar, in all of my years looking for films deemed "cruel and unusual punishment" in 49 of the 50 states, this is the first hardcore sex-cum-gore film I've seen. (Excepting, of course, Tinto Brass' **Caligula** [1980], a film whose hardcore footage was added after the fact. What also separates this from Brass' big-budget porn classic is that here the two ever popular taboos are married within the same scenes, making for some extremely distasteful viewing.)

Hardgore wastes no time in cutting to the quick. A "nymphomaniac w/masochistic tendencies" is admitted to an institution, and before she can finish unpacking her bags, she's caught giving her nurse a tongue-lashing (and vice versa). They stop long enough for the nurse to give her the "get the hell out of here while you can" spiel, but the girl—exhibiting her only act of masochism during the film's running time—stays put, intent on screwing or getting screwed by whoever crosses her path.

Pretty soon, the intentions of the institution are made clear. During what are assumed to be "bad dreams," the new girl is exposed to sadistic orgies put on by the Chief Psychologist (dressed as the devil wearing what looks like a large daisy), and witnesses such atrocities as a woman getting it doggy-style as her head is lopped off by a guillotine. She doesn't fare much better while awake. While her and a nurse are having fun with a vibrator, someone ups the voltage (guess they didn't question as to why it was plugged into an electric generator), electrocuting the nurse. (As smoke is pouring out of her crotch, she screams—rather unconvincingly—"Call my mother! Call the doctor! Call the fire department!" and you can't help but wonder if this was supposed to be intentionally funny.)

The film goes from one extreme to another; one minute you'll be forced to endure such scenes as a doctor explicitly raping a corpse in a room that could only be described as an abattoir, and in the next you'll be laughing your ass off at the bargain-basement contrivances. (A hallucination sequence depicting airborne dildos—complete with sparklers—is only one of several ludicrous moments.)

Needless to say, the production values of this sleazy wonder are abysmal: chainsaw editing, actors who would have never had a chance doing legit horror films (let alone legit *porn* films), and a microphone boom which has much more stage presence than the aforementioned actors. And if the gore isn't extreme for you, the special effects people decided to keep the set pieces slicked down with more fake cum than is usually required in ten straight hardcore efforts.

Hardgore has to be seen to be believed... but you might want to think twice about it before taking my advice.

Harem Keeper of the Oil Sheiks *see* Ilsa—Harem Keeper of the Oil Sheiks

He Kills Night After Night After Night *see* Night, After Night, After Night

The Headless Eyes (1971)
Laviniaque Films, Inc. [USA]
DIR: Kent Bateman; PRO: Ronald Sullivan; SCR: Kent Bateman; EXP: David Bowman and Chandler Warren
STR: Bo Brundin, Mary Jane Early, Gordon Ramon, and Kelley Swartz
Approximately 80m; Color
VID: The Headless Eyes [Wizard Video; 78(80)m]
ADL: *He's out there... out of sight, and out of his mind!*

A cat burglar is caught in the act, and his eye is scooped out with a spoon by a none-too-happy victim. (Lucky for her it just happened to be lying on the endstand.) As a result of the accident, the ex-con is now a psychopathic artist with an eyepatch and a fetish for—dismembered eyes. (Well, at least he's discovered his artistic side, thanks to the psychological repercussions of the presumably painful and debilitating disfigurement. I mean, not just *anyone* would have the knack to make mobiles and paperweights out of such delicate objects.) How does he obtain his newfound art supplies? If you guessed "a spoon," you're right again! "I'm twisted," the down-on-his-luck thespian repeats incessantly to *anyone* who will listen; unfortunate for him, he's a bit of a sociopathic misanthrope, so there's nary a shoulder around for him to cry on. Until he meets *her*, that is.

Although mired in melodrama, there's something for every trash fiend. (Although I was a little surprised that, as sleazy as it was, no nudity abounds. Odd.) Gore is plentiful, and there is some very inventive photography. (Bloody eye-cam, rocking chair-cam, nausea-cam, etc.) And if the stripped down production values aren't enough to make you clamp yer nose shut, the stilted scripting, canned music, and jarring editing should do the trick.

This flick is so 70s, you can't help but love it. 🐱 🐱 🐱

Hell *see* Jigoku

Hell's Creatures *see* La Marca del Hombre Lobo

The Heritage of Caligula—An Orgy of Sick Minds *see* The Incredible Torture Show

Het Schrikkasteel der Zombies *see* La Notte del Terror

Hexen Bis Aufs Blut Gequält *see* Brenn, Hexe, Brenn

Hexen Geschändet und zu Tode Gequält [Witches Raped and Tortured to Death] (1972)
TV 13 [West Germany]
DIR: Adrian Hoven; PRO: Adrian Hoven; SCR: Fred Denger and Adrian Hoven; DOP: Ernst W. Kalinke; EXP: Horst Hachler; MUS: Sonoton Musikverlag
STR: Lukas Ammanni, Johannes Buzalski, Enrica Bianchi Colombatto,

Anton Diffring, Harry Hardt, Adrian Hoven, Percy Hoven, Dietrich Kerky, Astrid Kilian, Reggie Nalder, Rosy-Rosy, Ellen Umlauf, and Jean-Pierre Zola
AKA: Curse of the Devil; Mark of the Devil II; Mark of the Devil Part 2
Approximately 90m; Color
VID: Mark of the Devil II [Video Dimension; 88(87)m]
ADL: *10 scenes that you will POSITIVELY not be able to stomach!*

This—a lukewarm sequel to the unjustly maligned **Brenn, Hexe, Brenn** (1970) aka **Mark of the Devil**—treads similar ground, yet is never given the opportunity to walk in its footsteps. Stripped of the former's visceral punch—let alone anything that could be taken as serious commentary on the separation of church and state—**Part II** gracelessly exploits the sadism prevalent during the time of the witchburnings, without justifying itself in the process. No longer is the power of the church a palpable injustice that threatens the livelihoods of anyone with the courage to speak against it; it is simply a plot device to string together one scene of cruelty after another. And it isn't even done well.

Production values are several notches below the standards set by its already primitive forerunner, and the lackluster performances only sully it further. (Even Nalder—essentially reprising his role, but under the more unlikely moniker of "Natas"—seem to be doing a bit of sleepwalking.) Also on the downside is the film's decision to replace much of the predicted gore with gratuitous scenes of rape. (It was hard enough to believe **Brenn, Hexe, Brenn**'s claim that the film was "banned in 21 countries," but **Part II**'s similar toutings are completely ludicrous.)

Of minimal interest, and only then to diehard fans of the witch-burning/inquisition subgenre.

Las Hijas de Dracula *see* **Vampyres, Daughters of Dracula**

The Hills Have Eyes (1977)
Blood Relations Company [USA]
DIR: Wes Craven; PRO: Peter Locke; SCR: Wes Craven; DOP: Eric Saarinen; SFX: Gregory M. Auer and John Frazier; MFX: Dave Ayres and Ken Horn; MUS: Don Peake
STR: Michael Berryman, Janus Blythe, Ethel Carter, Cordy Clark, Flora, Lance Gordon, Russ Grieve, Robert Houston, Susan Lanier, Peter Locke, Brenda Marinoff, Martin Speer, John Steadman, Striker, Virginia Vincent, Dee Wallace, and James Whitworth
AKA: **La Colina del Terror** [The

Hills of Terror]; **La Colline a des Yeux** [The Hills Have Eyes]
Approximately 89m; Color
VID: **The Hills Have Eyes** [Harmony Vision; 89m]; **The Hills Have Eyes** [Vestron Video; 87m]
ADL: *A nice American family. They didn't want to kill. But they didn't want to die.*

A family on their way to California decide to stop by their old silver mine situated near the remnants of a desert community. A gas station owner, about ready to pack up and hit the road himself, warns them to "stay on the main road." For reasons to be disclosed, he is reluctant to tell them that the hills are the stomping grounds for a family of inbred cannibals. They ignore the old man's warnings (of course), and quickly find themselves stranded in the middle of nowhere. With food becoming quite scarce, the rival family decides to prepare for hard times and take advantage of the meal on wheels.

This, Wes Craven's follow-up to the infamous **Last House on the Left** (1973), is a highly effective low-budget shocker in the same vein as **The Texas Chain Saw Massacre**. (The story, though, owes everything to the legend of the Sawney Beane clan, a family of cave-dwelling cannibals in fifteenth century Scotland who were thought to be responsible for the disappearance of at least a thousand victims—unwary travelers captured, robbed, and pickled by the monstrous criminals.) The production values are quite low, but—like that other film—this "grit" actually benefits the presentation, instilling a level of realism that cannot be found in slicker fare. The violence is brutal, although not gratuitous, and actually complements the tension as opposed to detracting from it (unlike so many splatter films made since).

Performances are also quite good for an independent horror film of this caliber. Dee Wallace appears in her first genre role—if not her first substantial role altogether—and Michael Berryman makes his debut as one of the bloodthirsty kinfolk, a role that made him something of a commodity in horror films. Even those players who didn't go on to have successful careers are more than adept in their parts, helping to establish sympathetic characters with which the viewer can relate.

The Hills Have Eyes is a testament as to what can be accomplished in the genre with a little innovation; it is because of this that the viewer may wish that someone take away Craven's financial backing so he would have to start again at square one and—hopefully—find a way to reclaim that which made him a director to be reckoned with early on. (Tobe Hooper and John Carpenter should be similarly divested of substantial funds, but that's neither here nor there.)

By the way, if you didn't know, **The Hills Have Eyes** spawned a turd of a sequel that is better left buried.

Hollywood Meat Cleaver Massacre (1976)

Cine Repertory Group, Inc. [USA]

DIR: Evan Lee; PRO: Ray Atherton; SCR: Ray Atherton and Keith Burns; DOP: Guerdon Trueblood; EXP: Julie Ellen Fine; MFX: Don Ling; MUS: Joe Azarello, Gary Ray, Ed Scannell, Steve Singer, and Jay Stewart

STR: Jim Bagdanas, Alisa Beaton, Robert Clark, J. Arthur Craig, Dorian Crane, John de Rose, Doug Ely, Miklos Gyulai, James Habif, Undine Hampton, Ken Horne, Larry Justin, Marge Kazan, Paul Kelleher, Lisette Kramer, Christopher Lee, Don Ling, Bob Mead, Phil Meyer, Drew Michael, Pat Nagel, Natasha, Ellen Nicklous, George Selin, Doug Senior, Carol Silverman, Steve Singer, Lyle Steven, Toni Telo, Guedon Trueblood, Guerdon Trueblood XIV, Dawna Walden, Ollie West, Woody Wise, Carol Wood, Ed Wood, and Charles Woodard

AKA: **Evil Force; Meatcleaver Massacre; Revenge of the Dead**

Approximately 84m; Color

VID: **Meatcleaver Massacre** [Catalina Home Video; 85(84)m]

ADL: *Four crazed killers butchered his Wife, Son and Daughter. From his hospital deathbed he called upon the POWER OF THE OCCULT for Revenge... And he got it, he REALLY got it!*

As implied by the adline, the plot concerns four losers who somehow managed to scrape up college tuition off their professor's family. (Although they callously forget to mention the senseless murder of their dog Poopers. How could they forget Poopers?) The teacher survives, but is left a seemingly braindead paraplegic. He summons the spirit of Morak, the Great Avenger, a Gaelic devil god that goes about dispatching the filthy lot. (Yes, sometimes with a meatcleaver. Or at least I *think* he did. The film is still a blur, to be quite honest with you.)

In both an introduction and an afterword that were obviously tacked on after the fact by a distributor who realized just what a lousy film this was, Christopher Lee graciously sacrifices all credibility and jabbers on about the supernatural, trying to give the film's hokey storyline some historical creedence. (Unfortunately, this extra seven minutes does nothing more than lull the viewer into something of a stupor, preparing them for the thankless task at hand.) Not that this low-rent shocker doesn't have its perks—an oppresive atmosphere, a very energetic soundtrack, and some gratuitous kneaded nipple shots—but the wooden direction, inept editing, unsympathetic characters, and laughable story make it a long eighty-four minutes indeed.

Fans of **The Demon Lover** may get some mileage out of this, but everyone else may want to continue relegating **Hollywood Meat Cleaver Massacre** to the pits of obscurity.

Holocausto Canibal [Cannibal Holocaust] (1979)

F.D. Cinematografica [Italy]
DIR: Ruggero Deodato; PRO: Franco di Nunzio and Franco Palaggi; SCR: Gianfranco Clerici; DOP: Sergio d'Offizi; SFX: Aldo Gasparri; MUS: Riz Ortolani
STR: Luca Giorgio Barbareschi, Salvatore Basile, Francesca Ciardi, Pio di Savola, Ricardo Fuentes, Robert Kerman, Paolo Paolini, Perry Pirkanen, Luigina Rocchi, and Gabriel Yorke
AKA: **Cannibal Massaker** [*Cannibal Massacre*]; **Grand Guignol Cannibale** [*Grand Guignol Cannibal*]; **Nackt und Zerfleischt** [*Naked and Mangled*]

Approximately 96m; Color
SND: Cannibal Holocaust [Lucertola Media (CD)]
VID: Cannibal Holocaust [Rex Films Video (PAL); 96m]
ADL: *They EAT and they are EATEN!*

Even though it contains obligatory (and nauseating) footage of animals being treated quite maliciously, **Holocausto Canibal** somehow transcends (however slight it may be) the whole cannibal epic subgenre. And it's even nastier than most... an achievement that shouldn't be taken too lightly.

Instead of the familiar linear approach that most of these (and other) films use, **Holocausto Canibal** decides to be a bit more daring by presenting its material as a montage of news footage, dramatization, and found film intended for a documentary to have been made by a band of roving filmmakers. Although not entirely convincing, this documentary footage is quite effective and adds a great deal of weight to what might otherwise be tired proceedings.

The gore is as extreme as it gets, but it is used sparingly until the unveiling of the final reels of the aforementioned found film. Although the similarly used theme of "primitive man being more civilized than the products of modern day society" has been invoked countless times in an attempt to justify the ensuing savagery, it seems particularly pertinent and even sincere in **Holocausto Canibal** if only because the unscrupulous film crew is particularly loathsome in their portrayal. (Of course—as in most cannibal epics—the filmmakers here are fairly hypocritical in their condemnations as they are exploiting the selfsame social strata and animal cruelty as their antagonists; they just do an admirable job at covering up their intentions.) Lamberto Bava was an assistant director.

Definitely not for all tastes (animal lovers, keep your fast forward button ready at all times), but if you lean towards this type of fare, it is definitely required viewing.

☠☠☠ 🐱🐱🐱

Holy Terror see Alice, Sweet Alice

El Hombre Lobo see La Marca del Hombre Lobo

El Hombre Que Vino de Ummo see Los Monstruos de la Noche

El Horriplante Bestia Humana [The Horrible Man-Beast] (1968)
Cinematografica Calderón S.A. [Mexico]
DIR: René Cardona; PRO: Alfredo Salazar; SCR: René Cardona and René Cardona, Jr.; DOP: Raúl Martinez Solares; EXP: Guillermo Calderón Stell; AST: Valerio Olivo; SFX: Javier Torres Torija; MUS: Antonio Diaz Conde
STR: Gerardo Cepeda, Juan Fava, Norma Lazareno, Carlos López Moctezuma, José Elias Moreno, Gina Morett, Noelia Noel, Javier Rizo, Armando Silvestre, and Austín Martinez Solares
AKA: **Gomar—The Human Gorilla**; **Horror y Sexo** [*Horror and Sex*]; **Night of the Bloody Apes**

Approximately 84m; Color
VID: **Night of the Bloody Apes** [Maljack Productions, Inc.; 84m]; **Night of the Bloody Apes** [Meteor Video; 82(84)m]
ADL: *Half Man, Half Beast, ALL HORROR!*

I usually don't like to give out more information about a film's proceedings than what is given on the video box, but I do make exceptions when the droll hype doesn't do justice to unbelievably bad films as this south-of-the-border wonder. A doctor attempts to save his dying son suffering from leukemia by performing a heart transplant (with actual heart surgery footage spliced in to sleazen things up a bit) utilizing the healthy organ from a full grown gorilla which he "borrows" from a nearby zoo. No complications seem to arise until the recovering young man changes into a hormonally-charged clay-faced beast that has a penchant for mutilating anyone who crosses his path. (The doctor has the half-baked notion that the animal's blood will "annihilate whatever is causing the cancer in the blood." I think it's safe to assume that he didn't get his medical degree from Harvard.) Of course, the murders are attributed to the AWOL ape. Oh, and did I mention that the girlfriend of the detective who is heading the investigation is a woman wrestler (In a 60s Mexi-film? Who would've thought?) who wears a red Catwoman costume? It's a shame she never gets to drag the creature into the ring, but I guess you can't have everything.

Yes, the whole thing is as bad as it sounds, but there's more. Gore is aplenty: Throats are torn open, skin and scalps are peeled off, and one poor soul even has his eyeball graphically plucked out before being permanently dispatched. (And as atrocious as the effects are, the makeup is even more abysmal.) There is also a fair amount of skin, more than what one would expect from a late 60s horror flick, anyway.

Inept performances, inane dialogue (not just bad dubbing) and incompetent direction all help secure this film a place in the annals of trash cinema. (Oh, and let's not forget the oboe-heavy score that one would swear was swiped from any number of H.G. Lewis films.) Favorite line of the film? "Suddenly an idea occurs to me, before it becomes too late!"

El Horriplante Bestia Humana deserves the flying recommendation of "it doesn't get much worse than this!" 🔪🔪🔪

Horror Castle *see* La Vergine di Norimberga

Horror Hospital (1973)

Noteworthy Films Limited [UK]
DIR: Antony Balch; PRO: Richard Gordon; SCR: Antony Balch and Alan Watson; DOP: David McDonald; MUS: De Wolfe

STR: Robin Askwith, Kenneth Benda, James IV Boris, Kurt Christian, Michael Gough, Martin Grace, George Herbert, Allan Hudson, Simon Lust, Skip Martin, Ellen Pollock, Dennis Price, Vanessa Shaw, Colin Skeaping, and Barbara Wendy

AKA: **Computer Killers; Doctor Bloodbath**

Approximately 90m; Color

VID: **Horror Hospital** [MPI Home Video; 90m]

A poor man's Mick Jagger (Robin Askwith) decides he needs a break and a hippie resort. (Namely "Hairy Holidays' Fun in the Sun for Under 30s." You should be able to date this flick on this alone.) He meets up with a girl on the train who happens to be going where he is, although it's to see her Aunt Harris. The resort is a ruse, though, to supply Dr. Storm (Michael Gough) with guinea pigs for his wacky experiments that turns the young into mindless zombies (not much of a stretch, as far as I can see), and the aforementioned Aunt Harris is the doctor's crotchety old assistant. This recipe for destruction also includes a smart-ass—but sometimes ingratiating—dwarf, a car

Horror Hospital

Hey, if you pause your VCR during one of the decapitation scenes, you can actually see a stagehand tossing one of the rubber props over the edge of the mobile guillotine blade.

equipped with blades that somehow manage to decapitate passers-by (forget the fact that it's only a couple of feet off the ground), and a seldom seen "monster" trolling the halls of the sanitarium in the wee hours of the morning.

Why everyone raves about this being such a clever parody of the horror genre is beyond me. **Horror Hospital**—besides being painfully dated—is a droll shocker that occasionally makes some well meaning, but usually ineffectual stabs at the clichés which even today threaten to drag the horror film down, kicking and screaming. (Maybe some of the pretentiousness comes with the fact Balch had done some collaboration with the notorious beat writer William S. Burroughs, whose works are still considered quite groundbreaking, and rightfully so.) Regardless, this movie works much better as a cheap schlock than anything else, and even then it proves to be fairly tiring. Furthermore, gore is relegated to the aforementioned decaps, save for one poor soul with raw hamburger smeared on his face.

Horror Hotel Massacre see **Eaten Alive**

Horror of Snape Island see **Tower of Evil**

Horror of the Werewolf see **La Maldición de la Bestia**

Horror of the Zombies see **El Buque Maldito**

Horror Rises from the Tomb see **El Espanto Surge de la Tumba**

Horror y Sexo see **El Horriplante Bestia Humana**

Hotel Erotica see **La Bestia Uccide a Sangue Freddo**

House of Blood see **Mansion of the Doomed**

House of Doom see **Los Ojos Azules de la Muñeca Rota**

House of Psychotic Women see **Los Ojos Azules de la Muñeca Rota**

House of Terror see **La Orgia de los Muertos**

The House of the Screaming Virgins see **The Incredible Torture Show**

The Human Beasts *see* El Carnaval de las Bestias

The Hunchback of the Morgue *see* El Jorobado de la Morgue

The Hunchback of the Rue Morgue *see* El Jorobado de la Morgue

I Drink Your Blood (1971)

Cinemation Industries, Inc. [USA]
DIR: David E. Durston; PRO: Jerry Gross; SCR: David E. Durston; DOP: Jacques Demarecaux; MFX: Irvin Carlton; MUS: Clay Pitts
STR: Bhaskar, Richard Bowler, Iris Brooks, Bruno Damon, John Damon, Ronda Fultz, Mike Gentry, Tyde Kierney, Lynn Lowry, Alex Mann, Elizabeth Marner-Brooks, Riley Mills, George Patterson, and Jadine Wong
AKA: **Bebere Tu Sangre** [*I Drink Your Blood*]; **Bebo Tu Sangre** [*I Drink Your Blood*]; **Die Satans-Bande** [*The Satan-Group*]
Approximately 83m; Color
VID: **I Drink Your Blood** [Flamingo Video; 83m]; **Bebere Tu Sangre** [Gran Video; 83m; In English w/Spanish subs]

A van full of hippie devil worshippers decide to stop off in the small town of Valley Hills, population 40, to wreak a little havoc. They beat an old veterinarian and drug him (LSD, natch) and the geezer's grandson retaliates by injecting rabid dog blood into the meat pies they purchase from a local bakery. Before long, they're foaming at the mouth and chopping up anyone or anything—dead or alive—that happens to be in their path. One of the girls gets gangbanged by construction workers at a nearby dam site, infecting them as well.

If you can handle the slough of animal carcasses littering the sets, than this unpleasant obscurity is a must-see for every trash fiend and 70s horror enthusiast (if you can manage to track down a copy of it, that is). There isn't anything *not* tasteless about this film; every grainy frame reeks of no-budget opportunism. (Director/scriptwriter Durston even manages to make some passing references to Manson and the Tate/la Bianca murders, still fresh in the memories of most Americans.) Even so, **I Drink Your Blood** manages to be fairly disturbing, and even quite shocking at times.

Picked up for distribution by Jerry Gross, the producer wanted to release it as part of a double-bill. After dusting off an old acquisition from 1964 (namely Del Tenney's **Voodoo Bloodbath**), Gross renamed this black and white

143 L'Iguana della Lingua di Fuoco

shocker as **I Eat Your Skin**, creating one of the most memorable double-bills in film history. Filmmaker Durston went on to direct only one more film, the VD epidemic melodrama **Stigma**, made a year later and starring Philip Michael Thomas, who went on to fame in TV's **Miami Vice**.

The Crazies, minus any artistic merit. (Coincidently, it co-stars Lynn Lowry, who was not only in *that* film, but another disease-minded shocker, David Cronenberg's **The Parasite Murders**.) 🐱🐱🐱

I Hate Your Guts *see* **Day of the Woman**

I Spit on Your Grave *see* **Day of the Woman**

I Wake Up Screaming *see* **The Comeback**

La Iguana *see* **L'Iguana della Lingua di Fuoco**

L'Iguana della Lingua di Fuoco [The Iguana with the Tongue of Fire] (1971)
Les Films Corona [France] Oceania [Italy] and Terra Filmkunst [West Germany]
  DIR: Riccardo Freda; SCR: Alessandro Continenza, Günther Ebert, and Riccardo Freda; DOP: Silvano Ippoliti; MUS: Stelvio Cipriani
  STR: Dominique Boschero, Valentina Cortese, Anton Diffring, Sergio Doria, Ruth Durley, Dagmar Lassander, Arthur O'Sullivan, Luigi Pistilli, Werner Pochat, and Renato Romano

AKA: La Iguana [*The Iguana*]; La Lengua de Fuego [*The Tongue of Fire*]
Approximately 91m; Color

A body of a woman—throat slashed and features disfigured beyond recognition with acid—is found in the trunk of an ambassador's car. The police are stumped because there is seemingly no motive, and this viewer was so nonplused about the whole thing that I decided not to waste my time trying to figure out the killer's identity.

This *giallo* thriller is not only convoluted, but truly unengaging. (Truly disappointing is that it was perpetrated by the selfsame director who gave us the groundbreaking piece of necrophilic gothica **L'Orribile Segreto del Dottor Hichcock** (1962), as well giving Mario Bava his start in the business.) The film suffers from an endless supply of obtrusive close-ups, some of the worst editing ever to accompany fight scenes, the forced inclusion of the film's title in the proceedings, and—here's my favorite—blaring musical clues that kick in when someone is shown to own a pair of black sunglasses, since

that is the killer's method of disguise. Needless to say, everyone in the film has a pair. (Profoundly funny that at one point—after a dozen such cues—the camera zooms onto a pair of some old woman's prescription eyeglasses sitting on a desk, but—since they're not sunglasses—no cue. Trust me, in the context of the film, it's a riot.)

As for the gore, the first and last of the murders committed are particularly graphic—even for the time—but all of the killings in the interim amount to little more than smeared fake blood on still-breathing actors.

Tedious in every sense of the word.

The Iguana with the Tongue of Fire see **L'Iguana della Lingua di Fuoco**

Ilsa—Harem Keeper of the Oil Sheiks (1976)

Mount Everest Enterprises, Ltd. [USA]
DIR: Don Edmonds; PRO: William J. Brody; SCR: Langston Stafford; DOP: Dean Cundey and Glenn Roland; MFX: Joe Blasco
STR: Victor Alexander, Tanya Boyd, Haji Cat, Uschi Digard, George Flower, Marilyn Joy, Sharon Kelly, Su Ling, Dea Martensen, Ivan Roars, Wolfgang Roehm, S. Stearns, Michael Thayer, Dyanne Thorne, Elke Von, and Bobby Woods
AKA: **Harem Keeper of the Oil Sheiks**
Approximately 92m; Color
VID: **Ilsa—Harem Keeper of the Oil Sheiks** [Videatrics; 91(92)m]

Everyone's favorite big-busted, whip-wielding ball-breaking bitch with a German accent is back. (That's *Eelza*, if you ask her.) Somehow, she managed to survive her imminent fate at the hands of a concentration camp victim from **Ilsa—She Wolf of the SS**, no worse for wear. Even though she has since changed vocations (as eluded to in the title), having traded medical experiments for white slavery, torture still seems to be a prerequisite. Her opposition this time out is—of course—a young, virile man, a prince-cum-spy who infiltrates the sheiks ranks. (He takes his time doing so, though, as he spends at least a third of the film on a plane to his destination.) Ilsa is not without her friends; here, she utilizes the deadly talents of two underfed, asskicking, man-hating martial artists who—besides running around the entirety of the film topless—are apparently responsible for Ilsa's company of eunuchs.

Both the sex and violence quotients are moved up a notch for this outing, although the production values are about on par with the original. (Like the third and only other official entry, **Ilsa the Tigress of Siberia**, some of the stock music used herein later showed up in George Romero's **Dawn of the Dead**.) There are several other familiar faces from the first film as well, although none but Thorne reprise their roles from **Ilsa—She Wolf of the SS**. And, yes, there are other familiar sights as well; to some people's chagrin, Thorne doesn't expose hers until the last third of the film. ("Her name's Ilsa," an official

Ilsa—She Wolf of the SS

tells the lead agent. "Anything on her?" he asks. Nothing, besides a very snug uniform, one may be inclined to respond.)

The gore—perpetrated by long time professional Joe Blasco—is meted out as disturbing, although most definitely gratuitous scenes of torture orchestrated by the title antiheroine. (The "sex bomb" is particularly bent, and is sure to draw some uncomfortable laughs from even the most jaded splatterpunks.)

Some noteworthy names involved with this production include cinematographer Dean Cundey (who went on to photograph many a John Carpenter film), and art director J. Michael Riva (who went on to a big career as one of Hollywood's most successful production designers).

If you haven't had the opportunity to check out any of the Ilsa flicks, this is as good a place as any to hop on board, especially since most of the films in the series are nearly impossible to track down through local sources.

Ilsa, la Belva delle SS *see* **Ilsa—She Wolf of the SS**

Ilsa—La Louve des SS *see* **Ilsa—She Wolf of the SS**

Ilsa—She Wolf of the SS (1974)

Aetas Film Produktions [USA]
DIR: Don Edmonds; PRO: David F. Friedman; SCR: Jonah Royston; DOP: Glenn Rowland; MFX: Joe Blasco
STR: Jo Jo Deville, Uschi Digard, George Flower, Rodina Keeler, Sharon Kelly, Gregory Knoph, Lance Marshall, Maria Marx, Tony Mumolo, Sandy Richman, Nicolle Riddell, Wolfgang Roehm, and Dyanne Thorne
AKA: **Ilsa, la Belva delle SS** [Ilsa, the She-Wolf of the SS]; **Ilsa—La Louve des SS** [Ilsa—The She-Wolf of the SS]
Approximately 90m; Color
VID: **Ilsa—She Wolf of the SS** [Videatrics; 95(90)m]

"The film you are about to see is based upon documented fact. The atrocities shown were conducted as 'medical experiments' in special concentration camps throughout Hitler's Third Reich. Although these crimes against humanity are historically accurate, the characters depicted are composites of notorious nazi personalities, and the events

WHO'S THAT WOMAN WITH HITLER?

portrayed have been condensed into one locality for dramatic purposes. Because of the shocking subject matter, this film is restricted to adult audiences only. We dedicate this film with the hope that these heinous crimes will never occur again."

Although a few "atrocity" flicks predate this classic women's concentration camp film, **Ilsa—She Wolf of the SS** precipitated a slough of like films, primarily originating in Italy. (This film also spawned three sequels—one of the unofficial variety—although these changed the settings with each entry.) Ilsa (played with sadistic glee by Dyanne Thorne, who had previously been in a number of straight sexploitation films) is the head of a concentration camp, and who oversees a series of experiments with which she will hopefully prove to her patriarchal superiors that women have a higher tolerance for pain and a much greater stamina than men. All the while, the natives are getting a little restless, due in part to a male prisoner stirring things up a bit, and whom Ilsa has her eyes on for more "personal reasons."

Released with an X rating, **Ilsa—She Wolf of the SS** contains no hardcore footage to officially qualify it for such, but boasts enough softcore sex and graphic violence to get the attention of most milquetoasts in the audience. This film established the formula for the entire series: sex, violence, more sex, more violence, even more sex, even more violence, and so on and so forth. Although the films ultimately offer some kind of moral in recompense for their sleazy excesses, they are obviously insincere, and are there simply to deter any detractors. (Of course, this did little good as the Ilsa series has a not altogether spotless reputation that still precedes it twenty years later.)

Some noteworthy "names" guest starring herein include big-breasted 70s porn starlet Uschi Digard, and B-actor George "Buck" Flower (hiding under the pseudonym "C.D. Lafleur').

On an interesting sidenote, the set used for this film was the self-same one used for TV's **Hogan's Heroes** a few years previous. It was immediately burnt down following the film's production.

Not at all politically correct, but definitely worth a look for all you exploitation fans.

Ilsa the Tigress of Siberia (1977)

Mount Everest Enterprises, Ltd. [Canada]

Ilsa the Tigress of Siberia

DIR: Jean Lafleur; PRO: Julian Parnell; SCR: Marven McGara; DOP: Richard Ciupka; SFX: Angelo Rizzo and André Trielli
STR: Tony Angelo, Gilbert Beaumont, Tommy Coady, Carol Down, Sonny Forbes, Nicole Fortin, Judy Galt, Henry Gamer, Greg Gianis, Anne Marie Guenette, Terry Haig, Lucie Hutchins, Michel René Labelle, Ray Landry, Jean-Guy Latour, Jorma Lindqvist, Michel Maillot, Joe Mattia, Howard Maver, Kirk McColl, Jacques Morin, Michel Morin, Carole Péloquin, Bertha Pierre, Dyanne Thorne, and Gil Vivian
AKA: **The Tigress**
Approximately 91m; Color
VID: **Ilsa the Tigress of Siberia** [American Video; 90(91)m]; **The Tigress** [Charter Home Video; 85m]
ADL: *From the frozen waste of Siberia to the metropolis of North America, this woman blazed a path of infamy!*

Siberia, 1953. Gulag 14 is a camp for political prisoners, run by the buxom ball-buster Ilsa. (Don't ask how she survived the first two films, or even if it's the same character. Might as well be, though.) Once the producers have milked this set for all it's worth (about forty minutes), the film jumps to Montreal, 1977, where Ilsa now runs a brothel—a cover for organized crime. A counterrevolutionary interred at the infamous Gulag 14, but who survived the massacre which pronounced its demise, stumbles across Ilsa's new operation while playing bodyguard for Russian hockey players.

Steeped in sex and violence, this film—much like its predecessors but maybe to an even greater degree—jumps maniacally between excessive gore to gratuitous softcore romps, and back again. Unfortunately, either the formula became tired, the producers ran out of new backdrops, or Dyanne Thorne tired of the role, as this was the last official entry in the series. (Jesús Franco Manera was responsible for the Thorne vehicle **Greta, Haus Ohne Männer** made the same year, and released under several different **Ilsa...** monikers to help cash in on this franchise's popularity. Despite the star and backdrop, it proved to be little more than a typical Franco WIP film, with an added emphasis on sadism.)

Production values are again improved over the previous entries, with a little more action thrown in to appeal to its intended testosterone-laden audience. Everything else, though, is business as usual ... so Ilsa fans rejoice!

At least one source cites that this film was produced by the unlikely pairing of Roger Corman and Ivan Reitman, although I have my doubts. (Maybe one or the other, but...)

A pinnacle of 70s sleaze.

In der Gewalt der Zombies *see* **Le Notti Erotiche dei morti Viventi**

The Incredible Melting Man (1977)

American International Pictures [USA]
DIR: William Sachs; PRO: Samuel W. Gelfman; SCR: William Sachs; DOP: Willy Curtis; EXP: Max Rosenberg; SFX: Rick Baker and Harry Woolman; MFX: Rick Baker; MUS: Arlon Ober
STR: Newell Alexander, Michael Alldredge, Janus Blythe, Westbrook Claridge, DeForest Covan, Burr de Benning, Jonathan Demme, Julie Drazen, Samuel W. Gelfman, Myron Healey, Dave Hull, Bonnie Inch, Mickey Lolich, Dorothy Love, Rosemary Lovell, Edwin Max, Keith Michl, Leigh Mitchell, Jennifer Mulaire, Alex Rebar, Stuart Edmond Rogers, Rainbeaux Smith, Ann Sweeny, Don Walters, Chris Whitney, and Lisle Wilson
AKA: **El Increible Hombre que se Derrite** [*The Incredible Melting Man*]
Approximately 85m; Color
VID: **The Incredible Melting Man** [Vestron Video; 85m]

The first manned trip to Saturn doesn't bode well for its single survivor. As can be ascertained from the title's subtle allusions, the astronaut has acquired an unprecedented infirmity, losing weight faster than the stand-ins in Jenny Craig commercials. (The only benefit is that he gets to drink human blood than having to subsist on those no-calorie frozen dinners.) I'd go into more detail, but I don't want to give away the last five minutes of the movie.

This 70s take on 50s B-science fiction (in particular **The First Man into Space**) was filmed wholly to display Baker's amazing effects work. (The progressive meltdown is even more impressive than anything in **The Devil's Rain** groundbreaking finale, a record not to be taken lightly.) Our anti-hero's bloody and pus-ridden countenance is, simply, a joy to behold. His handiwork is almost as remarkable; one victim—face half missing—looks like something out of real crime footage. Not to mention a messy decap and an eviscerated corpse. (A severed head—the product of the former—really gets around, covering more ground than the title character.) It's a shame they don't make films this "moist" anymore.

The Incredible Melting Man avoids extraneous footage early on, cutting to the quick and offering nothing even remotely resembling character development until a third into the film. There is some unintentional silliness: Not only does it proffer what has to be the most unnecessary split screen effect used in the 70s, but the most ridiculously staged chase scene ever. (A nurse—the melting man's first victim-to-

The Incredible Torture Show

be—runs down a *reeealy* long corridor in slow motion, the killer in short pursuit—if half a mile constitutes "short." In a panic, she throws herself through a glass door—who needs doorknobs?—and, without a beat, runs into the mutant bloodsucker. It's much worse than it sounds; trust me.)

Messy, downbeat fun for the entire family.

The Incredible Torture Show (1976)

Rochelle Films [USA]
DIR: Joel M. Reed; PRO: Alan C. Margolin; SCR: Joel M. Reed; DOP: Gerry Toll; SFX: Bob O'Bradovich; MFX: Bob O'Bradovich; MUS: Michael Sahl
STR: Alphonso, Athena Anderson, Janis Beaver, Judy Best, Arlana Blue, Michelle Craig, George Davalos, Louie de Jesus, Alan Dellay, Dan Fauci, Karen Fraser, Joann Friedman, Sharani Gomez, Juliet Graham, Carol Henry, Illa Howe, Robert Kirsh, Viju Krem, Carol Mara, Niles McMaster, Rita Montone, Seamus O'Brien, Ernie Pysher, Gail Renay, Saiyanidi, Lynette Sheldon, Linda Small, Helen Thompson, Evalyna Wade, Suzanne Wall, and Erica Wolfe

AKA: Blood Sucking Freaks; Bloodsucking Freaks; The Heritage of Caligula—An Orgy of Sick Minds; The House of the Screaming Virgins
Approximately 88m; Color
VID: **Bloodsucking Freaks** [Cult Video (PAL); 88m; In English w/Dutch subs]; **Bloodsucking Freaks** [Troma Team Video; 91(88)m; Director's Cut]; **Bloodsucking Freaks** [Vestron Video; 88m]; **The Heritage of Caligula—An Orgy of Sick Minds** [Magnum Entertainment; 88m]
ADL: *JOIN THE FUN!.. Human Dart Boards... Home Style Brain Surgery... Dental Hijinks!*

Sadly, this film (having risen to infamy under the equally subtle moniker of **Bloodsucking Freaks**) is director's best effort to date. Obviously inspired by H.G. Lewis' **The Wizard of Gore** (1970), Reed takes the *Grand Guignol* formula a little too seriously, reaching heights of sadism rarely seen even in splatter films, administering the sick goings-on with tongue planted firmly in cheek. (So over-the-top are the proceedings that it probably would have come across as a comedy even without the tasteless one-liners that punctuate the scenes of violence.)

The gore, which might not be nearly as graphic as Lewis' "worst," still manages to rate higher on the gag-o-meter. (One particular scene that would garner a big old "yuck" from even the more hardened fans involves a demented doctor removing a woman's teeth with a pair of pliers, shaving then drilling a hole in her head, and inserting a straw into the fresh orifice, blowing bubbles in the liquefied gray matter with childlike glee.) The production values are also a few steps of Lewis' work, not that it makes much of a difference. Even with twice the budget and with a more talented cast and crew behind the reigns, **The Incredible Torture Show** would still reek of absolute, unrepentant sleaze.

Shortly after the film's initial theatrical release, a number of women's groups attacked the film on the grounds that it promoted violence towards women. Even though there is no basis in fact that such films instigate misogynistic behavior in people already predisposed to it, one really can't blame them for getting up in arms. It is difficult to take the sexism and misogyny seriously when taken into context within the film as whole, it doesn't make it any less offensive or perturbing. Every female that is presented onscreen is immediately stripped, humiliated, tortured, and finally murdered… all for the purpose of entertainment.

Tasteless on all counts, and should most definitely be avoided by the easily offended. (Those who insist on checking it out should be prepared to take a shower immediately thereafter. And hopefully not a cold one.) ☠☠☠

El Increible Hombre que se Derrite see **The Incredible Melting Man**

Inferno (1960) see **Jigoku**

Innocents from Hell see **Alucarda—La Hija de las Tinieblas**

Inquisición [Inquisition] (1976)

Ancla Century Films [Spain] and Anubis Films [Spain]
DIR: Jacinto Molina Alvarez; PRO: Roberto P. Moreno; SCR: Jacinto Molina Alvarez; DOP: Miguel F. Milá; EXP: Martinez de Azcoitia; SFX: Pablos Péres; MUS: Máximo Baratas
STR: Tota Alba, Jacinto Molina Alvarez, Eduardo Calvo, Antonio Casas, Belen Cristino, Juan Luis Galiardo, Daniela Giordano, Antonio Iranzo, Tony Isbert, Eva León, Isabel Luque, Ricardo Merino, Jenny O'Neill, Mónica Randall, María Salerno, Julia Saly, and Loretta Tovar
Approximately 94m; Color
VID: **Inquisition** [Video City Productions; 90m]
ADL: *INHUMAN BESTIALITY! UNSPEAKABLE TORTURES! SHAMELESS BRUTALITY!*

Made a little late in the game, this entry in the inquisition/witch-burning subgenre is completely derivative, offering nothing new except the contribution of Spanish horror actor Paul Naschy (né Jacinto Molina Alvarez). Here, Naschy plays a judge who falls for the wiles of a young woman who, although not a witch at the onset, joins a coven, selling her soul to the devil. Predictably, the corrupt official is burnt at the stake for the selfsame crimes he had accused innumerable innocents of.

As could be ascertained, the story is inconsequential; everything in the film revolves around the scenes of nude women tortured into obtaining a false confession. (Although gore is sparse, there is one

unnerving scene involving nipple torture that is sure to make even the more hardened splatterpunks flinch. I did.) Unlike many similar films, Naschy (who also wrote and directed this film) does introduce real supernatural elements into the mix, offering one of the most abysmally staged black masses on record, and a charming—albeit horribly made up—goat-faced devil who oversees the aforementioned proceedings. Production values are typical of Spanish horror of the time, so—like everything else about the picture—pretty innocuous.

For torture freaks and Naschy aficionados only.

El Inquisidor [The Inquisitor] (1975)
Industria Andina Del Cine [Argentino] and Marlo Cinematografica [Peru]
DIR: Bernardo Arias; SCR: Gustavo Ghirardi and Pedro Marzzialetti; DOP: Carlos Bonnatti and Pedro Marzzialetti; EXP: Armando José Marimon, Fortunato Osvaldo, and Brown Prado; MUS: Tito Ribero
STR: Jorgelina Aranda, Maria Aurelia Bisutti, Rosalindo Bocanegra, Jorge Cacéres, Guillermo Campos, Eduardo Cesti, Antonio Cevalios, Williams Cornejo, Hernando Cortes, Julian Favre, Dorremori Fernández, Valerio Franco, Lucio Gálvez, Gutapercha, Francisco Herazo, Helena Huambos, Flavia López, Duilio Marzio, Heli Miñano, Juan Moy, Soledad Mujico, Guillermo Pafhurr, Ruth Razzetto, Robert Reid, Roberto Ronet, Mario Savina, Elena Sedova, Vita Vani, José Velázquez, Olga Zubarry, and Zulaika
Approximately 80m; Color
VID: **El Inquisidor** [Video Mex International; 80m; In Spanish]

Honestly, I haven't a clue as to what's going on here, and I have doubts that an English language edition would clarify it all that much. All I can tell you is that it's something about an overzealous cult that burns young women at the stake after torturing them for whatever reasons. Although a straightforward modern day witchhunting film for most of its running time, **El Inquisidor** does include some incongruous scenes of real hokum towards film's end.

The production values are passable, but the film was probably dated even at the time it was made with all of the go-go dancing and fuzzed out guitars. Gratuitous nudity is in abundance, and there is a fair amount of blood. (Although some of the gore leaves something to be desired, the charcoaled corpses of the supposed witches are fairly realistic and somewhat unnerving.) Quick, someone get me a translator. 🐾 🐾 🐾

Les Insatisfaites Poupées Érotiques du Dr. Hichcock see La Bestia Uccide a Sangue Freddo

Invasion der Zombies see Non Si Deve Profanare il Sonno dei Morti

The Island of Living Horror see Brides of Blood

Island of the Damned see ¿Quien Puede Matar a un Niño?

The Island of the Living Dead see Zombi 2

It Fell from the Sky see The Alien Dead

Jack el Distripador de Londres [Jack the Ripper of London] (1971)
Cinefilms S.L. [Spain] and International Apollo Films [Italy]
DIR: José Luis Madrid; PRO: José Luis Madrid; SCR: Jacinto Molina Alvarez, Tito Carpi, and José Luis Madrid; DOP: Diego Úbeda; MUS: Piero Piccioni
STR: Jacinto Molina Alvarez, Enrique Beltran, Franco Borelli, Alfonso Castizio, Orchidea de Santis, Victor Iregua, Patricia Loran, Maika, Renzo Marignano, Miguel Minuesa, Irene Mir, Paloma Moreno, Isidoro Novellas, Antonio Ramis, Andrés Resino, Carmen Roger, Teresita-Castizio, and Victor Vilanova

AKA: Jack the Ripper; Sette Cadaveri per Scotland Yard [*Seven Murders for Scotland Yard*]
Approximately 83m; Color

A series of Ripper-like murders points to horror star Paul Naschy (*né* Jacinto Molina Alvarez), here an ex-circus performer who wakes up after a drunken binge and finds himself snuggled up alongside a dead prostitute, with the cops knocking at his door, no less. (The real killer—obviously not Naschy—likes to cut out his victims' heart, storing them in big pickle jars. When time allows, he wastes no time in taunting police, even sending them the head of one of his victims in a hat box.)

Not one of his more engaging efforts, this Naschy vehicle is typical low-rent Spanish horror fare, with all of the *giallo* trappings intact. The proceedings are fairly uninteresting, not excluding the murders, despite the fact they are invariably punctuated by close-ups of gaping, but not always bloody stab wounds.

Highly obscure, but not worth the trouble it would take to track it down.

Jack l'Éventreur see Jack the Ripper—Der Dirnenmörder von London

Jack the Ripper (1971) see Jack el Distripador de Londres

Jack the Ripper (1976) see Jack the Ripper—Der Dirnenmörder von London

Jack the Ripper—Der Dirnenmörder von London [Jack the Ripper—The Prostitute Killer of London] (1976)

Cinemec-Produktion [Switzerland/West Germany] DIR: Jesús Franco Manera; PRO: Erwin C. Dietrich; SCR: Jesús Franco Manera and Nicolas Weisse; DOP: Peter Baumgartner; AST: Mark Rissi and Alfons Sinniger; SFX: Hans-Walter Kramski and Karlheinz Reiber; MUS: Walter Baumgartner
    STR: Angela Arndts, Lorli Bucher, Josephine Chaplin, Francine Custer, Otto Dornbierer, Regine Elsener, Herbert Fuchs, Hans Gaugler, Olga Gebhard, Klaus Kinski, Mike Lederer, Andreas Mannkopff, Peter Nüsch, Lina Romay, Friedrich Schönfelder, Esther Studer, Ursula von Wiehse, and Nicolas Weisse
    AKA: **Erotico Profondo** [*Deep Erotica*]; Jack l'Éventreur [*Jack the Ripper*]; Jack the Ripper; Jack the Ripper—The Harlot Killer of London; Sohon Teura Staja
    Approximately 95m; Color
    VID: **Jack the Ripper** [Vestron Video; 82m]; **Jack the Ripper—The Harlot Killer of London** [Elite Video; 88m]
    ADL: *Close your eyes and whisper his name...*

At first, it seems that most (if not all) of the facts concerning the infamous serial killings that inspired this film are sacrificed for the more sensational aspects of the crime, namely the sex and violence. Anyone familiar with the director's work will realize that his reasons for deviating from the facts are far more personal; Franco's agenda is not to make a film that complies with viewer expectations, but is with making exploitation films that comply with his own skewed, fetish-ridden visions. Although the sex and violence is gratuitous, it is complemented by a compelling case study of a sympathetic, albeit sick human being unable to control his own bent compulsions... and one can't help wondering if Franco is using himself as a springboard for the fictional character portrayed herein. It is also no surprise that the role seems tailor-made for Austrian actor Klaus Kinski; known for playing unbalanced villains, his portrayal of the tortured killer remains one of his best genre outings.
    As far as production values, this is by far one of Franco's better looking productions. (Although it still has its fair share of distracting close-ups, his penchant for zooms is kept in check.) True to form, though, this exercise in Grand Guignol inherently reeks of sleaze. (Many viewers will be surprised to find that the only available American print is shorn of

The Jekyll and Hyde Portfolio   154

thirteen minutes; even in its truncated form, **Jack the Ripper** more than qualifies for inclusion in this book. What exactly is still missing, I do not know, but it is difficult to imagine it being any nastier than this version is.)

Brutal, uncompromising exploitation fare from a questionable genius. ☠☠☠

Jack the Ripper—The Harlot Killer of London *see* **Jack the Ripper—Der Dirnenmörder von London**

The Jekyll and Hyde Portfolio (1971)

Xerxes Productions Ltd. [USA]
DIR: Eric Jeffrey Haims; PRO: Eric Jeffrey Haims; SCR: Donn Greer; DOP: Arch Archambault

STR: Nancy Ayers, René Bond, Terri Bond, Sebastian Brooks, Sandy Carey, Gray Daniels, Cathie Demille, Duane Grace, Donn Greer, Hump Hardy, Terri Johnson, Casey Larrain, Philip Lionel, Ric Lutz, Mady Maguire, Lexy Morrell, Melissa Ruiz, Eve Standish, John Terry, Jane Tsentas, and Nora Wieternik
AKA: Jekyll and Hyde Unleashed
Approximately 78m; Color

Here's an obscure little number: Someone is knocking off inmates at the Florence Nightingale Institute, an asylum for women. While the director, the twitchy Dr. Cabala, is off playing in his lab, the nurses take to feeling up and ogling the patients.

You think some of Andy Milligan's early films are exceptionally bad, **The Jekyll and Hyde Portfolio** isn't much better, and could easily be mistaken for one of that director's films were it not for the credits. The acting is god-awful (save for the presence of porn star René Bond, although even she can't salvage the dialogue), the editing migraine-inducing, the photography grainy and consisting of an abundance of pointless camera shots, and the score consists entirely of overly familiar stock music. Even worse, we are subjected to gratuitous frog dissection footage. (I swear the film would be ten minutes shorter if they deleted it all. And to make things worse, they drench the froggy carnage in at least a quart's worth of fake blood.) And let's not forget the narrated intro given by someone whose knowledge of psychology is whatever he managed to glean from abysmally written horror films.

The film's highlights include gory murders accompanied by carnival music, a hunchback who tries to steal away Paul Naschy's Lifetime Achievement Award for Profuse Drooling, and some reasonably realistic *and* erotic lesbian footage. (Sadly, René Bond wasn't involved in these scenes. Worse yet, Bond is the only actress who *doesn't* get nekkid in the film, whereas everyone else isn't on screen for more than ten seconds before they doff their tops. And *she's* the porn actress. Strange.)

Okay, so I enjoyed it. So sue me. 🐱🐱🐱

Jekyll and Hyde Unleashed *see* **The Jekyll and Hyde Portfolio**

Jigoku [Hell] (1960)
Shintoho [Japan]
DIR: Nobuo Nakagawa; PRO: Mitsugo Okura; SCR: Ichirô Miyagawa and Nobuo Nakagawa; DOP: Mamoru Morita
STR: Shigeru Amachi, Hiroshi Hayashi, Ukato Mitsuya, Fumiko Miyata, Torahiko Nakamura, Yoichi Numata, Jun Otomo, Kimie Tokudaiji, and Akiko Yamashita
AKA: **Inferno**; **Sinner to Hell**; **The Sinners of Hell**
Approximately 101m; Color

The first two thirds of this film is in an intense drama about human failings, and walks a fine line between clinical psychiatry and religious moralism. The last thirty-or-so minutes is, well, the reason I included **Jigoku** in the first place.

Applying striking imagery and lush photography, we—the viewers—are given a tour of the abyss, a Hell that owes as much to Orthodox Christianity as it does to Eastern mysticism. (Because of its approach, I'm inclined to make comparisons to José Mojica Marins'; not to discredit Marins for what he accomplished on such minuscule budgets, but this is the same material done right.) As we make our descent, the level of savagery builds. We are exposed to graphic depictions of every conceivable atrocity: beheadings, dismemberments, impalations, disembowelments, etc. (One extremely unsettling scene involves a rather nasty saw blade.) Sets are equivocably ominous: a lake of sulfuric acid and a field of swords offer additional opportunities to show just how vulnerable we are.

The special effects range from passable to downright unnerving in their realism. (This makes **Jigoku** exemplary in that, not only were gore films virtually nonexistent at the time, but that it took the rest of the world almost a decade to catch up with the quality of the work herein.)

Although certain aspects of the film are a bit dated (particularly the 60s soundtrack), it has held up reasonably well with the passage of time. (There is a 1979 remake which is—purportedly—much, much nastier, but I have yet to locate it.) Recommended. 🐱🐱🐱

El Jorobado de la Morgue
[The Hunchback of the Morgue] (1972)
Eva Film [Spain]
DIR: Javier Aguirre; PRO: Fran-

El Jorobado de la Morgue

cisco Lara Polop; SCR: Javier Aguirre, Jacinto Molina Alvarez, and Alberto S. Insua; DOP: Raúl Pérez Cubero; EXP: Francisco Lara Polop; SFX: Pablo Perez; MUS: Carmelo A. Bernaola
  STR: Victor Alcazar, Jacinto Molina Alvarez, Iris Andre, María Elena Arpón, Victoria Ayllon, Blaki, Dani Card, Sofia Casares, Saturno Cerra, Jose Luis Chinchilla, Alberto Dalbes, Manuel de Blas, Alfonso de la Vega, Kinito, Susana Latour, Javier Martin, Julio Martin, Antonio Mayans, Angel Menéndez, María Perschy, Antonio Pica, Ingrid Rabel, Antonio Ramis, Joaquin Rodriguez, Richard Santis, Fernando Sotuela, Susan Taff, Adolfo Thous, and Rossana Yanni
  AKA: **Le Bossu de la Morgue** [*The Hunchback of the Morgue*]; **The Hunchback of the Rue Morgue**; **The Rue Morgue Mascares**; **Die Stunde der Grausamen Leichen** [*The Hour of the Cruel Dead*]
  Approximately 84m; Color
  VID: **El Jorobado de la Morgue** [Manga Films (PAL); 84m]; **The Rue**

Morgue Massacres [All Seasons Entertainment; 90(82)m]
  ADL: *STATUS: DEATH AFTER ARRIVAL. CAUSE: MUTILATION.*

  This oddly contrived horror film is by far one of Naschy's (né Alvarez') goriest outings. What makes this one an interesting footnote in his career is that it isn't a vehicle for the actor, being relegated in a supporting role as the title hunchback. (Apparently, Naschy won the Georges Méliés Award for Best Actor for his unconvincing portrayal herein; not that he doesn't deserve recognition for his contributions to the genre, it is odd that he received it due to his work on *this* particular film.)
  The production values, surprisingly, are above average for Spanish genre films of the 70s, especially since **El Jorobado de la Morgue** is one of the more exploitive films he's been involved with. Furthermore, some of the special effects are quite convincing. This isn't even taking into account a stomach-churning scene depicting a cadaver's throat being cut. Naschy claimed in a recent interview that the corpse in question was real; although one is inclined to believe it after seeing the footage in question, one must also be a little skeptical since the same claims were made by or fabricated around other genre efforts which boasted similarly unnerving effects— Aristide Massaccesi's **Buio Omega** and Nacho Cerdá's **Aftermath** come immediately to mind. (I'll hold off on my "autopsy footage" warning

until after this rumor has been publicly confirmed.) As if to make the viewer question their own skepticism, live rats suffered for the sake of realism, being burned alive in front of the camera and worse. The only consolation we animal lovers have is that Naschy—who insisted on playing it for real—suffered numerous bites at the hands of the hungry rodents while filming these truly disturbing scenes.

Worthwhile viewing for Spanish horror enthusiasts, if one can stomach its irredeemably exploitive nature. 🐈 🐈 🐈

Jungle Holocaust see **Ultimo Mondo Cannibale**

De Kannibalen vallen Aan! see **Cannibal Ferox**

Kill and Go Hide see **The Child**

Killer's Moon (1978)
Rothernorth Limited [UK]
DIR: Alan Birkinshaw; PRO: Alan Birkinshaw and Gordon Keymer; SCR: Alan Birkinshaw; DOP: Arthur Lavis; MUS: John Shakespeare and Derek Warne
STR: Carol Binsted, Hilda Braid, Elizabeth Counsell, Alison Elliott, Anthony Forrest, Jo-Anne Good, Nigel Gregory, Jane Hayden, David Jackson, Christina Jones, Georgina Kean, James Kerry, Jayne Lester, Tom Marshall, Debbie Martyn, Lynne Morgan, Chubby Oates, Paul Rattee, Jean Reeve, Hugh Ross, Graham Rowe, Peter Spraggon, Charles Stewart, Lisa Vanderpump, and Edwina Wray
AKA: **Les Tuers du Clair de Lune** [The Moonlight Killers]; **Verschrikkelijke Schoolres**; **Voyage Scolaire Sanglant** [Bloody School Trip]

Approximately 92m; Color
VID: **Killer's Moon** [Electric Video (PAL); 92m]; **Killer's Moon** [VCL Communications; 92(88)m]
ADL: *AN ENDLESS NIGHT OF UNSPEAKABLE TERROR.*

Four buggy—and extremely horny—inmates ply their way out of their padded cells and hightail it into the countryside. Lo and behold, they are the recipients of some highly unstable "dream therapy"; apparently, three of the psychopaths are under the impression that they are in a shared dreamstate, and are thus given free reign to act out whatever twisted fantasies they wish to without the restraints of social inhibitions. They stumble across a bus load of young girls on a school outing forced to seek refuge in an old country inn; the screenwriter then permits the four nutters to rape and murder the underage fodder at their own convenience.

Killer's Moon would probably be a fairly innocuous psychos-on-the-loose outing were it not for its penchant for shocking the viewer with its distasteful contrivances. (Staged animal mutilation, underage rape and murder, etc.) As could be expected, there is gore to be had, although some of it seems unusually restrained in American prints. Aside from its exploitive nature, there is not much else to recommend. There is little or no suspense throughout (hindered, at least in part, by the fact that most of the scenes are either underexposed or overexposed). Granted, the "dream therapy" plot device is quite original and used to disturbing effect, but it isn't sufficient to carry the film. (Neither is the presence of a three-legged dog, also used to disturbing effect.) Of limited interest.

Krug and Company *see* Last House on the Left

KZ9—Lager di Sterminio *see* SS Camp Extermination

De Laatste Kannibalen *see* Ultimo Mondo Cannibale

Lady Dracula *see* Ceremonia Sangrienta

Lady Frankenstein *see* La Figlia di Frankenstein

Una Lagartija con Piel de Mujer *see* Una Lucertola con la Pelle di Donna

The Last Cannibal World *see* Ultimo Mondo Cannibale

Last House on Dead End Street *see* The Funhouse

Last House on the Left (1972)
The Night Company [USA]
DIR: Wes Craven; PRO: Sean S. Cunningham; SCR: Wes Craven; DOP: Victor Hurwitz; SFX: Troy Roberts; MUS: David Alexander Hess
STR: Marshall Ankler, Sandra Cassell, Jonathan Craven, Ray Edwards, Cynthia Garr, Lucy Grantham, David Alexander Hess, Martin Kove, Fred Lincoln, Jeramie Rain, Marc Sheffler, Gaylord St. James, and Ada Washington
AKA: **Grim Company**; **Krug and Company**; **Mondo Brutale** [**Brutal World**]; **Night of Vengeance**; **Sex Crime of the Century**
Approximately 91m; Color
VID: **Last House on the Left** [Vestron Video; 81m; R-rated version]; **Last House on the Left** [Vestron Video; 83m; Uncut edition]

Taking its cue from Ingmar Bergman's **The Virgin Spring** (1959), this—Wes Craven's directorial debut—is a highly disturbing, high voltage shock film that tells the quaint little story of two teenagers who are brutalized and imminently murdered by three thugs, and how the parents of one of the girls exact their revenge on the hooligans. Sure, it seems short on story, but the writing takes backseat to the in your face horror that exploits parents' fear for their children's well-being, and their fear of strangers.

Although Craven's film is by now fairly dated, and, in retrospect, seems almost unexemplary when placed alongside similar fare also released during a time of lax censorship laws, **Last House on the Left** was a harrowing film that successfully captured the ever-growing generation gap that formed in the wake of 60s rebellion. Many have written in depth on what set this film apart from so many others; even a book came out this year that focuses on this film, plumbing its allegory and socio-political mindset for all it's worth. This seems, if anything, a vain attempt to make the younger generation see what all the fuss was about; although Generation Xers can still appreciate the film on its merits as a disturbing horror film, it is doubtful they will ever truly see what the fuss was all about as **Last**

Legend of the Wolfwoman see La Lupa Mannara

Leichenhaus der Lebenden Toten see Non Si Deve Profanare il Sonno dei Morti

La Lengua de Fuego de la Iguana see L'Iguana della Lingua di Fuoco

Let Sleeping Corpses Lie see Non Si Deve Profanare il Sonno dei Morti

Let Them Die Slowly see Cannibal Ferox

Levende Doden in Het Lijkenhuis see Non Si Deve Profanare il Sonno dei Morti

House on the Left is truly a product of its times.

Although director Craven went on to become a very successful filmmaker, it is doubtful that he—like Tobe Hooper and his debut The Texas Chain Saw Massacre—will ever again create a film so powerful, and so lasting.

Recommended viewing.

Last House on the Left II see Antefatto

The Last Survivor see Ultimo Mondo Cannibale

The Legend of Blood Castle see Ceremonia Sangrienta

Legend of the Bayou see Eaten Alive

Una Libelula para Cada Muerto [A Dragonfly for Each Corpse] (1973)

Compagnia Cinematografica Astro [Spain] and Profilmes S.A. [Spain]

DIR: León Klimovsky; PRO: Modesto Perez Redondo; SCR: Jacinto Molina Alvarez; DOP: Miguel F. Milá; EXP: José Antonio Peréz Giner and Ricardo Sanz; SFX: Amobaq and Manuel Gomez; MUS: CAM

STR: Rafael Albaicin, Luis Alonso, Jacinto Molina Alvarez, Angel Aranda, Eduardo Calvo, José Canalejas, Juan Cazalilla, Ramón Centenero, Enrica Bianchi Colombatto, Cesar de Barona, Javier de Rivera, Beni Deus, María Kosti, Juan Madrigal, Anne Marie, Antonio Mayans, Susana Mayo, Ricardo Merino, Antonio Vidal Molina, Frances O'Flynn, Ingrid Rabel, Ernesto Vañes, and María Vidal

AKA: **Giustiziere Sfida la Polizia** [*The Executioner Challenges the Police*] Approximately 85m; Color

A junkie-slash-painter is hacked to death by a masked assailant while shooting up in what he thought was the safety of his luxurious studio. A streetwalker quickly follows suit. A dragonfly is left at the scene of both crimes, and an inspector doing his best Clint Eastwood impersonation (Alvarez) is put on the case. With his fashion designer wife at his side, he pursues a killer intent on eliminating the city's many "undesirables" in as messy a fashion as he can muster.

This—a Spanish attempt at the Italian *giallo* thriller—is enjoyable, although fairly derivative effort. The script offers lots of possible, but very unlikely, culprits for the viewer to wade through, a task that becomes so overwhelming that one can't help but let Naschy do the work for them. (Some of the more interesting characters include a very unconvincing stripper, and a professor with a penchant for necrophilia.)

Una Libeluna para Cada Muerto suffers from some extremely low-rent camerawork (maybe Mila didn't have the luxury of a steadycam, but he could have at least used a tripod) and other side effects of a low budget, but it is no less enjoyable as Eurotrash. (Although not overtly gory, there is probably enough blood spattering the walls to keep a splatterpunk's interest throughout.)

Lisa *see* The Axe

Lisa, Lisa *see* The Axe

The Living Dead *see* Non Si Deve Profanare il Sonno dei Morti

The Living Dead at the Manchester Morgue *see* Non Si Deve Profanare il Sonno dei Morti

The Lorelei's Grasp *see* Las Garras de Loreli

Lucertola con la Pelle di Donna, Una [A Lizard in a Woman's Skin] (1971)
Atlantida Films [Spain] Les Films Corona [France] and International Apollo Films [Italy]
DIR: Lucio Fulci; PRO: Edmondo Amati; SCR: Lucio Fulci, Roberto Gianviti, José Luis Martinez, and André Tranché; DOP: Luigi Küveiller; MFX: Carlo Rambaldi and Eugenio Ascani; MUS: Ennio Morricone
STR: Stanley Baker, Franco Balducci, Penny Brown, José Soara Bulco, Alberto de Mendoza, Lucio Fulci, Edy Galleani, Leo Genn, Gaetano Imbró, Mike A. Kennedy, Ezio Marano, Silvia Monti, Georges Rigaud, Jean Sorel, and Anita Strinberg
AKA: Carole; Un Lagartija con Piel de Mujer [*A Lizard in a Woman's Skin*]; Schizoid; Le Venin de la Peur [*The Venom of the Fear*]
Approximately 95m; Color
VID: **A Lizard in a Woman's Skin** [VIP (PAL); 100(95)m]

A woman begins to suffer from hallucinations (inevitably sexual in flavor), and goes to her shrink, but to no avail. Eventually, the waking dreams begin to take on a more sinister, more macabre tone. After having one where she sees herself knifing her lesbian neighbor, the woman actually turns up dead, killed in a similar fashion. With no suspects at hand, the police eagerly latch onto the woman after she comes forward about her strange visions, giving them a whole lot to chew on for about an hour's worth of screen time.

Director Fulci shows some real flare here, something sorely missed in much of his later, gorier work. (Most everything following **L'Aldilá** [1981] can be included in this generalization.) There is a good portrayal of early forensics work (something which didn't become commonplace until after TV's **Quincey**), and some sets, especially for the chase scenes. For those who like their sleaze, there is also an abundance of bare flesh, gratuitous even as far as early Eurotrash goes. On the downside, the production values are marred by an ungodly amount of wobbly, jerky camerawork

The most interesting aspect of the film, though, is the controversy which surrounded one of the gorier scenes involving an eviscerated dog, twitching and whimpering. The effects work was convincing enough that Fulci was taken to court on the grounds of animal abuse, and was only able to avoid a two year sentence after artist Rambaldi brought his prized mechanical dog into court. Needless to say, it is easy to see why people were fooled as the sequence is one of the more disturbing of its type ever staged.

An exemplary *giallo* thriller.

Macchie Solari [Sunspots] (1976)

Clodio Cinematografica [Italy]
DIR: Amando Crispino; PRO: Leonardo Pescarolo; SCR: Lucia Battistrada and Armando Crispino; DOP: Carlo Carlini; MUS: Ennio Morricone
STR: Carlo Cattaneo, Mimsy Farmer, Angela Goodwin, Ray Lovelock, Barry Primus, Massimo Serato, and Gaby Wagner
AKA: **Autopsy**; ¡Tension! The Victim;
Approximately 85m; Color
VID: **Autopsy** [Prism Entertainment; 90(85)m]
ADL: *HUMAN BODY PARTS HAVE NEVER BEEN SEVERED AND EXAMINED... SO COMPLETELY!*

Overwhelmed by her work, a med student (Mimsy Farmer) interning at a coroner's office is going a little buggy. (While on the job, she suffers from hallucinations involving corpses either bumping uglies with one another, or accosting her.) To make things worse, she discovers on her slab a woman who she had met the night before claiming to be a guest of her father's. The dead woman's brother—a race car driver turned priest following a tragic accident—shows up, insisting that his sister could not have killed herself. Since Ms. Farmer is currently completing a thesis on the differences between simulated and authentic suicides, as well as the fact that she is indirectly but still personally involved, she decides to investigate the case further.

The filmmakers set the film's tone by opening with a string of unrelated (staged) suicides, and—when

that doesn't seem to do the trick—uses real autopsy photos to even better effect. Part docu-drama, part psychological horror, part *giallo* thriller, **Macchie Solari** is an engaging—albeit fairly sleazy—Eurotrash offering. The whodunit aspects are unpredictable, and is interesting if only because of the aforementioned contrivances. Production values are standard, and the performances are palatable.

Gore is sparse, but the scenes set in the coroner's office are particularly nasty. (Had the setting been anywhere else, they would have been undeniably gratuitous.) And, just to keep things interesting, the viewer is treated to lots of skin, and even some implied necrophilia.

Eurotrash fans are sure to get something out of **Macchie Solari**; everyone else who happens to walk into the line of fire, though, could rightly be considered innocent bystanders.

Mad Doctor of Blood Island (1968)

Hemisphere Pictures Inc. [Philippines/USA]
DIR: Gerardo de Leon and Eddie Romero; PRO: Eddie Romero; SCR: Reuben Canoy; DOP: Justo Paulino; EXP: Kane W. Lynn; MUS: Tito Arevalo

STR: Alicia Alonzo, John Ashley, Alfonso Carvajal, Tony Edmunds, Cenon Gonzalez, Johnny Long, Quiel Mendoza, Tita Muñoz, Edward Murphy, Nadja, Ricardo Nipolito, Angelique Pettyjohn, Bruno Punzalan, Ronald Remy, Felisa Salcedo, Paquito Salcedo, and Ronaldo Valdez

AKA: **Tombs of the Living Dead**
Approximately 88m; Color
VID: **Mad Doctor of Blood Island** [Magnum Entertainment; 110(88)m]; **Tombs of the Living Dead** [Sinister Cinema; 83m]
ADL: *No waiting, No appointment. No escape!*

The film that made John Ashley a household name, **Mad Doctor of Blood Island** is the second in a series of wonderfully abysmal horror films based around the mythical "Blood Island" and opens with a butt naked native chased through the jungle and eventually torn apart by a crusty monster. (Watch out for those man-eating plants!) Shortly thereafter, Ashley and Pettyjohn arrive on the island to investigate a report concerning crazed natives with green

La Maldición de la Bestia

blood. There's a bad case of "chlorophyll poisoning" making the rounds, possibly precipitated by Dr. Lorca and his more than likely unorthodox experiments.

This has got to be one of the most amazing PG films ever released, as I seriously doubt that it could squeak by with an R in this day and age. Not only does the film contain a surprising amount of full-frontal nudity, **Mad Doctor of Blood Island** boasts what has got to be the nastiest gore in a 60s film outside of H.G. Lewis' patented atrocities. Hastily torn body parts are strewn about the sets, and we—the viewer—are treated to one of the nastiest pre–**Dawn of the Dead** eviscerations ever staged for our entertainment. Of course, one has to suffer from eyestrain provoked by the most overused zoom lens this side of Jesse Franco's, so be prepared for a migraine.

Besides the cool demeanor of Mr. Ashley, we are exposed to the ample charms of Ms. Pettyjohn (fresh from an appearance in TV's **Star Trek**, and ready to start a string of porn flicks using the pseudonym of "Heaven St. John"). Oh, and let's not forget the dirty dancing natives.

As if this film didn't already have enough going for it, it sponsored an interesting gimmick upon its theatrical release. Theatergoers were given a small vile of "green blood" (probably water and food coloring) and urged to "join the **Mad Doctor of Blood Island** in taking the oath of green blood."

What are you waiting for? Someone to tell you this is a *good* film? God forbid. 🐾🐾🐾 🐈🐈🐈

The Mad People *see* **The Crazies**

Madame Frankenstein *see* **La Figlia di Frankenstein**

Make Them Die Slowly *see* **Cannibal Ferox**

La Maldición de la Bestia *[The Curse of the Beast] (1975)*

ProFilmes S.A. [Spain]
DIR: Miguel Iglesias Bonns; PRO: Modesto Pérez Redondo; SCR: Jacinto Molina Alvarez; DOP: Tomás Pladevall; SFX: Alfredo Segoviano; MFX: Alfredo Segoviano; MUS: CAM
STR: Eduardo Alcazar, Jacinto

La Maldición de la Bestia   164

Molina Alvarez, Carmen Cervera, José Luis Chinchilla, Castillo Escalona, Pepita Ferrer, Indio González, Luis Induñi, Victor Israel, Ann Maria Mauri, Grace Mills, Veronica Miriel, Juan Oller, Ventura Oller, Salomon, Silvia Solar, Fernando Ulloa, Juan Velilla, and Gil Vidal
 AKA: **Dans les Griffes du Loup Garou** [*In the Claws of the Werewolf*]; **Hall of the Mountain King; Horror of the Werewolf; Night of the Howling Beast; The Werewolf and the Yeti**
 Approximately 95m; Color
 VID: **Hall of the Mountain King** [Majestic Home Video; 88(82)m]; **Night of the Howling Beast** [Super Video Inc.; 87m]

A scientific expedition into the Himalayas confirms the existence of the abominable snowman. Anthropologist Waldemar Daninsky is sent in, and... wait a minute. Having fought nearly every classic movie monster in the book, I don't see where he found the time to get his degree. But hold on... he doesn't become a lycanthrope until a third of the way into the film, meaning we're back to square one *again*. (Much like the **Ilsa** films, there's little or no continuity between the entries in the series, and that these are no more than different incarnations of the same character.)

Anyway, Daninsky gets separated from his party, but is saved from certain death by a pair of sisters who watch over a sacred cave he just so happens to stumble into. Much to his post-coital chagrin, the siblings have a penchant for human flesh and—under the light of the full moon—get *really* ugly. He, of course, kills them both in self defense, but not before he receives the predictable "love bite." Then he's off to save his friends from a group of despotic bandits who rape and or impale just about anyone who pisses them off. Obviously, the Yeti is the least of our angst-ridden hero's worries in this humdinger of an entry.

"El Hombre Lobo" strikes again in what is the eighth entry in this long-running series, and is easily one of the best—and goriest—of the lot. (Just to whet your appetites, one woman is skinned alive, one of the unfortunate party members is impaled from ass to shoulder blade, another is beheaded, etc.) Not only is the gore fairly extreme, but the sex is unexpectedly risqué for even a Naschy film with twice the quota of skin and even some softcore fellatio. Still, some things don't change. Our favorite lycanthrope still boasts the same tacky makeup effects as he did in every other film, and he is more than eager to rip open someone's face (as well as drool and spit up blood all over the setpieces when time allows for such frivolities).

Now if only the Yeti could have spun off into his own series...

The Man with Two Faces *see* **Dr. Jekyll and Mr. Blood**

The Man with Two Heads *see* **Dr. Jekyll and Mr. Blood**

Maniac at Large *see* **Passi di Danza Su una Lama di Rasoio**

La Mano Che Nutre la Morte [The Hand That Feeds the Dead] (1974)

Cine Equipe [Italy/Turkey]
DIR: Sergio Garrone; PRO: Amedeo Mellone; SCR: Sergio Garrone; DOP: Emore Galeassi; EXP: Vincenzo Iaccio; MFX: Carlo Rambaldi; MUS: Stefano Liberati and Elio Maestosi
STR: Bruno Arié, Luigi Bevilacqua, Stella Calderoni, Katia Christine, Marzia Damon, Romano de Gironcoli, Klaus Kinski, Carla Mancini, Alessandro Perrella, Osiride Pevarello, Carmen Silvia, Amedeo Timpani, and Pasquale Toscano
AKA: Ölümün Nefesi
Approximately 86m; Color
VID: La Mano Che Nutre la Morte [CVR (PAL); 86m; In Italian]

Retreading ground already staked out by Georges Franju's Les Yeux sans Visage (1959), La Mano Che Nutre la Morte deals with a doctor (the inimitable Klaus Kinski) experimenting with rather unethical skin graft procedures. Although derivative, the film handles the redundant material with more than a modicum of style, and offers Kinski the sort of role in which he works best: a man obsessed. (He remains fairly subdued until the end whereupon—predictably—the spittle begins to spatter the lens.) There is also something about a hunchback being driven mad with a tuning fork, but that's neither here nor there.

La Mano Che Nutre la Morte is an adeptly filmed, nicely photographed period piece that boasts some incongruous gratuity. The surgery footage—supplied by artist Carlo Rambaldi, later of E.T. fame—is fairly intense, some of it being downright disturbing to boot. There is also fair amount of T&A, with a rape scene and some lesbian play thrown in for good measure.

Since—to my knowledge, anyway—an English language print of this film does not exist, one's only exposure to this film is the untranslated Italian video release. Being a particularly talky film, only those truly infatuated with sleazy Eurogothic fare will want to go out of their way for this one. (Maybe someone will end up releasing a dubbed or subtitled version for the English speaking market in the near future; I'm dying to know what the damn ending was all about.)

Keep an eye out for a coffin with Ivan Rassimov's name on it. (I have no clue if the Italian actor was actually inside it or not; he kept pretty quiet if he was.)

Le Manoir de le Terreur see Le Notte del Terrore

Mansion of the Doomed (1975)

Charles Band Productions [USA]
DIR: Michael Pataki; PRO: Charles Band; SCR: Frank Ray Perilli; DOP: Andrew Davis; MFX: Stan Winston; MUS: Robert O. Ragland
STR: Donna Andresen, Richard Basehart, Simmy Bow, Sandy Champion, Barry Chase, Libby Chase, Jo Jo d'Amore, Al Ferrara, Katherine Fitzpatrick, Gloria Grahame, Lance Henriksen, Marilyn Joi, Sally Marr, Del Negro, Barbara Sloane, Arthur Space, Katherine Stewart, Trish Stewart, Patsy Sublime, and Vic Tayback
AKA: Eyes; Eyes of Dr. Chaney; House of Blood; The Terror of Dr. Chaney

Approximately 86m; Color
VID: **Mansion of the Doomed**
[United Home Video; 85(86)m]

A surgeon (Richard Basehart) is reluctant to perform organ transplants until his own daughter is blinded in a car accident. Out of desperation, he drugs his daughter's beau (Lance Henriksen), using him as a guinea pig for a procedure which will hopefully restore the young woman's sight. All goes well... for a while. Revealed to be only a temporary cure-all, the doctor's basement is quickly steeped in blind donors, most of whom are not at all happy about their predicament.

This early shocker from producer Charles Band exhibits adequate production values but boasts some strong performances, a few tense moments, and graphic eye surgery supplied by Stan Winston. (The stuff that isn't the real McCoy, anyway. Winston also proffers some fairly impressive empty eye socket effects, if only because he didn't settle with equipping the actors with black eye patches covered in fake blood like most.) As for the story, they might as well have just called it **Le Yeux sans Visage**, but, hey, that's exploitation for ya'. Richard Band was assistant director.

Directed by the guy who starred in **Grave of the Vampire** (1973) and **Zoltan... Hound of Dracula** (1977). 🎬🎬🎬

La Marca del Hombre Lobo
[The Mark of the Wolf Man] (1967)

Maxper P.C. [Spain]
DIR: Enrique López Eguiluz; PRO: Enrique López Eguiluz; SCR: Jacinto Molina Alvarez; DOP: Emilio Foriscot; EXP: Maximiliano Pérez-Flores; MUS: Angel Arteaga
STR: Rafael Alcántara, Jacinto Molina Alvarez, Carlos Casaravilla, Milagros Ceballos, Aurora de Alba, Antonio G. Escribano, Gualberto Galbán, Victoriano López, Manuel Manzanaque, Juan Medina, Ángel Menéndez, José Nieto, Leonid Orengo, Angela Rhu, Beatriz Savón, María Teresa Torralba, Julián Ugarte, Pilar Vela, Rossana Yanni, and Dianik Zurakowska.
AKA: **Les Fantômes de Dracula** [*The Ghosts of Dracula*]; **Frankenstein's Bloody Terror**; **Hell's Creatures**; **El Hombre Lobo** [*The Wolf Man*]; **Die Vampire des Dr. Dracula** [*The Vampire of Dr. Dracula*]; **Les Vampires du Dr. Dracula** [*The Vampires of Dr. Dracula*]
Approximately 93m; Color [3-D]
ADL: *Sickening Horror to Make Your Stomach Turn and Flesh Crawl!*

A couple of grave robbing gypsies remove a silver cross from the chest of Imre Wolfstein who was rumored to have been bitten by a werewolf in Tibet and forced to endure the "Curse of the Black Star." Revived, he kills them—among others—and is eventually brought down by villagers, but not before he bites ancestor Naschy (né Jacinto Molina Alvarez). Of course, he sprouts a rather nasty five o'clock shadow himself. Some vampires get wind of the situation and decide to use him for their own nefarious plans.

This is the first entry in the "El Hombre Lobo" series, as well as the film which essentially kickstarted the entire Spanish horror trend. (Due to strict reigns on cinema during the Franco regime, genre films made in this country were virtually unheard of.) Although it contains many of the trademarks of Naschy's later fare, it isn't nearly as sexy or gory as these films eventually became; still, there are enough hastily torn throats for it to make the book.

The film was originally released in the U.S. as **Frankenstein's Bloody Terror**, a misleading title, to be sure, but attached by distributors so they could fill "prebooking commitments" for what was supposed to be a Frankenstein film. (The opening credits were altered to reflect this, and the film itself redubbed, making a tenuous association by changing the Daninsky's family name to "Wolfstein..")

Of primary interest are the rumors surrounding the running time. Some sources claim that it originally clocked in at 133 minutes, but the longest print so far comes in at 93 minutes. This leads one to believe that someone misread its 1 hour 33 minute running time which would make it a staggering—and quite dubious—two hours and thirteen minutes long. To add some "credibility" to the claim, a fire razed Maxper Studios to the ground in 1970, destroying the original negatives. (Video Search of Miami's print, mislabeled at 100 minutes, doesn't hesitate to subscribe to the 133 minute version.) Sounds like an urban legend in the making to me, folks.

Mardi Gras Massacre (1978)

Production company unknown [USA]
DIR: Jack Weis; PRO: Jack Weis; SCR: Jack Weis; DOP: Don Piel, Jack McGowan, and Jack Weis; SFX: Mike Nahay; MUS: Westbound Records
STR: Gwen Arment, Butch Benit, Nancy Dancer, Curt Dawson, Cathryn Lacey, Wayne Mack, William Metzo, Laura Misch, and Ronald Tanet
Approximately 92m; Color
VID: Mardi Gras Massacre [VCII Home Video; 92m]

Someone is roaming New Orleans sacrificing "evil" women (prostitutes, of course) to a Peruvian god, possibly Quetzalcoatl (shades of Larry Cohen's **Q—The Winged Serpent**, sans a big flying snake).

While investigating the case, a homicide detective gets involved with an uppity pro, who (of course) is inevitably targeted by the killer. The story is fairly inconsequential, as it's the film's awkward, no-budget approach that makes the material interesting. Wooden performances complement the equally knotty script. If our antagonist didn't stop for so many dramatic pauses, **Mardi Gras Massacre** probably would have clocked in at about half the time. Another actor has to constantly consult the script on the desk before him, usually halfway into his lines. Oh, and let's not forget the rhyming pimp.

There's also lots of skin, some poorly choreographed fight scenes, and a coroner's meatwagon which is actually nothing more than a weathered suburban. And disco music. How can one forget the disco music?

Mardi Gras Massacre is a gorefest in the best H.G. Lewis tradition. There are multitudes of loving close-ups of evisceration. Forget the fact that, apparently, none of the women were born with ribcages, or that the same gore footage is recycled constantly throughout the film.

Somewhat charming. (**Blood Feast** by way of **Saturday Night Fever**?)

El Mariscal del Inferno [The Marshall of Hell] (1974)

Profilmes S.A. [Spain]
DIR: León Klimovsky; SCR: Jacinto Molina Alvarez; DOP: Francisco Sanchez; EXP: Nestor Gaffet and José Antonio Peréz Giner; SFX: E.E.C. and Eugenio Peñalver; MUS: Carlos Vizziello
STR: Jacinto Molina Alvarez, Simon Arriaga, Guillermo Bredeston, Eduardo Calvo, Carmen Carro, José Luis Chinchilla, Jeanette Christensen, Cesar de Barona, Tom de Mosul, Javier de Rivera, Ana Farra, Maria Giani, Luis Induñi, Graciela Kilson, Germán Kraus, Juan Madrigal, Emilio Mellado, Antonio Vidal Molina, Jaime Morano, Sandra Mozarosky, Francisco Nieto, Graciela Nilson, Antonio Orengo, Luis Gonzalez Paramo, Fernando Rubio, Norma Sebre, Joaquim Solis, Adela Vazquez, and Fernando Villena
AKA: **Devil's Possessed**
Approximately 88m; Color
VID: **Devil's Possessed** [All Seasons Entertainment; 90(88)m]
ADL: *Beware the Dungeons of Doom!*

This medieval period piece stars Paul Naschy (*né* Jacinto Molina Alvarez) as an usurper in training selling his soul to the black arts. Instead of a straightforward **Inquisición**-style knock-off, though, **El Mariscal del Inferno** is actually an exploitive retelling of the classic Robin Hood fable. You wouldn't be able to deduce this from the video box which depicts a cowled torturer standing over a bloody victim and poking him with an ominous pokything. The adline is similarly deceiving. There are a few scenes involving the marshall's torture chamber (from where these photos were taken), but these are far and few between.

The bloodshed that the film does contain gets more explicit as the film progresses, neatly complementing the escalating severity of the marshall's crimes, a byproduct of his efforts to gain political control. (Naschy's character is obviously based—albeit tenuously—on the historical figure Gilles de Rais. Why no one has done a faithful translation of this bloodied piece of history, I'll never know as it is rife with the stuff that exploitation filmmakers usually drool over.)

Naschy is as wonderfully unlovable as ever, having built his entire career on playing the part of the tortured monster (both physically and psychologically). Surprisingly, and most atypical for a Naschy vehicle, **El Mariscal del Inferno** is virtually sexless; there is not an ounce of bare flesh in sight, with all copulation transpiring offscreen. (It may have been trimmed by distributors, but you'd think that the violence would have befell the same fate were this the case.) In its stead, we get some poorly choreographed Errol Flynn–style swordplay (with a stand-in for Naschy, obvious in that the stunt double lacks the trademarked barrel chest), an incongruous soundtrack (rock music does not lend itself well to a film where something a little more baroque would have been appropriate), and abysmal dubbing.

Mark of the Devil see **Brenn, Hexe, Brenn**

Mark of the Devil II see **Hexen Geschändet und zu Tode Gequält**

Mark of the Devil 3 see **Alucarda—La Hija de las Tinieblas**

Mark of the Devil Part 2 see **Hexen Geschändet und zu Tode Gequält**

The Mark of the Wolfman see **La Marca del Hombre Lobo**

Martin (1979)

Braddock Associates [USA]
DIR: George A. Romero; PRO: Richard P. Rubenstein; SCR: George A. Romero; DOP: Michael Gornick; SFX: Tom Savini; MFX: Tom Savini; MUS: Donald Rubenstein

STR: John Amplas, Robert Barner, Pasquale Buba, Tony Buba, Harvey Eger, Stephen Fergelic, Christine Forrest, Ingeborg Forrest, J. Clifford Forrest, Jr., Michael Gornick, Al Levitsky, Lincoln Maazel, Nick Mastandrea, Frances Mazzoni, Carol McCloskey, Clayton McKinnon, Fran Middleton, Elayne Nadeau, Robert Ogden, Tony Pantanella, George A. Romero, James Roy, Tom Savini, Albert J. Schamus, Lillian Schamus, Douglas Serene, Jeanne Serene, Donna Siegal, Donald Soviero, John Sozansky, Regis J. Survinski, Vincent D. Survinski, Sarah Venable, and Tom Weber

AKA: **Wampyr** [Vampire]
Approximately 95m; B&W and Color
VID: **Martin** [Anchor Bay Antertainment; 96(95)m]; **Martin** [HBO Video; 95m]; **Martin** [Redemption Video (PAL); 94m]; **Martin** [Thorn EMI Video; 96(95)m]
ADL: *See it with someone you're sure of...*

Martin is a disturbing movie about a young man (Amplas) who suffers from a severe case of blood fetishism and who—for the sake of argument—thinks he's a real vampire. (The gothicized fantasies which loosely correspond to real events are

Martin

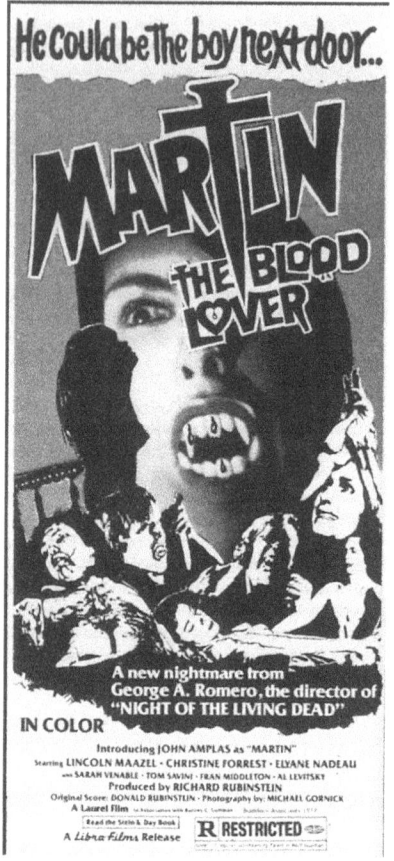

shown in black and white, and stylized after old horror films. It is the film's cold scientific approach coupled with these romanticized delusions that help make this film so far ahead of its time.) The psycho-sexual vampirism that is alluded to in other films is not only brought to the fore, but dissected for the more able-minded viewer.

After taking a routine victim on a train, Martin arrives in Pittsburgh to live with his venerable cousin Cuda. His cousin is convinced that Martin is *nosferatu*, the real McCoy. (Some of the film's more humorous—and compelling—moments revolve around Cuda trying to bring his bloodthirsty kin under control using more traditional methods: Crucifixes, garlic, etc.) A bit of a homebody, Martin becomes a popular guest ("The Count") on a phone-in radio talk show, trying to convince the public and a skeptical DJ that vampires—although real—are much different than the ones that grace the silver screen. Meanwhile, the sexually awkward Martin finds himself being seduced by a lonely wife who has no clue to his predilections.

By far, this is the best realistic vampire flick to date, and probably Romero's most artistic work as well.

Amplas is perfect in the title role, physically as well as emotively; one minute he's naive, almost cherubic. The next, he's cold and manipulative, exhibiting the same chameleon-like charisma as more successful serial killers. (You'd swear the film was tailor-made for the man, as it is impossible to imagine anyone else in the same role.)

The film also boasts Savini's first work for Romero. Although still a bit on the primitive side, the effects are about on par with that in **Dawn of the Dead** (1978), albeit on a much smaller scale. (It is amazing, though, how gory it is for a vampire flick. But, hey, with Romero and Savini, what did you expect?)

Also of note, the Italian release of **Martin** (released there as **Wampyr**) was instead accompanied by a soundtrack by the fusion-rock band Goblin, who also supplied the score for **Dawn of the Dead**.

Required viewing, unless your idea of an exemplary vampire film is **The Lost Boys**. 🐾🐾🐾

Massacre a la Tronconneuse see **The Texas Chain Saw Massacre**

Le Massacre des Morts-Vivants see **Non Si Deve Profanare il Sonno dei Morti**

Masscare Zombie see **Le Notte del Terror**

Meatcleaver Massacre see **Hollywood Meat Cleaver Massacre**

Le Messe Nere della Contessa

Dracula see **La Noche de Walpurgis**

Microwave Massacre (1979)
Reel Life Productions [USA]
DIR: Wayne Berwick; PRO: Craig Muckler and Thomas Singer; SCR: Thomas Singer; DOP: Karen Grossman; MUS: Leif Horvath
STR: Malvina Ackerman, Larry Allen, Allison, Sarah Alt, Elaine Barker, Luigi Bercovici, Debra Draper Berwick, John Beyrooty, Robert A. Burns, Phil de Carlo, Harry Evans, Brad Ford, Norman Friedman, Cindy Gant, Claire Ginsberg, John Harmon, Joel Hurwit, Rory Hurwit, Bill Ingwersen, Tonedeaf Jackson, Aaron Koslow, Al Mannino, Anna Marlowe, Karen Marshall, Craig Muckler, Dick Nibbler, Loren Schein, Bob Shebop, Marla Simon, Ed Thomas, Al Troupe, Jackie Vernon, Greg Walter, and Lou Ann Webber
Approximately 75m; Color
VID: **Microwave Massacre** [Midnight Video; 75m]; **Microwave Massacre** [Rhino Video; 76(75)m]
ADL: *A CREEPY COMEDY ABOUT CADAVERS AND CANNIBALISM.*

A construction worker (yesteryear comedian Jackie Vernon) reluctantly buys his wife a new microwave oven big enough *for the entire family*. He's fed up with the fact that she can't cook a "normal" meal, and—in a drunken fit of desperation—kills her, and—inevitably—eats her. Quickly acquiring a taste for *longpig*, he shares the newfound taste sensation with his unwary co-workers, but it seems there's not quite enough of his wife to go around as he had hoped.

This gore-drenched comedy is actually quite funny at times, although

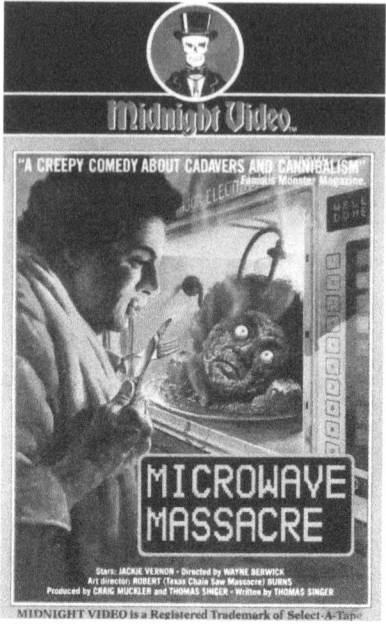

the humor is far from politically correct. And for those who care, **Microwave Massacre** is so damn late 70s: A wha wha peddle-heavy score, gratuitous T&A, and the like punctuate the sleazy, tongue-in-cheek proceedings. It's dumb, yes, but ingratiating nonetheless.

"The producers wish to express their thanks to microwave ovens, without which this movie would have taken much longer."

Model Massacre see **Color Me Blood Red**

Le Monde des Morts-Vivants see **El Buque Maldito**

Mondo Brutale see **Last House on the Left**

Mondo Cannibale II—Der Vogel-

mensch see **Ultimo Mondo Cannibale**

Los Monstruos de la Noche [The Monster of the Night] (1969)
Eichberg Film [West Germany] International Jaguar [Italy] and Producciones Jaime Prades [Spain]
DIR: Tulio Demichelli and Hugo Fregonese; PRO: Jaime Prades; SCR: Jacinto Molina Alvarez; DOP: Godofredo Pacheco; EXP: Jaime Prades; MFX: Rafael Ferrer; SFX: Antonio Molina; MUS: Franco Salina
STR: Jacinto Molina Alvarez, Peter Damon, Manuel de Blas, Angel del Pozo, Karin Dor, Ella Gessler, Craig Hill, Ferdinando Murolo, Fadja Nicol, Michael Rennie, Gene Reyes, Patty Shepard, Diana Sorel, and Luciano Tacconi
AKA: **Assignment Terror**; **Dracula Jagt Frankenstein**; **Dracula Vs. Frankenstein**; **El Hombre Que Vino de Ummo** [*The Man Who Came from Ummo*]; **Los Monstruos del Terror** [*The Monster of Terror*]; **Operacione Terror** [*Operation Terror*]
Approximately 89m; Color
VID: **Dracula vs. Frankenstein** [United American Video; 77m]

Aliens decide to conquer the world using, no, not a giant death ray or other earth-shattering device, but by reviving and utilizing the combined talents of Dracula, the Wolfman, Frankenstein's Monster, and the Mummy. Of course, the werewolf is none other than Paul Naschy (*né* Jacinto Molina Alvarez) as the indefatigable Waldemar Daninsky aka "El Hombre Lobo," the anti-hero of now over ten films. There's a bit more to it than that, but, really, what else do you need to know?

173   Il Montagna del Dio Cannibale

By sacrificing its gothic trademarks for more conventional monster mash antics, this—the third in Paul Naschy's popular "El Hombre Lobo" series—is by far one of the weakest, most awkward entries. By no means is this a denouncement of **Los Monstruos de la Noche**; if anything, the contrivances which evoke such "classics" as **House of Frankenstein** and **House of Dracula** (1944 and 1945, respectively) make it one of the more entertaining films of the lot.

Predictably, many of the scenes center around at least one of the four stock beasties, 60s interpretations of the classic Universal monsters. (Unfortunately, this leaves little screen time for Paul Naschy and his profuse drooling, but one can't have it all.) Sadly, all of the monsters are actually quite ineffectual; both Dracula and the Mummy come across as real pushovers, and the Frankenstein Monster just doesn't look all that scary with his sideburns and paste-on felt eyebrows. Oh, well; Daninsky didn't need the competition anyway.

Throw in a xenophobic conspiracy, some real-life surgery footage, and scads of gratuitous sex and violence, and you have a real barn-burner of a horror film. (As enjoyable as it is, though, it was best for the series that future installments brought Waldemar Daninsky's exploits back down to earth—so to speak—thus giving them *some* level of respectability, as dubious as it was.)

Be warned, though; the only English language print available stateside (clocking in at about 77 minutes) is nearly unwatchable, having been struck from a scratchy, poorly dubbed and hastily edited print that was further trimmed of all of its offensiveness in order to be shown on late-night television. Suddenly, bootlegs don't seem like such a bad option. 🎬🎬🎬

Los Monstruos del Terror *see* **Los Monstruos de la Noche**

Il Montagna del Dio Cannibale [The Mountain of the Cannibal God] (1977)

Dania Film [Italy] and Medusa Distribuzione [Italy]

DIR: Sergio Martino; PRO: Luciano Martino; SCR: Cesare Frugoni and Sergio Martino; DOP: Giancarlo Ferrando; MUS: Guido de Angelis and Maurizio de Angelis

STR: Ursula Andress, Claudio Cassinelli, Franco Fantasia, Stacy Keach, Carlo Longhi, Antonio Marsina, T.M. Munna, Luigina Rocchi, Akushla Sellajaah, Lanfranco Spinola, M. Suki, and Dudley Wanaguru

AKA: **Prisoner of the Cannibal God; Slave of the Cannibal God**

Approximately 99m; Color

VID: **Slave of the Cannibal God**
[Wizard Video; 86(84)m]
ADL: *THEIR CULT WAS DEATH... THEIR LUST WAS FOR BLOOD!*

A woman (Ursula Andress) goes to Papua New Guinea to find her husband, having vanished while on a secretive expedition. She enlists the aid of her hubby's best friend (Stacy Keach) to help her, who seems to know more about his friend's activities than he lets on. They make their way to the island of Roka, home to a sacred mountain revered by cannibalistic natives once thought extinct.

Although it takes a while for the cannibals to show their scarred hides, the film is well paced and offers enough surprises along the way to keep things interesting. The gore is also a long time coming, although the producers try to tide the viewer over by offering the perfunctory geeking, dishing up nauseating scenes of animal cruelty from the get-go.

Ursula Andress, one time wife of John Derek, is forced to endure similar indignities as that of another of John's wives Bo Derek, at JD's hands in the abysmal **Tarzan, the Ape Man** [1981]. Here, though, the ceremony marking the heroine's ascent into White Goddess-hood is much yuckier.

The only other real point of interest is that **Il Montagna del Dio Cannibale** is, as far as I can recall, the first film to include a cannibal dwarf. (Of course, the laws of exploitation demand that he be the most sadistic of the natives.)

If you're a fan of the genre, you know what you're getting into here.

🐱 🐱 🐱

La Morte Viene dal Buio *see* **Rivelazioni di un Maniaco Sessuale al Capo della Squadra Mobile**

Mosaico [Mosaic] (1973)

M.G.D. Film Productions [Italy]
DIR: Mario Mancini; PRO: Benedetto Graziani; SCR: Ferdinando di Leoni and Mario Mancini; DOP: Emilio Varriano; MFX: Carlo Rambaldi; MUS: Daniele Patucchi

STR: Umberto Amambrini, Gigi Bonos, Lemmy Carson, Dalila di Lazzaro, Bob Fiz, Dada Gallotti, Marco

Mariani, Fulvio Mingozzi, Gordon Mitchell, Ciro Papa, John Richardson, Renato Romano, and Marisa Traversi
    AKA: Frankenstein '80; Frankenstein 1980; Les Orgies de Frankenstein '80 [*The Orgies of Frankenstein '80*]
    Approximately 88m; Color
    VID: Frankenstein '80 [MPI Home Video; 90(85)m]
    ADL: *HE HAD A BONE TO PICK...*

A noted German surgeon, Rudolf Schwarz, has created a serum which prevents organ rejection following transplant procedure. An ailing woman is given hope by the medical breakthrough, but dies when the only bottle of the serum is stolen on the night of her heart surgery. Her brother is given permission by Dr. Schwarz to conduct an investigation, all the while someone is walking the streets, killing young women and pilfering their vital organs. Of course, no one even stops to question a certain Dr. Frankenstein who is also a resident surgeon in the hospital. (And why does *he* get a secret laboratory on the premises and nobody else does?) The murders are—another given—being committed by his latest creation which he has dubbed "Mosaic," a creature who seems to get a distinct pleasure out of feeling up the corpses before disemboweling them. (Much like **Black Frankenstein**, the monster's only sexual release is the murders themselves, making for a disturbing mix of titillation and violence.)

    Frankenstein '80 has all the trademarks of 70s Eurotrash: obnoxious zooms, a jazzy score, sleazy excesses, and the like. Production values are substandard, with a script that works overtime in trying to make it all work. (It doesn't, but that's okay.) The focus, of course, is on sex and violence, with the two usually intertwined. If a woman isn't shoving her breasts into the camera lens while being strangled by our patchwork beast, he's raping prostitutes or simply ogling the fresh cadavers. This is imminently followed by graphic scenes of the monster eviscerating them, the sometimes convincing effects consisting of no more than pig gut and red paint. (H.G. Lewis would be proud.) But, despite the film's charming itinerary, **Frankenstein '80** is actually quite forgettable. (If you enjoy it while it's on, I suggest you purchase a copy because you'll inevitably have to crack the case every year or two just so you can remember what it is that you *did* like about it in the first place.) And, yes, the scene with the monster beating a woman to death with a very large femur bone—garishly depicted on the video box—is actually in the film, but even this fact tends to fade from one's memory after a while.

Purportedly, the original version of this film includes numerable shots of the monster's enormous organ, but I have yet to corroborate this. For the sake of trash films everywhere, we can only hope this to be the truth.

For trash fiends only.

Mosquito der Schander [Mosquito of Shame] (1976)

Monarex Production [Switzerland] DIR: Marijan David Vajda; PRO: Chris D. Nebe; SCR: Marijan David Vajda; DOP: David Khan; EXP: Manfred Dome and Dominik Huser; MFX: Robert Jacob; MUS: David Llywelyn
STR: Fred Berhoff, Roswitha Geuther, Peter Hamm, Charly Hiltl, Marion Messner, Hary Olsbauer, Werner Pochath, Gerhard Ruhnke, Jony Soster, Ellen Umlauf, Karl Yblagger, and Birgit Zamulo
AKA: **Bloodlust**
Approximately 91m; Color

Having been abused by his father (and seeing him molest his sister as well), a young deaf mute grows up to be a not very well-adjusted adult now harassed by his co-workers. He plays with dolls, breaks into funeral homes, mutilates corpses, and leaves behind a bloody signature ("MQ" for "mosquito"). His crimes begin to escalate, cutting out and saving the corpses' eyes and the like; eventually,

he has a glass straw custom made so he can vampirize the cadavers as well. (The fact that he probably doesn't get more than a mouthful of formaldehyde doesn't seem to deter him.) All the while, he's in love with a flaky redhead who—save for the morbid tendencies—might even be worse off than him.

This low-budget but effective piece of filmmaking is ahead of its time in its depiction and dissection of a serial killer. Furthermore, the gore is fairly nasty, although some of the effects are not nearly convincing as others. (**Mosquito der Schander** is reminiscent of early Spanish horror fare, in particular such films as **Le Jorobado de la Morgue** [1972], both in execution, content, and the clinical look of the gore. Whereas Javier Aguirre's effort is an unrepentant exploitation film, Vajna's is a disturbing profile of a seriously deranged individual, and uses the staples of the exploitation film as a means to an end.)

An exceptional obscurity that warrants more attention.

Il Mostro è in Tavola ... Barone Frankenstein [The Monster and the Slab... Baron Frankenstein] (1973)

Compagnia Cinematografica Champion S.P.A. [France/Italy]
DIR: Antonio Margheriti and Paul Morrisey; PRO: Andrew Braunsberg; SCR: Antonio Margheriti and Paul Morrisey; DOP: Luigi Kuveiller; EXP: Carlo Ponti, Jean Pierre Rassam, and Jean Yanne; SFX: Carlo Rambaldi; MUS: Claudio Gizzi
STR: Liù Bosisio, Joe Dallesandro,

Il Mostro è in Tavola...

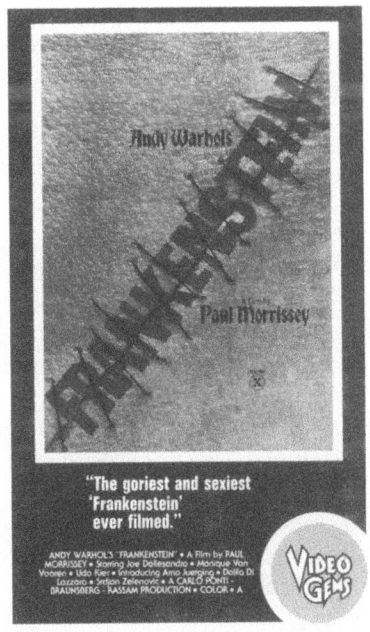

Dalila di Lazzaro, Nicoletta Elmi, Cristina Gaioni, Arno Juerging, Udo Kier, Marco Liofredi, Carla Mancini, Imelde Marani, Fiorella Masselli, Aleksic Miomir, Rosita Toros, Monique van Vooren, and Srdjan Zelenovic
AKA: **Andy Warhol's Frankenstein**; **Carne per Frankenstein** [*Flesh for Frankenstein*]; **Chair pour Frankenstein** [*Flesh for Frankenstein*]; **The Devil and Dr. Frankenstein**; **Flesh for Frankenstein**; **Frankenstein**; **The Frankenstein Experiment**; **Up Frankenstein**
Approximately 96m; Color
VID: **Andy Warhol's Frankenstein** [Air Video; 96m]; **Andy Warhol's Frankenstein** [3-D TV Corp.; 96m; In 3-D]; **Andy Warhol's Frankenstein** [Triboro Entertainment; 93m; R-Rated Version]; **Andy Warhol's Frankenstein** [Triboro Entertainment; 96m; Unrated Edition]; **Andy Warhol's Frankenstein** [Video Gems; 96m]

Considered too sordid, too garish by most art film lovers, and too pretentious and campy by horror fans, this oddly contrived take on Mary Shelley's novel is an adeptly made, often funny exploitation film that revels in gratuity. All of the perverse, psycho-sexual elements that were only hinted at in other Frankenstein films are brought to the fore; curiously enough, they don't seem out of place with the period costuming and gothic trappings.

Baron Frankenstein (Udo Kier) is an obsessive compulsive madman bent on creating a race of Nietzschean archetypes. His assistant Otto (Arno Juerging) is a necrophilic, bug-eyed psychopath. The baron's wife (Monique van Vooren), who is also his sister, is a sexually repressed woman obsessed with aesthetics. And their children are, well, they aren't quite right in the head either, as they like to sneak into daddy's lab and play around with the cadavers. Leave it to a testosterone-driven sheep herder (Joe Dallesandro) and his asexual friend (Srdjan Zelenovic) to mess up their happy little home life. (One learns early on that this film has its tongue planted firmly in cheek, as it's difficult *not* to notice that Dallesandro is running around 19th century Italy sporting a *very* Brooklyn accent.)

Mostro è in Tavola remains a cult favorite, even though most reviewers prefer to write it off completely. Obviously a joke wrapped up in a sometimes beautiful, sometimes blood soaked package, the film refuses to placate any single audience. The dialogue is purposefully stilted or awkward in its presentation. (Such lines as "To know death... you have to fuck life in the gall bladder"—intoned with as much profundity as Udo Kier can muster—is sure to catch the viewer off guard, giving them something worth repeating to friends the next day.) The picturesque photography is marred only by the occasional thrusting of something at the audience (usually breasts or viscera), as the film was originally made and released in 3-D. (How would you have liked to be a part of *that* unsuspecting audience?) Throw in a deliciously downbeat ending which has our hero bound helplessly, surrounded by the bodies of damn near everyone, and being encroached upon by the baron's "curious," scalpel-wielding progeny, and you've got my recommendation.

Although Morrisey receives sole directorial and screenwriting credit on most film prints, it has been cited by Margheriti himself in several interviews that he co-scripted and directed much of the film. Morrisey denies such claims, so it hasn't been fully substantiated. Regardless, he has been given co-credit for both.

If you liked this, check out **Dracula Vuole Vivere—Cerca Sangue di Vergine!**, made back to back with this film and featuring most of the key players, this time screwing with Bram Stoker's characters. ☠☠☠

Mountain of the Cannibal God *see* **Il Montagna del Dio Cannibale**

The Mummy's Revenge *see* **La Venganza de la Momia**

Mundo Canibal! Mundo Salvaje! *see* **Ultimo Mondo Cannibale**

Murder on the Bayou *see* **Eaten Alive**

Mutilated *see* **Shriek of the Mutilated**

The Mutilator (1979) *see* **The Dark**

Die Nacht der Blutigen Wolfe *see* **Dr. Jekyll y el Hombre Lobo**

Die Nacht der Reitenden Leichen *see* **La Noche del Terror Ciego**

Nacht der Vampire *see* **La Noche de Walpurgis**

Nackt un Zerfleischt *see* **Holocaust Canibal**

Die Nackte Gotin der Zombies *see* **La Orgia de los Muertos**

Necromaniac *see* Necrophagus

Necrophagus (1971)
International Films, S.A. [Spain]
DIR: Miguel Madrid; PRO: Tony Recoder; SCR: Miguel Madrid; DOP: Alfonso Nieva; SFX: Medina; MUS: A. Santisteban
STR: Franco Braña, John R. Clark, Titania Clement, Bill Curran, Catharine Ellison, Beatriz Elorieta, Antonio Jiménez Escribano, Yocasta Grey, Victor Israel, Beatriz Lacy, María Paz Madrid, Rosario Royo, and Marisa Shiero
AKA: **El Descuartzador de Binbrook** [*The Dismemberer of Binbrook*]; **Graveyard of Horror**; **Necromaniac**
Approximately 87m; Color
VID: **Graveyard of Horror** [Gee Video; 105(87)m]; **Graveyard of Horror** [Super Video; 88(87)m]; **Necromaniac** [All American Video; 88m]
ADL: *When the crypts are empty, the terror begins...*

A man loses his wife to a failed cesarean while he's away on business. Everyone seems to be hiding something, and are especially reluctant to tell him how she kicked it. Even the authorities refuse to exhume the body upon his insistence, so he takes the initiative and digs her up and— Surprise!—the coffin's empty. So is every other coffin in the graveyard. And somehow, his absent brother works into the equation.

With a silly premise and an even sillier monster at its disposal, **Necrophagus** is so bad it's almost laughable. This muddled mess includes flashbacks within flashbacks, recycled footage, abysmal editing, painfully obvious red herrings, inappropriate "shock music," cultists in Halloween masks, an asthmatic ghoul that looks like a turnip with teeth, and a very trying script. (At one point, a doctor insists that "bears don't eat meat at all." Not only that, but a police chief automatically assumes that a decapitation was the work of a monster, without any evidence pointing to such an irrational conclusion. I'd surely like to know where these two myopic imbeciles got their degrees.)

The film's only saving grace is that, despite a modern day setting, **Necrophagia** is mired in the sort of gothic atmosphere that makes Spanish horror fare so endearing. (One expects Paul Naschy to walk through at any given moment.)

Uninspired drudgery.

Next! *see* **Lo Strano Vizio della Signora Wardh**

The Next Victim *see* **Lo Strano Vizio della Signora Wardh**

Night, after Night, after Night (1969)
Dudley Birch Films Ltd. [UK]

DIR: Lindsay Shonteff; PRO: James Mellor; SCR: Dail Amber; DOP: Douglas Hill; MUS: Douglas Garnley
STR: Jacqueline Clerk, Shirley Easton, Peter Forbes-Robertson, John Gabriel, Carol Haddon, April Harlow, Bernard G. High, Gary Hope, Walter Horsbrugh, Simon Lack, Justine Lord, Linda Marlowe, Jack May, Elisabeth Murry, Michael Nightingale, Yvonne Paul, Terry Scully, Roy Skelton, Jack Smethurst, Donald Sumpter, and Gilbert Wynne
AKA: **He Kills Night after Night after Night**; **Night after Night**; **Night Slasher**
Approximately 88m; Color
VID: **He Kills Night after Night after Night** [Monterey Home Video; 87(88)m]
ADL: *He kills night after night after night... until you could almost set your watch by it!*

Someone is making short work of young women on London's streets. Things get even more serious when a police inspector's wife becomes a victim. Convinced that a young lady-killer is taking the term too literally, he begins hounding him relentlessly, his persistence unabating as the brutal murders continue.

This early entry in the first wave of slasher films is no doubt influenced by the *giallo* thriller, a genre which reached the selfsame year with Dario Argento's **L'Uccello dalle Piume di Cristallo**. The main difference, though, between this UK production and those other whodunits is that here "whodunit" is fairly obvious right off the bat; the scriptwriter probably realized this early on and decided not to expend any more energy trying to conceal the killer's identity.

This film also bears some resemblance to Peter Walker's horror films of the mid-70s in that it displays the same irreverence towards authority; even more pointed is that all aspects of the judicial system are held in contempt.

Night, after Night, after Night is particularly notable for being at least a few years ahead of its time as far as gratuity goes, exhibiting a level of sex and violence that really didn't become commonplace in such films until the early 70s. And it's just plain sleazy to boot.

Jorgé Grau Sola essentially covered the same material much, much better in his 1973 film **Pena de Murte** [*Penalty of Death*].

Night of the Blind Dead *see* **La Noche de las Muerte Ciego**

Night of the Blood Cult *see* La Noche de las Gaviotas

Night of the Bloody Apes *see* La Horriplante Bestia Humana

Night of the Death Cult *see* La Noche de las Gaviotas

Night of the Demon (1979)

Aldan Company Inc. [USA]
DIR: James C. Wasson; PRO: Jim L. Ball; SCR: Mike Williams; DOP: John Quick; SFX: Susan Brott; MUS: Stuart Hardy and Dennis McCarthy
    STR: Joy Allen, Bunny Bernhardt, Philip Boyd, Rob Camp, Bob Collins, Shannon Cooper, Michael J. Cutt, Shane Dixon, Eugene Dow, Lynn Eastman, Heather Eide, Virginia English, Richard Fields, Melanie Graham, Don Hurst, Ray Jarris, Paul Kelleher, Michael Lang, Greg Langdon, Jodi Lazarus, Reneta Lee, William F. Nugent, Mark Olay, Fred Owens, Mark Phelan, Kathy Stimac, Sally Swift, Dix Turner, and Terry Wilson
    Approximately 95m; Color
    VID: **Night of the Demon** [VCII; 97(95)m]
    ADL: *The ultimate horror has been conceived during the... Night of the Demon*

Under the direction of their college professor, six students are off in pursuit of a killer sasquatch—the selfsame creature responsible for the death of one of the girls' father. Although they don't seem to have much luck in tracking the elusive creature down, it doesn't seem to have any problem finding victims wandering near the reserve where it lives, knocking them off with as much contrived innovation as it can muster (with a little help from the screenwriter, of course).

Night of the Demon is the most brutal, and probably most inept bigfoot flick ever conceived. (That's saying a lot in reference to the latter.) The direction is perfunctory, which isn't encouraging when the actors have all the emotional range of lobotomized thespians with hangovers. (To compensate, it seems, there's a lot of footage of running feet. Just the feet.) Either because of the tight budget, or to pad out what they thought would be a shy running time, it looks as if no footage was left on the cutting room floor, and the entire finale-cum-massacre is played out in slow motion.

Not convinced yet? Okay, here's the *really* good stuff. There is absolutely no shortage of gratuitous sex and violence. Besides the nudity, offal is strewn liberally about the sets. Not only are the killings gory, but—as I alluded to earlier—quite imaginative, especially to have been perpetrated by a pissed off throwback. One biker gets his testicles ripped off by the furry critter while urinating alongside the road, and two girl scouts are forced to stab each other to death with their pen knives by the selfsame galoot. And let's not forget where he almost whips several people to death with one of their friend's intestines!

There's a bigfoot cult, sasquatch-vision and rocking chair-cam, a bigfoot rape which culminates—nine months later—with a half human offspring (actually, it's a baby doll covered in blood and mohair, but don't tell the filmmakers we know), and, best of all, is the creature himself

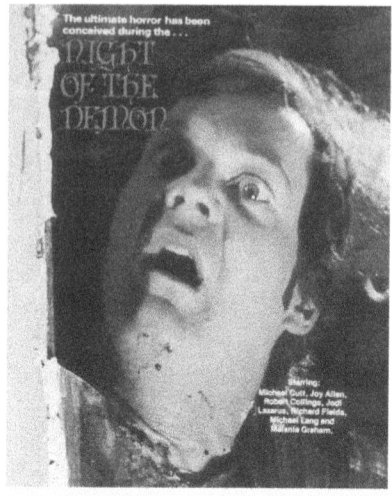

which could conceivably be passed of as Lou Ferrigno on a bad hair day.

By far, the best bigfoot gore film ever made.

Night of the Devils see **La Notte dei Diavoli**

Night of the Howling Beast see **La Maldicion de la Bestia**

Night of the Living Dead (1968)

Image Ten [USA]
DIR: George A. Romero; PRO: Karl Hardman and Russell W. Streiner; SCR: George A. Romero and John A. Russo; DOP: The Latent Image, Inc.; SFX: Tony Pantanello and Regis J. Survinski
STR: William Burchinal, Randy Burr, Bill Cardille, Sharon Carroll, Charles Craig, Alvin C. Croft, Frank Doak, Marilyn Eastman, Jack Givens, Karl Hardman, Ross Harris, Lee Hartman, S. William Hinzman, Steve Hutsko, Dave James, Duane Jones, George Kosana, A.C. McDonald, Joann Michaels, William Mogush, Judith O'Dea, Marc Ricci, R.J. Ricci, Richard Ricci, Jason Richards, Paula Richards, Judith Riley, George A. Romero, Kyra Schon, John Simpson, Ella Mae Smith, Phillip Smith, Samuel R. Solito, Herbert Summer, and Keith Wayne
AKA: **La Noche de los Muertos** [*The Night of the Dead*]
Approximately 96m; B&W
NOV: **Night of the Living Dead** by John A. Russo [Pocket Books]; **Night of the Living Dead** by John A. Russo [Warner Books]
VID: **Night of the Living Dead** [Anchor Bay Entertainment; 108(96)m]
ADL: *They keep coming back in a bloodthirsty lust for HUMAN FLESH!*

You know the story: A group of strangers wall themselves up in an isolated farmhouse, besieged by the walking dead and their insatiable appetite for human flesh.

Despite the simple premise, this low-budget Pittsburgh based production went on to become one of the most influential horror films of all time. Not only did it sire two superb sequels (and kick off the career of George A. Romero, a much-revered genre filmmaker), it inspired countless "zombie" films. No longer was the name applied only to the mythical, voodoo-spawned creatures that were showcased in films like **White Zombie** (1932) and **I Walked with a Zombie** (1943); "zombies" had come to be known as something quite different to the younger generations.

These creatures were no longer mindless slaves who struck fear simply with their crusty visage, but flesh-eating cadavers driven by nothing more than a primal urge to consume their living kin, created by everything from toxic spills to pathological maladies. They were now ghouls of the Atomic Age.

Much has been written about this film's socio-political subtexts, but—when all is said and done—**Night of the Living Dead** is a brutal, tense shocker whose power lies in its ability to tap into our primal fears. Dated by today's standards (black and white photography, restrained gore, the by-now formulaic proceedings), the film still retains much of its effectiveness as a shocker if only because of its sincerity, something lacking in most of the films that followed in its footsteps.

Although not nearly as gratuitous as H.G. Lewis' films were at the time, **Night of the Living Dead** is one of the first splatter films to successfully reach a mainstream audience, *and* garner some positive reviews from the press. By the time its sequel, **Dawn of the Dead**, came out ten years later, audience expectations had increased ten-fold, thanks to the progressively gorier outings cashing in on the selfsame gut-munching formula. Thirty years after Romero kickstarted the subgenre, the demand for gore has leveled off, but zombie flicks—whether they be over-the-top homegrown efforts or subdued mainstream offerings—remain. And rarely is there any mention of their Haitian cousins.

Required viewing.

Night of the Seagulls *see* **La Noche de las Gaviotas**

Night of the Sorcerers *see* **La Noche de los Brujas**

Night of Vengeance *see* **Last House on the Left**

Night Slasher *see* **He Kills Night, after Night, after Night**

Nights of Terror *see* **Le Notte del Terrore**

The Nights of the Werewolf *see* **La Noches del Hombre Lobo**

Nightstalker *see* **Don't Go Near the Park**

No Profanar el Sueño de los Muertos see Non Si Deve Profanare il Sonno dei Morti

La Noche de las Gaviotas
[The Night of the Seagulls]
(1975)

Ancla Century Films [Spain] and Profilmes S.A. [Spain]
DIR: Amando de Ossorio Rodríguez; PRO: Jose Angel Santos; SCR: Amando de Ossorio Rodríguez; DOP: Francisco Sánchez; SFX: Antonio Vidal Molina and José Gomez Soria; MFX: Cristobal Criado; MUS: Antón García Abril
STR: José Antonio Calvo, Jan Antonio Castro, Susana Estrada, Julia James, María Kosti, Sandra Mozarowsky, Victor Petit, Oscar Phens, Javierde Rivera, Julia Saly, Pilar Vela, María Vidal, and Fernando Villena
AKA: **Das Blutgericht der Reitenden Leichen** [*The Bloodlaw of the Riding Dead*]; **Night of the Blood Cult; Night of the Death Cult; Terror Beach**
Approximately 85m; Color
VID: **Night of the Death Cult** [Sony Video; 90(85)m]
ADL: *A village possessed by unspeakable evil...*

A doctor arrives with his wife in a small coastal village, much to

the chagrin of the town's inhabitants. It turns out his timing is impeccable, as the community is in the grip of the Templars, vampiric zombies that demand ritual sacrifice in return for the safety of the remaining townspeople. Partly out of desperation, the newcomers decide to go against the grain and—not only fend off the advances of the undead but deny them a young girl given up as an offering.

This, the fourth and final installment in Amando de Ossorio Rodríguez' impressive "Blind Dead" series, is another atmospheric shocker that could have only been made in the 70s. Despite reiteration, the crusty ghouls that punctuate each film are still effective and unnerving, a testament to the ingenuity of low budget filmmaking. Everything that has been said about the previous films (**La Noche del Terror Ciego, El Ataque de los Muertos sin Ojos,** and **El Buque Maldito,** 1971, 1973, and 1974, respectively) can be applied to La Noche de las Gaviotas as well. Cool stuff.

La Noche de las Muerte Ciego *see* La Noche del Terror Ciego

La Noche de los Brujos *[The Night of the Sorcerers] (1970)*

Profilmes S.A. [Spain]
DIR: Amando de Ossorio Rodríguez; PRO: José Antonio Pérez Giner and Luis Laso Moreno; SCR: Amando de Ossorio Rodríguez; DOP: Francisco Sánchez; EXP: Luis Laso Moreno and Ricardo Muñoz Suay; MUS: Fernando Garcia Morcillo
STR: Simon Andreu, Marisol Hernández, Barbara King, María Kosti, Jack Taylor, José Telman, and Loretta Tovar
Approximately 83m; Color
VID: **The Night of the Sorcerers** [Unicorn Video; 76m]

"Deep in the jungles of the Congo, a young English girl is captured by natives practicing black magic. As part of their voodoo ritual, the girl is beheaded and transformed into a vampire leopard witch. Immediately after an English patrol opens fire and kills all the natives. Sixty years later a wildlife expedition happens upon the area. A local trader tells the group about the terrible legend of the vampire leopard woman and that the dead natives return to life to celebrate their sorcery. He advises the group to leave, but they scoff at his story. That night the beautiful blonde photographer for the expedition goes to the sacrificial site. She is captured by the zombie natives and the vampire leopard woman who rakes her bosom with a whip and severs her head with a gleaming machete. Now there are two vampire leopard women. What follows is a macabre tale of violence, murder and rape as jungle drums beat out a rhapsody of terror and death."

Whew. No, the writers of the video box synopsis are not making this up. And, yes, it is even worse than it sounds.

Before making his mark with the Blind Dead series, director Amando de Ossorio Rodríguez made this feature. Although it boasts many of the same staples which became an integral part of the Blind Dead films, La Noche de los Brujos is a sad little shocker that evokes none of the same frissons. Furthermore, the film seems mired in racism and sexism, its proceedings relying entirely on one's xenophobia or fear of the opposite sex. And, as could be ascertained from the poorly written—but very accurate—synopsis, the supernatural aspects are too hokey to be effective, following only a stream of consciousness logic. And, yes, it's similarly gratuitous as his later films.

Definitely good for a few laughs, but disappointing considering the film's progenitor.

La Noche de los Diablos *see* **La Notte dei Diavoli**

La Noche de los Muertos *see* **Night of the Living Dead**

La Noche de Walpurgis [The Night of Walpurgis] (1970)
Hi-Fi Stereo 70 KG [West Germany] and Plata Films S.A. [Spain]
DIR: León Klimovsky; PRO: José Antonio Pérez Giner; SCR: Jacinto Molina Alvarez and Hans Munkel; DOP: Leopoldo Villaseñor; EXP: Modesto Pérez Redondo; SFX: Antonio Vidal Molina; MUS: Antón García Abril
STR: Jacinto Molina Alvarez, Ruperto Ares, Barta Barri, Bárbara Capell, Eduardo Chappa, Gaby Fuchs, Luis Gaspar, José Marco, Julio Peña, Rupert Piros, Andrés Resino, Yelena Samarina, Betsabe Sharon, Patty Shepard, and Maria Luisa Tovar
AKA: **Blood Moon**; **La Furie des Vampires** [*The Fury of the Vampires*]; **La Messe Nere della Contessa Dracula** [*The Black Masses of Countess Dracula*]; **Nacht der Vampire** [*Night of the Vampire*]; **La Nuit des Loup Garous** [*The Night of the Werewolf*]; **Vampirlerin Gecesi**; **The Werewolf vs. the Vampire Woman**; **The Werewolf vs. the Vampire Women**; **The Werewolf's Shadow**; **Werwolf's Shadow**
Approximately 95m; Color
VID: **Blood Moon** [Air Video; 90m]; **The Werewolf Vs. the Vampire Woman** [Something Weird Video; 95m; In English and Spanish; LBX]; **Werwolf's Shadow** [Express Home Video (PAL); 83m; In Spanish w/Greek subs; LBX]; **Werwolf's Shadow** [Video Memory (PAL); 83m; In Spanish w/Greek subs; LBX]
ADL: *Don't just be afraid... be terrified!*

A small town doctor makes a grave mistake while performing an autopsy when he removes two silver bullets from the corpse of one Waldemar Daninsky. (Even worse, he waited until a full moon to do the routine examination.) Several months later, two college students discover—with the help of host Daninsky—the tomb of a blood-drinking Hungarian countess. (No, it's not Elisabeth de Báthory, but it might as well be.) Not only are the two women unaware of Daninsky's malediction, they inadvertently revive the countess, now a vampire. (Removing the silver cross from her ticker was bad enough, but then they had to go and bleed all over the corpse.)

For those familiar with Spanish horror, this is a typical outing for

La Noche de Walpurgis

Paul Naschy (*né* Molina). Besides the wide selection of ghosts and ghouls (one of which looks suspiciously like one of Amando de Ossorio's Templars, even though this predates his Blind Dead films), there is also the welcome gratuity to spice up the old world horrors. Gore is fairly strong for the time—especially for Spanish cinema, which was still conservative at this point in time—and nudity is thrown in whenever the script allows. (The original title sequence focuses on a pair of exposed breasts with blood pooling between them. How's that for subtle?) Production values are a bit rough, marred further by cheesy sound effects and tacky slo-mo shots, but the whole mess coalesces into something so endearing that one can't help but look past its many inadequacies.

Usually I don't make mention of specific video releases—good or bad—but feel compelled to in this case. The longest, most complete version of this film available domestically (released as **The Werewolf vs. the Vampire Woman** from Something Weird Video) is, undoubtedly, the worst patchwork job I have ever had the displeasure of coming across. Spliced together from a complete Spanish print and a cut English print, this version is nearly unwatchable. The dialogue jumps back and forth from Spanish to English and back again, as does the soundtrack (when it isn't dropped completely in mid-scene, or repeated—skipping like a broken record—to fill in the silence). Why they didn't just subtitle the Spanish version, I don't know. The print is slightly letterboxed and from a fairly clean master, but this in no way compensates for the ineptitude one has to bear witness to.

This film was later remade (helmed by Naschy himself and boasting a much higher budget) as **El Retorno del Hombre Lobo** [*The Return of the Wolf Man*] in 1980, an attempt to begin anew. Sadly, the later film spawned only one sequel.

Trash horror at its best.

La Noche del Asesino *see* **El Retorno de Walpurgis**

La Noche del Buque Maldito *see* **El Buque Maldito**

La Noche del Hombre Lobo *see* **El Retorno del Hombre Lobo**

La Noche del Terror *see* **Le Notte del Terrore**

La Noche del Terror Ciego
[The Night of the Blind Terror] (1971)

Interfilme [Portugal] and Plata Films S.A. [Spain]
DIR: Amando de Ossorio Rodríguez; PRO: José Antonio Pérez Giner; SCR: Amando de Ossorio Rodríguez; DOP: Pablo Ripoll; EXP: Salvador Romero; SFX: José Gomez Soria; MFX: José Luis Campos; MUS: Antón García Abril

STR: María Elena Arpón, Simon Arriaga, Cesar Burner, Jose Camoiras, Carmen Cir, Juan Cortes, Lone Fleming, Rufino Ingles, Veronica Llimera, Antonio Orengo, Francisco Sanz, Maria Silva, Andres Speizer, and José Telman

AKA: **The Blind Dead**; **Crypt of the Blind Dead**; **Die Nacht der Reitenden Leichen** [*The Night of the Riding Dead*]; **La Noche de las Muerte Ciego** [*The Night of the Blind Dead*]; **A Noite do Terror Cego** [*The Night of the Blind Terror*]; **La Révolte des Morts-Vivants** [*The Revolt of the Living Dead*]; **Le Tombe dei Resuscitati Ciechi** [*The Tomb of the Resuscitated Blind*]; **Tombs of the Blind Dead**

Approximately 101m; Color
VID: **Tombs of the Blind Dead** [Anchor Bay Entertainment; 102(101)m; In Spanish w/English subtitles; LBX]; **Tombs of the Blind Dead** [Midnight Video; 90m]; **Tombs of the Blind Dead** [Paragon Video Productions; 86(87)m]; **Tombs of the Blind Dead** [Redemption Benelux (PAL); 97(101)m; LBX]

ADL: *Don't move... don't breathe... don't let them hear your heart beating...*

It's hard to be objective about a film one finds so utterly endearing, but here it goes. The story is inconsequential, and uses a formula similar to the one used in its three sequels: A handful of people stumble across the stomping ground of the legendary Blind Dead, the animated, bloodthirsty corpses of the infamous Templars burned at the stake centuries before for heresy. The desperate souls try to protect themselves from the blood-drinking zombies (*ala* **Night of the Living Dead**), but are hopelessly outnumbered.

If it was one thing that sets these films apart from all other zombie films, it is the revenants themselves. Unlike their blue-skinned kin, these lumbering corpses are little more than desiccated mummies that claw their way out of their graves each and every night, all but their bony hands and eyeless visages concealed by weathered robes. If this wasn't enough, de Ossorio and crew lay on the atmosphere, thick. Actual crumbling ruins are used for the Templars' resting place. The soundtrack consists of rumbling, Gregorian-like chants. Scenes of the Templars pursuing their prey on horseback are inevitably shown in slow motion, making the action that much more taut. **La Noche del Terror Ciego** even throws in a vampire—one of the Templars' victims—hunting down a young woman in a mannequin factory. The obsessive photography and lighting only accentuate the gothic trappings, further keeping the film from being written off as a simple low-budget shocker wallowing in its own gratuity.

This film was followed up by the equally impressive **El Ataque de los Muertos sin Ojos** [*The Attack of the Blind Dead*] two years later.

A Noite do Terror Cego *see* **La Noche del Terror Ciego**

Non Aprire Quella Porta *see* The Texas Chainsaw Massacre

Non Si Deve Profanare il Sonno dei Morti [Do Not Disturb the Sleep of the Dead] (1974)

Produzioni Cinematografica Flaminia [Italy] and Star Films S.A. [Spain]
DIR: Jorgé Grau Sola; PRO: Edmondo Amati and Manuel Pérez García; SCR: Sandro Continenza, Marcello Coscia, and Jorgé Grau Sola; DOP: Francisco Sampere; SFX: Luciano Bird; MFX: Gianetto di Rossi; MUS: Giuliano Sorgini
STR: Paul Benson, Anita Colby, Vera Drudi, Cristina Galbo, Gengher Gatti, Fernando Hildeck, Joaquim Hinjosa, Arthur Kennedy, José Ruiz Lifante, Ray Lovelock, Aldo Massasso, Isobel Mestre, Jeannine Mestre, Roberto Posse, Vito Salier, Paco Sanz, Giorgio Trestini, and Vincente Vega
AKA: **Breakfast at Manchester Morgue; Dejen Que los Muertos Duermen** [*Do Not Disturb the Sleep of the Dead*]; **Da Dove Vieni?; Don't Open the Window; Fin de Semana para los Muertos** [*Weekend for the Dead*]; **Invasion der Zombies** [*Invasion of the Zombies*]; **Das Leichenhaus der Lebenden Toten** [*The Morgue of the Living Dead*]; **Let Sleeping Corpses Lie; Levende Doden in het Lijkenhuis** [*Living Dead in the Morgue*]; **The Living Dead; The Living Dead at Manchester Morgue; The Living Dead at the Manchester Morgue; La Massacre des Morts-Vivants** [*The Massacre of the Living Dead*]; **No Profanar el Sueño de los Muertos** [*Do Not Disturb the Sleep of the Dead*]; **Weekend per i Morti** [*Weekend for the Dead*]; **Zombi 3 — Da Dove Vieni?**

Approximately 92m; Color
SND: Non Si Deve Profanare il Sonno dei Morti [Beat Records; Split LP w/Paura nella Cittá dei Morti Viventi]
VID: Dejen Que los Muertos Duerman [Video Games de Venezuala; 92m; In English w/Spanish subs]; The Living Dead [AEE Video; 87m]

An experimental device that uses ultrasonic radiation to destroy insects that threaten crop growth has an unfortunate side effect on the populace... at least those buried six feet under. Corpses within proximity of the device are revived and — even worse — have voracious appetites. And — as could be expected — those killed by the zombies are similarly affected.

By far, **Non Si Deve Profanare il Sonno dei Morti** is one of the best post–Night of the Living Dead gut-

La Notte dei Diavoli

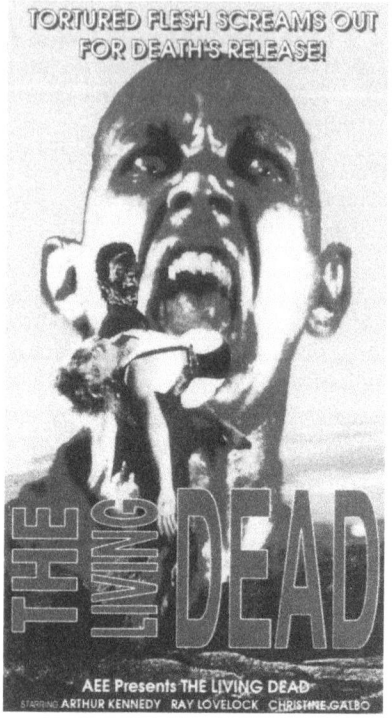

munchers, beat out only by Romero's own sequels (**Dawn of the Dead** and **Day of the Dead**, respectively). This engaging shocker exploits all of the familiar plot devices without reiterating the films it emulates, although plenty of films since have cannibalized Grau's effort with disappointing results. The low budget doesn't only *not* hinder the film, it actually adds to its effectiveness. With only the most primitive means at their disposal, the gore—which surpasses the gratuity in **Night of the Living Dead**—is quite convincing, and even more realistic than some of Tom Savini's effects work in **Dawn of the Dead**.

Whether the action is taking place in a crypt or the eluded-to Manchester Morgue, the atmosphere is laid on thick, itself creating a certain amount of tension long before the zombies poke their heads in the door. The remaining production values are pretty standard for both Italian and Spanish cinema at the time. (Forget the fact that most of **Non Si Deve Profanare il Sonno dei Morti** was filmed in English and, apparently, in the UK; it's spaghetti horror through and through, with some Spanish gothicism thrown in for good measure.)

For a film that has been released so many times under so many monikers, it's amazing that it has never had a stateside release on video. Regardless, it's worth going mail-order for. ☠☠☠

La Notte dei Diavoli [The Night of the Devils] (1972)

Copercines [Spain] Due Emme Cinematografica [Italy] and Filmes Cinematografica [Italy]
DIR: Giorgio Ferroni; PRO: Luigi Mariani; SCR: Eduardo Maria Brochero, Romano Migliorini, and Giambattista Mussetto; [Based on the short story "La Famille du Vourdalak" by Aleksej Tolstoj]; DOP: Manuel Berenguer Serra; EXP: Luigi Mariani; SFX: Carlo Rambaldi; MUS: Giorgio Gaslini
STR: Agostina Belli, Cinzia de Carolis, Teresa Gimpera, Roberto Maldera, Maria Monti, Stefano Oppedisano, Umberto Raho, Luis Suarez, Sabrina Tamborra, Rosita Toros, and William Vanders
AKA: **La Nuit des Diables** [*The Night of the Devils*]
Approximately 84m; Color

A man winds up in an institution, speechless and with amnesia. For some inexplicable reason, he gets antsy when anyone shuts off the lights. He receives a visitor who claims to know his identity; he sees her, goes berserk, and—through a series of convenient flashbacks—we find out why. While lost in the countryside, he smashes his car into a tree trying to avoid hitting a woman. He perchances across a group of peasants burying a bloodied corpse with a mummified baby, and the film is off and stumbling, becoming a gratuitously-inclined remake of Mario Bava's **I Tre Volta della Paura** (1963), or—more specifically—the third segment, both of which were inspired by a famous Tolstoy story.

The intro is particularly confusing, a montage of excess: A woman getting her face literally ripped apart by a shotgun blast; a man in a robe and skull mask feeling up faceless, nude women, some strung up; a heart being ripped out of a chest cavity. Of course, none of this has anything to do with the film in question, and seems to be tacked on simply to up the sleaze quotient and grab the audience's attention. It worked with me, anyway.

La Notte dei Diavoli is an enjoyable piece of gothic Eurotrash that boasts impressive sets, some haunting visuals, a downbeat ending, and some extremely intense gore for the time. Performances are palatable, and the rest of the production values at least as competent.

Not exceptional, but worthy of mention. 🐈 🐈 🐈

Le Notte del Terrore [The Night of Terror] (1979)

Esteban Cinematografica [Italy]
DIR: Andrea Bianchi; PRO: Gabriele Crisanti; SCR: Piero Regnoli; DOP: Gianfranco Maioletti; SFX: Gianetto de Rossi; MFX: Rosario Prestopino; MUS: Elsio Mancuso and Burt Rexon
STR: Antonietta Antnori, Renato Barbieri, Peter Bark, Roberto Caporali, Gian Luigi Chirizzi, Maria Angela Giordano, Simone Mattioli, Anna Valente, Karin Well, and Claudio Zucchetti
AKA: **Burial Ground; Hell Night; La Noche del Terror** [*The Night of Terror*]; **Le Manoir de la Terreur** [*The Manor of the Terror*]; **Massacre Zombie; Nights of Terror; Die Rückkehr der Zombies** [*The Return of the Zombies*]; **Het Schrikkasteel der Zombies; Zombi 3; Zombi Horror; Zombies**
Approximately 85m; Color
VID: **Burial Ground** [Vestron Video; 85m]
ADL: *You have to watch it to believe it!*

The strange goings-on at an archaeological site precipitate an ensuing mass of bloodthirsty zombies *al Italiano*.

In what has to be second worst spaghetti gut-muncher ever propagated (the absolute worst being Umberto Lenzi's **Incubo sulla Città Contaminata**), Le Notte del Terrore is little more than a tired knock-off of Lucio Fulci's **Zombi 2** (made the same year). The film sacrifices cohesion and logic for graphic gore effects; not much of a sacrifice when one realizes just how bad the effects are. (Buckets of juicy pig guts are used to cover up the latex seams, or—when that doesn't quite do the trick—the scenes are underexposed.)

The script is abysmal, and the proceedings tepid. (We won't even get into the silly incest subplot.) Favorite exchange? "Mark... what is it?" "I don't know." "It's horrible." "Whatever it is, it's not human." "I'm terrified, Mark." "C'mon." During this conversation, the two protagonists are just standing there as the zombie encroaches upon them. *Just standing there.* If anyone has ever deserved to die for their stupidity... (No, the *characters*, not the scriptwriter. But then again...) For zombie enthusiasts only.

💀💀💀

Le Notti Erotiche dei Morte Viventi [The Erotic Nights of the Living Dead] (1979)

Production company unknown [Italy]
DIR: Aristide Massaccesi; SCR: Aristide Massaccesi; DOP: Aristide Massaccesi; MUS: Marcello Giombini
STR: Dirce Funari, Laura Gemser, Luigi Montefiori, and Mark Shanon
AKA: **Demonia** [Demons]; **In der Gewalt der Zombies** [*In the Power of the Zombies*]; **Queen of the Zombies**
Approximately 106m; Color

Almost identical to **Dilizie Erotice** (1980) aka **Porno Holocaust** in every way, the single monster here is replaced by a number of low-rent zombies. (The gore is pretty typical of the genre, although the walking dead just love to ooze puss when poked with anything sharp.) The porn scenes are equally flaccid, and *Black Emanuelle* star Laura Gemser does little more than sit around and stare off into space. (She eventually gets enough energy so as to bite off one poor sap's member, but it's barely worth the effort—in respect to both her *and* the viewer.) The only "highlight" (which should say something about this film) is getting to see a somewhat talented woman remove a cork from a bottle with her vaginal muscles.

Painfully inept in every way, and only worth seeing for its geek value. XXX

Nueva York Bajo el Terror de los Zombi *see* **Zombi 2**

La Nuit des Diables *see* **Le Notte del Terrore**

Les Nuit des Masques *see* **Halloween**

Los Ojos Azules de la Muneca Rota [The Blue Eyes of the Broken Doll] (1973)

Profilmes S.A. [Spain]
DIR: Carlos Aured Alonso; PRO: José Antonio Peréz Giner; SCR: Carlos Aured Alonso and Jacinto Molina Alvarez; DOP: Francisco Sánchez; EXP: José Antonio Peréz Giner; MUS: Juan Carlos Calderón
STR: Jacinto Molina Alvarez, Pilar Bardem, Eduardo Calvo, Luis Ciges, Eva León, Diana Lorys, Inés Morales, María Perschy, Antonio Pica, and Antonio Ramis
AKA: **House of Doom**; **House of Psychotic Women**
Approximately 84m; Color
VID: **The Blue Eyes of the Broken Doll** [Cannon Video (PAL); 85(84)m]; **House of Psychotic Women** [Super Video; 91(84)m]; **House of Psychotic Women** [VidAmerica; 84m]

Hitchhiker Paul Naschy (né Jacinto Molina Alvarez) is picked up by a woman who wastes no time in offering him a job as a caretaker at an estate owned by her and her sisters. The three women all suffer from debilitating traits: One is scarred and missing half of her hand, another is bound to a wheelchair, and the third is, well, just plain horny. Oh, I almost forgot... they're all apparently nutters as well. (Hence the schlocky American retitling.) Our barrel-chested anti-hero makes his move on the lot of them; unfortunate for them, Naschy is an ex-con, just recently released for the murder of his wife. To make matters even stickier, he's still (occasionally) stricken by the compulsion to strangle the snot out of young women, making him the prime suspect in the eyes of the locals and the authorities when a string of murders occur. (All of them are young women, of course, but the difference in modus operandi—all of their eyes have been neatly removed by the killer—doesn't seem to sway anyone from believing it's our man Naschy.)

Ojos Azules de la Muneca Rota is typical Spanish fare, with an emphasis on sleaze and slack production values. Unfortunately, this *giallo*-style thriller is slow, offering little in the way of mystery, action, or gore until the last reel. What grue there is is enough to pass muster, but the scenes are far and few between, with the appropriated eyes shown only after the fact. (Yes, they're all blue, justifying the really nifty Spanish title.)

Despite what you make think of Naschy's acting ability (or lack thereof), one must grant him that he is always willing to take chances. (And I don't mean every time he opens his mouth, either.) Even though he is the star of this film, he doesn't hesitate in killing himself off well before the finale in order to make the script work.

Avoid the American releases of this flick as they all are missing footage vital in making this the sleazy gem it is. 🐈 🐈 🐈

Once Upon a Frightmare *see* Frightmare

Operacione Terror *see* Los Monstruos de la Noche

La Orgia de los Muertos [The Orgy of the Dead] (1972)

Petruka Films [Spain] and Prodimex Film [Italy]

La Orgia de los Muertos

DIR: José Luis Merino; PRO: Ramón Plana; SCR: Enrico Colombo and José Luis Merino; DOP: Modesto Rizzolo; EXP: Michael O'Hara; SFX: Julian Ruiz and Bianca Verdirosi; MUS: Francesco de Masi

STR: Jacinto Molina Alvarez, Pasquale Basile, Janis Brown, Jose Cardenas, María Pía Conte, Aurora de Alba, Charles Fay, Giusy Garr, Catherine Gilbert, Carla Mancini, Vickie Nesbitt, Alessandro Perrella, Charles Quiney, Isarco Ravaioli, Stelvio Rossi, Harold Stanley, Shirley Stanley, Leonora Vargas, Gerard Tichy Wondzinski, Marcella Wright, and Dianik Zurakowska

AKA: **Die Bestia aus dem Totenreich** [*The Beast from the Kingdom of the Dead*]; **Beyond the Living Dead; Bracula—Terror of the Living Dead; The Hanging Woman; House of Terror; Die Nackte Gottin der Zombies** [*The Night Goddess of the Zombies*]; **L' Orgia dei Morti** [*The Orgy of the Dead*]; **Les Orgias Macabres** [*The Macabre Orgies*]; **Orgy of the Demons; Return of the Zombies—Zombie 3; Der Totenchor der Knochenmänner** [*The Dead Chorus of Death*]; **Zombie 3—Return of the Zombies**

Approximately 91m; Color
VID: **Beyond the Living Dead** [Unicorn Video; 91m]; **The Hanging Woman** [Cinema Centre Films & Video Production; 90(91)m]; **The Hanging Woman** [Showcase Productions; 91m]; **The Hanging Woman** [Fabulous Flicks; 91m]; **The Hanging Woman** [United American Video Corp.; 90(91)m]; **House of Terror** [Wizard Video; 91m]; **Return of the Zombies—Zombie 3** [Edde Entertainment; 91m]

ADL: *FOR THE SQUEAMISH KEEP REPEATING IT CAN'T BE TRUE! CAN'T BE TRUE! CAN'T BE TRUE! CAN'T BE TRUE! CAN'T BE TRUE!*

The daughter of a man laid to rest breaks into his crypt to steal some documents from his person, and is accosted by an unseen assailant with bronchitis. The dead man's nephew comes to town and stumbles across his cousin's corpse hanging from a tree in front of the graveyard. Although the police rule out suicide, the killer's identity remains a mystery, but everyone knows it has something to do with a series of experiments the old man was financing... experiments concerning the re-animation of dead tissue.

This is one of the more engaging Spanish gothfests, and—as could be expected—was made with the participation of cult icon Paul Naschy (né Jacinto Molina Alvarez). Surprisingly, though, his role is relatively small as he plays Igor, a necrophilic gravedigger. Even more surprising is the lack of a hunchback. (Someone must've forgot to save the pillow from **El Jorobado de la Morgue**, made the same year. Luckily, they also forgot to salvage his frightwig from that film as well.) The production values are typical of the time period, and the gore is occasionally nasty. (There is one well-executed decap, and one scene that quite possibly utilizes real autopsy footage. If not, an unfortunate pig carcass was used as a stand-in.) Throw in a handful of blind zombies (no, not the Templars), some effective corpses, and a cheesy "hallucinatory" sex sequence which has the cinematography spinning his camera over the bed of the participants wildly.

Recommended for fans of splatter Español.

L'Orgia dei Morti see **La Orgia de los Muertos**

Les Orgies de Frankenstein '80 see **Mosaico**

Les Orgies Macabres see **La Orgia de los Muertos**

Orgy of Blood see **Brides of Blood**

Orgy of the Dead see **La Orgia de los Muertos**

Orgy of the Demons see **La Orgia de los Muertos**

The Parasite Murders (1976)
DAL-Reitman Productions [Canada]
DIR: David Cronenberg; PRO: Ivan Reitman; SCR: David Cronenberg; DOP: Robert Saad; EXP: Alfred Pariser; MFX: Joe Blasco; MUS: Ivan Reitman
STR: Kirsten Bishopric, Joan Blackman, Barry Boldero, Robert Brennen, Joy Coghill, Dorothy Davis, Silvie Debois, Fred Doederlein, Camille Ducharme, Kevin Fenlow, Sonny Forbes, Cathy Graham, Arthur Grosser, Paul Hampton, Edith Johnson, Nora Johnson, Lynn Lowry, Wally Martin, Alan Migicovsky, Ronald Mlodzik, Denis Payne, Charles Perley, Susan Petrie, Hanka Posnansko, Al Rochman, Felicia Shulman, Joe Silver, Barbara Steele, Vlasta Vrana, Roy Whittan, and Julie Wildman

AKA: **Frissons** [*Shivers*]; **Shivers**; **They Came from Within**

Approximately 87m; Color
VID: **Shivers** [Alpha Video (PAL); 87m]; **Shivers** [Anchor Bay Entertainment; 110(87)m]; **Shivers** [Avalanche Home Entertainment; 91(87)m; Director's Cut]; **They Came from Within** [Vestron Video; 87m]

ADL: *Going mad is just the beginning of the terror!*

The Parasite Murders

Starliner Towers, a self-sufficient apartment complex on a small, man-made island, offers more than just innumerable conveniences to its tenants. It can also tout itself as being the birthplace of a sexually transmitted parasite that confers to its host an insatiable libido. By the time the resident doctor tracks down the source of the strange occurrences plaguing the microcosm, it has become an epidemic that threatens to spread far beyond the building's walls.

David Cronenberg's directorial debut (as far as feature-length films go) help set the mold from which most of his later films were cast. His obsession with the flesh, and with the darker side of scientific progress, forms the foundation of his thought-provoking, bloodstained oeuvre. (His second film, **Rabid**, seems to be a natural extension of this shocker, and so forth.) From its disturbing opening which exposes the dark underbelly of a convenience-oriented society, Cronenberg fills the screen with a surreal viscerity previously unseen in most horror films. (It is no surprise that Romero's **Dawn of the Dead** deals with similar themes. By film's end, **The Parasite Murders** has become **Night of the Living Dead** by way of the promiscuous 70s.)

The low budget complements the shock effects, and adds to the unhealthy feel of the material. The repulsive phallic-like leeches that are a physical manifestation of the disease are quite impressive, as is some of the bladder effects, also by Joe Blasco. (Soon to become an abused effect in 80s and 90s genre fare, the bladder effects displayed in **The Parasite Murders** are still some of the best ever committed to screen.) And, of course, the story accommodates a fair amount of sex and violence, neither gratuitous, but the latter usually pretty intense.

On hand for downbeat festivities are Barbara Steele (scream queen icon of the 60s) and Lynn Lowry, the "Queen of Disease Films," as a nurse who eventually succumbs to the bug. (With such films as **The Crazies** and **I Drink Your Blood** to her credit, it's difficult not to label her as such.)

Recommended.

Pasos de Danza Sobre el Filo de una Navaja *see* **Passi di Danza Su una Lama di Rasoio**

Passi di Danza Su una Lama di Rasoio [Dance Steps on a Razor's Edge] (1972)

S.E.F.I. Cinematografica [Italy] and Producciones Balcazar S.A. [Spain] DIR: Maurizio Pradeaux; SCR: Alfonso Balcazar, Arpad de Riso, George Martin, and Maurizio Pradeaux; DOP: Jaime deu Casas; EXP: Francisco Balcazar; MUS: Roberto Pregadio

STR: Simon Andreu, Orlando Baralla, Salvatore Borgese, Anuska Borova, Carlo Carli, Robert Hoffman, Anna Liberati, Rodolfo Lolli, George Martin, Nerina Montagnani, Nieves Navarro, Serafino Profumo, Giovanni Pulone, Helga Lina Stern, Cristina Tamborra, and Rosita Toros

AKA: **Death Carries a Cane; Maniac at Large; Pasos de Danza Sobre el Filo de una Navaja** [*Dance Steps on a Razor's Edge*]; **Tormentor**

Approximately 91m; Color

VID: **Tormentor** [Wizard Video; 90(91)m]

ADL: *SCREAMING CAN'T SAVE YOU FROM HIS STEELY BLADE.*

Passi di Danza Su una Lama di Rasoio is a chauvinistic *giallo* thriller that could quite possibly be more convoluted than most of its peers. Besides the run-of-the-mill whodunit meanderings mired in red herrings and unconvincing coincidences, we are treated to scads of pointless softcore sex scenes and graphic throat slashings. The barely competent production values include painful close-ups and—exclusively for the English-speaking market— remarkably bad dubbing. (When the lead heroine remarks that she's "got to go pee pee," you wonder of the people responsible for the translation really take their job seriously.)

The film's only, and I mean *only* high point is Wizard Video's box art. The cover sports a photo of a nude woman sprawled out, split up the middle (let's see someone get away with that *now*), and a painting of a killer sporting a gleaming blade standing overhead. The back depicts two tense scenes with the aforementioned killer confronting a potential victim, and one with himself being confronted by the police. All fine and dandy, except these are all scenes from an entirely different film, namely Jesús Franco Manera's **El Sadico de Notre Dame** (1974/1979) which was also released by Wizard Video under the title **Demoniac**. (That video release sports a cover which is completely incongruous, so one wonders if the art department at Wizard—shall we say—fouled up somewhere along the line. After reading the video box synopsis for their release of **Anthropophagus II** aka **Monster Hunter**, this seems to be a perfectly valid assumption.) Don't bother.

Penetration (1976)

Production company unknown [Italy/U.S.A]
DIR: Roberto Bianchi Montero; PRO: Eugene Florimont; SCR: Luigi Angelo, Sergio Canevari, Italo Fasan, Roberto Bianchi Montero, and Francesco Vanorio; DOP: F. Rossi; MUS: Giorgio Gaslini
STR: Chris Avram, Eufemia Benussi, Bruno Boschetti, Luigi Ciavarro, Angela Covello, Jessica Dublin, Nino Foti, Farley Granger, Phillipe Hersent, Annabella Incontrera, Sylva Koscina, Fabrizio Moresco, Nieves Navarro, Krista Nell, Paul Oxen, Sandro Pizzorro, Irene Pollmer, Kim Pope, Harry Reems, Luciano Rossi, Tina Russell, Andrea Scotti, Ivano Staccioli, Benito Stefanelli, Marc Stevens, and Silvano Tranquilli
AKA: **Bad Girls**

Running time unknown; Color
ADL: *The ultimate X crime*

This film is actually Roberto Bianchi Montero's **Rivelazioni di un Maniaco Sessuale al Capo della Squadra Mobile**, released in the United States with unrelated hardcore inserts two years after its initial theatrical release. XXX

La Perversa Senora Ward *see* **Lo Strano Vizio della Signora Wardh**

Pesticide *see* **La Raisins de la Morte**

Petrification *see* **La Plus Longue Nuit du Diable**

Phantasm (1978)

New Breed Productions, Inc. [USA]
DIR: Don Coscarelli; PRO: D.A. Coscarelli; SCR: Don Coscarelli; DOP: Don Coscarelli; SFX: Paul Pepperman; VFX: Modern Film Effects and The Westheimer Co.; MUS: Fred Myrow and Malcolm Seagrave
STR: David Atntzen, A. Michael Baldwin, Reggie Bannister, Bill Cone, Lynn Eastman, Lawrence Rory Guy, Susan Harper, Ken Jones, Terrie Kalbus, Kathy Lester, Laura Mann, Ralph Richmond, Myrtle Scotton, Mary Ellen Shaw, and Bill Thornbury
AKA: **The Never Dead**
Approximately 88m; Color
VID: **Phantasm** [Magnetic Video Corporation; 90(88)m]; **Phantasm** [Nelson Entertainment; 88m]

Phantasm

ADL: *Where the dead are no longer that way...*

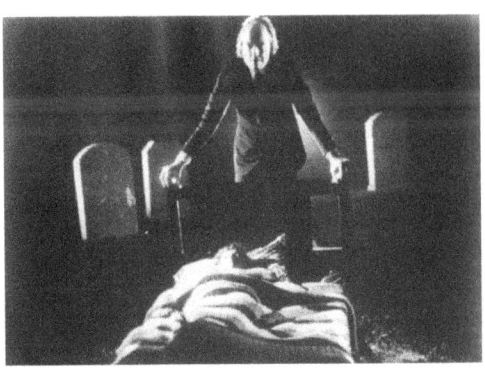

A man is killed while doing the nasty in a graveyard. The authorities claim it was a suicide, although his friend's younger brother begins to think otherwise when he witnesses some strange goings-on at the cemetery following the services. He eventually convinces his brother after bringing back some "evidence," and the two of them team up with an ice cream vending, guitar playing, ponytail wearing friend (Reggie Bannister) in order to get the bottom of the inexplicable events which involve grave robbing and alien conspiracies.

Despite its shortcomings, **Phantasm** still manages to be an unpredictable and spooky experience twenty years after its initial release. (For which it received an X-rating, due solely to a fairly bloody scene involving a flying sphere, a drill bit, and some poor hick's receding hairline.) This surreal exercise is splatter and science fiction ballyhoo manages to capture the ingenuity and intensity that is rarely realized in films boasting much higher budgets.

Although one's suspension of disbelief is constantly put to the test, the film's lack of logic actually contributes to the film's nightmarish quality. The viewer's tendency to relate to the just-as-confused heroes is of sufficient momentum to keep their interest. One is even quick to look past the film's rough edges: In-consistent performers, stilted dialogue, jolting editing, and some hokey, dime-store effects are its more noticeable detriments. (As for the latter, the adjective of "dime-store" is not just figurative as a bug used in one of the more effective sequences was purchased from a small variety store. Apparently, the one they wanted for the scene wasn't big

Michael Baldwin, Bill Thornbury, Reggie Bannister, Kathy Lester

enough, so they had to settle with a larger—and inherently cheaper-looking—stand-by.)

Highlights include a soundtrack which—when not depending on church organ drones—is on par with John Capenter's earlier outings, and a truly creepy performance from one Angus Scrimm (*né* Lawrence Rory Guy) as "The Tall Man," one of cinema's more memorable bogeymen.

Phantasm is an engaging film that surpasses its limitations; apparently, there must've been some interest as filmmaker Coscarelli has just finished **Phantasm IV—Oblivion** as of this writing.

Piranha (1978)

New World Pictures [USA]
DIR: Joe Dante; PRO: Jon Davison; SCR: John Sayles; DOP: Jamie Anderson; EXP: Roger Corman and Jeff Schechtman; SFX: Jon Berg; MFX: Rob Bottin and Vincent Prentice; VFX: Adam Beckett; MUS: Pino Donaggio
STR: Belinda Balaski, Bruce Barbour, Paul Bartel, Barry Brown, Jack Cardwell, Shannon Collins, Richard Deacon, Bradford Dillman, Virginia Dunnam, Hill Farnsworth, Bruce Gordon, Eric Henshaw, Guich Koock, Kevin McCarthy, Heather Menzies, Dick Miller, Shawn Nelson, Jack Pauleson, Robyn Ray, Roger Richman, Bill Smillie, Janie Squire, Barbara Steele, Michael Sullivan, Melody Thomas, Robert Vinson, and Keenan Wynn
Approximately 89m; Color
VID: **Piranha** [Warner Home Video; 89m]
ADL: *Lost River Lake was a thriving resort until they discovered... PIRANHA*

A mutant strain of piranha is created by the government for purposes of biological warfare, but—after being kept under wraps for several years—it is inadvertently let loose upon an unsuspecting resort community. An assortment of B-actors are on hand to convince others of the unseen menace, or become fish food. (Qualifying for the latter half is also an entire camp full of young children, making this film even more endearing to bent individuals like myself.)

This fun, often tense little nature-gone-berserk flick was made back in the days when Roger Corman and his crew of able hands churned out quality B-films; it is of little surprise that director Joe Dante and scriptwriter John Sayles eventually hit the big time, although neither ever came close to capturing the charm of their earlier efforts.

Piranha reiterates the formula established by **Jaws**, but manages to do this with a modicum of intelligence *without* sacrificing all of the

staples important to drive-in fare. The gore is occasionally nasty, and there's even a cute stop-animation critter thrown into the works.

A popular favorite, **Piranha** inspired not only two sequels, but a remake seventeen years after the fact.

Porno Holocaust *see* **Le Notti Erotiche de Morti Viventi**

Les Poupées du Professeur Hichcok *see* **Bestia Uccide a Sangue Freddo, La**

Les Poupées Sanglantes du Docteur X *see* **La Bestia Uccide a Sangue Freddo**

Prey (1977)
Tymar Film Production Limited [UK]
DIR: Norman J. Warren; PRO: Terence Marcel and David Wimbury; SCR: Max Cuff; DOP: Derek V. Browne; EXP: Kevin J.J. O'Driscoll; MFX: Harry Hampton; MUS: Ivor Slaney
STR: Glory Annan, Sandy Chinney, Jerry Crampton, Sally Faulkner, Eddie Stacey, and Barry Stokes
AKA: **Alien Prey**; **Le Zombie Venu d'Ailleurs** [*The Zombie That Came from Elsewhere*]
Approximately 85m; Color
VID: **Alien Prey** [Comet Video; 85m]; **Alien Prey** [VEC; 85m]; **Prey** [Arthouse Video [PAL]; 74m]
ADL: *Their unearthly hunger makes us all... ALIEN PREY*

Two lesbians in an isolated country house unknowingly take in a stranded alien. Although he seems normal enough, he occasionally gets real ugly and can only eat raw meat. (Human, preferably.)

Not much of a story, huh? By mid-way, the girls decide to dress their xenophagic guest in drag; he doesn't put up much of a fight, if only because there's no one else around to kill, and there's still a good forty minutes of the running time to kill. The murders are fairly gory (six in all by film's end), but this and the softcore sex can sustain the droll proceedings for any length of time.

The cast seems capable enough, but the crew isn't nearly as experienced. Worst of all, when the alien shows his true face, he looks like an extra from the musical **Cats**, sans a silly tail.

A sleazy—but uneventful—shocker from the man who brought us the more engaging (but no less schlocky) **Inseminoid** four years later.

Prisoner of the Cannibal God see Il Montagna del Dio Cannibale

Profondo Rosso [Deep Red] (1975)

Seda Spettacoli [Italy]
DIR: Dario Argento; PRO: Claudio Argento; SCR: Dario Argento and Bernardino Zapponi; DOP: Luigi Kuveiller; EXP: Claudio Argento; SFX: Germano Natali and Carlo Rambaldi; MUS: Giorgio Gaslini and Goblin
STR: Aldo Bonamano, Clara Calamai, Giuliana Calandra, Liana del Balzo, Nicoletta Elmi, Vittorio Fanfoni, Dante Fioretti, David Hemmings, Geraldine Hooper, Gabriele Lavia, Iacopo Mariani, Glauco Mauri, Piero Mazzinghi, Furio Meniconi, Macha Meril, Fulvio Mingozzi, Daria Nicolodi, Eros Pagni, Lorenzo Piani, Salvatore Puntillo, and Piero Vida
AKA: **Bloedlink** [*Bloodlink*]; Deep Red Hatchet Murders; Les Frissons de l'Angoisse [*The Shudders of Anguish*]; The Hatchet Murders; Rojo Oscuro [*Deep Red*]; The Sabre-Tooth Tiger; Suspiria—Part 2
Approximately 121m; Color
VID: **Deep Red** [Columbia Video; 105m; W/Japanese subs; LBX]; **Deep Red** [Fletcher Video (PAL); 105m]; **Deep Red** [Redemption Video (PAL); 121m]; **Deep Red Hatchet Murders** [Thorn EMI/HBO Video; 100m]; **Profondo Rosso** [Domo Video; 121m; In Italian w/Japanese subs]
ADL: *When the screaming starts and the blood begins to flow... Pinch yourself and keep repeating I'm at the movies! I'm at the movies! I'm at the movies! I'm at the movies!*

A psychic "sees" a long forgotten murder committed by a member of her audience while giving a demonstration. She is brutally dispatched, at home, that selfsame night with a meat cleaver. The murder is witnessed by a pianist (David Hemmings) who—unknowingly—saw who committed the crime, but can't recall the exact details. With the aid of a journalist (Daria Nicolodi), he tries to piece together the clues, aware that the killer has targeted him as well.

Profondo Rosso is not only one of Dario Argento's best films, it is also one of the best *giallos* made since the genre was initiated by Mario Bava in 1964 with **Sei Donne per l'Assassino**. Utilizing all of the elements from said films (a masked, black-gloved killer; a series of seemingly random, usually innovative murders; et al.), Argento backs up the mind-boggling mayhem with stylistic flourishes that distract the viewer from any flaws that may result from the convoluted script. Although the director's previous films are also exemplary entries in the genre, it is here his distinct style reaches full maturity, and the first time the camera itself becomes a major player in the cast. The visual intensity that marks this film became a recognizable element in all of his works since (although it is quite lacking in his work following the outstanding **Opera**, made twelve years later).

Profondo Rosso also marks the first time Argento took his already violent tendencies to gore-drenched extremes. Not content with slit throats and the like, **Profondo Rosso** depicts not only graphic hackings, but one of the more ingenious decapitations offered to an unsuspecting audience. Unlike many films that followed suit, though, the murders are not just gratuitous, but quite disturbing... a talent many of Argento's peers obviously don't have.

The film also boasts one of Goblin's most impressive scores, and is the first collaboration between the director and the prog-rock outfit (whose name would become synonymous with Argento and his work). Opening with a haunting theme that has been copied by other film composers too numerous to mention, it quickly gives way to one of Goblin's most frenetic, jazzy scores, not only accompanying the action but incorporating itself with the proceedings.

Highly recommended.

Il Profumo della Signora in Nero [The Perfume of the Lady in Black] (1974)

Euro International Films [Italy]
DIR: Francesco Barilli; PRO: Giovanni Bertolucci; SCR: Francisco Barilli and Massimo d'Avack; DOP: Mario Masini; MUS: Nicola Piovani

STR: Nike Arrighi, Daniela Barnes, Gabriele Bentivoglio, Maurizio Bonuglia, Ugo Carboni, Mimsy Farmer, Sergio Forcina, Roberta Gadringher, Luigi A. Guerra, Jho Jhenkins, Donna Jordan, Carla Mancini, Orazio Orlando, Alexandra Paizi, Mario Scaccia, and Renata Zamengo

Approximately 100m; Color

An overworked scientist (Mimsy Farmer) intent on winning the Nobel Prize begins to suffer from hallucinations that reflect a troubled childhood. Is it a psychological response, fraught over her mother's suicide? Or are the occurrences actually supernatural in origin?

This bloody *giallo* is a paranoid "everyone *is* out to get me" thriller that boasts the presence of Mimsy Farmer, who even for her puts in an exemplary performance. (Not surprisingly, her role is similar to the one she had in Armando Crispino's **Macchie Solari** the same year, so she might've still been in character for all we know.) Overall, the production values are above average for early 70s *Italiana*, with an emphasis on striking photography and eerie atmosphere.

As with many Italian thrillers at the time, the violence is quite heavy-handed, although most of the gore is relegated to the last reel. Of note, there are some nasty meatcleaver murders (à la **Profondo Rosso**) and an evisceration, the likes of which didn't become commonplace until **Dawn of the Dead** four years later.

If you have a hankering for exemplary giallos, then **Il Profumo della Signora in Nero** is worth sniffing out.

Psycho Puppet *see* **Delirium** (1977)

Queen of Black Magic *see* **Ratu Ilmu Hitam**

Queen of the Zombies *see* **La Notti Erotiche de Morti Viventi**

In Quella Casa Buio Omega *see* **Buio Omega**

¿Quien Puede Matar a un Niño? [Who Could Kill a Child?] (1975)
Penta Films [Spain]
DIR: Narciso Ibañez Serrador; PRO: Manuel Perez; SCR: Narciso Ibañez Serrador [Based on the short story "El Juego" by Juan José Plans]; DOP: José Luis Alcaine; SFX: Sixto Rincoin; MUS: Waldo de los Rios
STR: Javier de la Camara, Lourdes de la Camara, Maria Durille, Lewis Fiander, Luis Mateos, Roberto Nauta, Prunella Ransome, and José Luis Romero
AKA: **Death Is Child's Play; Island of Death; Island of the Damned**
Approximately 114m; Color
VID: **Island of Death** [NK Video (PAL); 87m]

A married couple (and their unborn child) touring Europe visits the island of Almanzora just off the coast of Venice. Oddly enough, no one on the island is old enough to sport pubic hair; they just run into one suspicious kid after another. Eventually, they come across what remains of some of the adults, and find themselves fearing for their lives.

¿Quien Puede Matar a un Niño? is something of a rarity: a low-budget shocker that is both grisly and suspenseful, and is intelligently written without sacrificing any of its visceral intensity. (Although the impetus behind the murders is never fully explained, the screenwriters sadly decide to imply that they are supernatural in origin instead of being some sort of scientific aberration.)

The film relentlessly dissects one of our most ingrained taboos, as implied by the title. (Not only does the director take to heart my cinematic credo of "kill off children at each and every opportunity," he also took it to an unprecedented extreme.) Having stripped them of their innocence, these children are now to be judged solely on their value as human beings, although the parents-to-be have difficulty accepting this psychology, even at the expense of their own well-being.

Production values are typical of Spanish fare at the time, but the engaging themes and adept direction make it seem that much better. There is some gore, the highlight being a disturbing piñata scene involving a fresh corpse and a scythe.

With that spooky-looking girl from Amando de Ossorio's Rodríguez' **La Endemoniada** (1974).

Rabid (1976)

The Dilbar Syndicate [Canada]
DIR: David Cronenberg; PRO: John Dunning; SCR: David Cronenberg; DOP: René Verzier; EXP: André Link and Ivan Reitman; SFX: Al Griswold; MFX: Joe Blasco Makeup Association and Byrd Holland
STR: Terry Angelo, Julie Anna, Monique Belisle, John Boylan, Jeanette Casenare, Marilyn Chambers, Valda Dalton, Lynne Deragon, Victor Desy, Terry Donald, Richard Farrell, Miguel Fernandes, Basil Fitzgibbon, Marcel Fournier, Patricia Gage, John Gilbert, Bob Girolami, Harry Hill, Una Kay, Kathy Keefler, Denis Lacroix, Isabelle Lajeunesse, Yvonne Lecompte, Grant Lowe, Sherman Maness, Kirk McColl, Gary McKeehan, Peter McNeill, Jack Messinger, Ron Miodzik, Frank Moore, Allan Moyle, Louis Negin, Malcolm Nelthorpe, Robert O'Ree, Madeline Pageau, J. Roger Periard, Susan Roman, Terrence G. Ross, Howard Ryshpan, Terry Schonblum, Joe Silver, Bob Silverman, Murray Smith, Riva Spier, Jerome Tyberghlen, Greg van Riel, Vlasta Vrana, Mark Walker, and Carl Wasserman
AKA: **Rage**
Approximately 90m; Color
NOV: **Rabid** by Richard Lewis [Mayflower Books]
VID: **Rabid** [Warner Home Video; 90m]

A motorcycle accident victim is rushed to the nearby Keloid Institute (which specializes in plastic surgery) for an immediate life-saving surgery. Taking advantage of the situation, a doctor decides to try out an experimental procedure, replacing internal tissue with a skin graft that has been treated by a solution that makes it morphogenetically neutral. Although comatose, everything seems to be going okay until she displays a phallic spur protruding from an anus-like opening beneath her armpit, and a thirst for human blood. Worse still, anyone she taps is stricken by an incurable rabies-like disease that is spread from person to person.

Although unrelated, this film picks up thematically where **The Parasite Murders** left off, offering a more brutal, but ultimately less nihilistic view of science gone awry. (Instead of molding itself after **Night of the Living Dead**, this film—Cronenberg's second mainstream effort—seems to tread the same territory as Romero's later **The Crazies**.) The gore is more gratuitous, and the production values are upped a notch (save for some annoying stock music, in particular the orchestral hits that punctuate scenes otherwise intense).

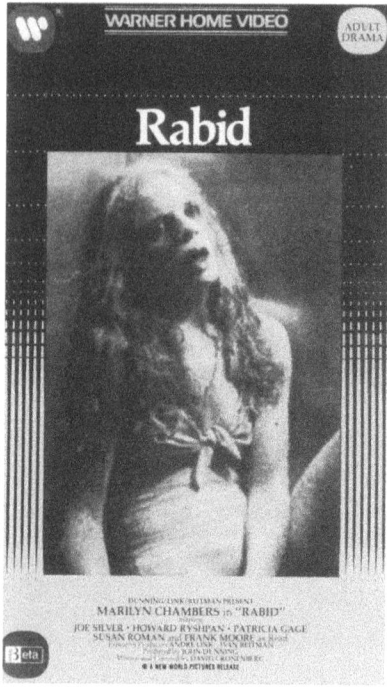

Rage *see* Rabid

Les Raisins de la Mort [The Grapes of the Dead] (1978)

Les Films ABC [France] Off Productions [France] and Rush Productions [France]
DIR: Jean Rollin; PRO: Claude Guedj; SCR: Jean-Pierre Bouyxou, Christian Meunier, and Jean Rollin; DOP: Claude Becognée; SFX: Yannick Josse, Raphael Moronjiv, and Alfredo Tiberi; MUS: Philippe Sissmann
STR: Paul Biscaglia, Jean-Pierre Bouyxou, Patricia Cartier, Michel Herval, Serge Marquand, Felix Marten, François Pascal, Marie-Georges Pascal, Mirella Rancelot, Jean Rollin, Olivier Rollin, Evelyne Thomas, Patrice Valota, and Brigitte van Meerhaegue
AKA: **Foltermühle der Gefangenen Frauen** [*The Torture Mill of Women Prisoners*]; **Pesticide**
Approximately 87m; Color
VID: **Les Raisins de la Mort** [Video Search of Miami; 84m; LBX]

Of historical interest is that **Rabid** marks the first "legit" screen appearance of Marilyn Chambers, star of **Behind the Green Door** and a handful of other adult "classics." For those who don't know, she received her notoriety by starring in the aforementioned filming shortly after modeling for Ivory Snow detergent; I guess someone found offense to a porn star appearing on a nationwide product, with a baby, representing the girl next door. (Her straight career also ended with this film; considering that her performance barely passes muster, it's no surprise.)

Cronenberg continued the trend—albeit on a more claustrophobic level—with **The Brood** (1979), another highly effective shocker.

A woman and her friend are accosted on a train by a sprayer exposed to a pesticide whose side effects include skin slip and an appetite for destruction. Her traveling partner is killed, and she jumps the train and wanders off into the desolate countryside. Apparently, it's become an epidemic; following several close encounters with death, the young woman stumbles across a small town where all hell has broken loose, thanks to the pesticide and the resulting tainted wine.

Although cited as a zombie flick, **Les Raisins de la Mort** owes little to George Romero's **Dawn of the Dead** (1978) and everything to his earlier effort **The Crazies** (1973).

There is some graphic gore, but it is (thankfully) more subdued than the rubbery carnage that appears in Rollin's later films like **La Morte Vivante** (1982). (Still, some of the makeup—in particular the cheesy facial applications—leave something to be desired, but a brutal decap helps make up for this.) Unfortunately, the film isn't nearly as haunting or surreal as his more accomplished efforts, instead relegating itself to being a derivative shocker.

All in all, though, **Les Raisins de la Mort** is an engaging film from France's most accomplished horror filmmaker.

Ratu Ilmu Hitam [Black Magic Queen] (1979)

Rapi Films [Indonesia/Philippines]
DIR: Liliek Sudjio; PRO: Sabirin Kasdani; SCR: Subagio S. and Inam Tantowi; DOP: Asmawi; SFX: E.L. Badrun; MUS: Gatot Sudarto
STR: Ali Albar, Dorman Borisman, Mien Brojo, I.M. Damsyk, Adang Mansyur, W.D. Muchtar, Alan Naury, Teddy Purba, Tizar Purbaya, Belkiez Rachman, Jufri Sardan, Soendoro, Gordon Subandono, Bu Subekto, Doddy Suskma, Suzzanna, Sofia W.D., Siska Widowati, and Jafar Free York
Approximately 85m; Color
AKA: **Black Magic III**; **Black Magic Terror**; **Queen of Black Magic**
VID: **Black Magic Terror** [Twilight Video; 85m]

Ratu Ilmu Hitam—standard Asian trash with the perfunctory revenge motif—doesn't really pick up steam until the second half of the film when all of the mumbo-jumbo hullabaloo finally kicks in, resulting

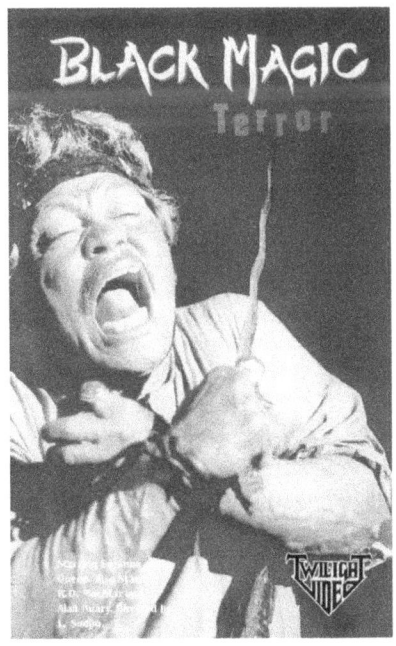

in heaping handfuls of chop socky grue. (Sure enough, we get one of those wonderful "floating head" vampires; this time around, though, we are treated to the accursed victim ripping his own head off first! Usually the departure is not nearly as painful.) Of course, you have to wade through inept dubbing and bland melodrama to get to any meat, but this is the price we must pay for, well, a really bad film.

Unfortunately for this flick, it's not nearly as memorable as other entries in the genre. (With only *one* scene of some poor schmuck throwing up live snakes and insects, it's sorely lacking when pitted against its peers.) What I will commend this film for, though, is the exceptional lack of animal cruelty which is not only commonplace but a staple to said films (including the other, unrelated films in the infamous **Black Magic** series).

If you like what you see here—but can stomach the animal butchery—check out such exemplary films (relatively speaking, of course) as **Devil Sorcery** (1988) and **Mystics in Bali** (1987) to see just how wild this stuff gets.

For Asian horror aficionados only.

Raw Meat *see* Deathline

Realazione a Catena *see* Antefatto

The Red Tide *see* Blood Tide

The Reincarnation of Isabel *see* Riti, Magie Nere e Segrete Orge nel Trecento...

La Reincarnazione *see* Riti, Magie Nere e Segrete Orge nel Trecento...

El Retorno de Walpurgis [The Return of Walpurgis] (1973)

Lotus Films [Spain] and Producciones Escorpion [Mexico]
DIR: Carlos Aured Alonso; PRO: Luis Mendez; SCR: Jacinto Molina Alvarez; DOP: Francisco Sánchez; EXP: Luis Mendez; SFX: Paul Percy; MUS: Angel Arteaga
STR: Jacinto Molina Alvarez, Eduardo Bea, Eduardo Calvo, Fabiola Falcón, Ana Farra, Sandalio Hernández, José Manuel Martín, Jorge Matamoros, Antonio Vidal Molina, Inés Morales, Felicidad Nieto, Maritza Olivares, Santiago Ribero, Ana Maria Rossie, Patty Shepard, María Silva, Pilar Vela, José Yepes, and Elsa Zabala

AKA: Curse of the Devil; La Noche del Asesino [*The Night of the Killer*]; Return of the Werewolf
Approximately 87m; Color
VID: Curse of the Devil [United American Video; 80m]

An inquisitor—one of Waldemar Daninsky's ancestors—kills the husband of Elisabeth de Báthory, so the countess pleads with Satan to grant her revenge and—Voilà—instant curse. Daninsky sends Báthory to the stake, and his bloodline ends up paying. On Walpurgis Night, a heroine gets a post-coital surprise from his ancestor, and from there on it's angst city for Waldemar, who is unable to disclose his little problem to his one true love.

This, one of the poorer made "El Hombre Lobo" outings, is still lots of fun with the prerequisite blood and titillation. As per usual, Paul Naschy (*né* Jacinto Molina Alvarez) mopes around the sets, waiting for the cue to sprout hair and drool profusely. Once again, El Hombre Lobo's origin has been rewritten, although the blame is always laid at the feet of the notorious Báthory, a staple of 70s horror films rooted in European legend. Unfortunately, it's all pretty rote by this time, but future installments tried to up the ante by pitting Daninsky against such antagonists as Dr. Jekyll and the Yeti. (Having already introduced—and disposed of—such stock monsters as Dracula, the mummy, and the Frankenstein Monster in the 1969 entry **Los Monstruos de la Noche,** potential rivals seemed to be at a minimum.)

For Paul Naschy aficionados only.

Retorno del Terror Ciego see El Ataque de los Muertos sin Ojos

Le Retour des Morts-Vivants see El Ataque de los Muertos sin Ojos

Return of Blackenstein see Blackenstein

Return of the Blind Dead see El Ataque de los Muertos sin Ojos

Return of the Exorcist see Un Urlo dalle Tenebre

Return of the Werewolf see El Retorno de Walpurgis

Return of the Zombies see La Orgia de los Muertos

The Revenge of Dracula see Dracula vs. Frankenstein (1971)

Revenge of the Dead see Hollywood Meat Cleaver Massacre

Revenge of the Living Dead (1972) see Children Shouldn't Play with Dead Things

La Révolte des Morts-Vivants see La Noche del Terror Ciego

Riti, Magie Nere e Segrete Orge nel Trecento... [Rites, Black Magic and Secret Orgies of the 14th Century...) (1972)

G.R.P. Cinematografica [Italy]

DIR: Renato Polselli; SCR: Renato Polselli; DOP: Ugo Brunelli; MUS: Romolo Forlai and Gianfranco Reverberi
STR: Anna Ardizzone, Dunca Balsor, Krista Barrymore, Gabriele Bentivoglio, Rita Calderoni, Tano Cimarosa, William Darni, Max Dorian, Vittorio Fanfoni, Stefamia Fassio, Mickey Hargitay, Marisa Indice, Bonini Marcello, Consolata Moschera, Cristina Perrier, and Raoul Traucher
AKA: Black Magic Rites—Reincarnation; The Ghastly Orgies of Count Dracula; The Reincarnation of Isabel; La Reincarnazione
Approximately 98m; Color
VID: **The Reincarnation of Isabel** [Redemption U.S.A; 98m; In Italian w/English subs; LBX]

To be painfully blunt, there is no story, no real narrative to speak of. This movie simply offers bits of filler between scenes of gratuitous sex and violence. We have cultists (sporting green greasepaint, red jammies and black capes) sacrificing young girls to Isabella, a dead nun who was once the lover of Count Dracula. This scenario allows this pointless exercise in sadistic sexploitation to show lots of writhing nude women having their hearts removed and the like. (The unadulterated chaos this film offers is oddly reminiscent of some of José Mojica Marins' Brazilian atrocities, but lacks the presence of a Coffin Joe to keep things engaging.)
 As far as its technical aspects, we have abysmal continuity, innumerable anachronisms (chain link fences in the Dark Ages?), cheesy effects (rubber bats and snakes being pulled with strings), migraine-inducing edits (in

case the "earthquake-cam" didn't do the trick), and enough Christmas tree lights illuminating the set to blind Mario Bava. Oh, and the dialogue: "Vampires need blood that's not comtaminated [sic] by human semen."

Essentially lost for nearly twenty years, one wonders why someone was motivated to actually track down a complete print of it, let alone unleash it on an unsuspecting public. I own it.

Ritual dos Sádicos [Ritual of the Sadists] (1969)

Multifilmes [Brazil]
DIR: José Mojica Marins; PRO: Giorgio Attili, José Mojica Marins, and Jorge Michel Serkeis; SCR: Rubens Francisco Lucchetti and José Mojica Marins; DOP: Giorgio Attili; SFX: Nilcemar Leyart
STR: Ângelo Assunção, Ronaldo Beibe, Andréia Bryan, João Callegaro, Ozualdo Candeias, Maurice Capovilla, José Carlos, Maria Cristina, Emília Duarte, Jaciara Ducena, Jairo Ferreira, Jandira Gabriel, Graveto, Sérgio Hingst, Mário Lima, Annik Malvil, Marcio Marcel, José Mojica Marins, Stela Maris, Claudio Marques, Dante Miná, Paulo Morandi, Ítala Nandi, Helena Nogueira, Palito, Walter C. Portella, Carlos Reichenbach, Luiz Renato, Lurdes Ribas, Jairo Rodrigues, Rosemeire Thiago, and Roney Wanderney
AKA: The Beast Awakens; O Despertar da Besta [*The Awakening of the Beast*]
Approximately 92m; B&W and Color
VID: The Awakening of the Beast [Something Weird Video; 92m]

After some really cool comic book credits, we get to see a woman shooting up (in her foot) while a group of dumbfounded men watch, the room wallpapered with busty girlie pics. Sated, she begins stripping to a 45rpm. Her makeshift audience offers her a pot, in which she apparently urinates. And from here on out, the strangeness doesn't let up for one minute, with more drug use, as well as the usual horrific images associated with Coffin Joe's patchwork atrocities. (The more horror-oriented footage—culled mostly from the director's other films—doesn't begin to rear its ugly head until the last half of the film, and even then the gore is a long time coming.) Intermixed with all of this (using some truly hyper editing) are numerous TV interviews with Coffin Joe himself (José Mojica Marins).

It may be the purest form of artistic expression, and could conceivably be an essay on the tenuous relationship between the sexes, or maybe chemical dependency, or maybe just assume that it's another whacked Coffin Joe effort and leave it at that. (Sorry, but the penis monster—no it doesn't look like a penis, it's actually a *real* penis made up to look like a monster—did it for me. Or maybe it was the Coffin Joe ass caricatures. Yes ... caricatures of Coffin Joe, painted on people's asses. Regardless, it's not Fellini.)

Hey, the band White Zombie saw fit to borrow some samples from this film for their **Astro-Creep 2000** album, so it's got *some* merits.

Rivelazioni di un Maniaco Sessuale al Capo della Squandra Mobile [Revelations of a Sex Maniac to the Chief of Police] (1974)
William Mishkin Motion Pictures [Italy]
DIR: Roberto Bianchi Montero; PRO: Eugene Florimont; SCR: Luigi Angelo, Sergio Canevari, Italo Fasan, Roberto Bianchi Montero, and Francesco Vanorio; DOP: F. Rossi; MUS: Giorgio Gaslini
STR: Chris Avram, Eufemia Benussi, Bruno Boschetti, Luigi Ciavarro, Angela Covello, Jessica Dublin, Nino Foti, Farley Granger, Phillipe Hersent, Annabella Incontrera, Sylva Koscina, Fabrizio Moresco, Nieves Navarro, Krista Nell, Paul Oxen, Sandro Pizzorro, Irene Pollmer, Luciano Rossi, Andrea Scotti, Ivano Staccioli, Benito Stefanelli, and Silvano Tranquilli
Approximately 83m; Color
AKA: **La Morte Viene dal Buio**; **Penetration** (1974/1976); **The Slasher**; **The Slasher ... Is the Sex Maniac!**; **So Sweet, So Dead**
VID: **The Slasher** [Monterey Home Video; 83m]
ADL: *He Has the Whole Town Afraid of the Dark*

This simple-minded *giallo* thriller's sole impetus is the depiction of unfaithful women being sliced to ribbons while in various stages of undress. The very first frame depicts a nude woman, sprawled across a bed, throat slit and breast slashed; the cinematographer strays from this scene only when prompted to do so by necessary exposition. (Needless to say, it's pretty sleazy even without the hardcore sex footage that was added for its American re-release.) Technically, the whole kit and caboodle is painfully average, with unsavory characters across the board. The sexist politics also make it that much more painful to watch. (All women are adulterous whores deserving of their fate, whereas all men are either simply opportunistic, or justified in their hatred of women.)

This film was also released in the U.S.—as **Penetration**—with unrelated hardcore inserts two years after its initial theatrical release. The new footage features such porn luminaries as Harry Reems, Kim Pope, Marc Stevens, and Tina Russell.

Unpleasant stuff, but not in a *good* sort of way.

Rojo Oscuro *see* **Profondo Rosso**

Rückkehr der Reitenden Leichen, Die *see* **El Ataque de los Muertos sin Ojos**

Die Rückkehr der Zombies *see* **Le Notte del Terrore**

The Rue Morgue Massacres *see* **El Jorobado de la Morgue**

SS Campo de Sexo y Violencia *see* **SS Campo Extermination**

SS Campo Extermination [SS Extermination Camp] (1976)
Three Stars 76 [Italy]
DIR: Bruno Mattei; PRO: Marcello Berni; SCR: Giacinto Bonacquisti, Aureliano Luppi, and Bruno Mattei; DOP: Luigi Ciccarese; EXP: Tommy Polgár; MUS: Alessandro Alessandroni
STR: Giovanni Attanasio, Titti Benvenuto, Gabriele Carrara, Dino

SS Campo Extermination

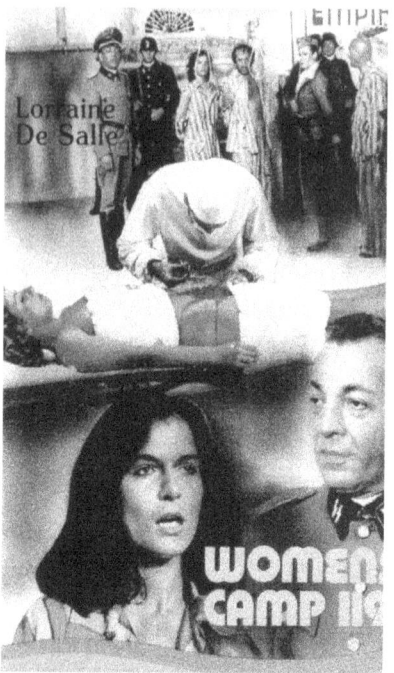

Chiappini, Ennio Cialone, Marina d'Aunia, Lorraine de Salle, Ria de Simone, Miriam Gravina, Eva Hutzar, Gotha Kopert, Manuela Murta, Monica Nikel, Pino Pupella, Nello Rivié, Ivano Staccioli, and Sonia Viviani
AKA: **Le Camp des Filles Perdues** [*The Camp of Lost Women*]; **KZ9 — Lager di Sterminio**; **SS Campo de Sexo y Violencia** [*SS Camp of Sex and Violence*]; **SS Extermination Love Camp**; **Women's Camp 119**
Approximately 110m; Color
VID: **Women's Camp 119** [Empire Video (PAL); 102(110)m; In English w/Dutch subs; LBX]

A nazi doctor at a women's camp is having doubts about the ethical nature of the experiments they perform "in the name of science." (Such experiments include uterus transplants to cure sterile German women, and bringing clinically dead soldiers back to life with sex. Thermal conduction and heat migration play a part in the latter.)

Usually I tend to avoid such films unless, like the Ilsa series, they're particularly repellent. **SS Camp Extermination** ends up making **Ilsa—She-Wolf of the SS** look like an episode of **Hogan's Heroes**. Without a doubt, this is the last say in sleazy nazi atrocity films; although many of these films are brutal in their depiction of scientific sadism, I have yet to find another nearly as graphic in its portrayal of the infamously bloody experiments. (The "highlight" here is an *estremamente disgustoso* uterus removal scene that is guaranteed to make more than a few stomachs churn.)

Typical for films in the genre, production values are low and performances subpar. (One needs a few hits of Dramamine just to make it past the camerawork, believe you me.) Anachronisms abound as well.

As for the important stuff, we get flagellation, rape, gang rape, lesbian rape, bootlicking, catfighting, and necrophilia. Now if that isn't enough, the filmmakers decided to ground it in reality by inserting real WWII atrocity footage, medical textbook disease pics, and an ending that contains retrospectives on real SS officers. But wait... did I mention this was a love story?

Sexist, racist, homophobic, and just in plain bad taste.

SS Extermination Camp *see* **SS Campo Extermination**

The Sabre-Tooth Tiger *see* Profondo Rosso

La Saga de los Draculas [The Saga of the Draculas] (1972)

Profilmes S.A. [Spain]
DIR: León Klimovsky; PRO: José Antonio Perez Giner; SCR: Lazarus Kaplan; DOP: Francisco Sánchez; EXP: José Antonio Perez Giner and Ricardo Muñoz Suay; AST: Andres Vich; MUS: A. Ramirez Angel, Johanne Sebastian Bach, and Daniel J. White
STR: Manuel Barrera, Ramón Centenero, Luis Ciges, Javier de Rivera, Henry Gregor, Tony Isbert, María Kosti, Narciso Ibañez Menta, Mimi Muñoz, J.J. Paladino, Ingrid Rabel, Pepe Riesco, Betsabé Ruiz, Tina Sainz, Helga Lina Stern, Cristina Suriani, Fernando Villena, and Elsa Zabala
AKA: Dracula—The Bloodline Continues; The Dracula Saga
Approximately 92m; Color
VID: Dracula—The Bloodline Continues [All Seasons Entertainment; 91m]; The Dracula Saga [Something Weird Video; 92m]

Dracula and his clan members invite his pregnant granddaughter and her husband to his castle, who find themselves waylaid on the trip when they stumble across an unconscious woman who sports the latest in teeth marks on her throat and breasts. Local townspeople write it off as an animal attack, but it doesn't make them any less leery of his granddaughter's relatives, none of whom has aged a lick in the time she was away from home.

This is an effective and well-photographed period piece that—being an early 70s Spanish production—boasts blood and boobs aplenty. (With an added emphasis on the latter.) There are few surprises early on, but it begins to kick in at the halfway mark, offering some twisted takes on the genre. (The screenwriter also decided to call upon history—in particular, the bloodied history of Dracula's real life counterpart Vlad Tepes of Walachia—in order to ground the more fantastical elements.) The film also benefits from Narciso Ibañez Menta, who makes an extremely effective-looking count.

Unfortunately, the film is not without its cheese. Dracula wears a big stupid cape, and is aided by a crusty-faced cyclopean ghoul (the product of a failed human/vampire coupling). The heroine has dreams about being pursued by someone wearing a big fluffy bat mask. And—of course—the usual corny conventions to which most older vampire flicks adhere.

It's surprising Paul Naschy didn't show up for this one, at least as a token hunchback. (Everyone's favorite ex-wrestler-turned-horror-film-icon can be found, though, playing the Count in Javier Aguirre's *El Gran Amor del Conde Dracula*, made the same year.)

Du Sang pour Dracula *see* **Dracula Vuole Vivere—Cerca Sangue di Vergina!**

Sangeria *see* **Zombi 2**

Sanguella *see* **Zombi 2**

Satan *see* **Brenne, Hexe, Brenn**

Satan's Black Wedding (1974)

Production company unknown [USA]
DIR: Steve Millard; PRO: Tamara Brown; SCR: Steve Millard; DOP: Paul Rogers; MFX: Yvonne Cory; MUS: Roger Stein
STR: Greg Braddock, Barrett Cooper, Osa Danam, Georgia Lemaster, Don Lipsey, Lisa Milano, Ray Myles, Lisa Pons, and Zarrah Whiting
Approximately 59m; Color
VID: *Satan's Black Wedding* [World Video; 61(59)m]
ADL: *A Blood Marriage of Ghouls!*

Under orders from a vampire, a writer slits her wrists after finishing her last book, **High Satanic Rites**. (Boy, she had a lot of red paint in them veins, I tell you.) Her brother flies in from Hollywood and begins his own investigation, convinced

that something is amiss concerning his sister's death. (Gee, maybe the fact that her body was missing a finger had something to do with the authorities ruling out her death as a suicide.) Before you can say "boo," though, she's back, snarling and sporting the biggest, clumsiest pair of dime-store fangs the prop department could muster up.

Even more obscure than Millard's charming **Criminally Insane** (1973) is this no-budget wonder. Unfortunately, it lacks the presence of a Priscilla Alden (crazy fat Ethyl herself) to keep things truly interesting. Otherwise, **Satan's Black Wedding** is about as "competent" as Millard's previous effort: Bargain-basement production values (the 16mm film stock and plastic Halloween fangs should clue you in right away to the level of professionalism we're dealing with here), struggling stage actors, and a spotty script are just the tip of the iceberg. Charming, really.

Despite the nonexistent budget (or maybe *because* of it), this is one of the bloodier vampire films to see the light of day in the 70s. (Of course, had they not squandered most of the funds on red paint, they might've been able to afford better fangs, but these are the sacrifices one must make for their art.)

Satan's Black Wedding shouldn't disappoint the more desperate trash fiends already scraping bottom; everyone else will simply ask "why?"

Satan's Bloody Freaks *see* Dracula vs. Frankenstein (1971)

Satan's Daughters *see* Vampyres

Satans-Bande, Die *see* I Drink Your Blood

Schizo (1976)
Heritage Ltd. [UK]
DIR: Peter Walker; PRO: Peter Walker; SCR: David McGillivray; DOP: Peter Jessop; MUS: Stanley Myers
STR: Paul Alexander, Victoria Allum, Stephanie Beacham, Raymond Bowers, Lindsay Campbell, Terry Duggan, John Fraser, Lynne Frederick, Wendy Gilmore, Pearl Hackney, Colin Jeavons, Diana King, John Leyton, John McEnery, David McGillivray, Robert

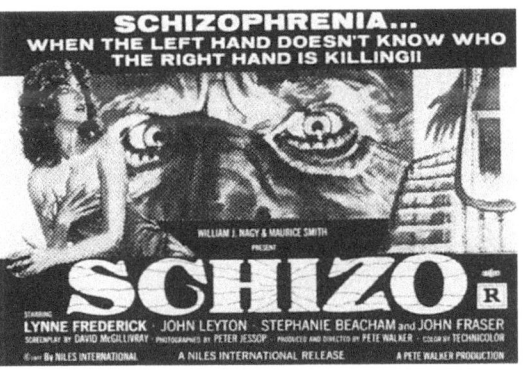

Mill, Tricia Mortimer, Primia Townsend, Jack Watson, Queenie Watts, and Victor Winding

AKA: Amok; Blade of the Ripper; Blood of the Undead

Approximately 108m; Color
VID: Schizo [Interglobal Home Video; 109(108)m]; Schizo [United Home Video; 109(108)m]

ADL: *Schizophrenia... when the left hand doesn't know who the right hand is killing!!*

An old man is perturbed by a wedding announcement in the paper, and goes about harassing the ice skater–cum–newlywed. (Wedding gifts are fine and all, but leaving a bloody butcher knife by the cake might be a little unprecedented.) It turns out that he was put away for murdering the young woman's mother many years before, and it looks like he wants to continue the tradition.

The production values are clean, the editing is often inspired, and—for the most part—**Schizo** is representative of Walker's later work. Unfortunately, it is overlong, and not as unpredictable as one would expect. Worst of all, though, is its unabashed exploitive nature. Like other films, **Schizo** perpetuates the misrepresentation of schizophrenia as multiple personality disorder, and even equates MPD with psychopathic disorders. (A narrator makes these erroneous claims at the start of the film, citing these as documented facts when they are completely unsubstantiated.)

To add insult to injury, there is also some unnecessary hokum thrown into the mix. Still, fans of Peter Walker's films will not be disappointed as the brutal, sometimes gratuitous violence and downbeat twists his name has become synonymous with are present, ready to delight those with a taste for British splatter.

Schizoid (1971) see **Una Lucertola con la Pelle di Donna**

Schizophrenic Murderer see **Frightmare**

Das Schloß der Blauen Vögel see **La Bestia Uccide a Sangue Freddo**

The School That Couldn't Scream see **Cosa Avete Fatto a Solange?**

Het Schrikkasteel der Zombies see **Le Notte del Terrore**

Scream Bloody Murder (1972)

Brian Roberts Productions [USA]
DIR: Marc B. Ray; PRO: Marc B. Ray; SCR: Larry Alexander and Marc B. Ray; DOP: Stephen Buruji; EXP: Brian Roberts; MUS: Rockwell

STR: Ron Bastone, Gloria Earl, Paul Ecenia, Suzette Hamilton, Fred Holbert, Nick Kleinholz III, Robert Knox, Lorence Lea, Marlena Lustik, Leigh Mitchell, Neil Redrick, Bailey Reynolds, Paul Vincent, and Nancy Whetmore

AKA: **Asesino** [*Murderer*]; The Captive Female; Claw of Terror
Approximately 86m; Color
VID: **Scream Bloody Murder** [United Home Video; 90(85)m]; **Scream Bloody Murder** [VGI; 90(85)m]
ADL: *Filmed in violent vision and gory color! So horrifying you need a blindfold to see it!*

A boy gets his hand severed in a tractor accident where his father is killed as well. Traumatized, he is put away for a few years, and has his missing limb replaced by a hook. Years later, he's out, homicidal and sexually maladjusted. After killing his mother and her new husband in a fit of jealous rage, he starts out

La Semana del Asesino

Rosso in un Labirinto do Vetro

La Semana del Asesino [The Wages of a Killer] (1973)

Truchado Films [Spain]
DIR: Eloy de la Iglesia; PRO: Joe Truchado; SCR: Eloy de la Iglesia and Anthony Fos; DOP: Raul Artigot; AST: Louis Gomez; SFX: Baquero; MUS: Fernando Garcia Morcillo
STR: Charlie Bravo, Rafael Hernandez, Lola Herrera, Vicky Lagos, Ismael Merio, Vincente Parra, Eusebio Poncela, Emmanuela Beltrán Rabola, and Valentin Tornos
AKA: **Apartment on the 13th Floor; The Cannibal Man; Week of the Killer**
Approximately 94m; Color
VID: *The Cannibal Man* [Redemption Video (PAL); 94m; LBX]

An initially homophobic slaughterhouse worker bludgeons a taxi driver to death after a skirmish where he refused to pay his tab. His girlfriend promises to leave him unless he goes to the police, so he strangles her. He tells his brother about the murders, and he goes down for the count as well. *Then*, his brother's fiancée comes calling... not a smart move on her part. *Then* his brother's fiancée's father, and, well... pretty soon he's run out of room under his bed, so he starts stacking the putrefying corpses like cord wood on *top* of the mattress. All the while, a neighbor who has a crush on our local butcher has been witnessing the murders through his apartment window. (Our killer doesn't seem to pay any mind to the fact his one-story across country, leaving a trail of corpses, until he settles in a small town where he falls in love with a prostitute. Convincing her he is wealthy, he tries backing up his story by killing a rich widow and her maid and taking over their mansion. Inevitably, he abducts the object of his affection, but everything goes to hell when the old woman's doctor comes a calling.

This trashy splatter flick is, at times, almost interchangeable with **Poor Albert and Little Annie** (aka **I Dismember Mama**), made the year before and graced by the same level of cut-rate production values. Outside of its intrinsic value to trash fiends and aficionados of low-rent 70s horror, there isn't much to recommend. Gore is charmingly shoddy, the acting bad and dialogue stilted, and—like **Poor Albert and Little Annie**'s infamous retitle—the stylish 70s moniker is the best thing going for it.

Sdejen Que los Muertos Duermen *see* **Non Si Deve Profanare il Sonno dei Morti**

The Secret Killer *see* **Gatti**

house has a skylight, or that there's a condominium only a stone's throw away looking down on his place.) Of course, the love stricken voyeur uses this knowledge to his advantage, at least for the time being.

Although **La Semana del Asesino** tries desperately to be more than an exploitation film, it's much too shallow to succeed on any other level. The killer's motives are vague, and the reasons behind his psychological decline unclear. (He doesn't exhibit the traits of a "typical" serial killer, and his desensitization to the violence he commits seems somehow linked to the slaughterhouse for which he works.) On top of all of this, homosexuality is looked upon as deviant behavior, surpassed in its abnormality only by the killer's own loathsome habits.

Technically, the film has some flare, although it is often marred by an extremely inappropriate jazzy soundtrack. The gore is particularly brutal, despite some cuts made by British censors to Redemption's print. The biggest crime made in connection with this film, though, is the erroneous English title; **The Cannibal Man** is a completely misleading moniker as there is not even a mention of anthropophagia.

Worth a look, especially if you're in the mood for some vintage Spanish gore. 🐈 🐈 🐈

Seven Murders for Scotland Yard *see* **Jack el Destripador des Londres**

Sex Crime of the Century *see* **Last House on the Left**

Sexy Cat (1972)

Titanic Films [Spain]
DIR: Julio Perez Tabernero; PRO: Julio Perez Tabernero; SCR: Julio Perez Tabernero; DOP: Alfonso Nieva
STR: Luis Agudin, Germán Cobos, Samuel de Benito, Marques del Toro, Lone Fleming, Pablo Hoyo, Monica Kolpek, Emilio Laguna, Antonio Vidal Molina, Antonio Orengo, Tomas Torres, Maria Villa, and Dianik Zurakowska
Approximately 75m; Color
VID: **Sexy Cat** [Telecine Video; 75m]

A distraught comic book creator hires a private dick to prove that he is the rightful creator of "Sexy Cat," a leather-clad villainess with a penchant for violent murders. Shortly thereafter, the artist is found with his throat slit by an unknown assailant with a Venetian dagger. The investigator approaches the man who is launching the stolen creation as a TV series, befriending the show's star in the process. Not only is she killed as well, but it looks like the fictional character Sexy Cat is herself responsible.

This is an engaging comic book murder-mystery that boasts some rather graphic splatter scenes for the time period. (Sure, H.G. Lewis had already been plumbing the depths of gore for several years, and to a greater extreme, but he was an exception to the rule.) Production values are below average, but only the rather sterile sets (reminiscent of most early porn films) are debilitating.

An interesting, rather fun Spanish obscurity. 🐈 🐈 🐈

Ship of Zombies *see* El Buque Maldito

Shivers *see* The Parasite Murders

Shriek of the Mutilated (1974)

AM Films [USA]
DIR: Michael Findlay; PRO: Ed Adlum; SCR: Ed Adlum and Ed Kelleher; DOP: Roberta Findlay; SFX: Ortun; MFX: Maxim Kinsky
 STR: Ivan Agar, Luci Brandt, Alan Brock, Darcy Brown, Warren d'Oyly-Rhind, Tawm Ellis, Tom Grail, Michael Harris, Morton Jacobs, Dwight Marfield, Harriet McFaul, Jack Neubeck, Jimmy Silva, Marina Stefan, Jennifer Stock, and a bunch of other actors whose names are too small to read.
 AKA: Mutilated
 Approximately 81m; Color
 VID: **Shriek of the Mutilated** [Iver Films Services Ltd.; 81m]; **Shriek of the Mutilated** [Lightning Video; 85(81)m]
 ADL: *College students seeking The Abominable Snowman find a cult of killers on an island of terror!*

God, I despise it when a video company feels the need to give a blow by blow account of a film when the filmmakers have made a valiant attempt to catch the viewer off guard. Part of the joy—if not necessity—of watching a horror film is to be surprised at the unexpected turn of events. (A rarity in itself, I assure you.) Any suspense is completely lost when viewers are forewarned of every last detail in advance, and it is because of microcephalic distributors that I purposefully avoid reading the backs of the video boxes. The story? If you can resist reading the back of the box, suffice it to say that

Shriek of the Mutilated (lovely title, that) involves a group of college students that go to an island retreat in order to investigate the legendary Sasquatch. Of course, they soon find themselves prey to the legendary—but apparently bloodthirsty—walking shag rug.

Maybe I shouldn't be getting so upset when the film in question is one of such a low caliber. Despite its slapdash look and threadbare production values, **Shriek of the Mutilated** is an innovative, well paced, and fun little shocker that belies the "talents" behind it. (Many will recognize the co-conspirating Findlays as those responsible for not only a string of very politically incorrect sexploitation films from the 60s, but the film which eventually became the infamous **Snuff**. Adlum and

Kelleher were responsible for the atrocious but still amusing **Invasion of the Blood Farmers**, to which this bears many similarities.) Wonderfully contrived, and using everything that it's got at its disposal, **Shriek of the Mutilated** falls in the same category as such films as Hennenlotter's **Basket Case**.

A must for fans of low-rent 70s horrors.

Sinner to Hell *see* **Jigoku**

The Sinners of Hell *see* **Jigoku**

Sisters of Satan *see* **Alucarda—La Hija de las Tinieblas**

The Sixth Gate of Hell *see* **The Comeback**

The Slasher *see* **Rivelazioni di un Maniaco Sessuale al Capo della Squadra Mobile**

The Slasher... Is the Sex Maniac! *see* **Rivelazioni di un Maniaco Sessuale al Capo della Squadra Mobile**

Slaughter (1970)
Selected Pictures [Argentina]
DIR: Michael Findlay; PRO: Jack Frost and Michael Findlay; SCR: Michael Findlay and Roberta Findlay; DOP: Roberta Findlay; AST: Roberta Findlay; MUS: Rick Howard
Approximately 80m; Color

Slaughter centers around a Manson-inspired cult and the events leading up to a mass murder obviously inspired by the "Helter Skelter" tragedy. (The only major departure here was that **Slaughter** was staged in Brazil and not the more appropriate Hollywood.)

Satán (or Seytan, either one would probably work) is a well-groomed, gibbering guru who heads a "family" which consists entirely of four (soon five, then four again) biker sluts who spend their off hours disciplining truant members and skinny dipping with their savior. Their vague plans involve guaranteeing the impregnation of a well-known sexploitation actress and sacrificing the unborn child; it is never made clear what the *point* to all this is. (At least Manson's nefarious ploy was grounded in logic, as precarious as it was.)

The fictional actress in question, Terry London, has just recently arrived in South America with her manager-cum-boyfriend Maximilian Marsh for a bout of location shooting. (The alleged film is never shown in production, and the actress is shown spending her time "sleeping in.") Conveniently, a previous one-night-stand of hers lives just down the river, and they resume their "sleeping in" behind Max's back. During one of their romps amid the stir of a Mardi Gras–like festival, Marsh is stabbed to death by an initiate of Seytan's... seemingly to no one's chagrin.

In a punctuated effort to make sure the script catches up to the real-life spree that inspired it, the actress's new boyfriend's spurned girlfriend joins the cult, and allows her new-found friends access to her ex-lover's villa. (Conveniently, their timing is impeccable as they inadvertently crash a drunken party.) They perform an unpleasant *coitus interruptus* on the boyfriend while he is *in flagrante* with a guest's wife. (With his permission, of course.) Saving the best for last, they track down the actress—who is unexpectedly caught doing the nasty as well... with her boyfriend's sexagenarian father—and proceed to carry out their pointless vengeance.

The film **Slaughter** is all that could be expected from the horrendously inimitable Michael and Roberta Findlay: poor editing and camerawork (the film being too often over- or underexposed), incompetent direction, and low-key bloodshed. The post-synch dubbing is also a Findlay trademark; not only is it below par when compared to cut-rate chop-sockey flicks (which says a lot since *they're* not filmed in English as this was), the voice-overs are done by the same crew employed for such Findlay wonders as **A Thousand Pleasures** (1968). (This crew—whom I assume include the Findlays' talents—apparently put in a lot of overtime. I seriously doubt more than four people were responsible for the voices of the dozen-or-so speaking roles herein.)

To stretch out an obviously shy running time, footage is recycled (although not to the extent of **Plan Nine from Outer Space**), and stock footage is often employed, particularly in the aforementioned Mardi Gras-style festivities. (While we're on the subject of "stock" material, cheesy canned music comprises the bulk of the soundtrack, including an excruciatingly repetitive "Born to Be Wild"-style riff which accompanies any and all scenes with the biker sluts on their hogs.)

Unlike earlier Findlay productions, anything of a deviant sexual nature is barely exploited... actually, anything sexual in general. Nudity is relegated to a few topless scenes, and the sparse but overdrawn sex scenes show everything *but* the two people involved. (Not that you really *want* to see any of the actors take off their clothes, but...) Sadly, the sick and twisted charms of **A Thousand Pleasures** or **Satan's Bed** are nowhere to be found, leaving only the incompetent production values and an inability to live up to its unprecedented hype as the infamous **Snuff** six years later.

Slaughter Hotel see **La Bestia Uccide a Sangue Freddo**

Slave of the Cannibal God see **Il Montagna del Dio Cannibale**

Snuff (1976)

Selected Pictures [Argentina] August Films [USA] and Monarch Releasing Corporation [USA]
DIR: Michael Findlay and Simon Nuchtern; PRO: Jack Frost and Allan Shackleton; SCR: A. Bochin, Michael Findlay and Roberta Findlay; DOP: Roberta Findlay and Carter Stevens; MUS: Rick Howard
STR: Tina Austin and Brian Cary (Remember, "The actors and actresses who dedicated their lives to making this film were never seen or heard from again.")
AKA: **American Cannibale**

Snuff

Approximately 82m; Color
AOV: **Snuff** [Astral Video (PAL); 82m]; **Snuff** [Cult Video; 82m]
ADL: *The film that could only be made in South America... where life is cheap!*

To avoid being reiterative, I refer back to the review for the 1970 film **Slaughter** for an indepth synopsis. This version of the film concerns only the last several minutes of the action which were tacked on almost six years later.

Picking up where the family members are about to off the luckless Sharon Tate stand-in, the film cuts abruptly to footage depicting a film crew wrapping up the scene in question. Unconvincing doubles for the actors walk off stage, leaving the crew and an unidentified stagehand behind. Who we assume to be the director (wearing a *"viva es muerte"* T-shirt) solicits the unsuspecting girl into a bout of heavy petting, and the remaining crew members begin documenting the escapades. The stagehand freaks out once she realizes what's going on and begins to fight off his now unwelcome advances, all to no avail. Right on cue, the aroused filmmaker begins raving and drooling, and with his crew's help he proceeds with the expected bloodshed.

He produces a knife, to which the girl screams "you're not serious... you're not *really* going to do it!" (Of course he's not *really* going to do it, as the unconvincing special effects prove to anyone who's made it this far through the film.) After cutting up her shoulder, he wastes no time in snipping off her pinkie with wire cutters, sawing off her hand with a circular saw conveniently hidden under the bed, and—just when you thought they had expended their allotted budget for latex rubber and red paint—he eviscerates her. Holding

Spawn of the Slithis

their involvement, but everything to do with the five minutes tacked onto the end and the propagation of the **Snuff** hoax by Mr. Shackleton. And the Findlay fans that *are* in the know probably don't care a whole lot as **Slaughter** is easily one of their most uninteresting films when taken on its own terms, even as tasteless as it may be.

In regards to Simon Nuchtern and Carter Stevens, reports are vague as to exactly who acted as director and cinematographer for the new footage.

Sohon Teura Staja *see* **Jack the Ripper—Der Dirnenmörder von London**

Les Sorcières Sanglantes *see* **Brenn, Hexe, Brenn**

the excavated viscera up for the inept cameraman, the screen goes black. Inexplicably, you hear the following exchange:

"Shit... we've run out of film. Shit!"

"Did you get it? Did you get it all?"

"Hm-Hmmm... yeah. Yeah... we got it all. Let's get out of here."

History is made with a simple conversation that could just as easily been an exchange between Mr. Shackleton and one of his investors.

What's truly ironic about this film is that it is undeniably the Findlays' most well known work—except that no one but hardcore film buffs are aware of their hand in its production. It's also ironic that the film's popularity has nothing to do with

Spawn of the Slithis (1977)

Fabtrax Films [USA]

DIR: Stephen Traxler; PRO: Paul Fabian and Stephen Traxler; SCR: Stephen Traxler; DOP: Robert Caramico; EXP: Dick Davis; MUS: Steve Zuckerman

STR: Mello Alexandria, Alan Blanchard, Prudie Butler, Dale Caldwell, Dave Carlton, J.C. Claire, Gregory Clemmons, Daphne Cohen, Abraham Columbus, Win Condict, Don Cummins, Drew Deeter, Gary Dyer, Alisa Estes, Dennis Lee Falt, Ed Fournier, Rocky Fumarelli, Marcus Harvey, John Hatfield, Stephen J. Hoag, Michael Hudson, Jack Kelly, Hy Pyke, Wendy Rastattar, David Ridenour, Ken Stimson, and Alejandro Vass

AKA: **Slithis**

Approximately 86m; Color

VID: **Slithis** [Media Home Entertainment; 86m]

ADL: *Hell hath no fury... like Slithis.*

A nuclear leak cooks up a hulked-out **Creature from the Black Lagoon** clone that would never make it as poster boy for **The Vegetarian Times**. Before viewers have the opportunity to reach for the fast forward button on their remote, our testy little friend has gone from killing stray dogs to ripping apart the residents of Venice, California... for many of whom it doesn't seem to be much of a stretch. Of course, nobody believes the poor souls in the film who've actually *seen* the creature, so it's their duty as concerned citizens to nip the problem in the bud before he actually goes after someone who matters.

The script is awful, and the editing during the action sequences is handled with about as much adeptness as if the Slithis had done the work himself. There are only two death scenes an hour into the film, but the red stuff finally kicks in, offering the splatterpunks some nasty, after-the-fact gore. (Unfortunately, quite a bit of the "red stuff" is nothing more than smeared red paint; it worked for H.G. Lewis, so why not?) The high point—of course—is the monster himself, a groovy pre-**Humanoids from the Deep**-style denizen who has the excusable habit of biting off more than he can chew.

Throw in lots of disposable shocks, a slough of low-rent actors trying—and often failing—to keep a straight face throughout the laughable proceedings, and the most neurotic police chief that ever graced a feature film, and you have my recommendation.

Starlight Slaughter *see* **Eaten Alive**

Strano Vizio della Signora Wardh, Lo *[The Strange Vice of Mrs. Ward] (1970)*

Copercines [Italy] and Devon Film [Spain]

DIR: Sergio Martino; PRO: Antonio Crescenzi and Luciano Martino; SCR: Eduardo Maria Brochero and Ernesto Gastaldi; DOP: Emilio Foriscot; MUS: Nora Orlandi

STR: Cristina Airolda, Carlo Alighiero, Bruno Corazzari, Marella Corbi, Alberto de Mendoza, Luis de Tejada, Miguel del Castillo, Edwige Fenech, Manuel Gill, George Hilton, Brizio Montinaro, Pouchie, Ivan Rassimov, and Mira Vidotto

AKA: **Blade of the Ripper; Next!; The Next Victim; La Perversa Senora Ward** [*The Perverse Mrs. Ward*]

Approximately 91m; Color
VID: **Blade of the Ripper** [Regal Video; 90(88)m]; **Blade of the Ripper** [Saturn Productions Ltd.; 90(88)m]

A woman is trying to shake a brutal ex-lover with whom she had indulged in some dangerous S&M games, and apparently getting married to someone else isn't doing the trick. Meanwhile, someone is carving up young women in the area with a straight razor, and there seems to be some connection between the killer and the aforementioned newlywed.

Although not an exemplary *giallo* thriller, **Lo Strano Vizio della Signora Wardh** is an unpredictable offering, throwing enough twists and turns at the viewer to keep their interest. There is some graphic violence in keeping with Italian genre fare at

the time as well, but nothing you haven't seen before.

Includes a note that reads "Il tuo vizio e una stanza chiusa e solo io ne ho la chiave" (Your vice is a locked room and only I have the key), a line which the director liked so much he used that as the name for an unrelated film he made in 1972.

Die Stunde der Grausamen Leichen see **El Jorobado de la Morgue**

Suspiria (1977)

Seda Spettacoli [Italy]
DIR: Dario Argento; PRO: Claudio Argento; SCR: Dario Argento; DOP: Luciano Tovoli; EXP: Salvatore Argento; SFX: Germano Natali; MUS: Dario Argento and Goblin
STR: Eva Axen, Joan Bennett, Miguel Bosè, Flavio Bucci, Allesandra Capozzi, Salvatore Capozzi, Stefania Casini, Diana Ferrara, Jessica Harper, Margherita Horowitz, Susanna Javicoli, Udo Kier, Cristina Latini, Barbara Magnolfi, Jacopo Mariani, Fulvio Mingozzi, Alfred Rainó, Franca Scagnetti, Renato Scarpa, Rudolf Schundler, Sarafina Scorcelletti, Giuseppe Transocchi, Alida Valli, Claudia Zaccari, and Renato Zamengo
AKA: **Alarido** [*Scream*]
Approximately 100m; Color
VID: **Suspiria** [Fox Lorber Home Video; 95(94)m; LBX]; **Suspiria** [Magnum Entertainment; 97(98)m; Unrated Edition]; **Suspiria** [Magnum Entertainment; 97(98)m; Unrated Edition; LBX]
ADL: *The only thing more terrifying than the last 12 minutes of this film are the first 80.*

Just so we can cut to the quick, the opening credits are accompanied by the following narration. "Suzie Banyon decided to perfect her ballet studies in the most famous school of dancing in Europe. She chose the celebrated Academy of Friedburg." Unfortunate for her, it is the home of one of the "Three Sisters"—specifically Mater Suspiriorum, "The Mother of Sighs"—who runs a coven of witches who occasionally prey upon the students.

Argento's most famed film is a nightmarish offering that sacrifices everything even remotely resembling logic or a coherent storyline for surreal staging and violent imagery. Its sheer visual intensity is a testament to what can be accomplished by a filmmaker solely through the visuals. The setpieces are awashed with filtered lights, framed by unsettling architecture, and eventually

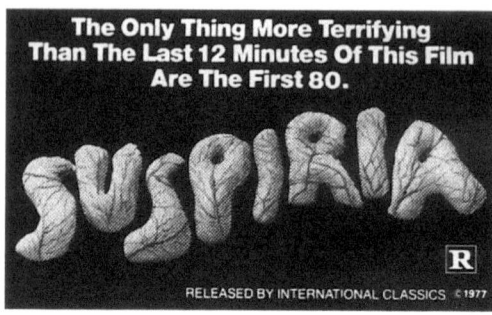

splashed by fake blood, maggots, and pig gut. **Suspiria** is Argento at his most balletic, each murder choreographed with the precision of a dancer's well-rehearsed routine. The whole of the film is accompanied by an impressive (and ear-rupturing) score from cohorts Goblin, and shows the full range of their collective talent. Performances are also good, with such luminary genre actors as Joan Bennett (TV's **Dark Shadows**) and Udo Kier (**Il Mostro è in Tavola... Barone Frankenstein** and **Dracula Cerca Sangue di Vergine... Mori di Sete** aka **Andy Warhol's Dracula** and **Andy Warhol's Frankenstein**, both 1973).

After having attained the American distribution rights, 20th Century-Fox found themselves "em-

barrassed" by their purchase, and released **Suspiria** through the bogus company of International Classics so as to take the heat off of them when it fared poorly at the box-office. **Suspiria** went on to become one of their more profitable films, and a cult classic to boot.

Maybe not Argento's best film, but easily his most representative.

Suspiria Part 2 see **Profondo Rosso**

Swamp of the Blood Leeches see **The Alien Dead**

Teenage Dracula see **Dracula Vs. Frankenstein** (1971)

Tension! see **Macchie Solari**

Terror Beach see **La Noche de las Gaviotas**

Terror Caníbal [Cannibal Terror] (1979)

Eurociné [France/Spain]
DIR: Julio Pérez Tabernero; SCR: Ilona Kunesova; DOP: Alan Hardy; MUS: Jean-Jacques Lemètre
STR: Burt Altman, Annabelle, Monique Delaunay, Antoine Fontaine, Stan Hamilton, Antonio Jover, Michel Laury, Gerard Lemaire, Amparo Marsilla, Olivier Mathot, Antonio Mayans, Montserrat Salvador, Silvia Solar, and Chris Yebenes
Approximately 93m; Color

In case Jesse Franco's **Mondo Cannibale** left you wanting more

227 The Texas Chain Saw Massacre

(more of the same, to be precise), here's another lousy Spanish cannibal epic that not only was produced by Eurociné as well, but was probably filmed back to back with Franco's turd. (In fact, it looks like both actually share some of the exact same footage as well, but I don't have a strong enough constitution to watch either one of them again to find out. Since Franco's film was released a year later, it may have simply pilfered some scenes from this sad film.) Yes, we are once again treated to the convincing performances of the fine, fine actors who played the parts of the supposedly South American primitives. Granted, many of them have sideburns and mustaches, and possess beer bellies (something I seriously doubt the natives would—call it a hunch), and all are obviously of European descent. Oh, and don't let the tacky KISS-style makeup deter you either.

Cannibal Terror might have qualified—like many of the other cannibal films—as a hardgore production, but there is only one graphic (albeit extremely graphic) scene in the first seventy minutes, and this same is recycled later for similar killings. (Wrap a pig carcass in an actor's clothing, and you have the extent of their effects budget.)

Is it any surprise that cannibal films died out, oh, not too long after *these* paeans of ineptitude were released?

Terror Castle *see* **La Vergine di Norimberga**

The Terror of Dr. Chaney *see* **Mansion of the Doomed**

Terror on Blood Island *see* **Brides of Blood**

Terror sin Habla *see* **Frightmare**

De Terugkeer der Gemaskerde Lijken *see* **El Ataque de los Muertos sin Ojos**

The Texas Chain Saw Massacre (1974)
Vortex, Inc. [USA]
DIR: Tobe Hooper; PRO: Tobe Hooper; SCR: Tobe Hooper and Kim Henkel; DOP: Daniel Pearl; EXP: Jay Parsley; SFX: Lynn Lockwood and Dorothy Pearl; MFX: W.E. Barnes; MUS: Wayne Bell and Tobe Hooper
STR: Marilyn Burns, Robert Courtin, William Creamer, Allen Danziger, John Dugan, John Henry Faulk, Jerry Green, Ed Guinn, Gunnar Hansen, Joe Bill Hogan, Perry Lorenz, Teri McMinn, Edwin Neal, Paul A. Partain, Jim Siedow, and William Vail
AKA: **Masacre en Cadena** [*Masacre in Chain*]; **Massacre a la Tronconneause** [*Massacre with a Chainsaw*]; **Non Aprire Quella Porta** [*Don't Open That Door*]; **The Texas Chainsaw Massacre**
Approximately 83m; Color
VID: **The Texas Chainsaw Massacre** [Astral Video; 84(83)m]; **The Texas Chainsaw Massacre** [MPI Home Video; 84(83)m]; **The Texas Chainsaw Massacre** [Media Home Entertainment; 84(83)m]; **The Texas Chainsaw Massacre** [Video Treasures; 84(83)m]; **The Texas Chainsaw Massacre** [Wizard Video; 84(83)m]
ADL: *Who will survive and what will be left of them?*

"The film which you are about to see is an account of the tragedy which befell a group of five youths,

The Texas Chain Saw Massacre

in particular Sally Hardesty and her invalid brother, Franklyn. It is all the more tragic in that they were young. But, had they lived very, very long lives, they could not have expected nor would they have wished to see as much of the mad and macabre as they were to see that day. For them an idyllic summer afternoon drive became a nightmare. The events of that day were to lead to the discovery of one of the most bizarre crimes in the annals of American history, the Texas Chain Saw Massacre."

Okay, so the above claims made by the film are completely bogus (resulting, interestingly enough, in one of the bigger urban legends to center around a horror film), but no one can deny this film for being one of the most visceral, most innovative horror films in cinematic history. Although much of its power has been sapped by the flood of copycats that followed in its wake, it still remains an unrelenting piece of filmmaking on all counts.

Loosely (very loosely) based on the case of the infamous Wisconsin cannibal and necrophile Ed Gein, **The Texas Chain Saw Massacre** recounts the story of a vanload of teens being methodically stalked and killed when they encroach on the property of the Sawyer family, comprised of The Hitchhiker, a twitchy, scarfaced, straight razor-wielding psycho; Leatherface, an oversized, chainsaw-wielding mute with a penchant for deathmasks; The Cook, the sanest of the lot but still buggy by these liberal standards; and Grandpa, the venerable patriarch of the butchering clan. The performers play their parts to the hilt, but in no way become cartoon caricatures of themselves, making for some of the most convincingly portrayed psychopaths ever to grace a horror film.

Made on an extremely low budget, the lack of finances appears to have benefited the production in every way. The almost *cinema vérité* approach gives the film a documentary-like look, insinuating itself as if the events were filmed as they happened, and not staged. The dilapidated farmhouse and setpieces look authentic in every way, furthering the illusion as well. The lack of splashy effects forced the effects artists to rely more on innuendo than outright grue; amazingly, many people today who have seen the film insist they have seen something exceptionally gory, when in fact it is mild not only by today's standards, but by those set in the early 70s by independent splatter fare. The nerve-shattering score—reminiscent of

some later industrial music—also adds to the tension, making the harrowing proceedings almost unbearable to watch. When one sees how everything fell into place, it is no wonder that **The Texas Chain Saw Massacre** became the cult classic it did.
   A damn near perfect film.

The Texas Chainsaw Massacre *see* **The Texas Chain Saw Massacre**

They Came from Within *see* **The Parasite Murders**

They're Coming to Get You (1971) *see* **Dracula vs. Frankenstein**

They're Coming to Get You (1972) *see* **Tutti i Colori del Buio**

This Night I Will Possess Your Corpse *see* **Esta Noite Encarnarei No Teu Cadáver**

Three on a Meathook (1972)
   On the Hook Corporation [USA] DIR: William B. Girdler; PRO: John Asman and Lee Jones; SCR: William Girdler; DOP: William Asman; EXP: Joseph Schulten; SFX: Richard Fowler; MFX: J.G. Patterson, Jr.; MUS: American Xpress, Dynamic Productions, and William B. Girdler
   STR: Madelyn Buzzard, Smith Haynie, Charles Kissinger, Kiersten Laine, James Pickett, John Shaw, Hugh Smith, Sterry Steiner, Alice Summers, Marsha Tarbis, Carolyn Thompson, Linda Thompson, and Thomas Todd
   Approximately 77m; Color
   VID: **Three on a Meathook** [New Horizons Inc.; 85(77)m]; **Three on a Meathook** [New Pacific Pictures;

85(77)m]; **Three on a Meathook** [Regal Video; 85(77)m]
   ADL: *Prime candidates for murder!*

   Four girls on a boating trip break down and find themselves spending the night in an old farmhouse owned by a young man and his reluctant host of a father. Before the night is through, all four are brutally murdered, with the father putting the blame on his son and his blackouts.
   Like many films (**The Texas Chain Saw Massacre** and **Psycho** included), **Three on a Meathook** is loosely based on the real life exploits of necrophile-cum-cannibal Ed Gein, a Wisconsin farmer with a psychotic attachment to his mother. Borrowing only specific elements from the case, **Three on a Meathook**

is actually much closer to Peter Walker's later—and much more compelling—film **Frightmare** (1974).

Although an adequate low-budget shocker, the film suffers from the fact that too much time is spent on romancing and not enough on the more horrific aspects. (I know this sounds fairly misanthropic, but when watching a film with such a coy moniker, one wants to be reminded on occasion that a meathook *does* play a part in the proceedings.) There are a few nasty gore scenes (including one of the more ingeniously executed decapitations), but they are few and far between, with the bulk of the bloodshed relegated to the initial massacre. (The rough production values could be easily overlooked had they piled on the grue a little more.)

An interesting film, even though its notoriety *is* its most interesting facet.

The Tigress *see* **Ilsa the Tigress of Siberia**

Todos los Colores de la Oscuridad *see* **Tutti i Colori del Buio**

Le Tombe dei Resuscitati Ciechi *see* **La Noche del Terror Ciego**

Tombs of the Blind Dead *see* **La Noche del Terror Ciego**

Tombs of the Living Dead *see* **The Mad Doctor of Blood Island**

The Toolbox Murders (1977)
Cal-Am Productions [USA]

BIT BY BIT...BY BIT HE CARVED A NIGHTMARE!

DIR: Dennis Donnelly; PRO: Tony di Dio; SCR: Robert Easter, Neva Friedenn, and Ann N. Kindberg; DOP: Gary M. Graver; MFX: Ed Ternes; MUS: George Deaton

STR: Robert Bartlett, Nicholas Beauvy, Betty Cole, Aneta Corsaut, George Deaton, Don Diamond, Tim Donnelly, Marciee Drake, Wesley Eure, Pamelyn Ferdin, Robert Forward, Gil Galvano, Evelyn Guerrero, John Hawker, Faith McSwain, Cameron Mitchell, Kelly Nichols, James Nolan, Kathleen O'Malley, Victoria Perry, Alisa Powell, and Marianne Walter

Approximately 94m; Color
VID: **The Toolbox Murders** [United Home Video; 93(94)m]; **The Toolbox Murders** [VCI Home Video; 93(94)m]; **The Toolbox Murders** [Video Treasures; 93(94)m]; **The Toolbox Murders** [Vipco (PAL); 90(93)m]
ADL: *Bit by bit... by bit he carved a nightmare!*

Someone is putting their toolbox to good use in an apartment building run by Cameron Mitchell and his nephew Wesley Eure (Will from TV's **Land of the Lost**). After half the tenants have been made short work of in various grisly fashions (limit one tool per customer), a young girl is abducted, and her brother starts his own investigation with the help of the owner's nephew.

There are some interesting and unorthodox approaches to the otherwise typical stalk 'n' slash material, as well as a few other kickbacks (at least in the eyes of trash film aficionados). Cameron Mitchell as a Bible-spouting, lollipop-sucking, nails-on-chalkboard-singing psychopath whose favorite tune is "Sometimes I Feel like a Motherless Child" is one. Wesley Eure and his ability to single-handedly lay waste to any film he's in with his overacting is another. Seeing a handful of well known porn stars getting the Black & Decker treatment isn't far behind, either.

On that note, it's easy to look past the misogynistically-staged murders (one is "nailed," another "drilled," another "hammered," et al.) when the rest of the film is so awkward. Despite everything, the whole mess proves to be rather engaging, both as a thriller and as an enjoyably shoddy production. And the gore is, well, fairly brutal, predating other such toolbox "classics" as **Driller Killer** and **Nail Gun Massacre**.

The film also claims to be based on a real series of events that happened in 1967; how substantial these claims are, I can only guess.

Throw in an incongruous soundtrack, and as much T&A as the story can withstand, and you have ... well, you have **The Toolbox Murders**, so take it or leave it.

Tormentor *see* **Passi di Danza Su una Lama di Rasoio**

Torso *see* **I Corpi Presentano Tracce di Violenza Carnale**

Torture Dungeon (1970)

Constitution Films, Inc [UK/USA]
DIR: Andy Milligan; PRO: William Mishkin; SCR: John Borske and Andy Milligan; DOP: Andy Milligan; SFX: Walter Terry
STR: Helen Adams, Haal Borske, George Box, Jeremy Brooks, Susan Cassidy, Patricia Dillon, Neil Flanagan, Robert Fucello, Patricia Garvey, Dan Lyra, Richard Mason, Jeremy Mishkin, Maggie Rogers, Dan Tyra, and Donna Whitfield
AKA: **Dungeon of Death**
Approximately 80m; Color
VID: **Torture Dungeon** [Midnight Video; 80m]
ADL: *AN UNBELIEVABLE ORGY OF TERROR!*

The story here in this medieval period piece is inconsequential because yer just gonna' fast-forward through it anyway. Made back to back with Milligan's **The Bloodthirsty Butchers**, **Torture Dungeon** has everything in common with that equally abysmal effort, save maybe for the fact that the viewer will identify even less with the characters in this film. (At least *some* of the players

Incompetent fare reserved exclusively for diehard Milligan fans.

Der Totenchor der Knochenmänner see La Orgia de los Muertos

Toutes les Couleurs du Vice see Tutti i Colori del Buio

Tower of Evil (1972)

Grenadier Films [UK]
DIR: Jim O'Connolly; PRO: Richard Gordon; SCR: Jim O'Connolly; DOP: Desmond Dickinson; EXP: Joe Solomon; MUS: Kenneth V. Jones
STR: Fredric Abbott, Robin Askwith, George Colouris, Mark Edwards, Derek Fowlds, Candace Glendenning, Bryant Haliday, John Hamill, Gary Hamilton, Jill Haworth, William Lucas, Mark McBride, Anna Palk, Dennis Price, Marianne Stone, Anthony Valentine, Jack Watson, and Serretta Wilson
AKA: **Beyond the Fog; Horror of Snape Island**
Approximately 90m; Color
VID: **Tower of Evil** [Interglobal Video; 86(90)m]; **Tower of Evil** [MPI Video; 90(89)m]
ADL: *A night of pleasure becomes a night of terror!*

in **The Bloodthirsty Butchers** were reasonably engaging. Not here, though.) The period costuming here is also a step down; whereas—despite other anachronisms—**The Bloodthirsty Butchers** was reasonably convincing in this respect, the costumes here look like leftovers from a high school play production. (This analogy keeps arising in respect to Milligan's films.)

So, read the review for that other film to get an idea of what to expect. In addition to that, the gratuity here is, well, much more gratuitous, and the inept camerawork, well, much more inept. (I don't know about you, but I picture a stumbling wino trying futilely to focus on the action at hand, and finally falling over, exhausted, camera still running.)

Two brine-swilling fisherman discover a corpse—arm severed and besieged by crabs—on the shore of Snape Island. In a nearby lighthouse, they perchance upon the single survivor, a little buggy after her and her friends were all but massacred while visiting the deserted isle. A doctor manages to pull her out of her catatonic stupor (drugs and hyptnotism, the modern wonders that they are) and finds her recounting a rather bizarre story. To clear her name of any murder charges (in her delirium, she had made short work of one of the aforementioned sailors, so it was assumed she did the same of her friends) she and a group of professionals go back to the scene of the crime, a little leery of history repeating itself. Oh, did I mention the legend that a vast Venetian treasure is supposedly hidden somewhere on Snape Island?

Having obviously inspired Aristide Massaccesi's **Anthropophagous** (*aka* **The Grim Reaper**) (1980), this early UK shocker by Jim (**Valley of the Gwangi**) O'Connolly is admirable on almost all counts. Although now a bit dated and predictable, **Tower of Evil** is still an engaging shuttered house-style mystery, made even more enjoyable by a slough of early 70s excesses: above average gore effects (of which there is a fair amount), an abundance of nekkid hippie chicks, and a lot of groovy sideburns. (A pair of which is sported by Robin Askwith, who also starred in **Horror Hospital** with Michael Gough, an uneventful pastiche of horror films made a year later.)

Definitely worth seeking out, and surprisingly tough to find considering that this film was largely public domain in the 80s and released by every bargain-minded video label and their grandmother. (Fans of Amando de Ossorio Rodríguez' horror fare in particular should get something out of this sometimes nasty little film, even if there are no Templars lumbering about the sets.)

Trap Them and Kill Them *see* **Emanuelle e gli Ultima Cannibali**

Der Triebmörder *see* **La Bestia Uccide a Sangue Freddo**

Les Tueurs du Claire de Lune *see* **Killer's Moon**

Il Tuo Vizio È una Stanza Chiusa e Solo Lo Ne Ho la Chiave [Your Vice Is a Closed Room and Only I Have the Key] (1972)
Lea Film [Italy]
DIR: Sergio Martino; PRO: Luciano Martino; SCR: Adriano Bolzoni, Ernesto Gastaldi, and Sauro Scavolini [Based on the short story "The Black Cat" by Edgar Allan Poe); DOP: Giancarlo Ferrando; MUS: Bruno Nicolai
STR: Enrica Bonaccorti, Bruno Boschetti, Armelinda de Felice, Edwige Fenech, Daniela Giordano, Angela la Vorgna, Carla Mancini, Marco Mariani, Nerina Montagnani, Franco Nebbia, Luigi Pistilli, Ivan Rassimov, Riccardo Salvino, and Anita Strindberg

AKA: Excite Me; Eye of the Black Cat; Gently Before She Dies
Approximately 92m; Color
VID: Gently Before She Dies [World Sales Intra Films; 94m; LBX]

A writer who cheats on his wife and degrades her relentlessly in public finds himself a suspect in a series of murders, one of the victims being their maid. During all of this, the not-so-happily married couple takes in the man's philandering cousin, who eventually beds both the husband *and* wife, and not in that order.

Now, would you have guessed this to be an adaptation of Poe's "The Black Cat?" Well, the source material probably takes up all of a scattered ten minutes of the running time, but the writer does own a black cat, and—in a role reversal—the wife cuts out its eye, and eventually inters it with her husband's corpse in the basement, where it is promptly found by the police due to the beast's caterwauling.

Unfortunately, the film is painfully lackluster despite its complexities, the production values being almost innocuous. There are some extremely graphic cleaver choppings and throat slashings (even by early *giallo* standards), but the effects are fairly primitive. Oh, and the completely anticlimactic motorcycle accident scene deserves a mention, as I have never seen one executed in such a nonplused fashion.

Vaguely interesting, at best.

Tutti i Colori del Buio [All the Shades of Darkness] (1972)

Compagnia Cinematografica Astro [Italy] Lea Film [Spain] and National Cinematografica [Italy]
DIR: Sergio Martino; PRO: Mino Loy; SCR: Ernesto Gastaldi and Sauro Scavolini; DOP: Giancarlo Ferrando and Miguel F. Milá; MUS: Bruno Nicolai
STR: Dominique Boschero, Renato Chiantoni, Vera Drudi, Tom Felleghi, Edwige Fenech, George Hilton, Lisa Leonardi, Marina Malfatti, Carla Mancini, Nieves Navarro, Luciano Pigozzi, Maria Cumani Quasimodo, Ivan Rassimov, Georges Rigaud, and Julián Ugarte
AKA: **L'Alliance Invisible** [*The Invisible Alliance*]; **Day of the Maniac; Demons of the Dead; Un Stranha Orchidae con Cinque Gocce di Sangue** [*A Strange Orchid with Five Drops of Blood*]; **They're Coming to Get You; Todos los Colores de la Oscuridad; Toutes les Couleurs du Vice** [*All the Colors of Vice*]
Approximately 90m; Color
VID: **Day of the Maniac** [VidAmerica; 89m]

A woman loses her grip on reality after losing her unborn child in an automobile accident. She begins having dreams of a man knifing a woman who turns out to be her mother. Suddenly, the selfsame man begins showing up everywhere—her psychiatrist's office; the subway; the park; and at her solicitor's office—carrying a hatchet and what appears to be a dog's head. Of course, no one believes her claims of being stalked. A friend suggests she go to a Sabbat in order to "get her head together." There, she meets a bunch of losers covered in pancake makeup sacrificing small dogs and drinking their blood. She succumbs, and becomes the center of attention in an impromptu orgy. Only forty minutes into the film we are, and I bet

Two Thousand Maniacs

you're thinking it won't get any stranger than this, huh?

Opening with a rather wacky dream sequence involving a guy in drag that would make John Waters wince, a pregnant hag draped across a chair, and the knifing of a nude woman by the aforementioned crones, the film retains a hallucinatory stance even when focusing on the "reality" of the situation. In other words, this is another sleazy "Who

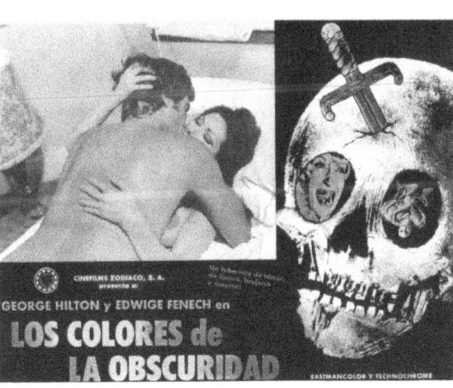

cares whodunit, just what the hell is going on?" *giallo* thriller from Italy (of course) that boasts kaleidoscopic effects, tacky editing, and some slo-mo knifings that are graphic even as far as most early 70s Euro-fare goes.

Not good, but interesting, to say the least.

Twitch of the Death Nerve *see* **Antefatto**

2000 Maniacs *see* **Two Thousand Maniacs**

Two Thousand Maniacs (1965)

Box Office Spectaculars [USA]
DIR: Herschell Gordon Lewis; PRO: David F. Friedman; SCR: Herschell Gordon Lewis; DOP: Herschell Gordon Lewis; MUS: Herschell Gordon Lewis
STR: Jeffrey Allen, Gary Bakerman, Linda Cochran, Mark Douglas, Jerome Eden, Yvonne Gilbert, William Kerwin, Michael Korb, Shelby Livingston, Connie Mason, Ben Moore, Vincent Santo, and Andy Wilson
AKA: **2000 Maniacs**
Approximately 70m; Color
SND: **Two Thousand Maniacs** [Rhino Records; Split-LP w/**Blood Feast**]
VID: **2000 Maniacs** [Comet Video; 70m]; **Two-Thousand Maniacs** [Rhino Video; 70m]

Unsuspecting travelers are rerouted through Georgia to Pleasant Valley, a small town that is in the midst of celebrating their centennial. Unbeknownst to the sidetracked tourists, the inhabitants are the ghosts of townspeople that were killed in a massacre during the Civil War a hundred

years previous. Worse yet, they want revenge, and they stringently adhere to the credo of "no one is innocent."

This, the second gore film by Herschell Gordon Lewis and David F. Friedman (the first being the 1963 celluloid atrocity **Blood Feast**), is technically a better film, and is a bit more restrained in its approach, but this is neither here nor there. **Two Thousand Maniacs** is yet another no-budget, no holds barred shocker aimed at the jaded drive-in crowd. Rubber prosthetics and pig offal drenched in red paint are thrust into the camera's eye. Although a few films predated Lewis' gore-drenched offerings, it could be said with little doubt that he was the first splatter filmmaker, as films of this orientation were the primary focus of his career until he bowed out of filmmaking in 1972.

On an interesting side note, it is rumored that the film was originally planned as **20,000 Maniacs**, but the budget didn't allow for such an excessive cast.

H.G. Lewis promptly followed up this one with **Color Me Blood Red** (1966).

La Ultima Casa a la Izquierda *see* **Last House on the Left**

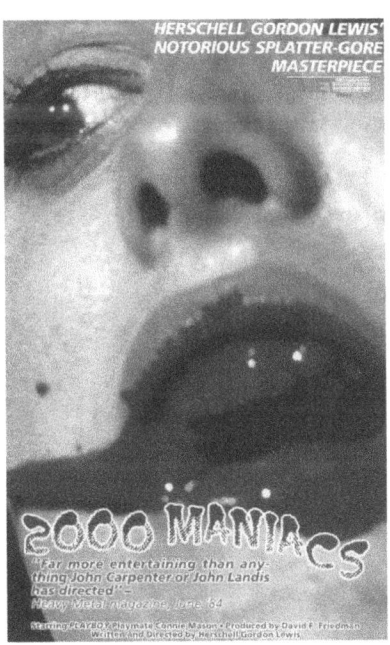

Ultimo Mondo Cannibale [The Last Cannibal World] (1976)

Erre Cinematografica [Italy]
DIR: Ruggero Deodato; PRO: Giorgio Carlo Rossi and Giovanni Masini; SCR: Tito Carpi, Gianfranco Clerici, and Renzo Genta; DOP: Marcello Masciocchi; MFX: Paolo Ricci; MUS: Ubaldo Continiello
STR: Massimo Foschi, Me Me Lai, Ivan Rassimov, Judy Rosly, Shamsi, Sheik Razak Shikur, and Suleiman
AKA: Cannibal; Cannibals; Cannibal Massacre; Carnivorous; Le Dernier Monde Cannibale [*The Last Cannibal World*]; Jungle Holocaust; De Laatste Kannibalen [*The Last Cannibals*]; The Last Survivor; Mondo Cannibale II—Der Vogelmensch [*Cannibal World II-The Birdman*]; Mundo Canibal! Mundo Salvaje! [*Cannibal World! Savage World!*]
Approximately 92m; Color
VID: **Cannibal** [Meteor Video; 88(83)m; LBX]; **Jungle Holocaust** [Video City Productions; 90(92)m]

"This is the true account of the series of events that led to the discovery of a stone age tribe on the island of Mindanao. The ceremonies and rituals portrayed were all experienced or witnessed by the central character, Robert Harper." A search for a downed plane turns up the fact that the missing crew has been, well, eaten by the aforementioned stone age tribe with bad table manners. (Etiquette is not one of their finer points.)

This, Deodato's first foray into the third-world cannibal genre (he followed it up three years later with the exceptional **Holocausto Canibal**), is a fairly convincing, sometimes disturbing, and usually exploitive offering that helped pave the way for an entire slough of like films in the 70s. Gore is pretty soft, as is the requisite animal cruelty. (A scene involving what looks like a Komodo dragon being swallowed whole by a really, *really* big snake looks more like legit documentary footage instead of staged animal brutality.) Although some of the sexual politics make sense within the context of the primitive culture, it still seems very "piggish" and is sure to offend anyone even remotely sympathetic with the current bane of political correctness.

Technically, it's about as could be expected from such a production, although it does boast an extremely unsettling feast sequence. (The second such scene loses much of its impact, though, thanks to a wholly inappropriate score.) Otherwise, **Ultimo Mondo Cannibale** will surely bore those splatterpunks with little interest in such films. 🐱🐱🐱

The Undertaker and His Pals (1967)

Howco International [USA]
DIR: Tom L.P. Swicegood; PRO: Ted V. Mikels; SCR: Tom L.P. Swicegood; DOP: Andrew Janczak; EXP: David C. Graham; SFX: Steve Harkus; MUS: Johnny White
STR: Karen Ciral, Rick Cook, Ray Dannis, Florence Dupre, Charles Fox, Sally Frei, Marty Friedman, Rad Fulton, Vince Harris, Barbra Heart, Robert Lowery, Tiffany Shannon Ohara, Larrene Ott, Jack Rydon, and Dodre Warren
Approximately 60m; B&W and Color
VID: **The Undertaker and His Pals** [MTI Home Video; 70(60)m]
ADL: *A macabre story of two mo-*

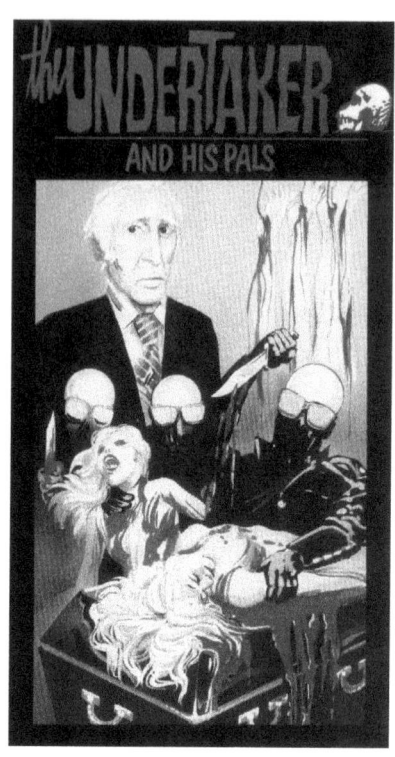

torcycle-riding, knife-wielding, shiv-shaving, eye-gouging, arm-twisting, chain-lashing, scalpel-flashing, acid-throwing, gun-shooting, bone-breaking, pathological nuts and their pal the undertaker...

The owner of the Shady Rest Funeral Parlor joins forces with two diner owners (one a pre-med student who appears to be doing a bad Dick Miller impersonation) in order to drum up business. At night, they go out, killing young women and stealing certain pieces of their anatomy to use as the special of the day, while the mortician gouges their loved ones for every penny he can.

This H.G. Lewis-esque gore comedy (which, in many ways, seems to have inspired Jackie Kong's **Blood**

Diner [1987], even though that film cites **Blood Feast** as its direct inspiration) is a fun, dated number that would have faded into complete obscurity were it not for its wonderful ad campaign and timely video release. The jokes are pretty stale and or downright silly (the victims are "Miss Lamb," "Miss Poultry," et al.), but there are a few truly funny, inspired moments. (The chase scene which punctuates the finale seems to be about fifteen years ahead of its time, poking fun at the fact that no matter how slow the killer is, and no matter how fast the victim is, the killer invariably catches up.)

The gore is fairly messy, as is most the production values. (Again, the comparison to Lewis' films is unavoidable.) But, unless 60s trash floats yer boat, I doubt you'll get much out of it.

O Universo de Mojica Marins [The Universe of Mojica Marins] (1978)

Production company unknown [Brazil]
DIR: Ivan E.S. Cardoso
STR: José Mojica Marins
AKA: **The Universe of Coffin Joe**
Approximately 25m; B&W and Color
VID: **Ivan Cardoso's Shocking Shorts** [Something Weird Video; 98(25)m]

This short documentary on José Mojica Marins (*aka* Coffin Joe) intersplices clips from the director's movies with behind-the-scenes footage, scrapbook photos, interviews and other live appearances.

(Much of this, interestingly enough, is narrated by the filmmaker's own mother. How's that for nepotism?) This sketch of Brazil's premiere splatter filmmaker is the main feature on the tape **Ivan Cardoso's Shocking Shorts**, which also includes trailers and innumerable outtakes from Cardoso's other as well as some of his early short films. (The latter come across as mostly worthless home movies; there ain't a script in sight, I assure you.)

"The cinema is my religion," Mr. Marins states proudly. Amen to that.

Up Frankenstein *see* **Il Mostro è il Tavola ... Barone Frankenstein**

Un Urlo dalle Tenebre [A Cry in the Dark] (1975)

Manila Cinmatografica [Italy]
DIR: Franco lo Cascio and Elio Pannaciò; PRO: Luigi Fedeli; SCR: Franco Brocani, Aldo Crudo, and Elio Pannaciò; DOP: Maurizio Centini and Franco Villa; SFX: Giancarlo Serravalle; MUS: Giuliano Sorgini
STR: Richard Conte, Franco Garofalo, Patrizia Gori, Mimma Monticelli, Filippo Perego, Françoise Prévost, Elena Svevo, Guiuseppe Tallarico, Jean-Claude Verné, and Sonia Viviani
AKA: **Bacchanales Infernales** [*Infernal Bacchanals*]; **L'Exorcista N.2** [*The Exorcist 2*]; **Naked Exorcism; The Possessor; Return of the Exorcist**
Approximately 88m; Color
VID: **The Possessor** [Wizard Video; 89(87)m]
ADL: *Nothing can satisfy her unholy hungers.*

What a mess this is. First we open to the flashbacks of a nun being

Urlo dalle Tenebre is probably the cheesiest entry in an already sorry subgenre. Outside of the oft-mentioned staples and utterly derivative script, we also have to suffer through a gratuitous discotheque scene. (Talk about insult to injury.) The only, and I mean *the only* inspired part of the film is the mock *cinema vérité*-style footage of a sanitarium that is—surprisingly—quite effective.

Although relatively tame, gore is nastier than what can be found in most of its **Exorcist**-inspired peers (hence my bothering to include it in this book) if only because the filmmakers probably pushed the envelope as much as their censorship laws would allow. If you go out of your way to see this, though, you're really scraping bottom.

Die Vampire des Dr. Dracula *see* **La Marco del Hombre Lobo**

Vampire Playgirls *see* **Gran Amor del Conde Dracula**

Les Vampires du Dr. Dracula *see* **La Marco del Hombre Lobo**

The Vampyre Orgy *see* **Vampyres**

Vampyres (1974)

Essay Films Ltd. [UK]
DIR: José Ramón Larraz; PRO: Brian Smedley-Aston; SCR: Diana Daubeney; DOP: Harry Waxman; MFX: Colin Arthur; MUS: James Kenelm Clarke

STR: Murray Brown, Michael Byrne, Gerald Case, Brian Deacon, Anulka Dziubinska, Sally Faulkner, Margaret Heald, Douglas Jones, Karl Lanchbury, Bessie Love, Marianne Morris, and Elliott Sullivan

indoctrinated into a Satanic cult and impregnated. (Given, the Black Mass adheres to Anton LaVey–style psychodrama more than most, but it's still pretty gosh darn cheesy.) This cuts to a teenage boy tied to his bed, doing his best Linda Blair impersonation by verbally abusing his sister-cum-nun. We then find out that these events were precipitated by his taking photographs of an unwary nude redhead by a waterfall, only—when developed—she's nowhere to be seen. Really spooky, uh huh. The kid inadvertently kills his girlfriend, then starts having wacky, incestuous hallucinations involving his mother and the elusive redhead. Before long, the potty mouth sets in, the bed's a-spinning, and the furniture's a-flying.

Not only is this *another* shameless rip-off of **The Exorcist**, Un

Vampyres

AKA: **Blood Hunger; Las Hijas de Dracula** [*The Daughters of Dracula*]; **Satan's Daughters; The Vampyre Orgy; Vampyres, Daughters of Dracula**
Approximately 86m; Color
VID: **Vampyres** [Cineplex (PAL); 84m]; **Vampyres** [M.I.A. Video (PAL); 84m]; **Vampyres** [Rank Video Library (PAL); 84m]; **Vampyres, Daughters of Dracula** [Magnum Entertainment; 84m; R-Rated Version]; **Vampyres, Daughters of Dracula** [Magnum Entertainment; 86m; Unrated Edition]
ADL: *Their lips are moist and very, very red!*

Two women are shot to death by an unknown assailant while having sex. They come back shortly thereafter as sex-starved vampires who lure unsuspecting men (and occasionally couples) back to their castle. (Although most leave alive—albeit a little drained—one poor sap keeps coming back for more, despite the consequences.)

One of Larraz' more consistent, more atmospheric efforts, this

gothic-drenched vampire flick makes accommodations for the requisite 70s-style gratuity. Although not deserving of the original X rating it received, **Vampyres** is chock full of skin, softcore sex (including some vampiric *ménage à trois*), and splashy bloodletting. Production values are better than would be expected, especially the graceful camerawork and authentic staging. Performances are similarly noteworthy.

Although it is an excellent example of what exploitation films can accomplish, **Vampyres** has inexplicably acquired something of a cult following. (There was even a one-shot magazine-style book from Draculina Publishing that focused specifically on this production, which has had numerous printings. If you find this film of any interest, I recommend the book, as it says much more about the film than I ever could.)

Vampyres, Daughters of Dracula
see **Vampyres**

La Venganza de la Momia
[The Vengeance of the Mummy] (1973)
Lotus Films [Spain] and Sara Films [Spain]
DIR: Carlos Aured Alonso; PRO: Julian Esteban and Luis Mendez; SCR: Jacinto Molina Alvarez; DOP: Francisco Sánchez; MUS: Alfonso Sanisteban and CAM
STR: Javinto Molina Alvarez, Pilar Bardem, Eduardo Calvo, Celia Cruz, Luis Dávila, M. Cruz Fernandez, Luis Gaspar, Jose Monne, Rina Ottolina, Fernando Sánchez Polack, Ann Mary Pool, María Silva, Juan A. Soler, Helga Lina Stern, Jack Taylor, and José Yepes
AKA: **The Mummy's Revenge**
Approximately 91m; Color
VID: **The Mummy's Revenge** [Unicorn Video; 91m]

Amen Ho-Tep, a particularly cruel pharaoh (vampirism and cannibalism not the least of his crimes), is poisoned and interred alive by his servants. (His just as bloodthirsty queen is saved this fate and promptly executed.) The tyrant's mummy is found by Eurotrash favorite Jack Taylor and crew almost two-thousand years later, whereupon the cursed pharaoh is resurrected by a descendant (also played by Spain horror icon Paul Naschy né Jacinto Molina Alvarez). The dry rot-ridden fiend (wearing as much eye-liner in death as he did in life) takes advantage of his newfound freedom and begins scouring London for virgins.

This gory rehash of the by-now familiar storyline is updated to accommodate the sexual and violent excesses of the uninhibited 70s. (Nudity abounds, and the title antagonist is given superhuman strength so as to crush human heads with his fists—these scenes rivaling anything in H.G. Lewis' opus **The Gore-Gore Girls**.) Production values are on par with most Spanish productions from the time, although the budget is stretched a bit thin when it comes to the flashbacks of ancient Egypt. Naschy is not at his best, probably due to the fact he doesn't get to brood here like he does in the "El Hombre Lobo" films. (Angst is most definitely his strongest suit. Next to drooling profusely, that is.)

More enjoyable than most 70s mummy nonsense, if only because of the gratuity. (Karloff *still* kicks ass.)

Le Vénin de la Peur *see* Una Lucertola con la Pelle di Donna

La Vergine di Norimberga [*The Virgin of Nuremburg*] (1964)

Atlantica Cinematografica [Italy]
DIR: Antonio Margheriti; PRO: Marco Vicario; SCR: Ernesto Gastaldi, Edmond T. Greville, and Antonio Margheriti [Based on the novel **The Virgin of Nuremburg** by Frank Bogart]; DOP: Ricardo Pallotini; EFX: Antonio Margheriti; MUS: Riz Ortolani
STR: Anna delli Uberti, Jim Dolen, Christopher Lee, Luciana Milone, Rosan Podestà, George Rivière, Lucille Saint-Simon, Leonardo Severini, Mirko Valentin, Patrick Walton, and Carole Windsor
AKA: **Back to the Killer; Castle of Terror; Die Gruft der Lebenden Leichen** [*The Crypt of the Living Corpses*]; **Horror Castle; Terror Castle; La Vierge de Nuremberg** [*The Virgin of Nuremburg*]
Approximately 83m; Color
VID: **The Virgin of Nuremburg** [Panther Entertainment; 83m]

A woman marries the descendant of an infamous torturer and, while staying in the family castle, starts seeing strange things: specters, corpses popping up at the most inconvenient times, and so forth. Undeterred by her hubby's reasoning, she begins nosing about, and finds out the castle is also harboring someone who stalks the halls at night wearing a black hood and red cape, and who likes to abduct young women whom he tortures in a secret crypt. Confronted with these claims, everyone starts acting suspicious—the maid, the castle's war-scarred custodian, even her husband—so it's up to the new lady of the house to figure out who is responsible in order to save her own skin.

La Vergine di Norimberga is not only an exemplary gothic film

Le Vergini Cavalcano la Morte see **Ceremonia Sangrienta**

Verschrikkelijke Schoolreis see **Killer's Moon**

The Victim see **Macchie Solari**

Victims! (1979)

Tumbleweed Productions [USA] DIR: Jeff Hathcock; PRO: Jeff Hathcock; SCR: John O'Hara; DOP: David Essex; MFX: Alice Campbell; MUS: Glenn Barley
STR: Robert Axelrod, Ken Blazer, Kathy Brothen, Phil de Carlo, Ray Gabriel, Chris Hammond, Richard Hathcock, Ava Kauffman, Denize Kazan, Larry Keye, Dee Kwan, Don Miller, Joan Phillips, Phil Pierce, Les Reed, Lee Richards, Pam Richards, Ann Richardson, Don Sangil, Geri Schlessel, Alan Scott, Jim Simpson, Janet Warren, and Lonny Withers

from accomplished Italian filmmaker Antonio Margheriti, it is also particularly gruesome for its time. In addition to some extremely grisly surgery footage, we see the end product of a spike-laden iron maiden (the title "Virgin of Nuremburg"), as well as one poor soul whose nose has been chewed off by a very hungry rodent. Not as splashy as a Herschell Gordon Lewis flick, but still nasty.

Production values are excellent, with lush photography and above-average performances. (Hammer star Christopher Lee plays the aforementioned disfigured caretaker, and—like many of his roles—creates an ominous, demanding presence without uttering a single word.) The atmosphere is so thick you can cut it with a halberd; if dark, foreboding castles and secret passages are your thing, you shan't be disappointed by this exemplary addition to the genre.

Not to be confused with Margheriti's bloodless spook flick **La Danza Macabre** (1963), which was also released under the painfully generic title **Castle of Terror**.

Approximately 76m; Color
VID: **Victims!** [Simitar Entertainment Inc.; 85(76)m]
ADL: *Four girls alone in the desert. They all became his ... Victims!*

After opening with numerous scenes of women being brutally murdered by a man in drag, the film cuts to a young woman being raped by redneck hooligans (apparently escaped mental patients), then cuts to a gratuitous shower scene, and then ... well, you get the picture. Eventually, something akin to a "story" evolves out of all of this, but it seems circumstantial at best. Essentially, **Victims!** is typical rape and revenge fare, prevalent in the liberal 70s (with more of an emphasis on rape than revenge, I might add).

The same director later made the similarly repellent **Night Ripper!** a few years later, but chose not to waste any celluloid on that effort and shoot it on video.

At its best, **Victims!** is poorly made exploitation fare with nothing of interest to anyone except misogynists and or indiscriminate filmgoers.

La Vierge de Nuremberg *see* **La Vergine di Norimberga**

Voyage Scolaire Sanglant *see* **Killer's Moon**

Watch Me When I Kill *see* **Il Gatto dagli Occhi di Giada**

Week of the Killer *see* **La Semana del Asesino**

Weekend per i Morti *see* **Non Si Deve Profanare il Sonno dei Morti**

The Werewolf and the Yeti *see* **La Maldición de la Bestia**

The Werewolf vs. the Vampire Woman *see* **La Noche de Walpurgis**

The Werewolf vs. the Vampire Women *see* **La Noche de Walpurgis**

The Werewolf's Shadow *see* **La Noche de Walpurgis**

What Have You done to Solange? *see* **Cosa Avete Fatto a Solange?**

When the Screaming Stops *see* **Las Garras de Loreli**

White Cannibal Queen *see* **Mondo Cannibale** (1979)

Who's Next? *see* **Cosa Avete Fatto a Solange?**

Wide-Eyed in the Dark *see* **Gatti Rossi in un Labirinto di Vetro**

The Wizard of Gore (1970)
Mayflower Pictures, Inc. [USA]
DIR: Herschell Gordon Lewis; PRO: Herschell Gordon Lewis; SCR: Allen Kahn; DOP: Herschell Gordon Lewis; EXP: Fred M. Sandy; SFX: Herschell Gordon Lewis; MUS: Larry Wellington
STR: Karin Alexana, Don Alexander, Eskander Ameripoor, David Atlas, Charlotte Bell, Monika Blackwell, Sally Brody, Karen Burke, Sherry Carson, Judy Cler, John Elliot, Stephen Field,

The Wizard of Gore

Kack Gilbreth, Corinne Kirkin, Patty la Du, Phil Laurenson, Wayne Ratay, Jim Rau, Eric Kelner Raynard, Sheldon Reis, Ray Sager, and Julie Yager
Approximately 95m; Color
VID: **The Wizard of Gore** [Continental Video; 96(95)m]; **The Wizard of Gore** [Midnight Video; 96(95)m]
ADL: *An astounding achievement in bizarre entertainment!*

A low-rent magician, Montag (Ray Sager), garners something of a reputation for his stage show. Not because he's such a capable illusionist, but because the volunteers he uses during his sets are found shortly thereafter, killed in a gory fashion similar to their bloodless dispatching on stage. (The viewer, though, gets to see what the audience doesn't, complete with gore: One woman is cut in half ... with a chainsaw, another has a metal stake pounded through her head, two young girls are forced to swallow swords, et al.) Apparently, Montag's power far exceeds pulling a rabbit out of his hat, as he has the ability to not only hypnotize the entire audience, but resuscitate his murdered victims long enough for them to walk off the stage before they, well, fall to pieces. It's all up to a talk show host (Judy Cler) and her skeptical boyfriend to get to the bottom of the unexplainable murders.

Although one of Lewis' most innovative, most surreal films, **The Wizard of Gore** is also one of his most incompetent productions ... to the delight of trash film aficionados everywhere. Every aspect of the production is abysmal, making for more unintentional laughs than any Ed Wood film could muster. The dialogue is painfully stilted, and their delivery equally hackneyed. The camerawork is the sloppiest to ever grace a Lewis production. The score sounds unfinished and or out of tune much of the time. And the gore is little more than sheep entrails piled atop shoddy rubber prosthetics, or rubber masks carelessly attached to Styrofoam heads, or, well, you get the point. (One of his goriest, **The Wizard of Gore** is second only to his swan song **The Gore Gore Girls**—made two years later—in sheer gratuity.) And it sports one of the most whacked shock endings to ever grace a horror film. (Talk about a real head scratcher.)

Anyone who has any appreciation for truly, *truly* bad films is recommended to track this puppy down. You're friends may not like you much afterwards, but you'll be

guaranteed many, many hours of enjoyment out of this celluloid atrocity.
☠☠☠

Woodoo—Die Schreckensinsel der Zombies see **Zombi 2**

Young Dracula see **Dracula Vuole Vivere—Cerca Sangue di Vergina!**

A Young Girl for the Cannibals see **Mondo Cannibale** (1979)

Zombi 2 [Zombie 2] (1979)

Variety Film [Italy]
DIR: Lucio Fulci; PRO: Fabrizio de Angelis and Ugo Tucci; SCR: Elisa Briganti; DOP: Sergio Salvati; SFX: Gianetto de Rossi; MFX: Gianetto de Rossi; MUS: Fabio Frizzi and Giorgio Tucci.
STR: Ugo Bologna, Pier Luigi Conti, Stefania d'Amario, Tisa Farrow, Auretta Gay, Richard Johnson, Olga Karlatos, Ian McCulloch, and Monica Zanchi
AKA: L'Enfer des Zombies [*The Inferno of the Zombies*]; **The Island of the Living Dead**; **Nueva York Bajo el Terror de los Zombi** [*New York Bay the Terror of the Zombies*]; **Sangeria**; **Sanguella**; **Woodoo—Der Schreckensisnel der Zombies** [*Voodoo—The Horrible Island of Zombies*]; **Zombie II**; **Zombie 2—The Dead Are Among Us**; **Zombie Flesh Eaters**
Approximately 91m; Color
SND: **Zombie** [Blackest Heart Media; Double-bill w/**Cannibal Ferox**]
VID: **Zombie** [Anchor Bay Entertainment; 91m]; **Zombie** [Wizard Video; 93(91)m]; **Zombie 2—The Dead Are Among Us** [Edde Entertainment; 91m]; **Zombie Flesh Eaters** [VIPC (PAL); 89m]
ADL: *We are going to eat you!*

A boat wanders into Hudson Bay carrying the remains of partially eaten crew members and a couple of voracious zombies. Meanwhile, a woman and three acquaintants set sail for an uncharted island where her father is conducting scientific ex-

periments concerning life after death, a perfect place since voodoo is a prevalent factor there. Before long, dead natives and—eventually—the corpses of conquistadors with poor table manners begin attacking *en masse*, eating the uninvited guests.

Obviously made in an attempt to cash in on the popularity/notoriety of George Romero's **Dawn of the Dead** (and released in Europe with a sequel-connoting moniker, since **Dawn of the Dead** was released thereabouts as **Zombi**), **Zombi 2** embraces the politics but avoids flagrant reiteration. Here, the flesh-eating ghouls are not the product of a mutant virus brought back by a returning space probe (or some other scientific cause), but old fashioned mumbo-jumbo. Of course, the results are inevitably the same, both in respect to reviving the dead, and the eventual takeover of modern civilization by pseudo-cannibalistic corpses.

It also differs in that, whereas Romero's is social commentary, offering pointed stabs at consumerism and the like, Fulci's in an unrepentant horror film, with high intensity gore being its major impetus. Although **Zombi 2**'s bloodshed is just as over-the-top as that found in Romero's film, there is no humor to temper it, and is often more grueling because of it. (Had the effects been more up to par with Tom Savini's groundbreaking work, it may have proved to be nearly unwatchable.) Bodies are eviscerated, eyes are pierced, hapless victims torn limb from limb, all in close-up detail and with as much fake blood as the effects department could afford. It may not be art, but it is as visceral as the genre gets.

Due at least in part to this film's box-office success, director Fulci went on to helm a whole string of ultra-violent shockers up until his death in 1996, including a handful of other zombie-oriented films. (The most infamous of these being the "Gates of Hell" series which is comprised of **Paura nella Città dei Morti Viventi** and **L'Aldilá**, 1980 and 1981, respectively.)

It doesn't get much nastier than this. ☠☠☠

Zombi 3—Da Dove Vieni? *see* **Non Si Deve Profanare il Sonno dei Morti**

Zombi Horror *see* **Le Notte del Terrore**

Zombie *see* **Zombi 2**

Zombie II *see* **Zombi 2**

Zombie 2—The Dead Are Among Us *see* **Zombi 2**

Zombie 3 *see* **Le Notte del Terror**

Zombie Child *see* **The Child**

Zombie Flesh Eaters *see* **Zombi 2**

Zombie Horror *see* **La Notte del Terrore**

Le Zombie Venu d'Ailleurs *see* **Prey (1977)**

Zombies *see* **Le Notte del Terrore**

Zombies—Dawn of the Dead *see* **Dawn of the Dead**

Appendix 1

Snuff: The Making of an Urban Legend

Note: An earlier version of this exposé appeared in **Skeptical Inquirer**, *V23#3, May/June 1999; CSICOP.*

Suburban myths are epidemic. For many of us, our tedious existence is made to seem that much more bearable by the mere presence of such guilty pleasures. For others, they are very real, and hold as much—if not more—power than fears which can be justified. And they are a means for us to indulge even our most morbid inclinations by the simple act of relaying well-worn accounts that fall somewhere between the idioms of gossip and campfire tales. It can be rightfully said that they are the folklore of the industrial generation.

Even those individuals unfamiliar with the concept of urban legends (or suburban myths, depending on the locale) have more than likely been responsible for disseminating and perpetuating such tales which defy debunking. The baby alligator which is flushed down the toilet, only to survive and breed in the sewers beneath the city streets. The nameless old woman who decides to dry off her beloved poodle by throwing it in the microwave for a few short minutes... with predictably nasty results. The nameless young woman who visits the tanning salon one too many times, and—after being unable to get rid of a noxious odor clinging to her person—discovers that her insides are rotting as a result of being cooked. These are but three of innumerable myths perpetuated by everyone from young children too young to understand their significance, to businesspeople gossiping around the water cooler during their breaks.

And, like living languages, urban legends change, both as a result from misrepresentation (the laws of chaos are undeniably inherent to hearsay), and as a means of evolution, adapting to fit the environment of those cultivating it. Yet, despite their stubborn existence, no one can ever offer any proof outside of it having happened to "a friend of a friend." So widespread are these snippets of delusion, so ingrained in our culture, they are now looked upon as something more integral to our lives than mere idle gossip. Recognizing the importance of these tales, modern folklorist Jan Harold Brunvand began collecting them in their various forms, and by the late 80s had authored at least seven books on the subject, and was responsible for a nationally syndicated bi-weekly column that recounted such tales. He found out that he had his hands full, though, as he probably spent just as much time writing about them as he did fending off the claims of those mythical "friends of a friend."

Although an occasional nuisance to those aware of their erroneous nature, urban legends rarely have much impact on our society. But what if such a tale grew to an unprecedented level of acceptance that it actually had a substantial effect on the mindset of the public? What if it became responsible for the dissemination of unsubstantiated claims that created a nationwide panic, generating results much like those of yelling "fire" in a crowded theater, yet on a much grander scale? What if such a tale was responsible for single-handedly creating a myth that would become a cinematic bogeyman of unheralded proportions? Such, it seems, is the history of the snuff film.

Urban legends cover all facets of life, including cinema. And since the two major themes underlying urban legends are sex and death, it seems only natural that the genre of the horror film is particularly rife with lore. Being a convenient scapegoat for numerous societal woes since its conception, and being vilified on the same grounds as rock music and comic books, horror films are a perfect breeding ground for such myths. Stories abound, ranging from the innocuous (rumors still persist that **King Kong vs. Godzilla** [1963] was released with two different endings, with Kong winning in the stateside release, whereas Godzilla triumphs in the Japanese version), to the downright macabre. (Many horror fans still think that such films as **Le Jorobado de la Morgue** [1972], **Buio Omega** [1980], and **Der Todesking** [1990] utilize real corpses to supplement the staged effects, despite documentation to the contrary. Because of the inaccessibility of many foreign films—especially low budget productions such as these—it is easy to see how such rumors can persist.) Some of these legends remain fairly obscure, relegated to being spread word of mouth by naïve, uninformed fans. Others persist outside the fan following, infiltrating mainstream America.

Of the latter variety, one of the more popular myths involves the film **The Texas Chain Saw Massacre** (1974). There is a lingering misconception that purports that this low-budget production was indeed based on a real story as it so coyly claims in an opening statement. In truth, it is loosely—if not *tenuously*—based on the exploits of one Edward Gein, a Wisconsin farmer who had a filthy habit of raiding graveyards and making lampshades out of its clientele. Evidence that he practiced cannibalism and necrophilia on occasion cannot be overlooked either, although a chainsaw was *not* involved. As for similarities between these crimes and Tobe Hooper's unrelenting horror film, they are far and few between. (Alfred Hitchcock's 1960 **Psycho** actually bears a much greater resemblance to the case, despite the fact that author Robert Bloch claims he knew nothing of Gein's heinous crimes before writing the novel that inspired the film.)

The claims of **The Texas Chain Saw Massacre** has imbedded itself so deeply in our culture that people are more than just convinced of its authenticity. Even to this day, I am approached by individuals claiming—in all sincerity—that they actually *knew* someone or have met someone from Texas who "lived just down the road from where it all happened." Granted, most of them are not horror fans, *per se*, yet most are well-educated people who are not only ignorant of the facts, but have taken the word of someone they felt inclined to believe.

Despite the inevitable frustration with having to reiterate the facts to those who adhere to these misconceptions, one can find humor in the claims inspired by **The Texas Chain Saw Massacre**. It is essentially harmless, and remains an excellent example of how gullible people can be, how they adapt their reality to suit erroneous information offered to them as fact. It is also a testament to how our culture embellishes reality, for whatever reasons.

The legend of the snuff film, on the other hand, lacks the humor of its slightly older sibling, and is a prime example of the weaknesses in our belief system.

The term "snuff" in reference to a specific genre of filmmaking where the actors are supposedly killed for the benefit of the viewer has been credited to Ed Sanders in his book **The Family—The Story of Charles Manson's Dune Buggy Attack Battalion** [Panther Books, 1976], and was used to describe unsubstantiated claims that Manson and his followers may have been involved in perpetrating such crimes; this is unlikely, though, as the movie predates the book in question.

A quarter century after the Sanders book, many people who have heard of—but have never seen—the movie **Snuff** insist that it *does* contain actual footage of human death and mutilation. Even those individuals who do not recall the controversy have been indelibly affected by it, as belief in "snuff" films persist to this day. Many people attest to the existence of snuff films even though no has ever actually *seen* one; authorities, it seems, also have nothing more concrete than vague rumors about the alleged production and distribution of snuff films as well. It is not at all surprising that most of the rumors concerning the existence of snuff films did not surface until *after* this film made the headlines.[1]

It is safe to say that anybody who has seen **Snuff** (which is obscure, but far from unavailable) knows how ludicrous these claims are, at least with respect to this specific production. Not only is the gore obviously fake, but the execution of the special effects is painfully inept. **Snuff** is nothing more than a grand marketing scheme that made a shameless little splatter film into one of the most profitable—and notorious—films ever conceived. The clever ad campaign is obviously tongue in cheek, but somehow millions of theater-goers were snagged by the notion "But what if it *is* real?" and it seems that their morbid curiosity got the best of them. Were the producers actually aware of America's obsession with the macabre? (One would only have to watch the evening news or catch sight of a gaggle of rubberneckers driving by a bloody highway accident to realize just how fascinated we are by death in its many forms.) Or did they simply view it as a clever dare all to attract a few extra ticket sales? As it turns out, the latter seems closer to the truth. Whatever the motives, it worked, to the absolute joy of the promoters—and to the chagrin of those who would inevitably be confronted with the chore of debunking the hoax in the years to come.

The film's origin dates back several years before its "auspicious" release in 1975. In 1971, filmmakers Michael and Roberta Findlay helmed a production in Argentina called **Slaughter**, a modest little film that was made for a little over $30,000. Although various sources have cited it to be an unfinished production, it *did* have a theatrical run, albeit brief. (**Slaughter** played no more than three theaters prior to October of 1975; obviously, promotion was not their strong suit.) How this came about is uncertain; with the exception of an abrupt end— quite possibly snipped to accommodate the splashier finale tacked on years later—it is obviously a complete production.

Slaughter did its damnedest to exploit the still-steaming remains of the Manson Family's involvement with the Tate/La Bianca murders, although much artistic license is taken. The film is generally more accessible than the Findlays' other films—**The Touch of Her Flesh** (1967), **A Thousand Pleasures** (1968), et al.—but this was not much of a stretch. (Even as far as sexploitation goes, their contributions to the genre were exemplary in their perversity and sheer audacity.) Fans of their films—especially **A Thousand Pleasures**—will not only recognize some of the familiar faces (and voices, some of the actors being dubbed by those involved in the aforementioned film, the Findlays among them), but the overwhelmingly awkward dialogue as well. Unlike these other lowbrow productions, though, **Slaughter** was not destined to languish in the pits of obscurity. Far from it.

In 1972, Allan Shackleton, a research engineer-turned-film producer had bought the world distribution rights for **Slaughter** through his Monarch Releasing Corporation, a distribution house that specialized in sexploitation fare. He was still "scratching to recoup a shaky investment in a rotten film" (Lynch, 1976) three years later when it caught the attention of someone who mistook the proceedings in his film as something more sinister than it was. Instead of setting the record straight, Mr. Shackleton played up on the false assumptions. Gambling on the three I's (implication, inference, and innuendo), he then launched an elaborate campaign that avoided a conviction to the authenticity of the atrocities in the film.

On December 1, 1975, Allan Shackleton sent out the first of several press releases aimed to pique people's interest. Unfortunately for him, Michael Findlay caught sight of it and immediately realized that it was *his* film **Slaughter** (now retitled under the more succinct, monosyllabic moniker **Snuff**) that was behind the escalating furor. Findlay approached the distributor about contract renegotiations (as he was obviously not getting a big enough piece of the pie), but was unsuccessful in his pleas for more money. He did, however, almost succeed in exposing the entire scam during a crushing interview; Shackleton immediately paid him off, and he did not hear from Michael again.[2]

Shackleton took the next step of distributing fake newspaper clippings that detailed the efforts of a fictional "Vincent Sheehan" and the retired attorney's crusade against the film through a newly formed organization called Citizens for Decency. Unbeknownst to him, though, there really already *was* a group called Citizens for Decency, but this did little to deter the real organization from rallying behind Shackleton's fictional do-gooder. If anyone from the group had checked Sheehan's credentials, they evidently did not make it publicly known.

Amidst the national hysteria, critics everywhere were writing articles condemning the unreleased film, endorsing its authenticity sight unseen and giving it whatever credibility it had previously lacked. At this point, no one had actually seen the movie save for a few disgruntled theater-goers who had happened to catch it during its short term run as **Slaughter**. Even more ironic, the notorious finale that would give the film the weight it needed and guarantee it a place in the history books had not even been filmed yet.

The scene that punctuates the Findlays' all-but-forgotten film was shot for $10,000 in a Manhattan loft by Simon Nuchtern of August films during the course of a single day. This new footage featured a film crew (supposedly the selfsame individuals responsible for **Slaughter**) who wrap up their production by mutilating, dismembering, and eventually eviscerating the leading lady (who bears no resemblance to the previous actress). At the pinnacle of her bloody demise, the cameraman conveniently runs out of film, although the audio track continues to record their panicked voices even after everything has faded to black.

And then it unofficially became cinematic history.

Snuff opened January 16, 1976, and was met by as many curiosity seekers as it was by ardent protesters. Theaters were besieged by staunch feminists, egged by angry picketers, and it was not uncommon for the small grindhouses to receive bomb threats on a daily basis. Instead of deterring would-be ticket buyers, though, it only fanned the flames of public interest. In the first week of its New York run, **Snuff** grossed $66,000, and outsold such hits as **One Flew Over the Cuckoo's Nest** for three weeks straight (Smith, 1982).

The controversy finally caught the attention of the legal system, forcing the film to carry a disclaimer that clearly stated that no one was harmed during the production of said film. Reluctantly, Shackleton went along with it, but eventually recounted his admittance, reverting to his statement that the public should be left to decide **Snuff**'s authenticity for themselves. Years later, Shackleton finally fessed up (sans coercion), but by that time no one wanted to listen—to him or anyone else it seemed. Not only had the notoriety of the film snowballed to unprecedented proportions, but it had become accepted "fact" that snuff films were a national scourge and no amount of debunking would change the public's mindset.

The incidental showing of **Slaughter** that sparked Shackleton's decision to play up the sordid implications of the snuff myth lead to Detective Joseph Horman's claims that the New York Police Department had "reliable sources attesting to the circulation of snuff films," which he erroneously referred to as "slasher" films. Apparently, he said, interested individuals were paying $200 a piece—some sources cite a mere $150—for private screenings of an eight reel, 8mm production which was rumored to have been filmed in Argentina. This unverified account could easily be traced back to **Slaughter**, although it had been greatly embellished by the time it had reached the authorities. This single rumor became the only evidence on which the entire **Snuff** hoax—and the snuff movie scare—was rooted.

The Los Angeles Police Department did an investigation into the phenomenon, and admitted that they could not find even the *slightest* evidence that snuff films actually existed. They later denied this statement, saying that no investigation was ever initiated by them, possibly in an attempt to defend themselves against the harassment of a public who that believed otherwise. Reporters who actually followed up on the rumors (as opposed to just accepting the authenticity of the films on hearsay) came up empty handed as well. Every individual who felt morally obligated to unearth a bona fide snuff flick failed in their attempts to do so. Still, the majority of the population was convinced that snuff films were a multi-million dollar racket that was upsetting the country's already shaky moral foundations. It was only after **Snuff** had run its course and the continued inability of the authorities to find evidence of snuff films that the hysteria died down and some people began doubting their convictions. Unfortunately, it had become so ingrained in our culture that, for future generations and those too young to understand its significance, snuff films would transgress the line from hoax to urban legend.

Twenty-four years later, the myth remains.

Even to this day, anti-smut campaigners use **Snuff** and snuff films in general as artillery to defend their moralistic crusades. Even many hardline feminists use snuff films as an example of patriarchal suppression (as if there weren't *enough* documented cases attesting to the psychological, sexual, and physical abuse of women). Such books as **The Age of Sex Crime** by Jane Caputi, **Outrageous Acts and Everyday Rebellions** by Gloria Steinem, and **Take Back the Night—Women on Pornography** by Laura Lederer make the presumption that snuff films are a given in this day and age; some even go so far as to suppose that snuff films are the logical conclusion for those individuals jaded by more traditional forms of pornography. Even Linda Lovelace, star of the groundbreaking adult film **Deep Throat** (1972), testified to the US Attorney General's Commission on Organized Crime that "women acting in porn films were being murdered on camera or after filming when they were deemed of no further use." (Kerekes, 1995). (Many, though, don't take her claims very seriously, and feel that she spent many years previous trying to vilify the adult film industry in an effort to assuage the guilt of her contribution to popularizing pornography.) Unfortunately, the decision on the part of some hardline feminists to rely on hearsay only exposes their ignorance of the facts or purposeful dissemination of long-debunked propaganda. Those individuals willing to cross the line and try to dispel the myth find themselves avoiding the slings and arrows of their detractors while they themselves are forced to convince individuals who cannot see beyond their own faith and gullibility. Unfortunately, in an age of sound bites, this is a task easier said than done.

The snuff film controversy is suspiciously similar to that of the current trend to blame many of our societal woes on Satanic cults and their sexual and psychological abuse of children; one cannot discount the possibility that there *may* be isolated incidents of both real snuff films and Satanic ritual abuse, but—insofar—there is no substantial proof as to the existence of either. (As of late, these two mythical scourges have become strange bedfellows; where one is "discovered," the other is seemingly not far behind, as if they could somehow validate each other's existence.)

Despite the sometimes chastising tone of this article towards the man responsible for **Snuff**'s conception, Shackleton should be commended for his ingenuity and his success at riling up a sometimes lax populace. (Especially in the 1970s, a decade known for its lack of political correctness.) Had he actually claimed the authenticity of the film like so many government authorities, angry citizens-turned-activists, and (especially) the media, he would have been no better. When it gets right down to it, his worst crime is being opportunistic.

In a perfect world, no one would have taken his inferences with anything more than a grain of salt, and if they had, the illusion would have been quickly dispelled on an individual and community level. Unfortunately, though, **Snuff**'s shameless promotion created a tidal wave of hysteria that latched on to a culture's deep-rooted ignorance, and flourished in a media-driven society that is quick to publicize the sordid and sensational. Furthermore, our society's cathartic dependence on the macabre—on our fascination with all things concerning death—only strengthened its roots.

Even today, there are rumors of "snuff" sightings, sometimes instigated by the filmmakers themselves. The most recent example involves a Japanese series of gory shot-on-video productions released under the collected title of **Za Ginipiggu** [Guinea Pig], several of the installments having been directed by the infamous *manga* artist/writer Hideshi Hino, known in the states for such comic book graphic novels as **Panorama of Hell** and **Hell**

Baby. (The first film in the series was even accompanied by the disclaimer "The producers received this video. There was no accompanying information. We are researching name, age, and other information about the girl and her three killers." Sound familiar?) Apparently, someone was showing a copy of the third installment, **Chiniku No Hana** (1990), at a Hollywood party circa 1991 where it caught the eye of actor Charlie Sheen. Convinced he had seen an actual snuff film, he immediately contacted the MPAA (Motion Pictures Association of America) and—before they could substantiate the claims—he "got involved in a subsequent movement to stop any kind of import distribution for the films" (Weisser and Weisser, 1997). The film was traced back to Chas Balun, a film reviewer who also moonlighted as a video bootlegger; of course, the atrocities in the film were proven to be fake. The incident made headlines, though, and was even spotlighted on ABC's **20/20**. Instead of the film being confined to the pits of obscurity like—we can assume—Mr. Sheen had hoped, the furor only fueled the fire of interest in this no-budget splatter film, giving it a cult status it did not deserve. This same film sparked similar controversy in Great Britain in 1992, the owner of the confiscated "video nasty" fined for nothing more than mild obscenity charges when it proved to be the low-rent hoax that it was.

Yet it is not only the claims of deceived individuals that help to perpetuate the myth; every time that snuff films are even mentioned in modern fiction and cinema, they are giving credence to the rumors, playing on the reader's or viewer's assumptions that they are real to begin with. Not only have snuff films become a common staple in many sordid crime novels written in the last twenty years (even by such respected mystery writers as Rex Miller and Andrew Vachss), it has become popular subject for innumerable exploitation and horror films. **Emanuelle in America** (1976), **The Last House on Dead End Street** (1977), **Effects** (1979), **Holocausto Canibal** (1979), **Video Violence… When Renting Is Not Enough** (1986), **Shiryo No Wana** (1988), **The Art of Dying** (1991), **Midnight 2 – Death, Sex and Videotape** (1993) and even the exemplary productions **C'Est Arrivé Près de Chez Vous** (1992), **Mute Witness** (1994), and the Hollywood hit **8mm** (1999) starring Nicolas Cage are just a few of the countless titles which milk the urban legend for all it's worth. Even if the existence of actual snuff films are validated at a later date, it is safe to say that there are more films *about* snuff films than there are actual snuff films in existence.

Of course, this issue begs the question: Should novelists and screenwriters avoid the subject altogether because it helps to perpetuate the myth? No, and why should they? Writers deal with fiction, and the suspension of disbelief is an integral part of any good novel or film. Putting any sort of disclaimer on each and every piece of entertainment that chooses to exploit this and other myths is a ludicrous notion; people should not have to be told that what they are reading or viewing has no basis in fact, as the label of "fiction" already establishes this.

The media, on the other hand, has a responsibility to the public, not so much with the dissemination of information, but with the dissemination of facts. Unfortunately, fanciful stories and alleged hearsay are usually more interesting than cold reality and facts, as urban legends have shown beyond any shadow of a doubt.

As an individual who appreciates a good put-on *and* enjoys trashy films, I will continue — like many others — to relish **Snuff** for what it is: a sleazy little time-waster whose charms reflect a decade that wasn't afraid of pushing the envelope, even if it meant sacrificing good taste. Others, refusing to see the great **Snuff** hoax for what it was, will remember it only as the end of a nation's innocence.

Endnote

1. Of course, pseudo-documentaries like **Faces of Death** do not meet the full criteria because the real deaths they do depict weren't staged specifically for the film itself, but culled from various incidental sources — newsreel footage, home movies that inadvertently committed such tragedies to film, etc. (Although much on that particular series was proven faked sometime after the fact.) One such shockumentary, **Snuff Video — Volume Red** (1997) from Flatline Productions,

even goes so far as to redefine snuff films to include such incidentals in the attempt to justify its erroneous moniker.

2. Michael died several years later while on his way to Europe to demonstrate a new, portable 3-D camera. His helicopter slammed into the roof of the Pan-Am building; he was decapitated, and his investment suffered a similarly dehabilitating fate. Roberta Findlay, whom he had split up with shortly before the unfortunate accident, went on to direct a string of reasonably successful hardcore porn films: **Angel Number 9** (1979), **The Playgirl** (1982), **Glitter** (1983), to name but a few. She eventually returned to the slightly more legit market—at least in the eyes of mainstream America—of independent horror, producing such straight-to-video fare as **The Oracle** (1985), **Blood Sisters** (1987), and **Prime Evil** (1988). She retired from filmmaking shortly thereafter.

Appendix 2

Video Sources

The following are legitimate video companies:

A-Pix Entertainment 500 Fifth Avenue, New York, NY 10110

Alpha Video Distributors, Inc. Piscataway, NJ 08854

Anchor Bay Entertainment 500 Kirts Blvd., Troy, MI 48084 www.anchorbayentertainment.com

Avalanche Home Entertainment 578 Post Road East, Suite 712, Westport, CT 06880

Columbia/TriStar Home Video 10202 West Washington Blvd., Culver City, CA 90232-3195

Dead-Alive Productions 111 West Main Street, Mesa, AZ 85201

Entertainment Programs International 4230 Del Rey Avenue, Suite 507, Marina Del Rey, CA 90292

Film Threat Video PO Box 3170, Los Angeles, CA 90078-3170 www.filmthreat.com

Fox Lorber Home Video 419 Park Avenue South, New York, NY 10016

Full Moon Home Video 3030 Andrita Street, Los Angeles, CA 90065 (323) 468-0599 www.fullmoonpictures.com

Live Entertainment, Inc. 15400 Sherman Way, Van Nuys, CA 91406

Moore Video PO Box 5703, Richmond, VA 23220

Paramount Home Video 5555 Melrose Avenue, Hollywood, CA 90038

Program Power Entertainment 190 Pomona Avenue, Long Beach, CA 90803 (562) 621-9090 www.programpower.com

Republic Pictures Home Video 12636 Beatrice Street, Los Angeles, CA 90066-0930

Rhino Home Video 10635 Santa Monica Blvd., Los Angeles, CA 90025-4900 1-800-432-0020 www.rhino.com

Something Weird Video PO Box 33664, Seattle, WA 98133 (206) 361-3759 www.somethingweird.com

Synapse Films PO Box 1860, Bloomington, IL 61702 (309) 661-9201 www.synapse-films.com

Tai Seng Video Marketing 170 South Spruce Avenue, Suite 200, South San Francisco, CA 94080 1-800-888-3836 www.taisengentertainment.com

Appendix 2. Video Sources 260

Tempe Video PO Box 6573, Akron, OH 4312-0573

Troma Inc. Radio City Station, PO Box 486, New York, NY, 10101-0486 *www.troma.com*

Warner Home Video 4000 Warner Blvd., Burbank, CA 91522

World Artists Home Video PO Box 36788, Los Angeles, CA 90036-0788

The following are legitimate video distributors:

Cape Copy Center 631 Main Street, Hyannis, MS 02601 (508) 775-6500

Cinema Classics, PO Box 174, Dept. F, Village Station, New York, NY 10014 (212) 677-6309

Draculina PO Box 587, Glen Carbon, IL 62034 (800) 358-2755

EI Independent Cinema PO Box 371, Dept. SS, Glenwood, NJ 07418 (973) 509-9352

Liberty Home Video 11333 E. 60th Place, Tulsa, OK 74146 (800) 331-4077

Paul's Hobby Zone PO Box 650113, Dept. FG, West Newton, MA 02165

Scarlet Street Video PO Box 604, Glen Rock, NJ 07452

Science Fiction Continuum 1701 East Second Street, Scotch Plains, NJ 07076 (908) 322-2010 *store.yahoo.com/continuum*

Trash Palace PO Box 2565, Dept. CM, Silver Spring, MD 20915 (301) 681-4625

Water Bearer Films 48 West 21st Street, Suite 301, New York, NY 10010 (212) 242-8686 *www.waterbearer.com*

The following are small mail-order companies that sell tapes "from one collector to another;" anyone who knows better, though, refers to these entrepeneurs as "bootleggers." Although some of these people are fans-cum-businessmen who offer decent second-generation copies of films and prints currently unavailable in the United States at a reasonable price, many are unethical scumbags who have simply found a convenient way to make money off of another's endeavors. The publishers and I will not be held responsible for any transactions you may make with these individuals; suffice it to say, dealing with bootleggers is an extremely risky prospect. Unfortunately, it is the only way to get our grubby paws on these films short of scouring Europe or Asia for them. Furthermore, some of these titles have never been offered by legitimate sources anywhere, so until domestic labels see fit to fill the demand on more obscure titles, they're all we've got.

All of these companies have catalogs available, although—by the time this books sees print—many of them may have folded, or simply ran off with some poor sap's money. (Having been one of the latter victims on several occasions, I can't impart upon you enough just how perilous this business is for naïve fans.) Just remember the credo: Don't part with monies that you can afford to lose. You've been warned.

Alpha Blue Archives, Inc. Dept. PO Box 16072, Dept. Cult,

Oakland, CA 94610 *www.alphabluearchives.com*

Blackest Heart Media PO Box 3376, Antioch, CA 94531-3376 (925) 753-0169 *www.houseofhorrors.com*

The Blood Shed PO Box 16602, Baltimore, MD 21221

Blood Times Video PO Box 3340, Steinway Station, Long Island City, NY 11103-0340

European Trash Cinema PO Box 12161, Spring, TX 77391-2161 (281) 251-0637 *www.diabolik.demon.co.uk*

Filmfax Products PO Box 1900, Evanston, IL 60204 (847) 866-7155 *www.filmfax.com*

Foxx Entertainment Ltd. 3651 West Butler, Chandler, AZ 85226 (818) 783-2263

Luminous Film & Video Wurks PO Box 1047, Dept. PV, Medford, NY 11763 *www.lfvw.com*

Midnight Video 5010 Church Drive, Coplay, PA 18037 (610) 261-1756 *www.midnight1.com*

Phantom Video PO Box 7301, Jupiter, FL 33468

Sarjim Video Services 139382 Cedar Rd., #308-IN, University Heights, OH 44118 *www.sarjim.com*

Shocking Videos HC-77 Box 111, Hinton, WV 25951

Sinister Cinema PO Box 4369, Dept. C, Medford, OR 97501-0168 (541) 773-6860 *www.sinistercinema.com*

Tapes of Terror 11430 Mullins Drive, Dept. CM, Houston, TX 77035-2632

Threat Theatre PO Box 7633, Olympia, WA 98507-7633

Tropic Twilight Company 1142 Auahi Street, Suite 3203, Honolulu, HI 96814

Unearthly Video PO Box 681914, Dept. F, Orlando, FL 32868-1914

Video Dungeon PO Box 873, Tarpon Springs, FL 34688 *www.videodungeon.net*

Video Holocaust PO Box 3187, Waterbuy, CT 06705

Video Screams PO Box 443, Dept. F170, Bellefontaine, OH 43311

Video Search of Miami PO Box 16-1917, Miami, FL 33116 (888) 279-9773 *www.vsom.com*

The Video Vault 142 91st Street, Brooklyn, NY 11209

Video Wasteland 214 Fair Street, Berea, OH 44017 (440) 891-1920 *www.slaughter.net/wasteland/*

Witching Hour Video, Dept. G, PO Box 806, University Station, Lexington, KY, 40506-0025 *www.witchinghour.com*

Index

A & A Special Effects 104, 115
À Meia-Noite Levarei Sua Alma 37, 110
Abagnalo, George 42
Abbott, Fredric 232
Aber, Jeannine 62
Aberg, Sivi 94
Abril, Antón García 47, 68, 98, 122, 184, 186, 188
Ackerman, Forrest J. 100
Ackerman, Malvina 171
Adams, A. *see* Adamson, Al
Adams, Helen 231
Adamson, Al 100
Addobbati, Giuseppe 124
Adiutori, Patrizia 79
Adlum, Ed 219
Adorni, Guido 97
Adsit, Robert 125
Aetas Film Produktions 145
Aftermath 156
Agami, Isac 87
Agar, Ivan 219
Agnew, Decatur 91
Agudin, Francisco 73
Agudin, Luis 218
Aguirre, Javier 130, 155, 176, 214
Aielo, Robinson 37
Airoldi, Cristina 79, 224
Alarido 225
Alavi, Mori 74
Alba, Angelita 65
Alba, Tota 150
Albaicin, Rafael 159
Albain, Jr., Richard 115
Albar, Ali 207
Alberge, Betty 93
Albert, Jerry 60
Alberti, Sergio 73

Alcaine, José Luis 204
Alcántara, Rafael 166
Alcazar, Eduardo 163
Alcazar, Victor 109, 130, 156
Alcott, Robert 96
Aldan Company Inc. 181
Alden, Michael 104
Alden, Priscilla 83, 214
L'Aldilà 161, 248
Alessandroni, Alessandro 114, 211
Alexana, Karin 245
Alexander, Don 245
Alexander, Larry 216
Alexander, Newell 148
Alexander, Paul 215
Alexander, Victor 144
Alexander, William 72
Alexandria, Mello 223
Alexeievna, Inna 101, 124
Alexis, Nora 128
Alice, Sweet Alice 38
Alien 39
Alien Dead 41
Alien Prey 201
Alighiero, Carlo 224
Alldredge, Michael 148
Allen, Barbara 42
Allen, Carol 46
Allen, Chris 62
Allen, Gary 38
Allen, Jeffrey 235
Allen, Joy 181
Allen, Larry 171
Allen, Nancy 71
L'Alliance Invisible 234
Allied Artists 38
Allison 171
Allodi, Simonetta 68
Allum, Victoria 215
Almirall, Joan *see* Cozar, Juan Soler

Almirall, Rosa *see* Romay, Lina
Almodovar, Cristino 122
Alone in the Dark 97
Alonso, Carlos Aured 109, 192, 208, 242
Alonso, Luis 159
Alonzo, Alicia 162
Alphonso 149
Alt, Sarah 171
Altman, Burt 226
Alucarda 41
Alucarda—La Hija de las Tinieblas 41
Alvarez, Jacinto Molina 98, 109, 121, 130, 150, 152, 156, 159, 163, 166, 168, 172, 186, 192, 194, 208, 242
Alves, Anselmo 111
Alves, Marlene 111
AM Films 219
Amachi, Shigeru 155
Amambrini, Umberto 174
Amante, James *see* Band, Charles
Amaral, Salvador 110, 111
Amati, Edmondo 45, 160, 189
Amato, Chris 103
Amazzo, T. *see* Findlay, Michael; Nuchtern, Simon
Amber, Dail 180
Amer, Nicholas 93
American Cannibale 221
American International Pictures 148
American Xpress 229
Ameripoor, Eskander 128, 245
Ammanni, Lukas 134
Amobaq 122, 159

Index

Amok 215
Amorós, Francisco 121
L'Amour Parmi les Monstres 109
Amplas, John 85, 169
Amunsen, Barbara 120
Ancla Century Films 47, 68, 150, 184
Anderson, Athena 149
Anderson, Clyde *see* Alonso, Carlos Aured
Anderson, Jamie 200
Anderson, Tera 57
Andre, Iris 156
Andresen, Donna 165
Andress, Ursula 173
Andreu, Simon 185, 197
Andrews, Brian 132
Andy Warhol's Bad 42
Andy Warhol's Dracula 101
Andy Warhol's Frankenstein 115, 177
Angel, A. Ramirez 213
Angelo, Luigi 198, 211
Angelo, Terry 205
Angelo, Tony 147
Ankler, Marshall 158
Anna, Julie 205
Annabelle 226
Annan, Glory 201
Anneman, Bill 80
Anouchka *see* Lesoeur, Anouchka
Anouska *see* Lesoeur, Anouchka
L'Antéchrist 45
Antefatto 44
Anthropophagous 68, 233
Anthropophagus II 198
L'Antichristo 45
Antnori, Antonietta 191
Anton, Matthew 42
Antonelli, Roberto 124
Antonini, Alfredo *see* Band, Albert
Antunes, Édson 111
Anubis Films 150
Aparecida, Nelita 90, 111
Apartment on the 13th Floor 217
Appel, Efrem 107
Aranda, Angel 159
Aranda, Jorgelina 151
Arantes, Ariane 112
Archambault, Arch 154
Ardizzone, Anna 209
Ardow, Dean *see* de Nardo, Gustavo
Arent, Laurie 115
Arent, Lindsey 115

Ares, Ruperto 186
Arévalo, Tito 49, 162
Argento, Claudio 202, 225
Argento, Dario 39, 43, 45, 85, 125, 180, 202, 225
Argento, Salvatore 225
Arias, Bernardo 151
Arié, Bruno 165
Armand, Claude 120
Arment, Gwen 167
Armstrong, Hugh 88
Armstrong, Michael 64
Armstrong, Peter 54
Arndts, Angela 153
Arnold, Mal 56
Arpón, María Elena 156
Arriaga, Simon 168, 188
Arribas, Fernando 73
Arrighi, Nike 203
Arrow, Ann 61
Arroyo, Alexis T. 41
Arteaga, Angel 121, 166, 208
Arthur, Colin 240
Artigot, Raul 68, 217
Ascani, Eugenio 160
Ascot, Anthony *see* Carmineo, Giuliano
Asesino 216
Ashdown, Shirley 61
Ashley, John 49, 50, 65, 162
Askin, Leon 94
Askwith, Robin 46, 140, 232
Asman, John 229
Asman, William 229
Asmawi 207
Assignment Terror 172
Assunção, Ângelo 210
Astor, Eva 72
Astro-Creep 2000 210
Astro-Zombies 81
Asturias, Carpi 50
Asylum Erotica 52
Asylum of the Insane 45
At Midnight I'll Take Your Soul Away 37
El Ataque de los Muertos sin Ojos 47, 115, 185, 188
Atherton, Ray 137
Athon Productions 59
Atkins, Peter 117
Atkins, Tom 115
Atkyns, Norman 117
Atlantica Cinematografica 243
Atlantida Films 160
Atlas, David 245

Atntzen, David 198
Attanasio, Giovanni 211
Attili, Giorgio 37, 90, 110, 111, 210
Au Rendez Vous de la Mort Joyeuse 72
Auci, Giuseppe 106
Au-Delà du Désir 90
Auer, Gregory M. 71, 135
Auger, Claudine 44
August Films 221
Aulin, Ewa 73
Aumont, Tina 79
Aured, Carlos *see* Alonso, Carlos Aured
Austin, Tina 221
Austria 1700 64
Autopsy 161
Avalon, Frankie 50
Avan, Anoosh 74
Avco-Embassy Pictures Corp. 115
Avelar, J. *see* Marins, José Mojica
Avery, Anita *see* de Alba, Aurora
Avram, Chris 44, 198, 211
Avred, Charles *see* Alonso, Carlos Aured
The Awakening of the Beast 210
The Axe 48
The Axe Murders 48
Axelrod, Robert 244
Axen, Eva 225
Ayers, Nancy 154
Ayling, Denys 39
Ayllon, Victoria 156
Ayres, Dave 135
Azarello, Joe 137
Azevedo, Renato 110

Baal, Karin 81
Baccaro, Salvatore 107
Bacchanales Infernales 239
Bach, Dale E. 53
Bach, Johanne Sebastian 93, 213
Bach, Rebecca 84
Back to the Killer 243
Bad Girls 198
The Bad Lieutenant 103
Badejo, Bolaji 40
Badessi, Carlo 81
Badger, Russ 128
Badrun, E.L. 207
Baeza, Nina 60
Baeza, Thomas 103
Baffico, Jim 85
Bagdonas, Jim 137

Index

Bahia de Sangre 44
La Baie Sanglante 44
Bain, Dickson 61
Baird, Alecs 76
Baker, Carroll 42
Baker, Fred 85
Baker, Kent 46
Baker, Rick 148
Baker, Stanley 160
Bakerman, Gary 235
Balaski, Belinda 200
Balcazar, Alfonso 197
Balcazar, Francisco 197
Balch, Antony 140
Balducci, Franco 160
Baldwin, A. Michael 198
Ball, Jim 84
Ball, Jim L. 181
Ball, Robert 94
Ball, Warren 80
Ballen, Ruth 74
Ballesteros, Me Paz 73
Balsor, Dunca 209
Band, Charles 165
Band, Richard 166
Bannister, Reggie 198
Baquero 217
Baraghini, Giulio 51
Baralla, Orlando 197
Baratas, Máximo 150
Barbareschi, Luca Giorgio 138
Barbeau, Adrienne 115
Barbi, Vince 80
Barbieri, Renato 191
Barboo, Luis 47, 122
Barbosa, Almir 37
Barbosa, José 90
Barbosa, Natalina 90
Barbour, Bruce 200
Bardem, Pilar 192, 242
Barilli, Francisco 203
Bark, Peter 191
Barker, Clive 117
Barker, Elaine 171
Barkley, Catherine 104
Barley, Glenn 244
Barner, Robert 169
Barnes, Daniela 203
Barnes, Jake 104
Barnett, Charlie 84
Barnett, Laurel 74
Barolsky, Martin 71
Barr, Andrea 131
Barrel, William 61, 97
Barrera, Manuel 213
Barri, Barta 98, 186
Barros, Suzy 37
Barry, Barta *see* Barri, Barta

Barry, George 61
Barrymore, Krista 90, 209
Bartel, Paul 200
Bartlett, Robert 230
Bartoli, Luciano 79
Basch, David 91
Basehart, Richard 165
Basile, Pasquale 194
Basile, Salvatore 138
Basket Case 220
Bastone, Ron 216
Bateman, Kent 134
Bathory, Elizabeth *see* de Báthory, Elisabeth
Battistrada, Lucia 161
Baumgartner, Peter 153
Baumgartner, Walter 153
Bava, Lamberto 139
Bava, Mario 40, 44, 143, 210
Bay, Sara *see* Neri, Rosalba
Bea, Eduardo 208
Beacham, Stephanie 215
Beardley, Richard 114
Beast 50
The Beast Awakens 210
Beast of Blood 49, 65
Beast of the Dead 49
Beast of the Yellow Night 50
Beaton, Alisa 137
Beaumont, Gilbert 147
Beauvy, Nicholas 230
Beaver, Janis 149
Bebere Tu Sangre 142
Bebo Tu Sangre 142
Beckett, Adam 200
Beckman, Henry 66
Becognée, Claude 206
Bedell, Rodney 131
Behind the Green Door 206
Beibe, Ronaldo 210
Belbin, George 93
Belen Films 47, 68
Belisle, Monique 205
Belk, Reggie 62
Bell, Charlotte 245
Bell, Edith 82
Bell, Wayne 104, 227
Belli, Agostina 190
Belmonte, Liza 49
Beltran, Enrique 152
Belty, Frank *see* Vicario, Marco
Benda, Kenneth 140
Benfield, Jan 62
Benit, Butch 167
Bennett, Jack 96
Bennett, Joan 225
Benson, Paul 189
Benson, Steven *see* Massaccesi, Aristide

Bentivoglio, Gabriele 203, 209
Benussi, Eufemia 198, 211
Benussi, Femi *see* Benussi, Eufemia
Benvenuto, Titti 211
Bercovici, Luigi 171
Beresford, Al *see* Armstrong, Michael
Berg, Jon 200
Berger, Alex *see* di Silvestro, Salvatore
Berger, Marlene 128
Bergfeld, Garrett 91
Bergman, Ingmar 158
Bergson, Jerome 92
Berhoff, Fred 176
Bernaola, Carmelo A. 109, 130, 156
Bernard, Anna 94
Bernard, James 117
Bernhardt, Bunny 181
Berni, Marcello 211
Berry, Julian *see* Gastaldi, Ernesto
Berryman, Michael 135
Bert, Agnes 113
Bertelli, Lírio 90
Bertolucci, Giovanni 203
Bertoni, Suzy 48
Berwick, Debra Draper 171
Berwick, Wayne 171
Besser, Ben 54
Best, Judy 149
Die Bestia aus dem Totenreic 194
La Bestia de la Noche Amarilla 50
Bestia de Sangre 49
La Bestia Uccide a Sangue Freddo 51
Betti, Laura 44
Bevan, Stuart 46
Bevilacqua, Luigi 165
Bew, Corlee 128
Beyond the Darkness 68
Beyond the Fog 232
Beyond the Living Dead 194
Beyrooty, John 171
Bhaskar 142
Biamonte Cinegroup 45
Bianchi, Andrea 191
Bianchi, Giulio 107
Bichette, Marcelle 131
Bido, Anthony *see* Bido, Antonio
Bido, Antonio 124
Billian, Hans *see* Manera, Jesús Franco
Binsted, Carol 157

Bird, Luciano 189
Birkinshaw, Alan 157
Bisacco, Roberto 79
Biscaglia, Paul 206
Bishopric, Kirsten 195
Bisutti, Maria Aurelia 151
Bittner, Dicky 103
Black Christmas 77
The Black Frankenstein 53, 175
Black Magic Queen 207
Black Magic Rites—Reincarnation 209
Black Magic Terror 207
Black Magic III 207
Blackenstein 53
Blackman, Joan 195
Blackwell, Monika 245
Blade of the Ripper 215, 224
Blair, Linda 240
Blake, Frank *see* Braña, Franco
Blaki 156
Blanc, Erika *see* Colombatto, Enrica Bianchi
Blanchard, Alan 223
Blasco, Joe 144, 145, 195, 205
Blazer, Ken 244
The Blind Dead 188
Bloch, Charles B. 115
Bloch, Lars 107
Bloedige Heksenjacht 64
Bloedlink 202
Blond, Susan 42
Blood and Black Lace 44
Blood and Lace 54
Blood Bath 44
Blood Castle 74
Blood Ceremony 73
Blood Devils 49
Blood Diner 239
Blood Feast 37, 55, 129, 168, 236, 239
Blood Freak 57
Blood Freaks 57
Blood Hunger 241
Blood Moon 186
Blood of Frankenstein 100
Blood of the Undead 215
Blood Orgy 128
Blood Orgy of the She-Devils 81
Blood Relations Company 135
Blood Rites 125
The Blood Seekers 100
Blood Stalkers 59
Blood Sucking Freaks 149
Blood Tide 59

Bloodlust 176
Bloodstalkers 59
Bloodstalkers Ltd. 59
Bloodsucking Freaks 149
Bloodthirsty Butchers 60, 231
The Bloody Countess 74
The Bloody Exorcism of Coffin Joe 112
Bloom, John 100
Bloomfield, Mike 42
Blossom, Roberts 92
Blue, Arlana 149
The Blue Eyes of the Broken Doll 192
Das Blutgericht der Reitenden Leichen 184
Blutmesse der Zombies 109
Blutmesse für den Teufel 109
Blynn, Jeff 127
Blythe, Janus 104, 135, 148
Bocanegra, Rosalindo 151
Boccaccini, Guido 44
Boccelli, Dick 38
Bochin, A. 221
The Body Shop 49, 62
Boehme, Harry 76
Bogart, Frank 243
Bogart, Humphrey 72
The Bogeyman and the French Murders 72
Bohr, Robert *see* Valeri, Bruno
Bokun, Rich 103
Boldero, Barry 195
Boles, Barbara 94
Boles, Eric 94
Boles, Jim 94
Bolin, Nick 53
Bolkan, Florinda *see* Bulco, José Soara
Bolla, Robert *see* Kerman, Robert
Bologna, Ugo 247
Bolton, Lyn 56
Bolzoni, Adriano 233
Bonaccorti, Enrica 233
Bonacquisti, Giacinto 211
Bonamano, Aldo 202
Bonavia, Mike 41
Bond, René 154
Bond, Terri 154
Bonet, Charlie 95
Bonnanni, Roberto 44
Bonnatti, Carlos 151
Bonner, William 100
Bonns, Miguel Iglesias 163
Bono, Bona 106
Bonos, Gigi 174
Bonuglia, Maurizio 203
The Boogeyman 63

Borelli, Franco 152
Borgese, Salvatore 197
Boris, James IV 140
Borisman, Dorman 207
Bornman, Lawrence 120
Borova, Anuska 197
Borske, Hal 125, 231
Borske, John 61, 231
Borsky, Alexandra *see* Massaccesi, Aristide
Bosche, Peter 38
Boschero, Dominique 143, 234
Boschetti, Bruno 198. 211, 233
Bosè, Lucía 73
Bosè, Miguel 225
Bosisio, Liù 176
Le Bossu de la Morgue 156
Botenuth, Claudia 81
Bottin, Rob 115, 200
Bouchet, Barbara *see* Gutcher, Barbara
Bousman, Lena 128
Bouyxou, Jean-Pierre 206
Bow, Simmy 165
Bowden, George 80
Bowers, Raymond 215
Bowie, Les 117
Bowler, Richard 142
Bowman, David 134
Bowman, Ralph D. 95
Box, George 231
Box Office Spectaculars 77, 235
Boyd, Philip 181
Boyd, Tanya 144
Boyden, Raymond 63
Boylan, John 205
Boylan, Mary 38, 42
Bracula—Terror of the Living Dead 194
Braddock, Greg 214
Braddock Associates 169
Bradley, Doug 117
Bradley, Elizabeth 46
Bradley, Lynne 48
Bradley, Stephen 93
Braid, Hilda 157
Brait, Carla 79
Braña, Franco 47, 179
Brana, Frank *see* Braña, Franco
Brand, Neville 104
Brandon, Don 62
Brandt, Luci 219
Brandwira, Alex 90
Brandywine Productions 39, 75
Brasil, Arnaldo 111

Brass, Tinto 133
Braunsberg, Andrew 101, 176
Braunstein, Joseph *see* Larraz, José Ramón
Braverman, Jack *see* Frost, Jack
Bravman, Jack *see* Frost, Jack
Bravo, Charlie 217
Brayne, William 93
Brazolin, Arlete Lobo 110
Breakfast at Manchester Morgue 189
Bredeston, Guillermo 168
Breitenstein, Jochen 63
Brenn, Hexe, Brenn 64, 135
Brennen, Robert 195
Brenner, Joseph 123
Brent, Yom 131
Brian Roberts Productions 216
Briant, Shane 117
Brides of Blood 65
Brides of Blood Island 65
Brides of Death 65
Brides of the Beast 65
Briganti, Elisa 247
Brisman, Heskel 71
Brito, Marina 110
Britton, Christopher 66
Brocani, Franco 239
Brochard, Martine 123
Brochero, Eduardo Maria 190, 224
Brock, Alan 219
Brock, Patrick 78
Brodie, Don 53
Brody, David 95
Brody, Sally 245
Brody, William J. 144
Broek, Terry Ten 91
Brojo, Mien 207
Bronley, Sydney 117
Brood, The 66, *206*
Brook, Claudio 41
Brook, David 133
Brooks, Iris 142
Brooks, Jeremy 97, 231
Brooks, Ray 46
Brooks, Sebastian 154
The Brooks Group 71
Brophy, Bob 53
Brothen, Kathy 244
Brott, Susan 181
Brown, Barry 200
Brown, Clifford *see* Manera, Jesús Franco
Brown, Darcy 219
Brown, Janis 194

Brown, Murray 240
Brown, Penny 160
Brown, Ralph *see* Polselli, Renato
Brown, Roger 82, 107
Brown, Steve 103
Brown, Tamara 214
Browne, Derek V. 201
Brownrigg, S.F. 96, 97
Bruce, Kitty 42
Brumberger, Tom 95
Brundin, Bo 134
Brunelli, Ugo 89, 209
Brushay, Johanna 95
Brutal Nights 107
Bruzzi, Iris 111
Bryan, Andréia 210
Bryant, Curtis 76
Buba, Pasquale 85, 169
Buba, Tony 169
Bucci, Flavio 225
Bucher, Lorli 153
Buck Rogers 41
A Bucket of Blood 78
Buckley, Betty 71
Buenaventura, Angel 49
Buio Omega 68, 156
Bulco, José Soara 160
Bullo, Gianfranco 124
Buñuel, Juan 72
Buñuel, Miguel 73
El Buque Maldito 47, 68, 185
Burchinal, William 182
Burial Ground 191
Buried Alive 68
Burke, Karen 245
Burke, Mary Ellen 80
Burke, Peter 76
Burman, Carl 80
Burner, Cesar 188
Burns, Keith 137
Burns, Marilyn 104, 227
Burns, Robert A. 171
Burr, Randy 182
Burroughs, William S. 141
Buruji, Stephen 216
Butcher, Kim 119
Butchie 85
Butler, Prudie 223
Buzalski, Johannes 64, 134
Buzzard, Madelyn 229
Byrne, Michael 240

C, Andy 53
Caçador, Rosalvo 111
Caccatti, Sharon 85
Cacéres, Jorge 151
Cagne, Gil 101
Cal-Am Productions 230

Calamai, Clara 202
Calandra, Giuliana 202
Calderón, Juan Carlos 192
Calderoni, Rita 90, 209
Calderoni, Stella 165
Caldwell, Dale 223
California Axe Massacre 48
California Axe Murders 48
Califri, Emi 101
Caligula 133
Calixto, Aparecida 111
Callegaro, João 210
Calloway, Judy 62
Calvert, Toni 56
Calvo, Eduardo 150, 159, 168, 192, 208, 242
Calvo, José Antonio 184
CAM 159, 163, 242
Cambist Films 82
Camera 2 Productions 95
Camoiras, Jose 188
Camp, Eugene 91
Camp, Rob 181
Camp des Filles Perdues, Le 212
Campbell, Alice 244
Campbell, Lindsay 215
Campbell, Nicholas 66
Campos, Carlos 111
Campos, Guillermo 151
Campos, José Luis 47, 188
Canalejas, José 47, 188
Candeias, Ozualdo 210
Canevari, Sergio 44, 198, 211
Canibales 70
Cannibal 237
Cannibal Girls 69
Cannibal Holocaust 138
The Cannibal Man 217
Cannibal Massacre 237
Cannibal Massaker 138
Cannibals 237
Canning, James 115
Canon, Jack 180
Canosa, Michael 103
Canoy, Reuben 162
Cantenero, Ramon 47
Canter, Kieran 68
Cantner, George, Jr. 91
Cantudo, María José 109
Capell, Bárbara 186
Capitolina Produzioni Cinematografiche 45
Caporali, Roberto 191
Capovilla, Maurice 210
Capozzi, Allesandra 225
Capozzi, Salvatore 225
Capritti, Eolo 127
The Captive Female 216

Index

Caramico, Robert 53, 104, 223
Carboni, Ugo 203
Card, Dani 156
Cardenas, Jose 194
Cardew, Jane 46
Cardi, Toni 111
Cardille, Bill 182
Cardinali, Katia 90
Cardini, Anna 68
Cardona, René 139
Cardona, René, Jr. 139
Cardos, John 100
Cardoso 37
Cardoso, Ivan E.S. 239
Cardwell, Jack 200
Carey, Sandy 154
Cark, Jean 76
Carli, Carlo 197
Carlin, Ed 54
Carlin Company Productions 54
Carlini, Carlo 161
Carlos, José 210
Carlson, Leslie 92
Carlton, Beth 38
Carlton, Dave 223
Carlton, Irvin 142
Carmen, Vince 62
Carnage 44
Carne per Frankenstein 177
Carnival of Blood 71
Carnivorous 237
Carole 160
Carpenter, John 48, 63, 115, 132, 145
Carpenter, Randall 70
Carpi, Tito 152, 237
Carr, Camilla 96
Carr, Vicki 128
Carradine, John 63
Carrara, Gabriele 211
Carrera, Dorothea 64
Carrie 71
Carro, Carmen 168
Carrol, Regina *see* Gelfin, Regina
Carroll, Gordon 39
Carroll, Lane 82
Carroll, Sharon 182
Carson, David 104
Carson, Lemmy 174
Carson, Sherry 245
Cart, John *see* Massaccesi, Aristide
Carter, Betty *see* Manera, Jesús Franco; Romay, Lina
Carter, Ethel 135
Cartier, Patricia 206

Cartwright, Veronica 40
Carvajal, Alfonso 49, 162
Carvalho, Genê 37
Carvalho, José 110
Cary, Brian 221
La Casa d'Appuntamento 72
Casara, Carl *see* Casaravilla, Carlos
Casaravilla, Carlos 166
Casares, Sofia 156
Casas, Antonio 150
Case, Gerald 240
Case, Humbert 114
Casenare, Jeanette 205
Casey, Katie 63
Cash, Renata *see* Kasché, Renate
Casini, Stefania 42, 101, 225
Cassell, Sandra 158
Cassidy, Susan 61, 231
Cassinelli, Claudio 173
Cassner, Sergio *see* Armstrong, Michael
Castel, Pilar 81
Castizio, Alfonso 152
Castle, Fred *see* Manera, Jesús Franco
Castle, Nick 132
Castle of Terror 243
Castro, Jan Antonio 184
Cat, Haji 144
Catania, Betty 41
Cats 201
The Cat's Victim 124
Cattaneo, Carlo 161
La Cavalcata dei Morti Senza Occhi 77
Cavanaugh, Chick 75
Cazalilla, Juan 47, 109, 159
Ceballos, Milagros 166
Cekovsky, Turk 91
Cemetery Girls 130
Cemetery Tramps 130
Centenera, Andrés 50, 65
Centenero, Ramón 109, 159, 213
Centini, Maurizio 239
Century Studios 96
Cepeda, Gerardo 139
Cerdá, Nacho 156
Ceremonia Sangrienta 73
Ceri, Ettore 51
Cerra, Saturno 156
Cerulli, Fernando 51, 124
Cervera, Carmen 164
Cervi, Antonio 79
Cesti, Eduardo 151
Cevalios, Antonio 151

Chadwick, June 78
Chair pour Frankenstein 177
Chambers, Marilyn 205
Champion, Sandy 165
Chandler, Betty 96
Chaney, Debi 91
Chaney, Lon, Jr. 100
Chaplin, Josephine 153
Chappa, Eduardo 186
Charles Band Productions 165
Charlie's Angels 79
Chase, Barry 165
Chase, Norman 82
Chatfield, Pam 85
Chen, Lawrence *see* Sudjio, Liliek
Cherewchenko, Luba 128
Cheverie, Roy 82
Chiantoni, Renato 234
Chiappini, Dino 212
The Child 74
Children Shouldn't Play with Dead Things 75, 93
Childs, Andrea 103
Childs Associates Films Ltd. 48
Chiles, Lane 60, 127
Chin, Mary Ann 95
Chinchilla, José Luis 156, 164, 168
Chinney, Sandy 201
Chirizzi, Gian Luigi 191
Christensen, Jeanette 168
Christian, Kurt 140
Christian, Sven *see* Steckler, Ray Dennis
Christine 92
Christine, Katia 165
Christmas, Robert *see* Natale, Roberto
Christopher, Dennis 54
Chromage Productions Ltd. 93
Chronopolis, Chris 91
Cialone, Ennio 212
Ciardi, Francesca 138
Ciavarro, Luigi 198, 211
Ciccarese, Luigi 211
Ciges, Luis 109, 192, 213
Cimarosa, Tano 90, 209
Cine Eqipe 165
Cine Repertory Group, Inc. 137
Cinedistri 112
Cinefilms S.L. 152
Cinemagic Pictures 87
Cinemation Industries, Inc. 142

Cinematografica Calderón S.A. 139
Cinemec-Produktion 153
Cineproduzione Daunia 70, 51
Cipriani, Stelvio 44, 143
Cipriari, Massimo 106
Cir, Carmen 188
Ciral, Karen 238
Citti, Franco 124
City of the Walking Dead 124
Ciupka, Richard 147
Claire, J.C. 223
Claridge, Westbrook 148
Clark, Benjamin 75, 92
Clark, Bob *see* Clark, Benjamin
Clark, Cordy 135
Clark, Greydon 100
Clark, John R. 179
Clark, Robert 137
Clarke, James Kenelm 240
Clarke, Oliver J. *see* Massaccesi, Aristide
Claudiane 37
Claw of Terror 216
Clemens, Günter 64
Clement, David 70
Clement, Titania 179
Clementi, Anne Marie 106
Clemmons, Gregory 223
Cler, Judy 245
Clerici, Gianfranco 45, 138, 237
Clerk, Jacqueline 180
La Clinique de la Terreur 66
La Cliniques des Horreurs 52
La Cliniques des Ténèbres 52
Clinton, Mildred 38
Cliver, Al *see* Conti, Pier Luigi
Clodio Cinematografica 161
Coady, Simon 97
Coady, Tommy 147
Coal Miner's Daughter 72
Coates, Lewis *see* Cozzi, Luigi
Cobos, Germán 218
Cochran, Linda 235
Code Name Trixie 82
Coe, Barry 94
Coffin Joe *see* Zé do Caixão
Coghill, Joy 195
Cohen, Daphne 223

Cohen, David J. 50
Cohen, Emma *see* Rabola, Emmanuela Beltrán
Cohen, Gary 103
Cohen, Herman 125
Cohen, Larry 167
Colby, Anita 189
The Cold-Blooded Beast 52
Cole, Albert 100
Cole, Betty 104, 230
Cole, Celea-Ann 60
Cole, Rosalie 75
Coletta, Hallie 103
La Colina del Terror 135
Colli, Ernesto 45, 79
La Colline a des Yeux 136
Collings, Andy 80
Collins, Alan *see* Pigozzi, Luciano
Collins, Bob 181
Collins, Cathy 77
Collins, Jean *see* Romay, Lina
Collins, Roberta 104
Collins, Shannon 200
Colombatto, Enrica Bianchi 134, 159
Colombo, Enrico 194
Color Me Blood Red 77, 236
Colouris, George 45, 232
Columbus, Abraham 223
The Comeback 78
Comex Productions 113
Communion 38
Compagnia Cinematografica Astro 122, 159, 234
Compagnia Cinematografica Champion S.P.A. 79, 101, 176
Computer Killers 140
Conaught International 59
Conde, Antonio Diaz 139
Conde, Fabián 73, 121
Conder, Candi 77
Condict, Win 223
Condor International 114
Cone, Bill 198
Conners, April 97
Conrad, Jess 46
Consadine, John 95
Constantine, Tom 103
Constitution Films, Inc. 60, 97, 231
Conte, María Pía 194
Conte, Richard 239
Contello, Ellena 41
Contemporary Film-Makers 54
Conti, Pier Luigi 247

Continenza, Alessandro 143
Continenza, Sandro 73, 189
Continiello, Ubaldo 237
Contreras, Abel 41
Cook, Rick 238
Cook, Walton 82
Cools, Alan W. *see* Massaccesi, Aristide
Cooper, Alan 120
Cooper, Barrett 214
Cooper, Ronald 120
Cooper, Shannon 181
Copercines 190, 224
Coplestone, Geoffrey 106
Copple, Robert 83
Corazzari, Bruno 224
Corbi, Marella 224
Corey, Maggie 55
Corman, Roger 200
Cornejo, Williams 151
Cornell, Lydia 59
Corpi Presentato Tracce di Violenza Carnale, I 79
The Corpse Grinders 80
Corrigan, Shirley 98
Corsaut, Aneta 230
Cortes, Hernando 151
Cortes, Juan 188
Cortese, Valentina 143
Cortez, Jayme 90, 111
Cortijo, Basilio 73
Cory, Yvonne 214
Cosa Avete Fatto a Solange? 81
Coscarelli, D.A. 198
Coscarelli, Don 198
Coscia, Marcello 189
Cossins, James 88
Cotten, Joseph 114
Coulakis, John 103
Counsell, Elizabeth 157
Count Dracula's Great Loves 130
Countess Dracula 74
Courtier, Gene 56
Courtin, Robert 227
Cousar, James 53
Couty, Jean-Claude 113
Covan, DeForest 148
Covello, Angela 79, 198, 211
Cox, Doug 71
Cox, Michael 61
Cox, Steve 103
Crabbe, Buster 41
Crabtree, Toni 60
Craig, Charles 182
Craig, J. Arthur 137

Craig, Michelle 149
Crampton, Gerry 88
Crampton, Jerry 201
Crane, Dorian 137
Cranston, Joseph L. 80
Craven, Jonathan 158
Craven, Wes 135, 158
Crawford, David 85
Crawford, Dennis 120
Crawford, Wayne 127
The Crazies 82, 86, 143, 196, 205, 206
Crazy Fat Ethel II 84
Creamer, William 227
Creature from the Black Lagoon 224
Crescenzi, Antonio 224
Criado, Cristobal 184
Crimen sin Huella 127
Criminally Insane 83, 214
Crisalda 50
Crisanti, Gabriele 127, 191
Crisofani, Eleonora 127
Crispino, Armando 161, 203
Cristal, Perla 121
Cristina, Dina 110
Cristina, Maria 210
Cristino, Belen 150
Croft, Alvin C. 82, 182
Cromwell, Sam *see* Ippolito, Ciro
Cronenberg, David 66, 195, 205
Cronin, Paul 76
Cross, Raymond 97
Crudo, Aldo 239
Cruz, Celia 242
Cruz, Xavier 41
Crypt of the Blind Dead 188
Cubero, Raúl Pérez 130, 156
Cuff, Max 201
Culliford, James 88
Cullivan, Dana 57
Cummings, Richard 42
Cummins, Debbie 76
Cummins, Don 48, 223
Cundey, Christopher 115
Cundey, Dean 115, 132, 144
Cunilles, José Maria 123
Cunningham, Christopher 117
Cunningham, Sean S. 158
Curran, Bill 179
Currier, Bob 57
Currier, Dolores 57
Curse of the Cannibal Confederates 84
Curse of the Confederate Cannibals 84

Curse of the Devil 135, 208
The Curse of the Screaming Dead 84
Curtis, Alan 46
Curtis, Jamie Lee 115, 132
Curtis, Willy 148
Curzon, Fiona 119
Cushing, Harry C. 114
Cushing, Peter 117
Custer, Francine 153
Cusumano Mark 91
Cutt, Michael J. 181
Cyphers, Charles 115, 132

D.R. per le Communicazioni di Massa 68
Dachman, Alan J. 128
Dachman, Harry 128
Dachman, Norman 128
da Conceição, Shirley 90
da Cruz, João 90
Dadashian, Robert 74
Da Dove Vieni? 189
Dagmar, Jack 119
Dailey, Janet 103
Daisies, Anthony *see* Margheriti, Antonio
Daisika 93
Dalbes, Alberto 156
dall'Aglio, Matilde 107
Dallamano, Massimo 81
Dallesandro, Joe 43, 101, 176
Dalmas, Max *see* Dallamano, Massimo
Dalmos, Jack *see* Dallamano, Massimo
DAL-Reitman Productions 195
Dalton, Valda 205
Daly, Cindy 71
Daly, Jane 76
d'Amario, Stefania 247
d'Amato, Joe *see* Massaccesi, Aristide
Damon, Bruno 142
Damon, John 142
Damon, Marzia 165
Damon, Peter 172
d'Amore, Jo Jo 165
Damsyk, I.M. 207
Danam, Osa 214
Danati, Dario *see* Massaccesi, Aristide
Dancer, Nancy 167
Dania Film 173
Daniel, Roberto 73
Daniels, Gray 154
Daniels, Jack *see* Colombo, Enrico; Merino, José Luis

Dannis, Ray 238
Dans les Griffes du Loup Garou 164
Dantas, Sebastiana 110
Dante, Joe 200
Danza Macabre, La 244
d'Aram, Philippe 113
Danziger, Allen 227
Dardick, Ruth 95
Darel, Dominique 101
Dark Shadows 226
Darni, William 90, 209
Darren, Eva 65
Date with a Kidnapper 49
Daubeney, Diana 240
d'Aunia, Marina 212
d'Avack, Massimo 203
Davalos, George 149
David, Pierre 66
Davies, Doreen 97
Davies, Rupert 119
Dávila, Luis 242
Davis, Andrew 165
Davis, Dick 223
Davis, Dorothy 195
Davis, Elizabeth 131
Davis, Jim 100
Davis, Richard *see* Findlay, Michael
Davis, Ronald W. 104
Davison, Jon 200
Dawn, Vincent *see* Mattei, Bruno
Dawn of the Dead
Dawson, Anthony M. *see* Margheriti, Antonio
Dawson, Curt 167
Dawson, Freddie 127
Day, Baybi 103
Day of the Dead 83, 86, 189
Day of the Maniac 234
Day of the Woman 87
The Day the Screaming Stopped 78
Deacon, Brian 240
Deacon, Richard 200
The Dead Don't Die 65
de Alba, Aurora 166, 194
de Angelis, Fabrizio 106, 247
de Angelis, Guido 79, 173
de Angelis, Maurizio 79, 173
de Araújo, Wilson Gomes 110
de Arildo Iruam, Nivaldo 37
Death Carries a Cane 197
Death Is Child's Play 204
Death Line 88

Death Rides a Carousel 71
Death Trap 105
Deaton, George 230
de Azcoitia, Martinez 150
de Barona, Cesar 159, 168
de Barros, Abigail 111
de Báthory, Elisabeth 74, 186, 208
de Benito, Samuel 218
de Benning, Burr 148
de Blas, Manuel 68, 156, 172
Debois, Silvie 195
de Bran, Fernando 73
de Carlo, Phil 171, 244
de Carolis, Cinzia 190
de Castro, J.L. Bermudez 68
Deep Red 202
Deep Red Hatchet Murders 202
Deeter, Drew 223
de Felice, Armelinda 233
de Frank, Bob 103
de Gironcoli, Romano 165
Dei, Gianni 127
Dejen Que los Muertos Duermen 189
de Jesus, Louie 149
de la Camara, Javier 204
de la Camara, Lourdes 204
de la Iglesia, Eloy 217
de la Motte, Mischa 117
de Lara, Joe 113
Delaunay, Monique 226
de la Vega, Alfonso 156
Delavena, Jim *see* Madrid, José Luis
del Balzo, Liana 202
del Carmen, Maria 110
del Castillo, Miguel 224
del Duca, Giancarlo 127
de Leon, Gerardo 65,162
Delgado, Mary Sol 122
del Gre, Jese 85
Delia, Joseph 103
d'Elia, Luccia 68
de Lima, Nivaldo 110, 111
Delino, Joseph 131
Deliria 46
Delirio Caldo 89, 91
Deliríos de um Anormal 90, 112
Delirium (1972) 90
Delirium (1977) 9
Dellay, Alan 149
delli Uberti, Anna 243
de los Rios, Waldo 204
del Pozo, Angel 172
del Toro, Marques 218

de Luna, Alvara 130
Demarecaux, Jacques 142
de Marne, Dennis 97
de Martino, Alberto 45
de Masi, Francesco 194
de Melo, Messias 111
de Mendoza, Alberto 160, 224
Demichelli Tulio 172
Demille, Cathie 154
de Milo, Cardella 53
Demme, Jonathan 148
The Demon Lover 76, 139
Demonia 192
Demoniac 197
Demonoia 68
Demons of the Dead 234
de Mossul, Tom 73, 168
Denger, Fred 134
Denise, Denise 95
Dennis, Ray 80
Dennis-Leigh, Patrick 95
de Noble, Alphonso 38
Deodato, Ruggero 138, 237
de Oliveira, Leila 111
de Oliveira, Terezinha 110, 111
de Ossorio, Amando *see* Rodríguez, Amando de Ossorio
de Palma, Brian 71
de Palma, Cameron 72
Deragon, Lynne 205
de Rais, Gilles 169
Deranged 77, 92
Derek, Bo 174
Derek, John 174
de Riso, Arpad 97
de Rivera, Javier 122, 159, 168, 213
Le Dernier Monde Cannibale 237
de Rose, John 137
de Rossi, Gianetto 191, 247
de Salle, Lorraine 107, 212
de Santis, Orchidea 152
El Descuartzador de Binbrook 179
de Sica, Vittorio 101
Desideri, Gidia 51
de Simone, Ria 212
de Skram, Mike 62
de Souza, Clayber 90
de Souza, Osvaldo 110, 111
Desperate Living 43
O Despertar da Besta 210
de Sue, Joe 53
Desy, Victor 205
de Tejada, Luis 224
deu Casas, Jaime 197

Deus, Beni 159
The Devil and Dr. Frankenstein 177
Devil Sorcery 208
Deville, Jo Jo 145
The Devil's Eye 123
Devil's Possessed 168
The Devil's Rain 148
Devlin, Joan 133
Devon Film 224
de Wolfe 140
I Diabolici Amori di Nosferatu 130
Diak, Rodney 46
Diamond, Don 230
Diamond, Marcia 92
Diaz, Raymond 127
Diaz, Vic 50
di Bernardo, Giovanna 81
Dickinson, Desmond 232
Dickson, Hugh 88
Dickson, Jim 75
di Dio, Tony 230
Dietrich, Daniel 85
Dietrich, Erwin C. 153
Diffring, Anton 135, 143
Digard, Uschi 144, 145
di Geronimo, Bruno 81
di Lazzaro, Dalila 174, 177
The Dilbar Syndicate 205
di Leo, Fernando 51
di Leoni, Ferdinando 174
Dilizie Erotice 192
Dillman, Bradford 200
Dillman, Max *see* Dallamano, Massimo
Dillon, Patricia 231
di Nunzio, Franco 138
Dionisio, Silvia 101
di Rossi, Gianetto 189
di Savola, Pio 138
Disciple of Death 93
Disney, Will 82
Dixon, Judy 84
Dixon, Shane 181
Doak, Frank 182
do Caixão, Zé *see* Marins, José Mojica
Doctor Bloodbath 140
Dr. Butcher, M.D. 106
Dr. Death 95
Doctor Death—Seeker of Souls 94
Doctor Gore 49, 62
Doctor Gore's Body Shop 49, 62
Dr. Jekyll and Mr. Blood 97
Dr. Jekyll et le Loup Garou 98
Dr. Jekyll vs. the Werewolf 98

Index

Dr. Jekyll Vs. the Wolfman 98
Dr. Jekyll y el Hombre Lobo 98
Doederlein, Fred 195
d'Offizi, Sergio 138
Dolen, Jim 243
Dome, Manfred 176
Donaggio, Pino 71, 200
Donald, Terry 205
Donnegan, Jim 95
Donnelly, Dennis 230
Donnelly, Tim 230
Don't Go in the House 95
Don't Look in the Basement 96
Don't Open the Window 189
Dor, Karin 172
Doria, Sergio 143
Dorian, Max 209
Dorifer, Bettyr 111
do Ritmo, Titulares 111
Dorn, Lu 100
Dornbierer, Otto 153
dos Santos, Wilson 111
Dougherty, Frank 97–98
Douglas, Mark 235
Dow, Eugene 181
Down, Carol 147
Downe, Allison Louise 56, 128, 131
Downes, Anson 72
Doyle, David 78
d'Oyly-Rhind, Warren 219
Dracula—The Bloodline Continues 213
Dracula Cerca Sangue di Vergine e... Morì di Sete!!! 101, 226
Dracula Jagt Frankenstein 172
The Dracula Saga 213
Dracula Vs. Frankenstein (1969) 172
Dracula Vs. Frankenstein (1971) 99
Dracula Vuole Vivere—Cerca Sangue di Vergina! 43, 101, 178
Dracula's Blood 130
Dracula's Virgin Lovers 130
Dracup, Robert 96
Drake, Marciee 230
Drazen, Julie 148
Driggers, Jenny 62
The Driller Killer 103, 231
Drive-In Masscare 104
Driver, Linda 61
Drudi, Vera 189, 234
Duarte, Emília 210

Dubin, Alexis *see* Ross, Gaylen
Dublin, Jessica 198, 211
Ducena, Jaciara 210
Ducharme, Camille 195
Duckworth, Allen 41
Dudley Birch Films Ltd. 179
Due Emme Cinematografica 190
Dugan, John 227
Duggan, Terry 215
Dukes, C.A. 131
Dumont, Kátia 111
Dungeon of Death 231
d'Union, Sheila 117
Dunlop, Joe 93
Dunn, Eileen 95
Dunn, John 42
Dunnam, Virginia 200
Dunning John 205
Dupre, Florence 238
Durille, Maria 204
Durkin, Joe 55
Durley, Ruth 143
Durston, David E. 142
Duval, Henri-Pierre *see* Steckler, Ray Dennis
Dyer, Gary 223
Dynamic Productions 229
Dziubinska, Anulka 240
E.E.C. 168
Earl, Gloria 216
Early, David 85
Early, Mary Jane 134
Easter, Robert 230
Eastman, G.L. *see* Montefiori, Luigi
Eastman, George *see* Montefiori, Luigi
Eastman, Lynn 181, 198
Eastman, Marilyn 182
Easton, Shirley 180
Eaten Alive 104
Ebert, Günther 143
Ebert, Roger 87
Ecenia, Paul 216
Echols, Frank 61
L'Ecologia del Delitto 44
Eden, Jerome 56, 77, 235
Eden, Rolf 72
Edgerton, Earle 71
Edmonds, Don 144, 145
Edmunds, Tony 162
Edwards, Ray 158
Egan, Charles 83
Egan, Henry L. *see* Eguiluz, Enrique López
Eger, Harvey 169
Eggar, Samantha 66

Eguiluz, Enrique López 121, 166
Eichberg Film 172
Eide, Heather 181
Einhorn, Richard 95
Eisly, Anthony 100
Ekberg, Anita 72
Elder, John *see* Hinds, Anthony
Elea Cinematografica 127
Eley, John 51
Elis Cinematografica 124
Elliot, B.R. *see* Mabe, Byron
Elliot, John 245
Elliott, Alison 157
Ellis, Don 80
Ellis, Doreen 120
Ellis, Tawm 219
Ellison, Catharine 179
Ellison, Joseph 95
Ellorieta, Beatriz 179
Elmi, Nicoletta 44, 177, 202
Elsener, Regine 153
Ely, Doug 137
Emanuelle and the Last Cannibals 106
Emanuelle e gli Ultima Cannibali 68, 106
Emanuelle en America 107
Emanuelle in America 107
Emanuelle's Amazon Adventure 106
Emmanuelle Negra en America 107
Emge, David 85
Emory, Carol 91
Encore 78
Endemoniada, La 123, 204
L'Enfer des Zombies 247
Engel, Roger 100
Engleman, Roy 76
English, Virginia 181
Englund, Robert 105
Enigma Rosso 82
Ennis, Bill 62
Ernst, Ted 60
The Erotic Nights of the Living Dead 192
Erotico Profondo 153
Erre Cinematografica 237
Escalona, Castillo 164
Escribano, Antonio G. 166
Escribano, Antonio Jiménez 179
El Espanto Surge de la Tumba 109
Essay Films Ltd. 240
Essex, David 244

Index

Esta Noite Encarnarei No Teu Cadáver 90, 110
Esteban, Julian 242
Esteban Cinematografica 191
Estela Films S.A. 123
Estes, Alisa 223
Estrada, Blanca 68
Estrada, Susana 184
O Estranho Mundo de Zé do Caixão 90, 110
Estrella, Carmelita 65
Eure, Wesley 230
Euro International Films 203
Eurociné 226
Eva Film 155
Evans, Harry 171
Evil Force 137
Excite Me 234
Exorcisma Negro 90, 112
The Exorcist 45, 112, 240
L'Exorcista N.2 239
Expulsion of the Devil 72
Eye of the Black Cat 234
Eyeball 123
Eyes 165
Eyes of Dr. Chaney 165

F.D. Cinematografica 138
Fabbri, Ottavio 68
Fabian, Paul 223
Fabtrax Films 223
Failo, Linda 62
Fairfax, Deborah 119
Fairman, Churton 93
Falcón, Fabiola 208
Falcon, Faye *see* Falcón, Fabiola
Falcon International Productions 132
Falt, Dennis Lee 223
Famous Monsters of Filmland 101
Fanfoni, Vittorio 202, 209
Fantasia, Franco 173
Les Fantômes de Dracula 166
Farah, Carlos 111
Farbrother, Pamela 119
Farmer, Marva 53
Farmer, Mimsy 161, 203
Farnsworth, Hill 200
Farra, Ana 73, 168, 208
Farrar, Robert 96
Farrell, Amy 128
Farrell, Richard 205
Farren, Richmond 127
Farros, Lisa 83
Farrow, Tisa 247

Fasan, Italo 198, 211
Fascination 113
Fassio, Stefamia 209
Fauci, Dan 149
Faulk, John Henry 227
Faulkner, Sally 201, 240
Fauré, Daniel 53
Fava, Juan 139
Favre, Julian 151
Fay, Charles 194
Feagin, Hugh 96
Fedeli, Luigi 239
Feigen, Leslie 38
Feld, Gay 98
Félix, Sandoval 90
Felleghi, Tom 234
The Female Butcher 74
Fenech, Edwige 224, 233, 234
Fenlow, Kevin 195
Fennelly, Libby 38
Ferdin, Pamelyn 230
Fergelic, Stephen 169
Ferguson, John 66
Ferguson, Thomas 127
Fernandes, Miguel 205
Fernández, Dorremori 151
Fernandez, M. Cruz 242
Ferrando, Giancarlo 79, 173, 233, 234
Ferrante, Traci 87
Ferrara, Abel 103
Ferrara, Al 165
Ferrara, Diana 225
Ferreira, Elza 90
Ferreira, Jairo 210
Ferrer, José 59
Ferrer, Mel 45, 105
Ferrer, Pepita 164
Ferrer, Rafael 172
Ferroni, Giorgio 190
Fiander, Lewis 204
Fidenco, Nico 106, 107
Field, Stephen 245
Fields, Richard 181
La Figlia di Frankenstein 114
La Fille de Frankenstein 114
Filles Traquees 113
Filmes Cinematografica 190
Films 75 41
Les Films ABC 113, 206
Les Films Corona 143, 160
Fin de Semana para los Muertos 189
Findlay, Michael 219, 220, 221
Findlay, Roberta 220, 221
Fine, Julie Ellen 137

Finley, William 105
Finney, Joyce 103
Fioretti, Dante 202
Firebird Pictures Inc. 41
The First Man into Space 148
Fischer, Lee 54
Fisher, Terence 117
Fitze, John 103
Fitze, Paul 103
Fitzgerald, Nuala 66
Fitzgibbon, Basil 205
Fitzpatrick, Katherine 165
Fiz, Bob 174
Flagg, Cash *see* Steckler, Ray Dennis
Flanagan, Niel 125, 231
Flash Gordon 41
Fleming, Lone 47, 188, 218
The Flesh and Blood Show 46
Flesh for Frankenstein 177
Flood, Gerald 119
Flood, Michael 83
Flora 135
Flora Film 106
Florimont, Eugene 198, 211
Flower, George 104, 115, 144, 145
Flower, Verkina 104
Floyd, Drake *see* Massaccesi, Aristide
Flynn, Carol *see* Steckler, Ray Dennis
Flynn, Errol 169
Foam, John *see* Bava, Mario
The Fog 48, 115
Foits, Charlie 95
Folie Sanglante 68
Foltermühle der Gefangenen Frauen 206
Fontaine, Antoine 226
Forbes, Sonny 147, 195
Forbes-Robertson, Peter 180
The Forbidden 116
Force, Lewis J. *see* Shonteef, Lindsay
Forcina, Sergio 203
Ford, Brad 171
Foree, Ken 85
Forella, Michael 42
The Forgotten 96
Foriscot, Emilio 166, 224
Forlai, Romolo 209
Forrest, Anthony 157
Forrest, Christine 85, 169
Forrest, Ingeborg 169
Forrest, J. Clifford, Jr. 169

Forth, Jane 42
Fortin, Nicole 147
Forward, Robert 230
Fos, Anthony 217
Foschi, Carlo 107
Foschi, Massimo 237
Foster, Alan Dean 40
Foster, J. Byron 80
Foster, Robert *see* Mayans, Antonio
Foster, Zena 80
Foti, Nino 198, 211
Fournier, Ed 223
Fournier, Marcel 205
Fowlds, Derek 232
Fowler, Richard 229
Fox, Charles 80, 238
Fox, Joan 70
Foxe, Cyrinda 42
Fracari, Antônio 110
Fraile, Alfredo 98
Fraile, Francisco 98
Frampton, Harry 88
France, Richard 82, 85
Franci, Geni 111
Franck, A.M. *see* Manera, Jesús Franco
Franco, Jeff *see* Manera, Jesús Franco
Franco, Jesus *see* Manera, Jesús Franco
Franco, Maria Renata 107
Franco, Valerio 151
Franju, Georges 165
Frank, Jess *see* Manera, Jesús Franco
Frankel, Jon 91
Frankenstein 177
Frankenstein and the Monster from Hell 117
Frankenstein '80 175
Frankenstein en het Monster van de Hel 117
Frankenstein et le Monstre de l'Enfer 117
The Frankenstein Experiment 177
Frankenstein 1980 175
Frankenstein's Bloody Terror 166
Franklin, Roger D. *see* Deodato, Ruggero
Franklyn, Fred 115
Fraser, John 215
Fraser, Karen 149
Frazier, John 135
Freda, Riccardo 143
Freda, Richard *see* Freda, Riccardo
Frederick, Lynne 215

Frederick Productions 48
Freed, Gordon 53
Freedom Arts Picture Corporation 94
Freeman, Kenneth *see* Garrone, Sergio
Fregonese, Hugo 172
Frei, Sally 238
Freitas, Nádia 110
Frias, Rafael 73
Friberg, John 38
Friday the 13th 45, 132
Friedel, Frederick R. 48
Friedenn, Neva 230
Friedlander, Irwin 48
Friedman, David F. 55, 77, 129, 145, 235
Friedman, Joann 149
Friedman, Marty 238
Friedman, Norman 171
Frightmare 119, 230
Frightmare II 119
Frissons 195
Les Frissons de l'Angoisse 202
Frizzi, Fabio 247
Frohman, Lou 53
Frost, Jack 221
FRSCO Productions 53
Frugoni, Cesare 173
Fryer, Fredrick 127
Fucello, Robert 231
Fuchs, Gaby 64, 186
Fuchs, Herbert 64, 114, 153
Fuchsberger, Joachim 81
Fuentes, Ricardo 138
Fulci, Lucio 160, 247
Fuller, Louis *see* Fulci, Lucio
Fulton, Jessie Lee 96
Fulton, Rad 238
Fultz, Ronda 142
Fulvia Cinematografica 106
Fumarelli, Rocky 223
Funari, Dirce 106, 192
The Funhouse 120
Funicello, Annette 50
La Furia del Hombre Lobo 121
La Furie des Vampires 186
Furr, Candy 62
The Fury of the Wolfman 121
Fusco, Maria Pia 107
Fux, Herbert *see* Fuchs, Herbert

G., Johnny 95
G.R.P. Cinematografica 89, 209

Gabboa, Joonee 50
Gabriel, Jandira 210
Gabriel, John 180
Gabriel, Ray 244
Gadringher, Roberta 203
Gaeta, Paulo 110
Gaffet, Nestor 168
Gage, Patricia 205
Gains, Walter *see* Lenzi, Umberto
Gaioni, Cristina 177
Galanis, James 105
Galbán, Gualberto 166
Galbo, Christine *see* Galbo, Cristina
Galbo, Cristina 81, 189
Galdino, Lenira 90
Gale, Richard *see* Fulci, Lucio
Galeassi, Emore 165
Galiardo, Juan Luis 150
Gall, Edy *see* Galleani, Edy
Galleani, Edy 160
Gallego, Cesar 121
Gallotti, Dada 174
Galt, Judy 147
Galvano, Gil 230
Gálvez, Lucio 151
Gamer, Henry 147
Gant, Cindy 171
Ganton, Doug 70
Gaos, Lola 73
Garbo, Ingrid 130
Garcia, Eddie 49, 50
García, José 50
García, Manuel Pérez 189
Gardair, Vincent 113
Garnley, Douglas 180
Garofalo, Franco 239
Garr, Cynthia 158
Garr, Giusy 194
Las Garras de Loreli 122
Garret, Jane 51
Garret, Richard *see* Garrone, Riccardo
Garris, Letty 91
Garrison, Ellis 80
Garrone, Sergio 165
Garvey, Jack 91
Garvey, Patricia 231
Garza, Lily 41
Gaslini, Giorgio 190, 198, 202, 211
Gaspar, Luis 98, 186, 242
Gasparri, Aldo 138
Gass, Ronnie 131
Gastaldi, Ernesto 79, 224, 233, 234, 243
Gastia, Ruben 50

Gatsby, Marty 104
Gatti, Gengher 189
Gatti Rossi in un Labirinto di Vetro 123
Il Gatto dagli Occhi di Giada 124
Gaugler, Hans 153
Gavazzi, Mauro 127
Gay, Auretta 247
Gebhard, Olga 153
Das Geheimnis der Grunen Stecknadel 81
Gein, Ed 92, 228, 229
Das Geisterschiff der Schwimmenden Leichen 68
Gelber, Glen 91
Gelfan, Barney 100
Gelfin, Regina 100
Gelfman, Samuel W. 148
Gelso, Egidio 114
Gemser, Laura 106, 107, 192
Geneni Film Distribution 80
Genn, Leo 119, 160
Genta, Renzo 237
Gentil, Michael *see* Rollin, Jean
Gently Before She Dies 234
Gentry, Mike 142
Gerry, Bob 64
Gessler, Ella 172
Geuther, Roswitha 176
The Ghastly Ones 61, 125
The Ghastly Orgies of Count Dracula 209
Ghika 73
Ghirardi, Gustavo 151
The Ghost Galleon 68
Ghostbusters 70
Giallo a Venezia 127
Giani, Maria 168
Gianis, Greg 147
Gianviti, Roberto 160
Gibb, Kenneth Lloyd 104
GICO Cinematografica 106
Gierisch, Stefan 72
Giger, H.R. 40
Gilbert, Catherine 194
Gilbert, Gordon 76
Gilbert, John 205
Gilbert, Philip 54
Gilbert, Yvonne 235
Gilbreth, Kack 246
Giler, David 39
Gill, Manuel 224
Gillen, Arlene 92
Gillen, Jeffrey 76, 92

Gilmore, Wendy 215
Gimpera, Teresa 190
Giner, José Antonio Peréz 109, 159, 185, 186, 188, 192, 213
Ginsberg, Claire 171
Giombini, Marcello 192
Giordano, Daniela 150, 233
Giordano, Maria Angela 127, 191
Girdler, William B. 62, 229
Girolami, Bob 205
Girone, Remo 45
Giustiziere Sfida la Polizia 159
Givens, Jack 182
Gizzi, Claudio 101, 176
Glendinning, Candace 46, 232
Glenn, Montgomery *see* Tranquili, Silvano
Glickman, Paul 100
Glover, Gary 127
Goblin 68, 85, 125, 202, 225
Goch, Gary 76
God's Bloody Acre 127
Goeld, Paul 127
Goff, John F. 104, 115
Goffe, Rusty 93
Gói, Anadir 90
Gold, Harry 72
Goldberg, Daniel 70
Golden, Al 56
Golden, Sally Anne 38
Goldsmith, Jerry 40
Goldstein, Herb 60
Gomar—The Human Gorilla 139
Gomes, Ivair 110
Gomez, Louis 217
Gomez, Manuel 159
Gomez, Sharani 149
Gomide, Geórgia 112
Gonçalves, Orival 90
Gonneau, Pierre 95
González, Arturo 98
Gonzalez, Cenon 162
Gonzalez, Estanis 73
González, Indio 164
Good, Jo-Anne 157
Gooding, Rita 103
Goodwin, Angela 161
Gordon, Alan 70
Gordon, Bruce 200
Gordon, Gilian 63
Gordon, Lance 135
Gordon, Lawrence T. 71
Gordon, Lewis H. *see* Lewis, Herschell Gordon

Gordon, Richard 140, 232
The Gore Gore Girls 128, 242, 246
Gore in Venice 127
Gori, Patrizia 239
Gorman, Patrick 38
Gornick, Michael 85, 169
Gorsuch, Harry 91
Gough, Michael 140
Goya, Tito 42
Grace, Duane 154
Grace, Martin 140
Graham, Cathy 195
Graham, David C. 238
Graham, John Michael 132
Graham, Juliet 149
Graham, Melanie 181
Grahame, Gloria 55, 165
Graig, Dave 62
Grail, Tom 219
El Gran Amor del Conde Dracula 130, 214
Le Grand Amour du Comte Dracula 130
Grand Guignol Cannibale 138
Grandim, Sebastião 110, 111
Granger, Farley 198, 211
Granger, Gilbert *see* Galbán, Gualberto
Grant, Howard 63
Grantham, Lucy 158
Grattan, Alex *see* Mikels, Ted V.
Grau, George *see* Sola, Jorgé Grau
Grau, Jorgé *see* Sola, Jorgé Grau
Grave Desires 65
Grave of the Vampire 166
Graver, Gary M. 100, 230
Graver, Sean 100
Graveto 210
Graveyard of Horror 179
Gravina, Carla 45
Gravina, Miriam 212
Gray, Franca 73
Graziani, Benedetto 174
Green, G. *see* Gastaldi, Ernesto
Green, Jerry 227
Green, Ray 48
Greens, Gregory *see* Rodríguez, Amando de Ossorio
Greenwood, Paul 119
Greer, Donn 154
Gregor, Henry 213
Gregor, Manfred *see* Dietrich, Erwin C.

Index

Gregory, Jennifer 127
Gregory, Nigel 157
Grenadier Films 232
Greta, Haus Ohne Männer 147
Greville, Edmond T. 243
Grey, Yocasta 179
Grieve, Russ 135
Griffith, Myron 104
Griffith, Peter 132
Griffiths, Lucy 117
Grim Company 158
The Grim Reaper 68, 233
Grimaldi, Dan 94
Grinell, William 71
Grinter, Brad F. 57
Grinter, Randy, Jr. 57
Griswold, Al 205
Gross, Jerry 142
Grosser, Arthur 195
Grossman, Karen 171
The Gruesome Twosome 131
Die Gruft der Lebenden Leichen 243
Grutta, Dominik 57
Guazzo, Marco 38
Gudbye, Douglas 104
Guedj, Claude 206
Gueffen, Max 41
Guenette, Anne Marie 147
Guerra, Luigi A. 203
Guerrero, Evelyn 230
Guinn, Ed 227
Gummer, Christopher 84
Gurney, Sharon 88
Gutapercha 151
Gutcher, Barbara 72
Guy, Lawrence Rory 198
Gyulai, Miklos 137

Habif, James 137
Hachler, Horst 134
Hackett, Pat 42
Hackett, Tod *see* Ormsby, Alan
Hackney, Pearl 215
Haddon, Carol 180
Hagerty, Beverly 53
Haig, Terry 147
Haims, Eric Jeffrey 154
Hale, Lucy 38
Haliday, Bryant 232
Halinen, Tarja Leena 105
Hall, Arch, Jr. 80
Hall, Chuck 38
Hall, Scott H. 56, 77
Hall of the Mountain King 164
Haller, Richard *see* Massaccesi, Aristide

Halloween 63, 132
Hallucinations 78
Hallucinations of a Deranged Mind 90
Hamell, Jack 62
Hamill, John 232
Hamilton, Gary 232
Hamilton, Stan 226
Hamilton, Suzette 216
Hamm, Peter 176
Hammer Film Productions Limited 74, 94, 109, 117, 244
Hammill, Ellen 95
Hammond, Chris 244
Hampton, Harry 201
Hampton, Paul 195
Hampton, Robert *see* Freda, Riccardo
Hampton, Undine 137
The Hanging Woman 194
Hanley, Jenny 46
Hanners, Richard 75
Hansen, Gunnar 227
Hansen, Mark *see* Lewis, Herschell Gordon
Hardgore 132
Hardiman, Marguerite 93
Hardman, Karl 182
Hardstark, Michael 38
Hardt, Harry 135
Hardy, Alan 226
Hardy, Hump 154
Hardy, Martin *see* Martino, Luciano
Hardy, Stuart 181
Harem Keeper of the Oil Sheiks 144
Hargitay, Mickey 90, 114, 209
Hargreaves, Janet 117
Harkus, Steve 238
Harlow, April 180
Harmon, John 171
Harp, Helen *see* Arpón, María Elena
Harper, Jessica 225
Harper, Susan 198
Harris, Craig 63
Harris, John 71
Harris, Michael 219
Harris, Ross 82, 182
Harris, Tony 117
Harris, Vince 238
Harris, William 77
Harrison, John 85
Hart, John 53
Hartman, Lee 182
Harvey, Marcus 223
Harvey, Michael 96

The Hatchet Murders 202
Hatfield, John 223
Hathcock, Jeff 244
Hathcock, Richard 244
Haves, Eileen 125
Haviv, Ronit 87
Haviv, Yuri 87
Haward, David 105
Hawker, John 230
Hawkes, Steve 57
Hawkins, Dave 85
Haworth, Jill 232
Hayashi, Hiroshi 155
Hayden, Jane 157
Hayden, Lennie *see* Manera, Jesús Franco; Romay, Lina
Hayman, David 48
Haynie, Jim 48, 115
Haynie, Smith 229
Hazrd, Frank 103
He Kills Night After Night After Night 180
Heacock, Gary R. 80
The Headless Eyes 134
Heald, Margaret 240
Healey, Myron 148
Heart, Barbra 238
Heatley, Kevin 120
Hedburg, John 95
Hedman, Marina 107
Heidankova, Alena 64
Helhoski, Maria 103
Hell 155
Hell Night 191
Hellman, Frank *see* Manera, Jesús Franco
Hellraiser 117
Hemisphere Pictures Inc. 49, 65, 162
Hemmings, David 202
Henkel, Kim 104, 227
Hennessey, Anthony 119
Henriksen, Lance 165
Henry, Carol 149
Henshaw, Eric 200
Henson, Lin 95
Herazo, Francisco 151
Herbert, George 140
Herbert, Martin *see* de Martino, Alberto
Herbst, Andy 76
Heritage Ltd. 45, 78, 119, 215
The Heritage of Caligula— An Orgy of Sick Minds 149
Herman, Jeffrey 95
Hernández, Marisol 185
Hernandez, Rafael 217

Hernández, Sandalio 208
Hernandez, Vicky 122
Heroux, Claude 66
Herrera, Lola 217
Herschel, David 63
Hersent, Phillipe 198, 211
Herval, Michel 206
Hess, David Alexander 158
Hexen Bis Aufs Blut Gequält 64
Hexen Geschändet und zu Tode Gequält 134
Hicks, Bill 62
Hi-Fi Stereo 70 KG 64, 186
Higgins, Melissa 91
High, Bernard G. 180
Las Hijas de Dracula 241
Hilario, Teofilo 49, 50
Hilary, Jane 61
Hildeck, Fernando 189
Hill, Angela 98
Hill, Clayton 85
Hill, Craig 172
Hill, Debra 115, 132
Hill, Douglas 180
Hill, Harry 205
Hill, Walter 39
Hills, Beverly 65
Hills, David *see* Massaccesi, Aristide
The Hills Have Eyes 128, 135
Hiltl, Charly 176
Hilton, George 224, 234
Hilton, Joe 60
Hindle, Art 66
Hinds, Anthony 117
Hinds, Cindy 66
Hines, Charles 127
Hingst, Sérgio 210
Hinjosa, Joaquim 189
Hinzman, Bill *see* Hinzman, S. William
Hinzman, S. William 82, 182
Hipp, Paul 54
Hirsch, April 127
Hoag, Stephen J. 223
Hobart, Doug 59
Hodges, Robert 42
Hoffer, Jerry 76
Hoffman, Robert 197
Hogan, Joe Bill 227
Hogan, Percy 106
Hogan, Susan 66
Hogan's Heroes 146, 212
Holbert, Fred 216
Holbrook, Hal 115
Hold, John *see* Bava, Mario

Hold, John, Jr. *see* Bava, Lamberto
Holland, Byrd 205
Hollander, Adam 132
Hollar, Lloyd 82
Hollmann, Frank *see* Manera, Jesús Franco
Hollowell, Frank 104
Hollywood Meat Cleaver Massacre 137
Holm, Ian 40
Holm, Michael 64
Holocausto Canibal 138, 237
Holotik, Rosie 96
Holt, Jonathan 61
Holy Terror 38
El Hombre Lobo 51, 110, 121, 130, 164, 166, 172, 208, 243
El Hombre Lobo 166
El Hombre Que Vino de Ummo 172
Hooper, Geraldine 202
Hooper, Tobe 104, 227
Hope, Gary 180
Hopwood, Pat 127
Horn, Ken 135
Horne, Ken 137
Horowitz, Margherita 225
El Horriplante Bestia Humana 139
Horrocks, Tamara 42
Horror Castle 243
Horror Hospital 140, 233
Horror Hotel Massacre 105
Horror of Snape Island 232
Horror of the Werewolf 164
Horror of the Zombies 68
Horror Rises from the Tomb 109
Horror y Sexo 139
Horrors of Blood Island 49
Horsbrugh, Walter 180
Horton, Helen 40
Horton, John 88
Horton, Louise 38
Horvath, Leif 171
Hotel Erotica 52
House of Blood 165
House of Doom 192
House of Dracula 173
House of Frankenstein 173
House of Psychotic Women 192
House of Terror 194
The House of the Screaming Virgins 149
Houseman, John 115
Houston, Robert 135
Hoven, Adrian 64, 134
Hoven, Percy 135

Howard, Moe 95, 96
Howard, Rick 220, 221
Howco International 238
Howe, David 71
Howe, Illa 149
Howey, David 46
Howorth, Richard 103
Hoy, Drucilla 80
Hoyo, Pablo 218
Huambos, Helena 151
Huber, Lon 84
Hudiberg, Wendell 75
Hudson, Allan 140
Hudson, Michael 223
Hudson, Robert 127
Hughes, Fred 42
Hughes, Heather 57
Le 8ème Passager 40
Hull, Dave 148
Humanoids from the Deep 224
Humbert, Humphrey *see* Lenzi, Umberto
The Hunchback of the Morgue 156
The Hunchback of the Rue Morgue 156
Hunt, Barbara 42
Hunter, Dennis M. 95
Hunter, Max *see* Pupillo, Massimo
Hurd, Robert L. 53
Hurst, Don 181
Hurt, John 40
Hurwit, Joel 171
Hurwit, Rory 171
Hurwitz, Victor 158
Huser, Dominik 176
Huston, John 91
Hutchins, Lucie 147
Hutsko, Steve 182
Hutt, Karen *see* Digard, Uschi
Hutzar, Eva 212

I Dismember Mama 76, 217
I Drink Your Blood 83, 142, 196
I Eat Your Skin 143
I Hate Your Guts 87
I Spit on Your Grave 87
I Wake Up Screaming 78
I Walked with a Zombie 182
Iaccio, Vincenzo 165
Ibéria Filmes 110, 111
La Iguana 143
L'Iguana della Lingua di Fuoco 143
The Iguana with the Tongue of Fire 143

Igus, Darrow 115
Illusions, Inc. 38
Ilsa—Harem Keeper of the Oil Sheiks 144
Ilsa, la Belva delle SS 145
Ilsa—La Louve des SS 145
Ilsa—She Wolf of the SS 144, 145, 212
Ilsa the Tigress of Siberia 144, 146
Image Ten 182
Imbró, Gaetano 160
In de Greep van de Zombies 85
In der Gewalt der Zombies 192
In Quella Casa Buio Omega 68
Inanoglu, Ilker 44
Inch, Bonnie 148
Incontrera, Annabella 198, 211
The Incredible Melting Man 148
The Incredible Torture Show 130, 149
El Increible Hombre que se Derrite 148
Incubo sulla Città Contaminata 124, 191
Independent-International Pictures 99
Indice, Marisa 209
Induñi, Luis 98, 122, 164, 168
Industria Andina Del Cine 151
Indústria Cinematográfica Apolo 37
Inferno (1960) 155
Ingles, Rufino 188
Ingwersen, Bill 171
Innocents from Hell 41
Inquisición 150, 168
El Inquisidor 151
Inquisition 150
Les Insatisfaites Poupées Érotiques du Dr. Hichcock 52
Inseminoid 201
Insua, Alberto S. 130, 156
Interbest American Enterprises 63
Interfilme 188
International Apollo Films 152, 160
International Films, S.A. 179
International Jaguar 172
Invasion der Zombies 189

Invasion of the Blood Farmers 220
Ippoliti, Silvano 143
Iranzo, Antonio 150
Iregua, Victor 152
IRMI Films 83
Iruam, Arildo 37
Irving, Amy 72
Irving, Penny 78
Irwin, Mark 66
Isadore, Christine 95
Isbert, Tony 150, 213
Ishikawa, Mimi 84
Island of Death 204
The Island of Living Horror 65
Island of the Damned 204
The Island of the Living Dead 247
Israel, Victor 164, 179
It! The Terror from Beyond Space 40
It Fell from the Sky 41
Italian International Film 81
Ivan Cardoso's Shocking Shorts 239

J.E.R. Pictures Inc. 125
Jack el Distripador de Londres 152
Jack l'Éventreur 153
Jack the Ripper (1971) 152
Jack the Ripper (1976) 153
Jack the Ripper—Der Dirnenmörder von London 153
Jack the Ripper—The Harlot Killer of London 153
Jackel, Jim 77
Jackson, David 157
Jackson, Richard *see* Garrone, Sergio
Jackson, Roosevelt 53
Jackson, Tonedeaf 171
Jacob, Robert 176
Jacobs, Jay 115
Jacobs, Morton 219
Jacoby, Shari 115
Jagger, Mick 140
James, Dave 182
James, Jerry 127
James, Julia 184
James, Patricia 104
James, Ron 63
Jameson, Louise 93
Janczak, Andrew 238
Janos, Victor *see* Watkins, Roger
Janson, Frank 75

Janus Films, S.L. 130
Jaroslow, Ruth 42
Jarris, Ray 181
Jartin, Josefina 122
Jarvis, May 70
Javicoli, Susanna 225
Jaws 200
Jeavons, Colin 215
Jefferies, Jeannie 85
Jeffords, Vince 59
Jeffries, Richard 59
The Jekyll and Hyde Portfolio 154
Jekyll and Hyde Unleashed 154
Jerome-Fredric 125
Jessop, Peter 46, 78, 119, 215
Jhenkins, Jho 203
Jigoku 155
Joffrey, Johnny 114
John, Nicholas 119
Johnson, Edith 195
Johnson, James Lee *see* Manera, Jesús Franco
Johnson, James P. *see* Manera, Jesús Franco
Johnson, Jed 42
Johnson, Noel 119
Johnson, Nora 195
Johnson, Richard 78, 247
Johnson, Sandy 132
Johnson, Terri 154
Joi, Marilyn 165
Jones, Carolyn 105
Jones, Ceri 88
Jones, Christina 157
Jones, Douglas 240
Jones, Duane 182
Jones, Frank 48
Jones, Harold Wayne 82
Jones, Jack 78
Jones, James Earl 59
Jones, Ken 198
Jones, Kenneth V. 232
Jones, Lee 229
Jones, Richard 91
Jones, Tiffany 104
Jong, Slosson Bing 75
Jordan, Donna 203
El Jorobado de la Morgue 155, 176, 195
José, João 111
Joseph, Don 77
Josse, Yannick 206
Joston, Darwin 115
Journet, Dominique 113
Jover, Antonio 226
Joy, Marilyn 144
Joyner, Harry M. 62

Joyner, Kerry 62
Juego, El 204
Juerging, Arno 101, 177
Julio, Montserrat 98, 109
Jungle Holocaust 237
Jürgens, Curd 64
Justin, Larry 137

Kahn, Allen 245
Kaiser, Norman F. 120
Kalbus, Terrie 198
Kaler, Berwick 61, 98
Kalinke, Ernst W. 64, 134
Kalinski, Edward 119
Kalist, Mike 91
Kamini, Susana 41
Kamp, Louise 56
Kaplan, Henry 41
Kaplan, Lazarus 213
Kapusta, Tom 85
Karamesinis, Vassili 127
Karlatos, Olga 247
Karloff, Boris 243
Karlowsky, Robert 82
Karlsen, John 51
Karnz, Nancy 41
Karr, Tom 92
Karr International Pictures 92
Kasché, Renate 114
Kasdani, Sabirin 207
Katt, William 72
Kauffman, Ava 244
Kava, Lynn 127
Kawsh, Frank 128
Kay, Una 205
Kazan, Denize 244
Kazan, Marge 137
Keach, Stacy 173
Kean, Georgina 157
Kearns, Jerry 62
Keaton, Camille 81, 87
Kedrova, Lila 59
Keefler, Kathy 205
Keeler, Rodina 145
Keesee, Oscar 65
Keiler, Victoria 103
Keith, Sheila 78, 119
Kelleher, Ed 219
Kelleher, Paul 137, 181
Kelly, Jack 223
Kelly, Monika 80
Kelly, Sharon 144, 145
Kelsch, Ken 103
Kelsey, George 41
Kemper, Terry *see* Gimpera, Teresa
Kendall, Suzy 79
Kendall, Tony *see* Stella, Luciano

Kennedy, Arthur 45, 189
Kennedy, Mike A. 160
Kennedy, Pluto *see* Giombini, Marcello
Kennedy, William C. 82
Kenney, Sean 80
Kenny, Brendan 76
Kent, Gary 100
Kenton, Jules 114
Kerky, Dietrich 135
Kerman, Robert 138
Kerry, James 157
Kerwin, Barbara 131
Kerwin, Harry E. 127
Kerwin, William 56, 127, 235
Ketsch, Ken 95
Keye, Larry 244
Keymer, Gordon 157
Khan, David 176
Kibbee, Lincoln 105
Kier, Udo 64, 101, 177, 225
Kierney, Tyde 142
Kilian, Astrid 135
Kill and Go Hide! 75
Killen, Jim 128
Killer's Moon 157
Kilson, Graciela 168
Kimball, Bruce 100
Kimberley, Glen 71
Kindberg, Ann N. 230
King, Andrea 53
King, Arthur *see* Locke, Peter
King, Barbara 185
King, Diana 215
King, Perry 42
King, Stephen 71
Kingfish, Bunker 70
Kinito 156
Kinski, Klaus 51, 153, 165, 219
Kirby, Jessie 96
Kirkin, Corinne 246
Kirkpatrick, Harry *see* Lenzi, Umberto
Kirschner, William 80
Kirsh, Robert 149
Kirt Films International 71
Kirtman, Leonard 71
Kissinger, Charles 229
Kittay, R. Simon *see* Fulci, Lucio
K-L Productions 88
Kleemann, Gunter 87
Kleinholz III, Nick 216
Klimovsky, León 98, 159, 168, 186, 213
Knapko Pat 91
Kneelen, Sandy 57

Knight, Harold *see* Rizzolo, Modesto
Knowles, Michael 46
Knox, Robert 216
Kohlberg, Stanford S. 56
Kollins, Nikki 95
Kolpek, Monica 218
Konopka, Diane *see* Dianik, Zurakowska
Koock, Guich 200
Kopert, Gotha 212
Korb, Michael 235
Kosana, George 182
Koscina, Sylva 198, 211
Koslow, Aaron 171
Kosmo, Wanda 112
Kosti, María 159, 184, 185
Kostur, Jerry 66
Kotter, Allan 66
Kotto, Yaphet 40
Kove, Martin 59, 158
Kozman, Myron 91
Kraft, Evelyn 72
Kramer, Lisette 137
Kramer, Richard *see* Pallottini, Riccardo
Kramer Vs. Kramer 67
Kramski, Hans-Walter 153
Kraus, Germán 168
Kraus, Lee *see* Küveiller, Luigi
Kregar, Alex 120
Krem, Viju 149
Kress, Frank 128
Krimann, Verônica 111
Kristel, Sylvia 106
Kroeger, Jackie 128
Krog, Tim 63
Kronenberg, Bruce 127
Krug and Company 158
Kruger, Henry *see* Raho, Umberto
Krusz, Walter L. 96
Krut, Jim 85
Kulier, Günther 64
Kunesova, Ilona 226
Kurtz, Linda 71
Küveiller, Luigi 101, 160, 176, 202
Kwan, Dee 244
Kyle, David 132
KZ9—Lager di Sterminio 212

Laatste Kannibalen, De 237
Labelle, Michel René 147
la Blaque, Fib 125
Lacey, Cathryn 167
Lacey, Ronald 93
Lack, Simon 180

Lacroix, Denis 205
Lacy, Beatriz 179
Ladd, David 88
la Du, Patty 246
Lady Dracula 74
Lady Frankenstein 114
Lady Frankenstein, Cette Obsedée Sexuelle 114
Lafleur, C. D. *see* Flower, George
Lafleur, Jean 147
Un Lagartija con Piel de Mujer 160
Lagos, Vicky 217
Laguette, Lya 110
Laguna, Emilio 218
Lahaie, Brigitte *see* van Meerhaegue, Brigitte
Lahee, Sally 46
Lai, Me Me 237
Laine, Jimmy *see* Ferrara, Abel
Laine, Kiersten 229
Lajeunesse, Isabelle 205
Lamb, Joe B. 62
Lambert, Jane 83
Lambie, Joe 42
Lanchbury, Karl 240
Land of the Lost 231
Landau, Susan 42
Landi, Mario 127
Landry, Ray 147
Lane, Andrew 127
Lane, Anthony 127
Lane, Graddie 48
Lane, Gwenn 127
Lane, Lori 127
Lane, Mark *see* Masciocchi, Marcello
Lane, Sherri 131
Lang, Michael 181
Langdon, Donald 59
Langdon, Greg 181
Lanier, Susan 135
la Page, Brent 132
Larocca, Sonny 83
Larrain, Casey 154
Larrath, J.R. *see* Larraz, José Ramón
Larraz, Jonathan *see* Larraz, José Ramón
Larraz, José Ramón 240
Larraz, Joseph *see* Larraz, José Ramón
Larson, Nancy 127
Lasalle, Martin 41
la Salle, Richard 94
Lasky, Gil 54
Lassander, Dagmar 143
Lassick, Sydney 72

Last House on Dead End Street 120
Last House on the Left 136, 158
Last House on the Left II 44
The Last Survivor 237
The Latent Image, Inc. 182
Latini, Cristina 225
Latino, Nino 51
Latour, Jean-Guy 147
Latour, Susana 130, 156
Laurel Group 85
Laurence, Brian 120
Laurenson, Phil 128, 246
Lauria, Frank 38
Laurie, Piper 72
Laurie, Sandra 76
Laury, Michel 226
Lava, William 100
Laverne, Lulú *see* Manera, Jesús Franco; Romay, Lina
LaVey, Anton 240
Lavia, Gabriele 202
Laviniaque Films, Inc.
Lavis, Arthur 157
la Vorgna, Angela 233
Lawlor, Ray 70
Lawrence, Adam 104
Lawrence, Andrea 117
Lawrence, Jacqueline 98
Lawrence, Scott *see* Crawford, Wayne
Lawrence, Stephen 38
Lazareno, Norma 139
Lazarus, Jodi 181
Lazer, J.A. *see* Manera, Jesús Franco
Lea, Lorence 216
Lea Film 233, 234
Leary, D'Mara 95
Lease, Maria 100
le Bar, Bob 100
Lecompte, Yvonne 205
Lederer, Mike 153
Lee, Bernard 117
Lee, Christopher 88, 137, 243
Lee, Cosette 92
Lee, Evan 137
Lee, Leslie 48
Lee, Margaret 51
Lee, Patricia 77
Lee, Reneta 181
Lefleur, C.L. 83
Legacy of Horror 126
The Legend of Blood Castle 74
Legend of the Bayou 105

Das Leichenhaus der Lebenden Toten 189
Leigh, Janet 115
Leirier, John 41
Lemaire, Gerard 226
Lemaire, Jean-Marie 113
Lemaster, Georgia 214
Lemei, Cristiane 111
Lemètre, Jean-Jacques 226
Lemos, Carlos 68
La Lengua de Fuego 143
Lenzi, Umberto 123
León, Eva 150, 192
Leonardi, Lisa 234
Lester, Jayne 157
Lester, Kathy 198
Lester, Stephen 80
Let Sleeping Corpses Lie 189
Levende Doden in het Lijkenhuis 189
Levey, William A. 53
Levitsky, Al 169
Levy, Eugene 70
Lewicki, Richard 82
Lewis, Herschell Gordon 37, 49, 55, 62, 71, 77, 111, 112, 126, 128, 131, 140, 149, 168, 175, 183, 218, 224, 235, 238, 242, 244, 245
Lewis, Linda 41
Lewis, Michael 131
Lewis, Robert 128, 131
Lewis Motion Picture Enterprises 128
Leyart, Nilcemar 90, 210
Leyton, John 215
Liaman, Don 50
Libelula para Cada Muerto 159
Liberati, Anna 197
Liberati, Stefano 165
Lies, Lenny 85
Lifante, José Ruiz 189
Liles, James F. 115
Lillo, Ramón 47, 121
Lima, Mário 37, 110, 111, 210
Lincoln, Fred 158
Lincoln, George *see* Freda, Riccardo
Lind, Karin 53
Linden, Anne 125
Lindqvist, Jorma 147
Lindsey, Linda 62
Liné, Helga *see* Stern, Helga Lina
Ling, Don 137
Ling, Su 144
Link, André 205

Index

Liofredi, Marco 177
Lion, Mickey *see* Bava, Mario; Leone, Alfredo
Lionel, Philip 154
Lippert, Mario 72
Lipsey, Don 214
Lipsick, David 127
Lisa 48
Lisa, Lisa 48
Liska, Stephen 82
Little Warsaw Productions 84
Littrell, Charlotte 91
The Living Dead 189
The Living Dead at Manchester Morgue 189
The Living Dead at the Manchester Morgue 189
Livingston, Shelby 235
Llimera, Veronica 188
Llinas, Francisco 109
Lloyd-Pack, Charles 117
Llywelyn, David 176
Lôbo, Ênio 110
lo Cascio, Franco 239
Locke, Peter 135
Lockwood, Lynn 227
Logan, Humphrey *see* Lenzi, Umberto
Logan, Lyn 70
Lolich, Mickey 148
Lolli, Rodolfo 197
Lom, Herbert 64
Lommel, Ulli 63
Lon John Productions 104
Long, Johnny 49, 50, 162
Longhi, Carlo 173
Longo, Tiziano 51
Loomis, Nancy 115, 132
Lopes, Édson 111
López, Flavia 151
López, Victoriano 166
Loran, Patricia 152
Lord, Justine 180
Lorde, Athena 95
Lore, France 111
The Lorelei's Grasp 122
Lorenz, Perry 227
Lorys, Diana 192
The Lost Boys 171
Lotosky, Michael 70
Lotus Films 208, 242
Louis, Larry *see* Bava, Lamberto
Love, Bessie 240
Love, Dorothy 148
Love, Nicholas 63
Love, Suzanna 63
Love Me Deadly 95
Lovejoy, Harry 80

Lovell, Rosemary 148
Lovelock, Ray 161, 189
Lowe, Grant 205
Lowery, Robert 238
Lowry, Jane 38
Lowry, Lynn 82, 142, 195
Loy, Mino 234
Lubin, Hedda 128
Lucas, Ralph 74
Lucas, William 232
Lucchetti, Rubens Francisco 90, 111, 210
Una Lucertola con la Pelle di Donna 160
Lucisano, Fulvio 81
Ludman, Larry *see* de Angelis, Fabrizio
Luis Films 73
Luján, Verónica 121
Lukeart, Valerie 105
Lundy, Nell 70
Luppi, Aureliano 114, 211
Luque, Isabel 150
Lust, Simon 140
Lust for a Vampire 94
Lustik, Marlena 216
Lutz, Ric 154
Lynn, Justina 133
Lynn, Kane W. 49, 65, 162
Lynn, Kaye 127

M.G.D. Film Productions 174
Maazel, Lincoln 169
MacAdams, Rhea 96
Macchie Solari 161, 203
MacDonald, A.C. 82
MacDonald, Camille 76
MacIntyre, Jack 103
Mack, Wayne 167
MacKay, Jeff 48
MacPhail, Menda 128
Mad Doctor of Blood Island 49, 65, 162
Mad People, The 82
Madame Frankenstein 114
Madden, Peter 117
Madrid, José Luis 152
Madrid, María Paz 179
Madrid, Miguel 179
Madrigal, Juan 159, 168
Madur, Francis *see* Madrid, José Luis
Maestosi, Elio 165
Magee, Michael 66
Magier, Fanny 113
Magnolfi, Barbara 225
Magnotti, Alexis 87
Maguire, Mady 154
Magurean, Peter 50

Mai, Franka 113
Maien, Michael 64
Maika 152
Mailer, Claire 103
Maillot, Michel 147
Maioletti, Gianfranco 191
Maitland, Katherine 98
Malanowski, Tony 84
Malco, Paolo 124
Malcomson, Craig 98
Maldera, Roberto 190
La Maldición de la Bestia 163
Malet, Arthur 132
Malfatti, Marina 234
Mallone, Will 88
Malvil, Annik 210
Mamches, Valerie 76
The Man with Two Faces 98
The Man with Two Heads 98
Mancini, Carla 165, 177, 194, 203, 233, 234
Mancini, Mario 72, 127, 174
Mancuso, Elsio 191
Mancuso, Kevin *see* Massaccesi, Aristide
Mandrell, Gary 91
Maner, Jeff *see* Manera, Jesús Franco
Manera, Frank *see* Manera, Jesús Franco
Manera, Jesús Franco 108, 147, 153, 197, 226
Manero, Frank *see* Manera, Jesús Franco
Maness, Sherman 205
Maniac 96
Maniac at Large 197
Manila Cinematografica 239
Mann, Alex 142
Mann, Laura 198
Manning, Sean 95
Mannino, Al 171
Mannino, Vincenzo 45
Mannkopff, Andreas 153
La Mano Che Nutre la Morte 165
Le Manoir de la Terreur 191
Mansion of the Doomed 165
Manson, Charles 142, 220
Mansyur, Adang 207
Manz, Michael *see* Manzanaque, Manuel
Manzanaque, Manuel 166
Mara, Carol 149
Marani, Imelde 177

Index

Marano, Ezio 160
Marboeuf, Jacques 113
La Marca del Hombre Lobo 122, 166
Marcel, Marcio 210
Marcel, Terence 201
Marcello, Bonini 209
Marco, José 98, 121, 186
Mardi Gras Massacre 167
Marfield, Dwight 219
Margheriti, Antonio 101, 176, 243
Margolin, Alan C. 149
Maria, Ana 111
Maria, Denise 110
Mariani, Jacopo 202, 225
Mariani, Luigi 190
Mariani, Marco 174, 233
Marie, Anne 159
Marignano, Renzo 152
Marimon, Armando José 151
Marinoff, Brenda 135
Marins, Antônio 37, 110
Marins, Cármen 37, 110
Marins, José Mojica 37, 90, 110, 111, 112, 155, 209, 210, 239
Marins, Merisol 112
Maris, Allen 91
Maris, Peter 91
Maris, Stela 210
Maris, Stephanie 91
El Mariscal del Infierno 168
Mark of the Devil 50, 64, 135
Mark of the Devil Part 2 135
Mark of the Devil II 135
Mark of the Devil 3 41
The Mark of the Wolfman 166
Marlo Cinematografica 151
Marlowe, Anna 171
Marlowe, Linda 180
Marly, Florence 95
Marner-Brooks, Elizabeth 142
Marquand, Serge 206
Marques, Claudio 210
Marr, Sally 165
Marrocco, Gino 70
Mars Production Corporation 104
Marsh, Dennis 54
Marsh, Julian *see* Findlay, Michael
Marshall, Iris 77
Marshall, Karen 171
Marshall, Lance 145
Marshall, Tom 157

Marsilla, Amparo 226
Marsina, Antonio 173
Martel, Chris 131
Martellanza, Pietro 72
Marten, Felix 206
Martensen, Dea 144
Martin 82, 169
Martin, Andrea 70
Martin, Ashlyn 56
Martin, Femi *see* Benussi, Eufemia
Martin, Frank *see* Frumkes, Roy; Girolami, Marino
Martin, George 197
Martin, Javier 156
Martín, José Manuel 130, 208
Martin, Julio 156
Martin, Lawrence *see* Martino, Luciano
Martin, Skip 140
Martin, Wally 195
Martine, Gina 83
Martinez, José Luis 160
Martino, Francesco *see* Frumkes, Roy; Girolami, Marino
Martino, Luciano 173, 224, 233
Martino, Sergio 79, 173, 224, 233, 234
Martino, Walter 68
Martinov, Peter 114
Martins, Elidio 110
Martins, Guilhermina 111
Martyn, Debbie 157
Marx, Maria 145
Marz, Carolyn 103
Marzio, Duilio 151
Marzzialetti, Pedro 151
Masacre en Cadena 227
Masciocchi, Marcello 237
Mascolo, Louis 103
Masefield, Joseph R. 95
Masini, Mario 203
Masini, Giovanni 237
Maslansky, Paul 88
Mason, Connie 56, 235
Mason, Emily 128
Mason, Frank *see* de Masi, Francesco
Mason, Richard 231
Massaccesi, Aristide 45, 68, 81, 106, 107, 156, 192
Massacre a la Tronconneause 227
La Massacre des Morts-Vivants 189
Massacre Zombie 191

Massasso, Aldo 189
Masselli, Fiorella 177
Massimini, Giulio 107
Mastandrea, Nick 169
Mastorakis, Nico 59
Matamoros, Jorge 208
Mateos, Luis 204
Mather, Jack 92
Matheson, Judy 46
Matheus, Jimmy *see* Massaccesi, Aristide
Mathot, Olivier 226
Matson, Curtis 80
Mattei, Bruno 211
Mattei, Marius 72
Matthews, Anthony *see* Margheriti, Antonio
Matthews, Jordan B. *see* Mattei, Bruno
Mattia, Joe 147
Mattioli, Simone 191
Maudslay, Craig, Jr. 56
Mauri, Ann Maria 164
Mauri, Glauco 202
Maver, Howard 147
Max, Edwin 148
Maxper P.C. 166
May, Jack 180
May, Martha 123
Mayans, Antonio 156, 159, 226
Mayflower Pictures, Inc. 131, 245
Mayo, Susana 159
Mazzeo, Alcione 112
Mazzinghi, Piero 202
Mazzoni, Frances 169
McAdams, Al 76
McAdams, Ann 96
McAdams, Jane 76
McAllister, Ada 125
McBride, Mark 232
McCarthy, Dennis 181
McCarthy, Kevin 200
McCloskey, Carol 169
McCloskey, Patrick 85
McClure, Robert M. 62
McClurg, Edie 72
McColl, Kirk 147, 205
McComb, David 95
McCormack, Colin 88
McCulloch, Ian 247
McCully, Robert J. 82
McDonald, A.C. 182
McDonald, Cliff 83
McDonald, David 140
McDouglas, John *see* Addobbati, Giuseppe
McEnery, John 215
McFaul, Harriet 219

Index

McGara, Marven 147
McGhee, William 96
McGillivray, David 119, 215
McGoohan, Al *see* Birkinshaw Alan
McGowan, Jack 76, 92, 167
McGregor, Charles 42
McHeady, Robert 70, 92
McKeehan, Gary 205
McKendry, Maxime 101
McKinney, Austin 48
McKinnon, Clayton 85, 169
McLee, Joseph *see* Zaccariello, Giuseppe
McLorin, Robert *see* Migliorini, Romano
McMaster, Niles 38, 149
McMillan, W.G. 82
McMinn, Teri 227
McNeill, Peter 205
McSwain, Faith 230
Mead, Bob 137
Meatcleaver Massacre 137
Medigovich, Rod 75
Medina 179
Medina, Juan 166
Medusa Distribuzione 173
Meek, David 82
Mehaffey, Roy 62
Mei, Magda 37
Meier, Ernest 63
Meliande, Antônio 112
Méliès, Georges 156
Mellado, Emilio 168
Mellone, Amedeo 165
Mellor, James 180
Melo, Renato 37
Mendez, Luis 208, 242
Mendizabal, Sergio 122
Mendonça, Tânia 110
Mendoza, Quiel 65, 162
Menéndez, Ángel 73, 122, 156, 166
Meniconi, Furio 202
Mennard, Tom 46
Mennen, Albert *see* de Mendoza, Alberto
Mensch, Bill 91
Menta, Narcisco Ibañez 213
Menzies, Heather 200
Meredith, Penny 46
Merenda, Luc 79
Merighi, Ferdinando 72
Meril, Macha 202
Merino, José Luis 194
Merino, Manuel 109
Merino, Margarita 68

Merino, Ricardo 150, 159
Merio, Ismael 217
Merrill, Donna 131
Messe Nere della Contessa Dracula, La 186
Messina, Terri 55
Messinger, Jack 205
Messner, Marion 176
Mestre, Isobel 189
Mestre, Jeannine 189
Metcalfe, Ken 50
Metner, Karl 103
Metrolina Motion Picture Corporation 62
Metzger, Alan 42
Metzo, William 167
Meunier, Christian 206
Meyer, John R. 60
Meyer, Phil 137
Mezzetti, Maria Gabriella 106
Miami Vice 143
Michael, Drew 137
Michaels, Joann 182
Michl, Keith 148
Microwave Massacre 171
Middleton, Fran 169
Migicovsky, Alan 195
Migliorini, Romano 190
Mikacecci, Theo *see* Mikels, Ted V.
Mikels, Ted V. 80, 238
Milá, Miguel F. 47, 122, 150, 159, 234
Milano, Lisa 214
Milestone, Hank *see* Lenzi, Umberto
Mill, Robert 215
Millan, Antonio 123
Millard, Frances 83
Millard, Steve 83, 214
Miller, Beverly 49, 50
Miller, Carol 48
Miller, Cheryl 95
Miller, Dick 200
Miller, Don 244
Miller, Kenny 60
Miller, Linda 38
Miller, Magna 90
Miller, Marta *see* Miller, Mirta
Miller, Mirta *see* Miller, Mirtha
Miller, Mirtha 98, 130
Miller, Philip *see* Millard, Steve
Miller, Rick 91
Miller, Vany 111
Milligan, Andy 60, 97, 125, 154, 231

Mills, D. *see* Milligan, Andy
Mills, Grace 164
Mills, Kaly 71
Mills, Riley 142
Milone, Luciana 243
Miná, Dante 210
Miñano, Heli 151
Mingozzi, Fulvio 174, 202, 225
Minuesa, Miguel 152
Miodzik, Ron 205
Miomir, Aleksic 177
Mir, Irene 152
Miranda, Isa 44
Miranda, John 61
Miriel, Veronica 164
Misch, Laura 167
Mishel, George *see* Serkeis, Jorge Michel
Mishkin, Jeremy 231
Mishkin, William 61, 97, 231
Mitchell, Cameron 230
Mitchell, Gordon 174
Mitchell, Leigh 148, 216
Mitchell, Norman 117
Mitchell, Sanford 80
Mitchell, Stuart 76
Mitchell, Ty 115
Mitsuya, Ukato 155
Mixon, Bart 84
Miyagawa, Ichirô 155
Miyata, Fumiko 155
Mlodzik, Ronald 195
Mocen, Jeanne 128
Moctezuma, Carlos López 139
Moctezuma, Juan López 41
Moctezuma, Yolanda L. 41
Model Massacre 77
Modern Film Effects 198
Modesto, Sam 68
Mogush, William 182
Moinnes, Colin 95
Molin, James *see* Alvarez, Jacinto Molina
Molina, Antonio Vidal 98, 109, 159, 168, 172, 184, 186, 208, 218
Molina, Jacinto *see* Alvarez, Jacinto Molina
Molina, Vidal *see* Molina, Antonio Vidal
Molina, Vince *see* Molina, Antonio Vidal
Moll, Jack *see* Alvarez, Jacinto Molina
Mollison, Clifford 117

Molva, David *see* Alvarez, Jacinto Molina
Monarch Releasing Corporation 221
Monarex Production 176
Monash, Paul 71
Le Monde des Morts-Vivants 68
Mondo Brutale 158
Mondo Cannibale 226
Mondo Cannibale II—Der Vogelmensch 237
Monkel, Hank *see* Munkel, Hans
Monne, Jose 242
Monreale, Cinzia 68
Monster Hunter 198
Monstruos de la Noche, Los 172, 208
Monstruos del Terror, Los 172
Montagna del Dio Cannibale, Il 173
Montagnani, Nerina 197, 233
Monte, Mina 110
Montefiori, Luigi 192
Monteillet, Max *see* Soler, Juan A.
Montenegro, Mario 65
Montero, Roberto Bianchi 198, 211
Montes, Diana 121
Monti, Maria 81, 190
Monti, Silvia 160
Monticelli, Mimma 239
Montinaro, Brizio 224
Montone, Rita 149
Montossé, Muriel 113
Montreal, Rhodney 103
Moore, Ben 235
Moore, Frank 205
Moore, Micki 92
Morais, Avelino 37
Moral, Malcolm *see* Stevens, Carter
Morales, Inés 192, 208
Moran, Tony 132
Morandi, Armando *see* Rodríguez, Amando de Ossorio
Morandi, Paulo 210
Morano, Jaime 168
Morcillo, Fernando Garcia 185, 217
Moree, Sam 127
Moreno, Eduardo 41
Moreno, José Elias 139
Moreno, Luis Laso 185
Moreno, Paloma 152

Moreno, Ric 115
Moreno, Roberto P. 150
Moresco, Fabrizio 198, 211
Morett, Gina 139
Morgan, Felicite 63
Morgan, Jane *see* Romay, Lina
Morgan, Lynne 157
Morgan, Robert W. 59
Morgan, William 110
Morghen, John *see* Radice, Giovanni Lombardo
Morin, Jacques 147
Morin, Michel 147
Morita, Mamoru 155
Moronjiv, Raphael 206
Morrell, Anne 100
Morrell, Lexy 154
Morricone, Ennio 45, 81, 160, 161
Morris, Butch 103
Morris, Lee 57
Morris, Marianne 240
Morrisey, Paul 101, 176
Morrison, Steven 120
Morrow, Joe 95
Morse, Ben 59
Morte Viene dal Buio, La 211
Morte Vivante, La 113, 207
Mortimer, Tricia 119, 215
Morton, Joseph *see* Nieto, José
Mosaico 174
Moschera, Consolata 209
Moseley, Jerry 59
Mosquito der Schander 176
Moss, Stewart 95
Il Mostro è in Tavola ... Barone Frankenstein 43, 101, 176, 226
Motionarts 75
Mount Everest Enterprises, Ltd. 144, 146
Mountain of the Cannibal God 173
Moy, Juan 151
Moyle, Allan 205
Mozarosky, Sandra 168, 184
Muchtar, W. D. 207
Muckler, Craig 171
Mueller, Paul *see* Müller, Paul
Mujico, Soledad 151
Mulaire, Jennifer 148
Mulher, Violada 87
Müller, Paul 114
Muller, Paul *see* Müller, Paul

Multifilmes 210
The Mummy's Revenge 242
Mumolo, Tony 145
Mundo Canibal! Mundo Salvaje! 237
Munkel, Hans 186
Munna, T.M. 173
Muñoz, Mimi 213
Muñoz, Tita 162
Murder in Paris 72
Murder on the Bayou 105
Murolo, Ferdinando 172
Murphy, Edward 162
Murry, Elisabeth 180
Murta, Manuela 212
Music Industries 80
Mussetto, Giambattista 190
Mutilated 219
Myers, Stanley 78, 119, 215
Myles, Ray 214
Myrow, Fred 198
Mystics in Bali 208

Die Nacht der Blutigen Wolfe 98
Die Nacht der Reitenden Leichen 188
Nacht der Vampire 186
Nackt und Zerfleischt 138
Die Nackte Göttin der Zombies 194
Nadeau, Elayne 169
Nadja 162
Nagel, Pat 137
Nahay, Mike 167
Nail Gun Massacre 231
Naish, J. Carrol 100
Nakagawa, Nobuo 155
Nakamura, Torahiko 155
Naked Exorcism 239
Nalder, Reggie 64, 135
Nandi, Itala 210
Nardi, Gabriella 124
Naschy, Paul *see* Alvarez, Jacinto Molina
Naschy, Richard *see* Alvarez, Jacinto Molina
Nash, Paul *see* Alvarez, Jacinto Molina
Nashy, Paul *see* Alvarez, Jacinto Molina
Natale, Roberto 124
Natali, Germano 202, 225
Natasha 137
National Cinematografica 234
Naury, Alan 207
Naushaus, Newton 104
Nauta, Roberto 204

Navaron Films 103
Navarro, Nieves 106, 197, 198, 211, 234
Navarro, Pedro 65
Neal, Edwin 227
Nebbia, Franco 233
Nebe, Chris D. 176
Necromaniac 179
Necronomicon 40
Necrophagus 179
Negin, Louis 205
Negro, Del 165
Neilsen, Howard 120
Neilson, Bonnie 70
Neilson, Marcia 61
Nekromantik 68
Nell, Krista 198, 211
Nelson, Connie 100
Nelson, Miles *see* Klimovsky, León
Nelson, Shawn 200
Nelthorpe, Malcolm 205
Neri, Rosalba 51, 72, 114
Nesbitt, Vickie 194
Neto, Aníbal Massaíni 112
Neubeck, Jack 219
The Never Dead 198
New Breed Productions, Inc. 198
New Film Production 107
New World Pictures 42, 66, 200
Newman, Raoul H. *see* Raho, Umberto
Newton, Peter *see* Massaccesi, Aristide
Next! 224
The Next Victim 224
Nibbler, Dick 171
Nicholas, Martin Alan 41
Nichols, Anthony 87
Nichols, Kelly 230
Nichols, Paula 103
Nicklin, Charles 115
Nicklous, Ellen 137
Nicol, Fadja 172
Nicolai, Bruno 45, 72, 123, 233, 234
Nicolodi, Daria 202
Nieto, Felicidad 208
Nieto, Francisco 109, 122, 168
Nieto, José 166
Nieva, Alfonso 179, 218
Night after Night 180
Night, after Night, after Night 179
The Night Company 158
Night of the Blood Cult 184
Night of the Bloody Apes 139

Night of the Cruel Sacrifice 113
Night of the Death Cult 184
Night of the Demon 181
Night of the Devils 190
Night of the Howling Beast 164
Night of the Living Dead 47, 76, 82, 86, 182, 188, 189, 196, 205
Night of the Seagulls 184
The Night of the Sorcerers 185
Night of Vengeance 158
Night Ripper! 245
Night Slasher 180
Night Walk 77
Nightingale, Michael 180
Nights of Terror 191
Nikel, Monica 212
Nilson, Graciela 168
Nipolito, Ricardo 162
Nivaldo, José 90
No Profanar el Sueño de los Muertos 189
Noble, Ann 80
La Noche de las Gaviotas 184
La Noche de las Muerte Ciego 47, 188
La Noche de los Brujos 185
La Noche de los Muertos 182
La Noche de Walpurgis 186
La Noche del Asesino 208
La Noche del Buque Maldito 68
La Noche del Terror 191
La Noche del Terror Ciego 185, 188
Nocilli, Stefania 107
Noel, Noelia 139
Noel, Sophie 113
Nogueira, Helena 210
Nogueras, Sofia 73
A Noite do Terror Cego 188
Nolan, James 230
Non Aprire Quella Porta 227
Non Si Deve Profanare il Sonno dei Morti 74, 189
Norcross, Elaine 120
North, Noelle 72
Noteworthy Films Limited 140
La Notte dei Diavoli 190
Le Notte del Terrore 191
Le Notti Erotiche dei Morte Viventi 192
Novak, Harry H. 74
Novellas, Isidoro 152

Novelli, Armando 51
Nuber, Jack 127
Nuchtern, Simon 221, 253
Nueva York Bajo el Terror de los Zombi 247
Nugent, William F. 181
La Nuit des Diables 190
La Nuit des Loup Garous 186
La Nuit des Masques 132
Numata, Yoichi 155
Nunez, Nora 50
Nuova Linea Cinematografica 44
Nüsch, Peter 153
Nuvoletti, Giovanni 44

Oaks, Connie 95
Oas-Heim, Gordon 42
Oates, Chubby 157
O'Bannon, Dan 39
Obeda, Lauren 128
Ober, Arlon 148
Oblowski, Stefan *see* Mattei, Bruno
O'Bradovich, Bob 149
O'Brian, Donald 106
O'Brien, Seamus 149
Oceania 143
O'Dea, Judith 182
O'Donnell, Lee 76
O'Driscoll, Kevin J.J. 201
Odyssey 91
Off Productions 206
O'Flyinn, Frances 159
Ogden, Robert 169
O'Hanlon, George 132
O'Hara, James 103
O'Hara, John 243
O'Hara, Michael 194
Ohara, Tiffany Shannon 238
Los Ojos Azules de la Muneca Rota 192
Okura, Mitsugo 155
Olay, Mark 181
Olivares, Maritza 208
Oliver, Robert H. *see* Oliveros, Ramiro
Oliveros, Ramiro 72
Olivo, Valerio 139
Oller, Juan 164
Oller, Ventura 164
Olsbauer, Hary 176
Olson, Astrid 56
Ölümün Nefesi 165
O'Malley, Kathleen 230
On the Hook Corporation 229
Once Upon a Frightmare 119

Index

O'Neal, Vickie 62
O'Neill, Jenny 150
Opera 203
Operacione Terror 172
Oppedisano, Stefano 90, 190
O'Ree, Robert 205
Orengo, Antonio 122, 168, 188, 218
Orengo, Leonid 166
La Orgia de los Muertos 193
L'Orgia dei Morti 194
Les Orgias Macabres 194
Les Orgies de Frankenstein '80 175
Orgy of Blood 65
Orgy of the Dead 194
Orgy of the Demons 194
Orlandi, Nora 224
Orlando, Orazio 203
Ormsby, Alan 76, 92
Ormsby, Anya 76
Ornadel, Cyril 46
Orr, Patt 92
L'Orribile Segreto del Dottor Hichcock 143
Orsini, Umberto 45
Ortolani, Riz 138, 243
Ortun 219
Ortuño, Racquel 73
Osmand, Gordon D. *see* Rodríguez, Amando de Ossorio
Ossori, Amando *see* Rodríguez, Amando de Ossorio
Oster, Emil 94
Osth, Robert 95
Ostman, Karil 83
O'Sullivan, Arthur 143
Osvaldo, Fortunato 151
Otegui, Juan José 73
Otomo, Jun 155
Ott, Larrene 238
Otto, Gunter 72
Ottolina, Rina 242
Ottoni, Filippo 44
Owen, Bill 78
Owens, Fred 181
Owens, Jay 74
Oxen, Paul 198, 211

Pace, Richard 87
Pacheco, Godofredo 172
Packer, Eve 71
Pafhurr, Guillemo 151
Pageau, Madeline 205
Pagni, Eros 202
Paizi, Alexandra 203

Paladino, J.J. 213
Palaggi, Franco 138
Palance, Holly 78
Palito 110, 111, 210
Palk, Anna 232
Pallotini, Riccardo 114, 243
Pallotini, Richard *see* Pallotini, Ricardo
Pandemonium 39
Pani, Corrado 124
Pannaciò, Elio 239
Panorama Films 74
Panouzis, Nick 91
Pantanello, Tony 82, 169, 182
Paolini, Paolo 138
Papa, Ciro 174
Papafrantzi, Spyros 59
Papas, Xiro *see* Papa, Ciro
Papineau, Bernard 113
Papps, Stan *see* Papa, Ciro
Paradela, Carlos 68
Paramo, Luis Gonzalez 168
The Parasite Murders 83, 143, 195, 205
Pareto, Willy *see* Freda, Riccardo
Paris, David 60
Paris, Renee 42
Paris Sex Murders 72
Pariser, Alfred 195
Parker, Dalila *see* di Lazzaro, Dalila
Parker, MaLynda 82
Parker, Percy G. *see* Hoven, Adrian; Manera, Jesús Franco
Parkin, Tony 98
Parkinson, Tom 93
Parnell, Julian 147
Parra, Vincente 217
Parsley, Jay 227
Partain, Paul A. 227
The Partridge Family 97
Parys, Armand *see* Lewis, Herschell Gordon
Pascal, François 206
Pascal, Marie-Georges 206
Pasos de Danza Sobre el Filo de una Navaja 197
Pass, Anthony *see* Mattei, Bruno
Passi di Danza Su una Lama di Rasoio 197
Past, Linda 57
Pataki, Michael 165
Patrick Vive Ancora 127
Patterson, George 142

Patterson, J.G., Jr. 48, 62, 229
Patterson, Melody 55
Patterson, Nita 62
Patterson, Pat *see* Patterson, J.G., Jr.
Patucchi, Daniele 174
Paul, Yvonne 180
Pauleson, Jack 200
Paulino, Cicero 37
Paulino, Justo 49, 50, 162
Paura nella Città dei Morti Viventi 248
Pavon, Benito 130
Pawluk, Mira 70
Payne, Denis 195
Peake, Don 135
Pearl, Daniel 227
Pearl, Dorothy 227
Pellegrini, Ines 123
Péloquin, Carole 147
Pember, Ron 88
Peña, Julio 109, 130, 186
Pena de Muerte 74, 97, 180
Penafiel, Luis *see* Serrador, Narciso Ibañez
Peñalver, Eugenio 168
Penetration 198, 211
Penkert, Rainer 81
Pennese, Giuseppe 124
Penta Films 204
Pepperman, Paul 198
Percy, Paul 208
Perego, Filippo 239
Pereira, Augusto 110
Peres, Jorge 90
Péres, Pablos 150
Perez, Manuel 204
Perez, Pablo 68, 130, 156
Pérez-Flores, Maximiliano 166
Periard, J. Roger 205
Perilli, Frank Ray 165
Perley, Charles 195
Perrella, Alessandro 72, 165, 194
Perrici, Vítor 90
Perrier, Cristina 209
Perry, Victoria 230
Perschy, María 68, 156, 192
Person, Luís Sérgio 111
La Perversa Senora Ward 224
Pescarolo, Leonardo 81, 161
Peschi, Rosy 95
Pesticide 206
Peters, Luan 46
Petersen, Marlies 64

Index

Petit, Victor 184
Petrie, Gordon 88
Petrie, Susan 195
Petrovic, Alex 128
Petruka Films 193
Pettyjohn, Angelique 162
Pevarello, Osiride 165
Pezzin, Mario 68
Phalen, Robert 132
Phantasm 198
Phantasm IV—Oblivion 200
Phebus, Chester 76
Phelan, Mark 181
Phens, Oscar 184
Philip, Robert 76
Phillips, Joan 244
Phillips, Nick *see* Millard, Steve
Phillips, Paul 120
Photiou, Rania 59
Piani, Lorenzo 202
Pica, Antonio 156, 192
Picaro, Berlau 87
Picchi, Marcelo 112
Picciano, Anthony 103
Piccioni, Piero 152
Pickett, James 229
Piel, Don 167
Pierce, Phil 244
Pierre, Bertha 147
Pigozzi, Luciano 234
Pike, David 61
Pike, Dennis 66
Pioneer 123
Piovani, Nicola 203
Piranha 200
Piras, Cristina 124
Pirkanen, Perry 138
Piros, Rupert 186
Pisano, Berto 127
Pistilli, Luigi 44, 143, 233
Pitts, Clay 142
Pizzorro, Sandro 198, 211
Pladevall, Tomás 163
Plan Nine from Outer Space 101, 221
Plana, Ramón 47, 194
Planet of the Vampires 40
Plans, Juan José 204
Plata Films S.A. 121, 186, 188
Plato, Joe 85
Pleasence, Donald 88, 132
Plores, Maximiliano Perez 121
Plumey, Alain 113
Plummer, Christopher *see* Martino, Sergio
Plummer, Terence 88
Pochath, Werner 143, 176
Podestà, Rosan 243
Poe, Edgar Allan 233
Pointer, Priscilla 72
Polack, Fernando Sánchez 242
Polansky, Roman 101
Polesnek, Michael 60
Polgár, Tommy 211
Politoff, Haydée 130
Polk, Brigid 42
Pollack, Joe 91
Pollmer, Irene 198, 211
Pollock, Ellen 140
Polop, Francisco Lara 130, 156
Polselli, Renato 89, 209
Pomerantz, Earl 70
Pomeroy, Ada *see* Pometti, Ada
Pometti, Ada 72, 114
Poncela, Eusebio 217
Pons, Lisa 214
Ponti, Carlo 79, 101, 176
Ponti, Sal 94
Pool, Ann Mary 242
Poor Albert and Little Annie 217
Pope, Kim 198, 211
Pope, Tim 96
Porcelli, Claudia 63
Porky's 77
Porno Holocaust 192
Portella, Walter C. 210
Posnansko, Hanka 195
Posse, Roberto 189
The Possessor 239
Pouchie 224
Les Poupées du Professeur Hichcok 52
Les Poupées Sanglantes du Docteur X 52
Powell, Alisa 230
Powers, Douglas 48
Pradeaux, Maurizio 197
Prades, Jaime 172
Prado, Brown 151
Pratt, Jane 63
Pratt, Jill 124
Pregadio, Roberto 197
Prentice, Vincent 200
Prestopino, Rosario 191
Preuwet, Linda 57
Prévost, Françoise 239
Prey 201
The Prey 60
Price, Allan 70
Price, Dennis 140, 232
Primus, Barry 161
Prisoner of the Cannibal God 173
Probyn, Brian 117
Prodimex Film 193
Producciones Balcazar S.A. 197
Producciones Escorpion 208
Producciones Jaime Prades 172
Produções Cinemattográfica Indrkis Kruskops 37
Produzioni Cinematografica Flaminia 189
Profilmes S.A. 109, 122, 159, 163, 168, 184, 185, 192, 213
Profondo Rosso 125, 202, 204
Profumo, Serafino 197
Profumo della Signora in Nero, Il 203
Prowse, David 117
Psycho 92, 132, 229
Psycho Puppet 91
Puca, Antonio 73
Pueyo, Joaquín 73
Pugsley, William 100
Pulone, Giovanni 197
Puntillo, Salvatore 202
Punzalan, Bruno 49, 65, 162
Pupella, Pino 212
Purba, Teddy 207
Purbaya, Tizar 207
Pyke, Hy 223
Pyle, Jacqueline 48
Pysher, Ernie 149

Q—The Winged Serpent 167
Quasimodo, Maria Cumani 234
Quatermass, Martin *see* Carpenter, John
Queen of Black Magic 207
Queen of the Zombies 192
Quick, John 181
¿Quien Puede Matar a un Niño? 204
Quiney, Charles 194
Quinn, Tom 42

Rabel, Ingrid 156, 159, 213
Rabid 196, 205
Rabola, Emmanuela Beltrán 109, 217
Radaelli, Antonio 51
Radburn, Veronica 125
Rage 205

The Raggedy Man 72
Ragland, Robert O. 165
Raho, Humi *see* Raho, Umberto
Raho, Umberto 190
Rain, Jeramie 158
Rainer, Klaus 68
Rainó, Alfred 225
Les Raisins de la Mort 206
Rambaldi, Carlo 40, 44, 72, 101, 160, 165, 174, 176, 190, 202
Raminto, George *see* Martino, Sergio
Ramis, Antonio 152, 156, 192
Ramisladi, Carlos *see* Rambaldi, Carlo
Ramon, Gordon 134
Ramos, Ely, Jr. 65
Ramos, Luis 127
Ramos, Paula 110, 111
Rampin, Gaetano 124
Rancelot, Mirella 206
Randall, Dick 72
Randall, Mónica 150
Rangel, Vânia 37, 110
Ransome, Prunella 204
Raoul 90
Rapi Films 207
Rassam, Jean Pierre 101, 176
Rassimov, Ivan 165, 224, 233, 234, 237
Rastattar, Wendy 223
Ratay, Wayne 246
Rattee, Paul 157
Ratu Ilmu Hitam 207
Rau, Jim 246
Ravagnoli, Antônio F. 111
Ravaioli, Isarco 194
Raven, Mike 93
Raw Meat 88
Ray, Andrew 114
Ray, Esther 47
Ray, Fred Olen 41
Ray, Gary 137
Ray, Marc B. 216
Ray, Robyn 200
Rayburn, Bill 63
Raymond, Dianne 131
Raynard, Eric Kelner 246
Raynes, Louis 98
Razzetto, Ruth 151
Reazione a Catena 44
Rebar, Alex 148
Recoder, Tony 179
Red Bank Films 71
The Red Tide 59
Redfield, Mark 84

Redondo, Modesto Pérez 159, 163, 186
Redrick, Neil 216
Reed, Joel M. 149
Reed, Les 244
Reed, Oliver 66
Reel Life Productions 171
Reems, Harry 198, 211
Reeve, Jean 157
Regan, Willy S. *see* Garrone, Sergio
Regent, Willy S. *see* Garrone, Sergio
La Regina dei Cannibali 106
Regnoli, Piero 191
Regoli, Maria Piera 107
Reiber, Karlheinz 153
Reich, Matthew 42
Reichenbach, Carlos 210
Reichert, Jeanne 105
Reid, Robert 151
The Reincarnation of Isabel 209
La Reincarnazione 209
Reiniger, Scott H. 85
Reis, Nidi 111
Reis, Sheldon 246
Reitman, Ivan 70, 195, 205
Remy, Ronald 162
Renato, Luiz 210
Renay, Gail 149
Renay, Liz 53
Rennie, Michael 172
Renzullo, Michele 127
Resino, Andrés 152, 186
Resnick, Judith 71
El Retorno de Walpurgis 208
El Retorno del Hombre Lobo 187
El Retorno del Terror Ciego 47
El Retour des Morts-Vivants 47
Rettew, Joanne 60
Return of Blackenstein 53
Return of the Blind Dead 47
Return of the Evil Dead 47
Return of the Exorcist 239
Return of the Werewolf 208
Return of the Zombies— Zombie 3 194
Return to the Horrors of Blood Island 49
Revenge of Dracula 100
Revenge of the Dead 137
Revenge of the Living Dead 76
Reverberi, Gianfranco 89, 209

La Révolte des Morts-Vivants 188
Rexon, Burt 191
Rey, Barbara 68
Reyes, Gene 172
Reynolds, Bailey 216
Rhu, Angela 166
Rialto Film 81
Ribalta Filmes 90
Ribas, Lurdes 210
Ribeiro, Jeff 111
Ribero, Santiago 208
Ribero, Tito 151
Ricci, Bill 95
Ricci, Marc 182
Ricci, Paolo 237
Ricci, Richard 182
Ricci, Rudy 85
Rice, Frank 128
Rich, Hal 56
Rich, Kathy 38
Richards, Jason 182
Richards, Kyle 105, 132
Richards, Lee 244
Richards, Pam 244
Richards, Paula 182
Richards, Stony 63
Richardson, Ann 244
Richardson, Carl 76
Richardson, John 79, 123, 175
Richman, Roger 200
Richman, Sandy 145
Richmond, Ralph 198
Riddell, Nicolle 145
Ridenour, David 223
Riesco, Pepe 213
Rigaud, Georges 123, 160, 234
Riggins, Norman 41
Riley, Doug 70
Riley, Judith 182
Riley, Sheila 127
Rinaldi, Antonio 44
Rincoin, Sixto 204
Ripoll, Pablo 188
Rissi, Mark 153
Riti, Magie Nere e Segrete Orge nel Trecento... 90, 209
Ritual dos Sádicos 90, 210
Ritvo, Rosemary 38
Riva, Anna *see* Findlay, Roberta
Riva, J. Michael 145
Rivelazioni di un Maniaco Sessuale al Capo della Squadra Mobile 198, 211
Rivera, Javier 121
Rivers, Michael *see* Rivera, Javier

Index

Rivié, Nello 212
Rivière, George 243
Rizo, Javier 139
Rizzo, Angelo 147
Rizzolo, Modesto 194
Roars, Ivan 144
Roberts, Brian 216
Roberts, Bruce 82
Roberts, Bump 84
Roberts, Helene 120
Roberts, Kim 95
Roberts, Mark see Maldera, Roberto
Roberts, Roy 41
Roberts, Troy 158
Robinson, Sherry 131
Robinson, Yvonne 53
Robles, Nestor 50
Rocca, Antonino 38
Rocchi, Luigina 138, 173
Rocha, Lourenço B. 90
Rocha, Romeu 111
Rochelle Films 103, 149
Rochman, Al 195
Rockerfella, Roger see Deodato, Ruggero
Rockwell 216
Rodal, Angel 74
Rodrigues, Jairo 210
Rodrigues, Roque 110
Rodríguez, Amando de Ossorio 47, 68, 122, 184, 185, 188, 204, 233
Rodriguez, Joaquin 156
Rodriguez, Maria Nuria 47
Roehm, Wolfgang 144, 145
Roel, Adriana 41
Roger, Carmen 152
Rogers, Larry 95
Rogers, Maggie 125, 231
Rogers, Paul 214
Rogers, Stuart Edmond 148
Rogers, Tristan 46
Rojo Oscuro 202
Roland, Glenn 144
Roldan, Gloria A. see Alvarez, Jacinto Molina
Rollin, Jean 113, 206
Rollin, Olivier 206
Roman, Drew 38
Roman, Susan 205
Romano, Renato 72, 143, 175
Romanos, Richard 125
Romay, Lina 153
Romero, Eddie 49, 50, 65, 162
Romero, George A. 48, 82, 85, 169, 182, 205, 248

Romero, José Luis 204
Romero, Salvador 188
Romero, Tina 41
Romeu, Ismael Garcia 74
Romeu, Roque 110
Ronet, Roberto 151
Rons, John 54
The Roosters 103
Rosano, Robert 127
Rosati, Anna Maria 44
Rose, Jeremy 88
Rose, William L. see Oliveros, Ramiro
Rosenberg, Jerry 42
Rosenberg, Max 148
Rosenberg, Richard K. 38
Roskam, Cathy 42
Rosly, Judy 237
Ross, Gaylen 85
Ross, Gene 96
Ross, Hugh 157
Ross, Terrence G. 205
Rossetti, Marco 68
Rossi, F. 198, 211
Rossi, Giorgio Carlo 237
Rossi, Joseph 38
Rossi, Luciano 198, 211
Rossi, Sandro 51
Rossi, Stelvio 194
Rossie, Ana Maria 208
Rossington, Norman 88
Rossitto, Angelo 100
Rosy-Rosy 135
Roth, Lillian 38
Rothernorth Limited 157
Roussel, Gilbert see Mattei, Bruno
Rowe, Graham 157
Rowe, Jerry 125
Rowland, Glenn 145
Roy, Esperanza 47
Roy, James 169
Roy, Jose, Jr. 50
Royo, Rosario 179
Royston, Jonah 145
Rubens, Paola 44
Rubenstein, Donald 169
Rubenstein, Richard P. 85, 169
Rubio, Fernando 168
Ruchel, Esmeralda 110
Die Rückkehr der Reitenden Leichen 47
Die Rückkehr der Zombies 191
Rudley, Irv 59, 60
The Rue Morgue Masscares 156
Ruhnke, Gerhard 176
Ruiz, Betsabé 47, 109, 122, 213

Ruiz, Julian 194
Ruiz, Melissa 154
Ruschel, Esmeralda 111
Rush Productions 206
Russell, Tina 198, 211
Russo, John A. 182
Rustam, Mardi 100, 104
Rustam, Mohammed 104
Ruxton, Richard 84
Rydon, Jack 238
Ryshpan, Howard 205

S., Subagio 207
S.A.M. Productions, Inc. 104
S.E.F.I. Cinematografica 197
Saad, Robert 70, 195
Saaf, Chuck 103
Saarinen, Eric 135
Sabine, Winifred 117
The Sabre-Tooth Tiger 202
Sacchi, Robert 72
Sachs, Andrew 119
Sachs, William 148
Sacks, Lee 115
El Sadico de Notre Dame 197
Saeta, Eddie 94
La Saga de los Draculas 213
Sager, Ray 62, 128, 131, 246
Sahl, Michael 149
St. James, Gaylord 158
St. John, Nicholas 103
Saint-Simon, Lucille 243
Sainz, Tina 213
Saiyanidi 149
Sakowicz, Sig 105
Salazar, Alfredo 139
Salcedo, Leopoldo 50
Salcedo, Paquito 162
Salem's Lot 65
Salerno, María 150
Sales, Tabajara 111
Saletri, Frank R. 53
Salier, Vito 189
Salina, Franco 172
Salina, Tom see Massaccesi, Aristide
Salli, Marina 128
Salome 117
Salomon 164
Salvador, Montserrat 226
Salvati, Sergio 27
Salvino, Riccardo 107, 233
Saly, Julia 150, 184
Samarina, Yelena 186
Samiotis, Yannis 59
Sampere, Francisco 189

San José, Leandro 130
Sanchez, Ben 65
Sanchez, Carlos 127
Sánchez, Francisco 168, 184, 192, 208, 213, 242
Sanchez, Frank *see* Sanchez, Francisco
Sancho, Fernando 47
Sande, Peter 128
Sandin, Will 132
Sandkuhler, Steve 84
Sandler, Robert 70
Sandy, Fred M. 131, 245
Du Sang pour Dracula 101
Sangeria 247
Sangil, Don 244
Sanguella 247
Sanisteban, Alfonso 242
Sansoul, Jacques 113
Santis, Richard 156
Santisteban, A. 179
Santo, Vincent 235
Santoni, Espartaco 74
Santora, Tommy 103
Santos, Dario 110, 111
Santos, Jose Angel 184
Santos, Ponti 111
Sanz, Francisco 47, 188
Sanz, Paco 47, 189
Sanz, Ricardo 122, 159
Sara Films 242
Satan 64
Die Satans-Bande 142
Satan's Bed 221
Satan's Black Wedding 84, 214
Satan's Bloody Freaks 100
Satan's Daughters 241
Satrova, Anna 121
Saturday Night Fever 168
Saunders, Ervin 100
Saunders, Geraldine 120
Savina, Carlo 73
Savina, Mario 51
Savini, Tom 85, 92, 169
Savón, Beatriz 166
Sayles, John 200
Scaccia, Mario 45, 203
Scagnetti, Franca 225
Scandariato, Romano 106
Scannell, Ed 137
Scarpa, Renato 225
Scary Pictures Productions 70
Scavolini, Sauro 233, 234
Schamus, Albert J. 169
Schamus, Lillian 169
Schattyn, Lloyd 91
Schechtman, Jeff 200
Schein, Loren 171

Schiano, Natasha 63
Schiff, Marty 85
Schiraldi, Vittorio 124
Schirrira, Greg 103
Schizo 215
Schizoid 160
Schizophrenic Murder 119
Schlessel, Geri 244
Das Schloß der Blauen Vögel 52
Schmidt, Wolf 63
Schmidt, Wolfgang *see* Steckler, Ray Dennis
Schmidtke, Ned 82
Schneider, Christine 105
Schoener, Ingeborg 64
Schofield, Annabel 59
Schofield, John D. 59
Schon, Kyra 182
Schonblum, Terry 205
Schönfelder, Friedrich 153
The School That Couldn't Scream 81
Het Schrikkasteel der Zombies 191
Schulten, Joseph 229
Schultz, Harry 103
Schundler, Rudolf 225
Schwarz, Rainer 66
Schweitzer, Daniel 127
Scorcelletti, Sarafina 225
Scott, Alan 244
Scott, Ridley 39
Scott, Susan *see* Navarro, Nieves
Scott, Tony 82, 133
Scotti, Andrea 198, 211
Scotton, Myrtle 198
Scream Bloody Murder 216
Scrimm, Angus *see* Guy, Lawrence Rory
Scuffy 105
Scully, Terry 180
Seagrave, Malcolm 198
Sebastião, Tomás 37
Sebre, Norma 168
The Secret Killer 123
Seda Spettacoli 202, 225
Sedova, Elena 151
Seeman, John 133
Segall, Stuart 104
Segoviano, Abobaq 122
Segoviano, Alfredo 122, 163
Sei Donne per l'Assassino 44, 202
Seirli, Sofia 59
Selected Pictures 220, 221
Selin, George 137
Sellajaah, Akushla 173

Selzer, Milton 55
La Semana del Asesino 217
Senatore, Paola 107
Senior, Doug 137
Serato, Massimo 161
Serene, Douglas 169
Serene, Jeanne 169
Serio, Aldo 124, 127
Serkeis, Jorge Michel 111, 210
Serpiente de Mar 69, 123
Serra, Manuel Berenguer 190
Serrador, Narciso Ibañez 204
Serravalle, Giancarlo 239
Servals, Janis 98
Setembro, Walter 90
Sette Cadaveri per Scotland Yard 152
Severini, Leonardo 243
Sex Crime of the Century 158
Sexy Cat 218
Seymour, Sheldon *see* Lewis, Herschell Gordon
Sezonov, John 128
Shackleton, Allan 221
Shakespeare, John 157
Shamsi 237
Shanon, Mark 192
Shaper, Sue 119
Sharon, Betsabe 186
Sharvell-Martin, Michael 119
Shaughnessy, Alfred 46
Shaw, George Newman 48
Shaw, John 229
Shaw, Joseph 66
Shaw, Mary Ellen 198
Shaw, Michael 127; *see also* Soavi, Michele
Shaw, Vanessa 140
Shean, Darcy 95
Shearin, Anne 57
Shebop, Bob 171
Sheffler, Marc 158
Shelby, Joe 85
Sheldon, Lynette 149
Shelley, Mary 177
Shelly, Bob 91
Shelton, Deborah 59
Shepard, Patty 172, 186, 208
Sheppard, Patty *see* Shepard, Patty
Sheppard, Paula E. 38
Sherlock, Norman 104
Sherman, Adrian 127

Sherman, Gary A. 88
Sherman, Robert 76
Sherman, Samuel M. 100
Sherrill, Louise 55
Sherwood, Hal 125
Shields, Brooke 38
Shiero, Marisa 179
Shikur, Sheik Razak 237
Shintoho 155
Ship of Zombies 68
Shivers 195
Shonteff, Lindsay 180
Shore, Howard 66
Shotwell, Sandra 83
Shriek of the Mutilated 81, 219
Shulman, Felicia 195
Shulman, Gerald 127
Shulman, Randy 91
Shusett, Ronald 39
Siedow, Jim 227
Siegal, Donna 169
Signorelli, Tom 38
Silk, Jeff 78
Sill, Ron 57
Silla, Feliz 66
Silva, Ademir 111
Silva, David 41
Silva, Euripidesda 37
Silva, Jean 111
Silva, Jimmy 219
Silva, María 188, 208, 242
Silver, Joe 195, 205
Silverman, Bob 205
Silverman, Carol 137
Silverman, Robert 66
Silvestre, Armando 139
Silvia, Carmen 165
Simmerman, James Barry 91
Simões, Geraldo Martins 37
Simões, Ilídio Martins 37, 110
Simon, Dan L. *see* Manera, Jesús Franco
Simon, Marla 171
Simpson, Bill 62
Simpson, Jim 244
Simpson, John 182
Simpson, Ken 62
Sinclair, Sandra 56
Sinclaire, Crystin 105
Sinde, José María Gonzalez 73
Singer, Stephen 103
Singer, Steve 137
Singer, Thomas 171
Sinner to Hell 155
The Sinners of Hell 155

Sinniger, Alfons 153
Sipek, Francis 57
Siqueira, Antonia 111
Sissmann, Philippe 206
Sisters of Satan 41
The Sixth Gate of Hell 78
Sjostrom, Rik *see* Freda, Riccardo
Skaife, Michael *see* Madrid, Miguel
Skay, Brigitte 44
Skeaping, Colin 140
Skeggs, Roy 117
Skelton, Roy 180
Skerritt, Tom 40
Sklarey, Seth 76
Slander, Frank 131
Slaney, Ivor 201
The Slasher 211
The Slasher ... Is the Sex Maniac! 211
Slaughter 220, 222
Slaughter Hotel 52
Slave of the Cannibal God 173
Sledge, Franklyn 41
Slithis 223
Sloane, Barbara 165
Sly, Trixie 103
Small, Linda 149
Smeagle, Brian 92
Smedley, Robert 76
Smedley-Aston, Brian 240
Smethurst, Jack 180
Smillie, Bill 200
Smith, Dana 91
Smith, Debbie 57
Smith, Ella Mae 182
Smith, Geraldine 42
Smith, Hart 48
Smith, Howard 85
Smith, Hugh 229
Smith, Kim 82
Smith, Madeline 117
Smith, Maria 42
Smith, Marshall *see* Findlay, Michael
Smith, Murray 78, 205
Smith, R.L. *see* Lewis, Herschell Gordon
Smith, Rainbeaux 148
Smith, Susan 95
Sneak Previews 87
Snuff 120, 126, 219, 221
So Sweet, So Dead 211
Soares, Jofre 112
Soavi, Michael *see* Soavi, Michele
Soendoro 207
Sohon Teura Staja 153

Sola, Jorgé Grau 73, 180, 189
Solar, Silvia 123, 164, 226
Solar, Sylvia *see* Solar, Silvia
Solares, Austín Martinez 139
Solares, Raúl Martinez 139
Sole, Alfred 38
Soler, Joan *see* Soler, Juan A.
Soler, Juan A. 242
Soles, P. J. 72, 132
Solis, Joaquim 168
Solito, Samuel R. 182
Solnicki, Victor 66
Solomon, Bruce 76
Solomon, Joe 232
Solomon, Stephanie 76
Solway, Larry 66
Sonoton Musikverlag 134
Les Sorcières Sanglantes 64
Sorel, Diana 172
Sorel, Jean 160
Sorgini, Giuliano 189, 239
Soria, José Gomez 184, 188
Sorlano, Charo 130
Sorley, Janet 120
Soster, Jony 176
Sotis, Carla 111
Sotuela, Fernando 156
Soucie, Jerry 53
Southcombe, Bryan 98
Soviero, Donald 169
Sozansky, John 169
Space, Arthur 165
Spacek, Sissy 72
Spadaccino, Silvano 51
Spawn of the Slithis 223
Speck, Richard 53
Speel, Irene 131
Speer, Martin 135
Speizer, Andres 188
Spencer, James 50
Sperling, David 63
Spier, Riva 205
Spillman, Harry 82
Spingi, Marcello 127
Spinola, Lanfranco 173
Spivak, Gloria 71
Spraggon, Peter 157
Squire, Janie 200
Srymkovicz, Maria 95
SS Campo de Sexo y Violencia 212
SS Campo Extermination 211
SS Extermination Love Camp 212
Staccioli, Ivano 198, 211, 212

Index

Stacey, Eddie 201
Stafford, Langston 144
Stage Fright 46
Standish, Eve 154
Stanford, Pamela *see* Delaunay, Monique
Stanley, Harold 194
Stanley, Shirley 194
Stanton, Harry Dean 40
Star Films S.A. 189
Star Trek 163
Star Wars 118
Starke, John 42
Starlight Slaughter 105
Starnes, Leland 82
Stasionis, Nélson 110
Statz, Franklin 120
Stavrakos, Taso N. 85
Stavrou, Ari 59
Steadman, John 135
Steane, Grahame 98
Stearns, S. 144
Steele, Barbara 195, 200
Steeve, Allan W. *see* Tabernero, Julio Perez
Stefan, Marina 219
Stefanelli, Benito 198, 211
Stefen, Steffy 90
Steffen, Ben *see* Stefanelli, Benito
Stein, Roger 214
Steiner, Sterry 229
Stell, Guillermo Calderón 139
Stella, Luciano 47, 122
Stephens, Nancy 132
Stephenson, Pamela 78
Stern, Helga Lina 109, 122, 197, 213, 242
Steven, Lyle 137
Stevens, Carter 221
Stevens, Marc 198, 211; *see also* Marco, José
Stevens, Rory 72
Stevens, Sherri 91
Stevenson, Robert Louis 97
Stewart, Cathy 113
Stewart, Charles 157
Stewart, Howard 62
Stewart, Jay 137
Stewart, Katherine 165
Stewart, Trish 165
Stigma 143
Stimac, Kathy 181
Stimson, Ken 223
Stock, Jennifer 219
Stoeber, Irene 131
Stoeber, Karl 131
Stokes, Barry 201
Stoll, Günther W. 81

Stone, Ivory 53
Stone, Marianne 232
Stoney, Heather 88
Stoppi, Franca 68
Stouffer, Rod 85
Stover, Jay 85
Strada, Beto 90
The Strange Case of Dr. Jekyll and Mr. Hyde 97
The Strange World of Coffin Joe 111
Un Stranha Orchidae con Cinque Gocce di Sangue 234
Lo Strano Vizio della Signora Wardh 224
Stratton, John 117
Strebel, Monica 51
Streiner, Russell W. 182
Strickfadden, Ken 53
Striker 135
Strindberg, Anita 45, 160, 233
Strobel, John 115
Stroup, Edi 41
Stryker, Jonathan *see* Ciupka, Richard
Stuart, Adriano 112
Stuart, Walter 112
Studer, Esther 153
Die Stunde der Grausamen Leichen 156
Suarez, Luis 190
Suay, Ricardo Muñoz 109, 122, 185, 213
Subandono, Gordon 207
Subekto, Bu 207
Sublime, Patsy 165
Sudarto, Gatot 207
Sudjio, Liliek 207
Suki, M. 173
Suleiman 237
Sullivan, Elliott 240
Sullivan, Michael 42, 200
Sullivan, Ronald 134
Summer, Herbert 182
Summerfield, Jennifer 98
Summers, Alice 229
Sumner, Chuck 41
Sumpter, Donald 180
Suriani, Cristina 109, 213
Survinski, Regis J. 82, 169, 182
Survinski, Vincent D. 82, 169
Suskma, Doddy 207
Suspiria 43, 225
Suspiria—Part 2 202
Sutters, Cindy Lou *see* Steckler, Ray Dennis

Suzzanna 207
Svevo, Elena 239
Swadron, Marion 70
Swamp of the Blood Leeches 41
Swartz, Kelley 134
Sweeny, Ann 148
Sweeting, Berry 127
Swicegood, Tom L.P. 238
Swift, Clive 88
Swift, Sally 181
Swim, David 63
Swinton, Mary 66
Syviano, René *see* White, Daniel J.; Manera, Jesús Franco

Tabernero, Julio Pérez 218, 226
Tabor, Eron 87
Tacconi, Luciano 172
Taff, Susan 156
Taft, Ronald 55
Taker, Sam 57
Talbott, Michael 72
Tallarico, Guiuseppe 239
Tallo, Nick 85
Tamahine, Karina 98
Tambini, Catherine 63
Tamblyn, Russ 100
Tamborra, Cristina 197
Tamborra, Sabrina 190
Tanet, Ronald 167
Tantowi, Inam 167
Tanya's Island 39
Tarber, Jane 57
Tarbis, Marsha 229
Tarsk, Alexander 120
Tarzan, the Ape Man 174
Tasgal, Bill 87
Tate, Sharon 222
Tayback, Vic 55, 165
Taylor, Bill 115
Taylor, Jack 68, 98, 185, 242
Taylor, Kent 65
Taylor, Lanny 103
Taylor, Laurie S. 103
Tebar, Juan 73
Tedesco, Paola 124
Teenage Dracula 100
Telman, José 47, 122, 185, 188
Telo, Toni 137
The Tempter 45
Tenebre 45
Tenser, Tony 119
¡Tension! 161
Tepes, Vlad 74, 213
Tereba, Tere 42

Teresita-Castizio 152
Ternes, Ed 230
Terra Filmkunst 143
Terror Beach 184
Terror Caníbal 226
Terror Castle 243
The Terror of Dr. Chaney 165
Terror on Blood Island 65
Terror sin Habla 119
Terrore nello Spazio 40
Terry, John 154
Terry, Walter 231
De Terugkeer der Gemaskerde Lijken 47
Terzon, Lorenzo 114
Testi, Fabio 81
Tetrick, Ted 53
The Texas Chain Saw Massacre 92, 105, 136, 159, 227, 229
The Texas Chainsaw Massacre 227
Thayer, Michael 144
Thelman, Joseph *see* Telman, José
They Bite 123
They Came from Within 195
They're Coming to Get You 234
Thiago, Rosemeire 210
Thilpot, Julie 70
This Night I Will Possess Your Corpse 110
Thomas, Bill 91
Thomas, Ed 171
Thomas, Evelyn 113, 206
Thomas, Llewelyn 63
Thomas, Melody 200
Thomas, Philip Michael 143
Thompson, Carolyn 229
Thompson, Helen 149
Thompson, Linda 229
Thomson, Alex 88
Thorn, Patricia 98
Thornbury, Bill 198
Thorne, Dyanne 144, 145, 147
Thous, Adolfo 74, 156
A Thousand Pleasures 221
Three on a Meathook 81, 92, 229
Three Stars 76, 211
The Three Stooges 97
Thunhurst, W.L., Jr. 82
Tiberi, Alfredo 206
Tichy, Gerard *see* Wondzinski, Gerard Tichy

Tieken, Chris 75
Tierney, Lawrence 42
Tierney, Mike 91
Tierney, Tony 100
The Tigress 147
Tike, David 97
Tilbrook, Peg 82
Tiller, Lucy 98
Timpani, Amedeo 165
Tinling, Ted 38
Tinti, Gabriele 106, 107
Titanic Films 218
Toccafondi, Bianca 124
Todd, Mike 131
Todd, Sweeney 61
Todd, Thomas 229
Todos los Colores de la Oscuridad 234
Tohus, Adolfo 98
Tokudaiji, Kimie 155
Toll, Gerry 149
Tolstoj, Aleksèj 190
Tomada, Willie 65
Tomazina, Despina 59
Le Tombe dei Resuscitati Ciechi 188
Tombs of the Blind Dead 188
Tombs of the Living Dead 162
The Toolbox Murders 230
Torija, Javier Torres 139
Tormentor 197
Tornberg, Jeff 42
Tornos, Valentin 217
Torokvei, Rob 127
Toros, Rosita 177, 190, 197
Torralba, María Teresa 166
Torres, Tomas 218
Torso 79
Tortosa, Sylvia 122
Torture Dungeon 231
Toscano, Pasquale 165
Tosi, Mario 71
Der Totenchor der Knochenmänner 194
Tough, Dave *see* Manera, Jesús Franco
Toutes les Couleurs du Vice 234
Tovar, Dolores 74
Tovar, Loretta 47, 122, 150, 185
Tovar, Maria Luisa 186
Tovoli, Luciano 225
Tower of Evil 232
Townsend, Primia 215
Traeger, Herman *see* Friedman, David F.
Tranché, André 160

Trani, Maurizio 107
Tranquili, Silvano 74, 198, 211
Trans Europa Express 124
Transocchi, Giuseppe 225
Trap Them and Kill Them 68, 106
Traucher, Raoul 209
Traversi, Marisa 175
Travolta, John 72
Traxler, Stephen 223
I Tre Volta della Paura 191
Trestini, Giorgio 189
Tribus, Walter 68
Die Triebmörder 52
Trielli, André 147
Trieste, Leopoldo 44
Tripkou, Irini 59
Troisio, Antonio 123
Troop, B.M. 127
Troughton, Patrick 117
Troupe, Al 171
Truchado, Joe 217
Truchado Films 217
Trueblood, Guerdon 137
Trueblood Guerdon, XIV 137
Tsentas, Jane 154
Tucci, Giorgio 247
Tucci, Ugo 247
Tucker, Nora 120
Les Tuers du Clair de Lune 157
Tully, Brian 46
Tumbleweed Productions 244
Il Tuo Vizio È una Stanza Chiusa e Solo Lo Ne Ho la Chiave 233
Turbine Films Inc. 95
Turner, Dix 181
Turner, Gail 95
Turner, June 88
Turner, Mary Ann 98
Turner, Peter 78
Tutti i Colori del Buio 234
TV 13 134
The Twilight People 50
Twin Peaks 101
Twins 70
Twitch of the Death Nerve 44
Two Thousand Maniacs 235
2000 Maniacs 235
Tyberghlen, Jerome 205
Tymar Film Production Limited 201
Tyra, Dan 231
Tyrrell, Susan 42

Index

Ubeda, Diego 152
L'Uccello dale Piume di Cristallo 180
Ugarte, Julián 166, 234
Ulloa, Fernando 164
Ulrich, Ronald 70
Ultimo Mondo Cannibale 237
Umlauf, Ellen 135, 176
The Undertaker and His Pals 238
Underwood, Dennis 41
The Universe of Coffin Joe 239
O Universo de Mojica Marins 239
Up Frankenstein 177
Un Urlo dalle Tenebre 239

Vail, William 227
Vaira, Larry 85
Vajda, Marijan David 176
Vakero, Rafael 74
Valdesta 104
Valdez Ronaldo 162
Valente, Anna 191
Valentin, Mirko 243
Valentine, Anthony 232
Valladares, Vasco 42
Valle, Pierluigi Cervetti 106
Valley of the Gwangi 233
Vallí, Alida 45, 225
Vallini, Edmondo 68
Valota, Patrice 206
Die Vampire des Dr. Dracula 166
Vampire Playgirls 130
Les Vampires du Dr. Dracula 166
Vampirlerin Gecesi 186
The Vampyre Orgy 241
Vampyres 240
Vampyres, Daughters of Dracula 240
Vanderpump, Lisa 157
Vanders, William 190
Van der Veer Photo 94
Vañes, Ernesto 159
van Horn, John 100
Vani, Vita 151
Vanlint, Derek 39
van Meerhaegue, Brigitte 113, 206
Vannini, Giovanni 124
Vanorio, Francesco 44, 198, 211
van Riel, Greg 205
van Vooren, Monique 177
Vargas, Leonora 194

Variety Film 247
Varriano, Emilio 174
Vasquez, Valéria 37
Vass, Alejandro 223
Vaughan, Steve 57
Vazquez, Adela 168
Vega, Vincente 189
Vela, Pilar 166, 184, 208
Velázquez, José 151
Velilla, Juan 164
Venable, Sarah 169
La Venganza de la Momia 242
Le Venin de la Peur 160
Verdirosi, Bianca 194
La Vergine di Norimberga 243
Le Vergini Cavalcano la Morte 74
Verkruspe, Lois 95
Verné, Claude Jean 239
Vernon, Howard *see* Lippert, Mario
Vernon, Jackie 171
Verschrikkelijke Schoolres 157
Verzier, René 205
Vest, Julie Hauck 91
Vest, Sunny 91
Vest, Todd 91
Viana, Luiz Carlos 111
Vic, John 115
Vicario, Marco 243
Vich, Andres 213
Vico, Jorge 98
The Victim 161
Victims! 244
Vida, Piero 202
Vidal, Gil 164
Vidal, María 122, 159, 184
Vidal, Mary *see* Vidal, María
Vidotto, Mira 224
Vieira, Landro 37
La Vierge de Nuremberg 243
Vigo, Maria 74
Vilanova, Victor 152
Vilar, José 37
Villa, Franco 51, 127, 239
Villa, Maria 218
Villa, Pablo *see* White, Daniel J.
Villaseñor, Leopoldo 121, 186
Villena, Fernando 168, 184, 213
Villiers, Dan *see* White, Daniel J.
Vincent, Joan *see* Manera, Jesús Franco
Vincent, Larry 95

Vincent, Paul 216
Vincent, Virginia 135
Vinson, Robert 200
Viotti, Piera 72
The Virgin of Nuremburg 243
The Virgin Spring 158
Vivian, Gil 147
Viviani, Sonia 212, 239
Vivó, Enrique 74
Vizziello, Carlos 168
Vogan, Rich 41
Vogel, Carol 125
Vogel, Matt 95
Voges, Jennifer C. 91
Volonté, Claudio 44
Von, Elke 144
von Danwitz, Doris 64
von Mueller, Kristina 60
von Theumer, Ernst R. 114
von Wiehse, Ursula 153
Voodoo Bloodbath 142
Vorkov, Zandor *see* Engel, Roger
Vortex, Inc. 227
Voskanian, Robert 74
Voss, Philip 117
Voyage Scolaire Sanglant 157
Vrana, Vlasta 195, 205
Vuco, Olivera 65
Vukotic, Milena 101
Vulpiani, Mario 124

W.D., Sofia 207
Wade, Evalyna 149
Wagner, Gaby 161
Wagstaff, Elsie 117
Wakeford, Kent 94
Walden, Dawna 137
Waldfogel, Michael 127
Waldman Marion 92
Waldon, Regina 115
Walker, Mark 205
Walker, Peter 39, 46, 78, 119, 180, 215
Wall, Suzanne 149
Wallace, Dee 135
Wallace, Edgar 81
Wallace, Robert 74
Wallace, Tommy Lee 115
Walleman, Police Officer 91
Walsh, William J. 127
Walter, Greg 171
Walter, Marianne 230
Walters, Don 148
Walton, Barrie 131
Walton, Patrick 243
Wampyr 169
Wanaguru, Dudley 173

Index

Wanderney, Roney 210
Ward, Gil 57
Ward, Michael 117
Ward, Trey 76
Warden, Kay 131
Warne, Derek 157
Warner, Elyn 77
Warner, Robert 92
Warren, Chandler 134
Warren, Dodre 238
Warren, Harryette 96
Warren, Janet 244
Warren, Norman J. 201
Washington, Ada 158
Wasserman, Carl 205
Wasson, James C. 181
Watch Me When I Kill 124
Waters, John 43, 235
Watkins, Roger 120
Watson, Alan 140
Watson, Jack 215, 232
Watson, Jerry 60
Watteau, Myriam 113
Watterson, Ronald 48
Watts, Queenie 215
Waxman, Harry 240
Way, Pat 42
Wayne, Keith 182
Weaver, Sigourney 40
Webb, Stan 59, 60
Webber, Lou Ann 171
Weber, Tom 169
Week of the Killer 217
Weekend per i Morti 189
Weenick, Annabelle 96
Weil, Michael 38
Weinstein, Judy 127
Weis, Jack 167
Weisberg, Rochelle Gail 103, 104
Weisenborn, Gordon *see* Lewis, Herschell Gordon
Weiss, Shelly 100
Weisse, Nicolas 153
Welbeck, Peter *see* Towers, Harry Alan
Welch, Charles 42
Well, Karin 191
Weller, Mary Louise 59
Welles, Adam 114
Welles, Gretchen 131
Welles, Mel *see* von Theumer, Ernst
Wellington, Larry 131, 245
Wells, Jerold 117
Wendlandt, Horst 81
Wendy, Barbara 140
The Werewolf and the Yeti 164

The Werewolf Vs. the Vampire Woman 186
The Werewolf Vs. the Vampire Women 186
The Werewolf's Shadow 186
Werwolf's Shadow 186
West, Ollie 137
West, Robert *see* Findlay, Michael
Westbound Records 167
The Westheimer Co. 198
Wetherell, Virginia 93
What Have They Done to Solange? 81
What Have You Done to Solange? 81
When the Screaming Stops 122
Whetmore, Nancy 216
White, A. Frank Drew *see* Manera, Jesús Franco
White, Caren 105
White, Daniel J. 213
White, Frank Drew *see* Bianchi, Andrea
White, Johnny 238
White, Richard 70
White Zombie 182
Whiteman Peter 114
Whitfield, Donna 231
Whiting, Zarrah 214
Whitman, Stuart 105
Whitney, Chris 148
Whittan, Roy 195
Whitworth, James 135
Who Could Kill a Child? 204
Who's Next? 81
Wide-Eyed in the Dark 123
Widowati, Siska 207
Wieternik, Nora 154
Wilcox, Mary 50
Wildman, Julie 195
Wilhite, Dianne 131
Willhelm, John 48
William, Leo *see* Vilaseñor, Leopoldo
William Mishkin Motion Pictures 211
Williams, David 91
Williams, Don 125
Williams, Karen 60
Williams, Leon 95
Williams, Mike 181
Williams, Pat 95
Willoughby, Ronald 38
Willrich, Rudolph 38
Willy Wonka and the Chocolate Factory 96
Wilson, Andy 235
Wilson, Jim 98

Wilson, Lisle 148
Wilson, Serretta 232
Wilson, Terry 181
Wimbury David 201
Winchester, Barron 91
Winding, Victor 119, 215
Windsor, Carole 243
Winkler, Gary 88
Winkler, Suzanne 88
Winner, Vic *see* Alcazar, Victor
Winston, Stan 165
Winters, Bob 91
Wise, Woody 137
Withers, Lonny 244
The Wizard of Gore 62, 130, 149, 245
Wohlers, Tina 110
Wolfe, Erica 149
Wolkowicz, Emilia 81
Women's Camp 119 212
Wondzinski, Gerard Tichy 194
Wong, Jadine 142
Wood, Annabella 61
Wood, Carol 137
Wood, Ed 137
Wood, Edward D., Jr. 53, 246
Wood, Oliver 95
Wood, Thomas *see* Kerwin, William
Woodard Charles 137
Woodoo—Der Schreckensinsel der Zombies 247
Woods, Bobby 144
Woods, Denise 95
Woolf, Victor 117
Woolgar, Jack 88
Woolman, Harry 148
Worldwide 91
Wotruba, Michael *see* Massaccesi, Aristide
Wray, Edwina 157
Wright, Jay 63
Wright, Larry 57
Wright, Marcella 194
Wright, Tommy 119
Wyman, Dan 115
Wynn, Keenan 200
Wynne, Gilbert 180
Wynroth, Alan 103

X Film 73
Xerxes Productions Ltd. 154

Yablans, Irwin 132
Yablans, Mickey 132
Yager, Julie 246
Yalem, Richard 91

Index

Yamanouchi, Al 106
Yamashita, Akiko 155
Yanne, Jean 101, 176
Yanni, Rossana 130, 156, 166
Yarnall, Celeste 49
Yates, Chuck 60
Yblagger, Karl 176
Yebenes, Chris 226
Yellen, Peter 103
Yepes, José 208, 242
Le Yeux sans Visage 165, 166
Yonowsky, Maurice 38
York, Jafar Free 207
Yorke, Gabriel 138
Young, Burt 71
Young, Carmen 90
Young, Jack 66
Young, Raymond 46
Young Dracula 101
Youngman, Henny 128
Yule, John 46, 119
Yuma Films 41

Zabala, Elsa 98, 109, 208, 213
Zabalza, José Mariá 121
Zaccari, Claudia 225
Zaccariello, Giuseppe 44
Zaharia, Jack 82
Zamengo, Renato 203, 225
Zamulo, Birgit 176
Zanchi, Monica 106, 247
Zani, Eleonori 101
Zapponi, Bernardino 202
Zaracausca, Luzia 90
Zarchi, Meir 87
Zarchi, Tammy 87
Zarchi, Terry 87
Zbeda, Joseph 87
Zé do Caixão 37, 91, 110, 111, 112, 210
Zeferino, Maria Helena 90
Zeising, Lucinda 63
Zelenovic, Srdjan 177
Zittrer, Carl 76, 92
Zola, Jean-Pierre 135
Zoltan ... Hound of Dracula 166
Zombi—El Regreso de los Muertos Vivientes 85, 248
Zombi Horror 191
Zombi 2 77, 191, 247
Zombi 3 191
Zombi 3—Da Dove Vieni? 189
Zombie 85
Zombie Child 75
Zombie Flesh Eaters 247
Zombie II 247
Zombie 2—The Dead Are Among Us 247
Zombie 3—Return of the Zombies 194
Le Zombie Venu d'Ailleurs 201
Zombies 191
Zombies—Dawn of the Dead 85
Zorrilla, Pilar 121
Zubarry, Olga 151
Zucchetti, Claudio 191
Zuckerman, Steve 223
Zulaika 151
Zurakowska, Dianik 166, 194, 218

www.ingramcontent.com/pod-product-compliance
Ingram Content Group UK Ltd.
Pitfield, Milton Keynes, MK11 3LW, UK
UKHW041926140426
5217IPUK00014B/332